NATIVE REMOVAL WRITING

American Indian Literature and Critical Studies Series

NATIVE REMOVAL WRITING

Narratives of Peoplehood, Politics, and Law

Sabine N. Meyer

UNIVERSITY OF OKLAHOMA PRESS : NORMAN

This book is published with the generous assistance of the McCasland Foundation, Duncan, Oklahoma.

Portions of this book were previously published, in a form since revised, in the following works with permission of the publisher:

"In the Shadow of the Marshall Court: Nineteenth-Century Cherokee Conceptualizations of the Law." In *Twenty-First Century Perspectives on Indigenous Studies: Native North America in (Trans)Motion*, edited by Sabine N. Meyer, Birgit Däwes, and Karsten Fitz, 148–71. Copyright © 2015 by Routledge, New York. Reproduced by permission of Taylor & Francis Group.

"The Marshall Trilogy and Its Legacies." In *The Routledge Companion to Native American Literature*, edited by Deborah L. Madsen, 123–34. Copyright © 2015 by Routledge, New York. Reproduced by permission of Taylor & Francis Group.

"From Domestic Dependency to Native Cultural Sovereignty: A Legal Reading of Gerald Vizenor's *Chair of Tears*." In *Native North American Survivance, Memory, and Futurity: The Gerald Vizenor Continuum*, edited by Birgit Däwes and Alexandra Hauke, 119–34. Copyright © 2017 by Routledge, New York. Reproduced by permission of Taylor & Francis Group.

"From Federal Indian Law to Indigenous Rights: Legal Discourse and the Contemporary Native American Novel on the Indian Removal." *Law & Literature* 29.2 (2017): 269–90. Copyright © 2017 by Cardozo School of Law, reprinted by permission of Taylor & Francis Ltd., http://www.tandfonline.com, on behalf of Cardozo School of Law.

Library of Congress Cataloging-in-Publication Data

Names: Meyer, Sabine N., 1979– author.
Title: Native removal writing : narratives of peoplehood, politics, and law / Sabine N. Meyer.
Other titles: American Indian literature and critical studies series ; v. 74.
Description: First. | Norman : University of Oklahoma Press, [2022]. | Series: American Indian literature and critical studies series; volume 74 | Summary: "A monograph of fictional and non-fictional writings on Indian Removal to advance two central claims. First, Native American removal writings cannot be reduced to trauma narratives helping Native people work through the wounds of land loss and death. Second, Native Removal writings across the centuries need to be treated as a genre in its own right. By creating links between historical past, narrative present, and political future, these writers emphasize indigenous futurity: the political and cultural persistence, rather than the disappearance, of indigenous peoples"— Provided by publisher.
Identifiers: LCCN 2021028973 | ISBN 978-0-8061-8016-8 (hardcover) | ISBN 978-0-8061-7624-6 (paperback)
Subjects: LCSH: Indian Removal, 1813–1903. | Indians in literature. | Indians of North America—Legal status, laws, etc. | Indians of North America—Government relations.
Classification: LCC E98.R4 M49 2022 | DDC 810.9/897—dc23
LC record available at https://lccn.loc.gov/2021028973

Native Removal Writing: Narratives of Peoplehood, Politics, and Law is Volume 74 in the American Indian Literature and Critical Studies Series.

The paper in this book meets the guidelines for permanence and durability of the Committee on Production Guidelines for Book Longevity of the Council on Library Resources, Inc. ∞

Copyright © 2022 by the University of Oklahoma Press, Norman, Publishing Division of the University. Manufactured in the U.S.A.

All rights reserved. No part of this publication may be reproduced, stored in a retrieval system, or transmitted, in any form or by any means, electronic, mechanical, photocopying, recording, or otherwise—except as permitted under Section 107 or 108 of the United States Copyright Act—without the prior written permission of the University of Oklahoma Press. To request permission to reproduce selections from this book, write to Permissions, University of Oklahoma Press, 2800 Venture Drive, Norman OK 73069, or email rights.oupress@ou.edu.

For Markus and Benno

Contents

Acknowledgments ix

Introduction 1

CHAPTER 1 "Domestic Dependent Nations": Native Visions of Belonging and the Legal Ideology of Removal 24

CHAPTER 2 Property-Owning Individuals: Early-Twentieth-Century Removal Writing and the US Federal Indian Policy of Assimilation and Allotment 68

CHAPTER 3 Indigenous Rights Subjects: Native Removal Literature of the 1990s and the Limits of Domestic Law 102

CHAPTER 4 "Cherokee by Blood"? Contemporary Afro-Native Removal Literature and the Freedman Debate 138

CHAPTER 5 "Museumized" *indians*: Native Speculative Removal Fiction, Cultural Appropriation, and Indigenous Futurity 180

Epilogue 216

Notes 229
Works Cited 251
Index 275

Acknowledgments

I HAVE BEEN working on the project that has finally become this book for almost a decade. The research it involves was inspired by multiple conversations with colleagues and students in different locales and was funded by various organizations and institutions.

In spring 2011, I joined the American Studies Section of the Institute for English and American Studies at the University of Osnabrück, Germany. I owe tremendous thanks to the chair of American Studies at Osnabrück, Peter Schneck, who introduced me to the field of cultural legal studies and who has been an inspiring mentor through all these years. His probing questions and his enthusiasm about the intricate and manifold relations between law and culture have greatly contributed to my research and the evolution of this monograph. It was also in Osnabrück that for many years I had the opportunity to coordinate the Osnabrück Summer Institute for the Cultural Study of the Law (OSI), which brings together scholars from all over the world working at the intersection of law and culture. The conversations that took place in the context of the many summer institutes, as well as the research networks that grew out of them, shaped the way I think about the relation between law and culture and informed my methodological approach for this book. From the large number of participants and faculty members who have pushed the conversation in important directions, I wish to particularly thank Leti Volpp, Beth Piatote, Joseph Slaughter, Cindy Holder, Brook Thomas, Fiona Macmillan, Helle Porsdam, Claudia Lieb, Martin Zeilinger, Cristina Martinez, and the late and unforgettable Kay Schaffer.

Of immeasurable significance for this book was also my one-year fellowship at the Käte Hamburger Center for Advanced Study in the Humanities "Law as Culture." The center offered the ideal infrastructure for writing a book: an inspiring setting, peace and quiet, intellectually stimulating conferences and lectures, and wonderfully supportive staff.

ACKNOWLEDGMENTS

What is more, it facilitated the cross-disciplinary engagement and discussion that are so vital for a project like mine. I owe particular thanks to Werner Gephart, the Center's founding and codirector, for his competence and enthusiasm as well as his ceaseless efforts to create the best possible research environment, in particular for younger scholars such as myself. I also would like to thank my cofellows and the invited guests at the center, whose knowledge and expertise have shaped my work, in particular Tiziana Andina, Tim Shaw, Thomas Dreier, Daniela Bifulco, Judith Hahn, Marta Bucholc, Morag Grant, Greta Olson, Peter Goodrich, and Erika de Wet.

My research on Native Removal writing also became an independent subproject of a joint research venture titled "The Claims of History: Native and National Narratives of Land as Property in the U.S.," pursued by Peter Schneck and myself. Between 2016 and 2020, this project was funded by the German Research Foundation (DFG, project number ME 4712/1-1). I am immensely grateful for this funding, as it allowed me to solely concentrate on my research and enabled me to collaborate with like-minded scholars across the world. The workshop with our partners at the University of California, Berkeley, was certainly one of the most intense and fruitful engagements with scholars working in the field of cultural legal studies and fields related directly to the project. I want to thank Beth Piatote, Leti Volpp, Marianne Constable, Bryan Wagner, Devin Zuber, James Martel, Mark Antaki, and Chad Luck for their immensely helpful thoughts on my work and their numerous suggestions as to the directions my research could take. It was also extremely inspiring to attend Chris Tomlins's Law as Minor Jurisprudence in Historical Key symposium at Berkeley in 2016. I was also so fortunate to be able to present my work at both the annual conventions of the Association for the Study of Law, Culture and the Humanities (ASLCH) and at the University of Hong Kong, whose law-and-literature research group around Marco Wan, Scott Veitch, and Elaine Ho provided me with extremely valuable input.

The ideas and arguments presented in this book are also the result of extensive conversations and cooperation with dozens of other scholars, often in the context of conferences. Thanks in particular to Karsten Fitz and Birgit Däwes, with whom I have worked together extensively over the past years and whose respective work in Native American studies has been of great benefit to me. I also want to thank Kerstin Knopf and René

ACKNOWLEDGMENTS

Dietrich for inviting me to their wonderful conference Biopolitics–Geopolitics–Sovereignty–Life: Settler Colonialisms and Indigenous Presences in North America. Special thanks are also owed to other colleagues in Germany and the United States whose commentaries and thoughts about my work have been tremendously helpful to me; among them are Mark Rifkin, David Carlson, Kristina Baudemann, Hartmut Lutz, Robert Nichols, Simone Knewitz, Christina Meyer, and Jatin Wagle. I also want to thank Tom Holm, Joshua Nelson, David E. Wilkins, Marilyn Vann, and Gerald Vizenor for taking the time to correspond, talk, and meet up with a German scholar working in the field of Native American studies. Your perspective has influenced my work in important ways. In addition, I would like to acknowledge the work and time invested by the staff of the University of Oklahoma Press to turn my manuscript into a book. Special thanks go to Alessandra Tamulevich and Steven Baker for their professional management of the publication process from start to end and to the reviewers for their critical and insightful comments. Just when I was about to send off this manuscript to the publisher, I received a copy of Claudio Saunt's *Unworthy Republic: The Dispossession of Native Americans and the Road to Indian Territory* (Norton, 2020). I could not incorporate Saunt's astute findings into this book but am immensely grateful for this scholarly reappraisal of a US policy that has had such devastating effects on the lives of Native Americans.

Last but by no means least, I would like to thank my husband, Markus, for his love, support, and unwavering faith in me, and our little son, Benno, who does not quite yet understand that his mother likes writing books but who, through his curiosity, cheerfulness, and warmth, is a constant source of motivation, joy, and happiness. Thank you so much, Markus and Benno, from the depth of my heart!

While putting the finishing touches on the manuscript of this book, I was appointed professor of American studies at the University of Bonn—my first permanent job in German academia after many years of professional instability and insecurity. Hence I do not consider this book the end of a journey but the beginning of a new one with wonderful colleagues, students, and a stimulating research environment.

Introduction

DURING THE SUMMER of 2016, thousands of protesters, most of them Native Americans, set up camp in North Dakota to protest the Dakota Access Pipeline (DAPL), a 1,200-mile conduit to be built by Texas-based Energy Transfer Partners to transport as many as 570,000 barrels of crude oil per day from North Dakota to Illinois. Rerouted to travel underneath the Missouri River, the major source of drinking water for the Standing Rock Sioux, the pipeline has sparked resistance among tribal members, who fear leakage and the damage of their water supply and who complain that the pipeline traverses sacred burial grounds. At the beginning of December 2016, the #NoDAPL protesters achieved a remarkable victory when the US Army Corps of Engineers announced that it would look for alternative routes for the pipeline. In February 2017, however, newly inaugurated president Donald Trump issued a presidential memorandum directing the US Army Corps to end its search for alternatives. After failed attempts by the Cheyenne River Sioux and the Standing Rock Sioux to secure a restraining order against the pipeline in US district court, North Dakota state government officials set a deadline for the evacuation of the camp. On February 23, 2017, those unwilling to leave were forcibly "removed" by the National Guard and law enforcement officers in what one journalist called "a military-style takeover" (Wong; see also Archambault; Worland; Barrera).

In the legal-political struggle between the Standing Rock Sioux and the federal and state governments, the protesters—primarily Native activists but also occasionally their non-Native allies—frequently invoke Indian Removal. Indian Removal, as Stuart Banner explains in his seminal monograph *How the Indians Lost Their Land*, "conventionally denotes a distinct era in the history of the United States Indian policy, from the late 1820s through the early 1840s," when the federal government forcibly expelled more than eighty thousand Cherokees, Creeks, Choctaws,

Chickasaws, and Seminoles from the southeastern states to what is now Oklahoma.[1] The so-called Trail of Tears has evolved into the "enduring image" of this time period, having come to signify the US Army's internment and forced relocation of about sixteen thousand Cherokees in the fall and winter of 1838 and 1839 and the suffering and painful deaths of thousands on the trail west (191).

In the context of Standing Rock, the descendants of the relocated tribes have referred to Indian Removal in their appeals for intertribal solidarity. With the emphatic appeal "Standing with Standing Rock on the Trail of Tears," organizers from Tennessee sought to encourage Native Americans from the region to rally in support of their "brothers and sisters" at Standing Rock (James). Also citing the Trail of Tears were those wishing to place the events in North Dakota affecting Native Americans in greater historical perspective. The chairman of the Standing Rock Sioux, David Archambault II, characterized state incursions on the Standing Rock Reservation as "a familiar story in Indian Country" reminiscent of "unspeakable hardships in the past," a comment that prompted bloggers and journalists to read Standing Rock through the lens of Indian Removal (Archambault; see also "Remembering the Trail of Tears"). When the eviction deadline approached, Ruth Hopkins (Dakota, Lakota Sioux) tweeted on #NoDAPL: "Forced removal isn't just in the history books. It's happening tomorrow on treaty lands at Standing Rock." These words and many other speeches, blogs, editorials, tweets, and articles reveal that Native American protesters and activists view the conflict at Standing Rock as "the new Trail of Tears" (Barton).

The Native protesters and their supporters across the United States are not the first to invoke Indian Removal at a particular moment of crisis. In fact, their invocations need to be viewed as part of a century-old Native tradition of Removal narrations, fictional as well as nonfictional. Indian Removal has occupied the minds of Native American intellectuals and writers ever since the late 1820s. For Native Americans, it has functioned as a marker of a specific set of historical events and a policy involving particular tribal nations. At the same time, Removal has functioned as a trope—a synecdoche for settler colonial oppression, disenfranchisement, and dispossession of Native communities across hemispheres—starting with the "removals" taking place long before the Indian Removal era and reaching up to the "removals" of the present moment (see also Banner

227). Furthermore, the policy of Removal has brought forth a plethora of government reports, treaties, laws, and court rulings that have determined Native forms of belonging—the identities of Native collectives, the proprietary relationship of these collectives to the land, and their most intimate relations among one another—in order to secure settler colonial dominance.[2] Due to the exceptional impact of Indian Removal on Native forms of living, being, and belonging, as well as its perpetual incompleteness, Native American intellectuals and writers have engaged with Removal in poetry, short stories, and novels, as well as in political, journalistic, academic, and historical writings from the late 1820s until the present day.[3] Cherokee scholar and writer Daniel Heath Justice speaks of a *"consciousness of Removal,* the full embrace of history, pain, and continuing existence" that still haunts Native communities (*Our Fire* 171; italics in original). Thus it is not surprising that the prologue of *An American Sunrise: Poems,* a 2019 collection by Joy Harjo, the first Native American poet laureate of the United States, retells the Indian Removal story from both a Muscogee Creek and a pan-Native perspective. The prologue contains a map that depicts one trail of the Muscogee Creek Nation's forced relocation yet insists that this is only one of many Trails of Tears that tribal nations were forced to walk (xv, xvii).

This monograph conceptualizes the Native fictional and nonfictional writings that have emerged from the specific historical event of Removal as a distinct genre of Native literature. Critically engaging with Native Removal writings across the centuries, it advances two central claims. First, these writings cannot, and should not, be reduced to trauma narratives helping Native individuals and collectivities work through the wounds of past land loss, dislocation, massive suffering, and death. Rather than limiting themselves to the depiction of past Native victimhood and the horrors of the trail, or serving therapeutic purposes, the writings are articulations of Native peoplehood that respond to immediate political concerns. Native Removal narratives engage with the question of how Native collectives can define and assert their own Indigenous social, cultural, and legal-political forms of living, being, and belonging within the settler colonial order. They go back to the past not only to reframe that past from the perspective of those silenced and obscured but also to dynamically and critically engage with the Indigenous present and to imagine and enact a future. This future is envisioned as being decidedly Indigenous and thus the opposite of what Mark Rifkin has termed "settler futurity"—that is, the "institutionalized temporal narratives" "treat[ing] settler political and legal norms as a given" and making "Native peoplehood [appear] as an aberration whose endurance indicates less sovereignty than oddity" (*Settler Time* 75). By repossessing Removal, Native Removal writings challenge settler colonial historiography, commemorate resilience and strength, and extend the story of Indigenous peoplehood into the future.

Second, nonfictional and fictional Native Removal writings across the centuries need to be treated as a distinct genre to make legible their respective interventions into past and ongoing legal-political debates. My conjoined readings of Native works on Indian Removal and a wide range of legal texts from federal Indian law, international law, and tribal law demonstrate that these works and the law resonate with each other. This resonance produces forms of Native collective identity informed by both the formative force of law and the imaginative force of literature. Drawing on the history of Removal allows Native writers to reflect on the modes of subjectivity that the settler nation has created and imposed upon Native collectives, reaching down to the most intimate levels of interaction. It also enables them to point to the limits of settler colonial ascriptions and knowledge frameworks and to develop alternate modalities of living, being, and belonging, sometimes in dialogue with and at other times in opposition to settler colonial interpellations.

As I explain in more detail below, peoplehood has, since the turn of the century, been used increasingly by Native scholars as a meaningful category of Native self-representation. Peoplehood can be culturally specific, but it is also "universal to all Native American tribes and nations and possibly to all indigenous groups" (Holm et al. 12). Working with the concept of peoplehood thus allows scholars to make both tribally specific and pan-Native or pan-Indigenous arguments. Giving prominence to Indigenous worldviews and values and implying persistence, peoplehood is deemed a discourse of power that challenges the hierarchies underlying settler colonial designations such as race and nation (Holm et al. 15-17). Scholars have also highlighted the close relation between peoplehood and Native literature and the significance of peoplehood as a heuristic tool in the analysis of Native literature. Peoplehood, as Justice has emphasized, "is a fundamental concern of our literature"; hence "it should also be a fundamental concern of our criticism of that literature" ("'Go Away, Water!'" 152). While, according to Justice, all Indigenous literatures negotiate forms of peoplehood, Native writings about Indian Removal are particularly invested in questions of peoplehood because of their focus on place or territory, and eventually the loss thereof. Scholars generally agree that Native collective identity is inextricably tied to a particular place and to the (proprietary) relationship of the collective to that place.[4] Therefore Native writings dealing with Removal—a key transactional moment, when massive portions of tribal land forcibly changed hands—inevitably engage with Native relations to that land and (re)negotiate forms of Native belonging. Native Removal literature sheds light on the interstices between modes of land ownership and group identity. By creating links between historical past, narrative present, and imagined future, this literature repossesses and reinterprets Removal: rather than foregrounding the disappearance of Indigenous peoples, it emphasizes their political and cultural persistence.

Native reflections on peoplehood become resurgent particularly at moments of legal-political crisis, when Native identity and forms of social organization come under external and internal pressure. By *external pressure*, I mean settler colonial interventions in Native cultures and sociopolitical structures; by *internal pressure* I mean debates about the contours of Native peoplehood within Indigenous collectivities. Hence I developed my corpus of Native Removal writings with an eye to US domestic, international, and tribal legal-political developments across time. The individual chapters discuss how Native writers have responded to Native subjectivities produced by settler colonial law, international law, and tribal law, starting with the immediate reaction to Indian Removal and its aftermath (chapter 1) and moving on to Native Removal writings in response to the US Indian policy of assimilation and allotment (chapter 2), the emergence of the Indigenous rights subject in international law (chapter 3), the tribal definition of "Indianness" through the idiom of blood in the context of the Cherokee freedmen debate (chapter 4), and the increasing petrification of Native identity, history, and culture in response to settler colonial acts of Native cultural appropriation (chapter 5). All these chapters demonstrate that external and internal pressures are, more often than not, interrelated, with external pressures impacting Native social relations and forms of belonging.

INTRODUCTION

In selecting specific Removal writings, I was particularly drawn to writings that grapple with the law and its creation of subjectivities not only thematically but also formally, for instance by including maps, historical source material, legal documents, and autobiographical comments and anecdotes, and to writings that challenge the conventions of the genres they work in. The texts I chose all evoke the past—Indian Removal—while leaving the pressures of their contemporary moments largely unstated. Through close readings of the literary texts and their legal contexts, I show how the literary texts engage Removal to work through and articulate forms of Native peoplehood that can serve the present and move toward the future. My analysis thus insists upon a strong historical grounding of Removal writings to lay bare their radical visions and distinct aesthetics and to shed light on how historical and legal conditions shape the possibilities of the literary imaginary at any given moment.

The majority of Removal writings that I analyze are novels. The first Native American novel ever written, John Rollin Ridge's *The Life and Adventures of Joaquín Murieta* (1854), is an allegory of Removal and is deeply interested in imagining post-Removal forms of Native peoplehood within the legal framework of the settler state. The genre has become the primary medium for Native American writers for investigating the relation between the past and legal-political and ethical concerns in the present and has become a lens through which to reflect on new ways of understanding peoplehood moving forward. I place the Removal novels I selected—those by John Rollin Ridge, John Milton Oskison, Robert Conley, Diane Glancy, Sharon Ewell Foster, Zelda Lockhart, Blake Hausman, Stephen Graham Jones, and Gerald Vizenor—in conversation with nonfictional Removal writings. The speeches, letters, and memorials by leading Cherokee politicians John Ross, Elias Boudinot, and John Ridge are essential for a discussion of Native Removal writings, as they are the first Native responses to this US policy. Oskison's journalistic pieces are useful for developing a more precise idea of his politics. Finally, I was drawn to Rachel Caroline Eaton's 1914 historical monograph *John Ross and the Cherokee Indians* because it is the first extensive treatment of Removal by an Indigenous female academic. She combined the methods of Western historiography with Native ways of practicing history to produce an alternative history of Indian Removal.[5]

INTRODUCTION

Except for Lockhart (Choctaw), Jones (Blackfeet), and Vizenor (Anishinaabe), all these writers have Cherokee roots. This is not surprising given that political debates over Indian Removal focused on the Cherokees, as did most laws and court cases. Although neither the largest southern tribal community nor the one with the largest land base, the Cherokees lived on fertile land and were successful farmers who produced cotton and other crops. Hence Cherokee land, along with their livestock and houses, particularly attracted the settlers' greed (Banner 198–99). Moreover, Cherokee politicians played a significant role in these political and legal struggles due to their thorough familiarity with both the English language and the workings of Western law and politics (Perdue and Green, *Cherokee Nation* xiv). The ethnic origin of the authors, however, does not make their writings and their specific arguments about Cherokee collective identity less applicable to other Native communities, most of which have also experienced some form of "removal" and displacement by the US government.[6] By placing Cherokee Removal writings alongside Removal literature by authors from other Native nations, I show that Removal functions as a broader trope and conceptual framework extending beyond the Cherokees' historical experience with settler colonialism. My book thus engages yet also shows the limitations of nationalist approaches to Native literature.

Through my choice of topic, textual corpus, and methodology, I seek to complement and expand existing scholarship in various ways. First, conceptualizing Native Removal writing as a distinct genre encompassing texts across three centuries, and offering comparative readings of these texts, allows me to offer the first in-depth reflection on the important role that literature plays in Native acts of commemorating and repossessing Removal.[7] In his book *Monuments to Absence: Cherokee Removal and the Contest over Southern Memory*, Andrew Denson alerts us to acts of commemoration of Indian Removal that the tourist industry and cultural heritage workers have been engaging in since the 1920s. As he convincingly shows, white southerners could acknowledge Removal because it was a story of Native disappearance that established white settlers as the logical possessors of Native American land. "Commemoration of the Trail of Tears reflected and reinforced this idea of Indian absence" and was therefore uncontested history (8; cf. 5–6, 219).[8] Denson also hints at Native attempts to repossess and transform the history of Removal and to use it for their own purposes (9, 222). Native American acts of commemorating Removal emphasize tribal persistence, Native sovereignty, and Native presence; "their purpose is [thus] less to recognize the injustice of that episode than to strengthen Cherokee people and communities in the present" (222; cf. 194). While Denson is concerned with material monuments to absence or, in the case of Native American acts of commemoration, presence, this book focuses on Native writing as a practice of commemorating, repossessing, and transforming Removal. It uses writing to flesh out an argument that Denson merely hints at toward the end of his monograph: the significance of Removal for Indigenous identity formation and forms of belonging (214, 222).

Moreover, my law-and-literature approach to Native nonfictional and fictional Removal writing demonstrates the need for an alternative interpretive perspective on this particular genre. The few existing scholarly analyses of selected Native texts on Indian Removal view them through the prism of trauma. Daniel Heath Justice, Hsinya Huang, and Celia E. Naylor have conceptualized the Trail of Tears as a site of "massive trauma" that "continues to reverberate in the memory and cultural expressions of the Cherokees today" (Huang 217; Justice, *Our Fire* 47; Naylor, *African Cherokees* 1). For Huang, the presence of Indian Removal in Native literature "is a sign of the traumatic disorder in the past, the crime that has not been set right, and is therefore also a sign that the present psyche still suffers from that traumatic disorder" (219). In her view, Native Removal literature serves to heal the transgenerational wounds created by the settler colonial appropriation of Native lands and the forced relocation of entire communities. This primary focus on trauma and on the tribal psyche in the conceptual framing of Indian Removal and its literary representations has shaped the general perception of Removal literature. Joshua D. Miner points out that Indian Removal has begun "to form a discourse, an aesthetic of its own, within the larger arena of trauma discourse." Representations of Indian Removal, especially those by the forcibly relocated tribes, tend to be "'vanishing Indian' swan songs" that seek to satisfy "the American appetite for tragedy." They feature an "empty, sentimentalist Trail of Tears aesthetic" and thus "have produced a static representational field" that "limits narrative possibility and visionary peoplehood" (61, 69).

The interdisciplinarity of my own approach demonstrates that these narratives are not at all about "vanishing Indians" and are not limited to healing the wounds that Removal has inflicted on the tribal psyche. While they engage painful histories and portray Native characters as victims of settler aggression (how could they not?), they simultaneously emphasize Native agency and capacity for self-articulation and self-organization. These writings depict Removal as one foundational moment of a historical trajectory that began long prior to the arrival of Europeans on the North American continent and that extends into the present and future. Rather than constituting a "static representational field," they are unique articulations of Native peoplehood, shaped by the cultural and social backgrounds of their authors and by the particular moments at which they were produced.

Creating a corpus of Native Removal writings across the centuries and treating them as a distinct genre also enables me to examine texts that have never been read together before. It allows me to make visible their politics and the strong resonances between them. "Reading texts across the centuries," Stephanie Fitzgerald and Hilary E. Wyss emphasize, "creates a space from which to trace Native intellectual histories and practices in a number of different forms, a space where early and contemporary scholars and scholarship can meet" (272–73). It contributes to an "understanding of the interrelations between the literary and the political, the past and the present, and the varieties of expression" (272). Such an understanding is necessary to see Native Removal writings as far more than what Huang has called a "compulsive return" to the Trail of Tears called forth by a psychological disorder (Huang 219). My juxtaposition of Native Removal writings across time illustrates that rather than being "compelled" to return to Indian Removal, Native authors consciously activate the past to intervene in the legal-political struggles of the present and to imagine ways for Natives peoples to move into the future.

My study further adds to the field of Native literary studies by bringing attention to texts that have not yet received much scholarly attention, either because they are too recent (Hausman, Jones, Vizenor) or because they have long been deemed "assimilationist" or even aesthetically deficient (Eaton, Oskison, Conley). The latter judgment may be a result of the way scholars in Native literary studies approached Native literature. For until the 1990s, the dominant approaches were formalist, biographical, and ethnographical. According to Eric Cheyfitz, the scholarship produced up to that point largely focused on "the aesthetic or formal properties of Native texts in limited cultural contexts, while deemphasizing or ignoring the social, political, and historical contexts in which U.S. American Indian literatures take shape." Only in recent years has a more context-oriented scholarship emerged; it has been rethinking the nature, value, and function of Native literary texts (Cheyfitz 5; see also Herman 1–2). The nonfictional writings I selected have not generated much interest among scholars of Native literature either because of their general preference for contemporary fictional works (Fitzgerald and Wyss 271).[9]

Finally, by reading the Removal novels by Sharon Ewell Foster and Zelda Lockhart as African-Native American literature,[10] this book boldly expands Native American literature to include Indigenous-African American literary production. It demands the recognition of an understudied yet highly significant body of literature[11] and positions itself in favor of moving beyond what Jonathan Brennan has called "a monolithic system of dichotomous racial identity," which has resulted in African-Native American authors' classification as either African American or Native American and in "a scholarly myopia . . . clouding African-Native American studies in an often impenetrable fog" (39, 41).[12] In their Removal novels, Foster and Lockhart draw attention to an aspect of African-Native American history that has long been neglected by writers, scholars, and Native American communities themselves and that has been rediscovered in the last few years:[13] the enslavement of Blacks by Native Americans. Placing these novels alongside other Native texts on Indian Removal unearths new interpretative layers and makes visible what Justin Leroy has termed "the full scope of slavery and settlement's interconnected history" and the "mutually constitutive origins" of Indigenous dispossession and slavery (8).

LAW AND NATIVE AMERICAN LITERATURE

My conjoined readings of Native American Removal literature and selected legal texts locate my project within the budding field of law and Native American literature. Legal scholars such as Felix S. Cohen have long emphasized that "law dominates Indian life in a way not duplicated in other segments of American society" (*Handbook* [1982] vii). Scholars in the fields of legal history, politics, and Native American studies, in particular, have explored the manifold ways in which law has determined the construction of Native American identities and influenced Native American communities and legal traditions (see, e.g., Williams; Rosen, *American Indians*; Wilkins, *American Indian Sovereignty*; Deloria and Wilkins; Wilkins and Lomawaima; Deloria and Lytle; Duthu, *American Indians*; Robertson). While the impact of the law—and what all these scholars mean by "law" is federal Indian law—on Native lives has been widely acknowledged, until the turn of the twenty-first century, the relation between law and Native literature was not the focus of scholarly attention. In 2006 Cheyfitz deplored most readers' continued inability to recognize the significant influence of US law on Native American literatures. "The lack of awareness of the field of federal Indian law," he claimed, "is in large part due to the fact that while studies of U.S. Native American oral and written expression to date have alluded to federal policy in Indian matters, they have done so at best in a fragmentary way, and never in a way that argues the intimacy of law and literatures in this field" (6).

This book seeks to shed light on what Cheyfitz has termed the "imbrication" of Native American literature and the law—that is, the complex interplay between law and Native writings (100). The interdisciplinary nature of my analysis has made it imperative to build on the rich body of work in the areas of Native property rights, federal Indian law, and international law produced by scholars such as Matthew Fletcher, Stuart Banner, Tim Alan Garrison, Lindsay G. Robertson, David Chang, Vine Deloria, David E. Wilkins, Joseph Singer, David Getches, Robert A. Williams, Kenneth Bobroff, N. Bruce Duthu, Angela Riley, Kristen Carpenter, Rebecca Tsosie, Jeff Corntassel, Ronald Niezen, and James Anaya.

My work is also deeply influenced by and in conversation with the law-and-literature scholarship that has emerged in the field of Native American/Indigenous studies within the last decade.[14] The scholarship most relevant for my own interpretations of Native Removal writings is that by Mark Rifkin, Beth Piatote, Chadwick Allen, Cheryl Suzack, and David Carlson, who have explored the complex relationship between Native literature and federal Indian law and Native American literature's engagement with the modes of legal subjectivity imposed by the settler state. In addition, my research has been influenced by the recent scholarly turn to the complex relationship between Native literature and international as well as tribal law. Lee Schweninger and Joni Adamson have emphasized the importance of reading Native American literature in light of debates about Indigenous rights in international law. And in their study of Native forms of governance, Native legal scholars have increasingly emphasized the significance of stories and storytelling for the development of tribal law and tribal notions of sovereignty (Fletcher, "Looking" 3–4; Borrows 13–23, 46–54; Tsosie and Coffey 196; Singel). "Tribal law and culture," Fletcher claims, "are collections of stories. The same stories that scholars study as snapshots of tribal culture are also stories about a tribe's law" ("Looking" 3). Fletcher thus connects the literary and legal realms—aesthetics and politics. In a similar vein, their conjoined readings of law and literature have prompted Piatote and Rifkin to conclude that Native literary texts have, as Piatote puts it, a "deeply political dimension." Rifkin even views them as "forms of political theory" (Piatote, *Domestic Subjects* 11; Rifkin, *The Erotics of Sovereignty* 2). Such insights have had a formative impact on my understanding of Native literature as an important way to imagine (alternative) collective identities, which may or may not find their way into law. I view Native Removal writings as political interventions, challenging, complementing, and enhancing discussions that take place in the legal and political arena. While existing studies at the intersection of law and Native American literature tend to focus on one dominant body of law, it is the novelty of this book to think across multiple and simultaneous iterations of domestic, tribal, and international law.

PEOPLEHOOD AND NATIVE AMERICAN LITERATURE

Scholars working in the field of Native American studies have long been debating which terminology is most appropriate to describe Native collectivities. It is generally agreed upon that Native concepts of collective identification operate outside the basic tenets and assumptions of Western political thought.[15] As "indigenous normative systems inhabit the same territorial space as the official legal order," Native Americans have been constrained in using the Western legal-political language and the legal subjectivities produced by the settler state when struggling for their rights (Anderson 235; see also Rifkin, *Manifesting America* 6, 9).[16] Native Americans' employment of the term *sovereignty* for models of Indigenous governance may serve as a case in point. Native scholars such as Taiaiake Alfred criticize Natives' increasing reliance on this concept in their efforts for self-definition since the 1970s. Sovereignty, Alfred argues, is "an inappropriate concept" for Indigenous governance, as it is "rooted in adversarial and coercive Western notions of power" (*Peace, Power* 55–56, 59). "So long as sovereignty remains the goal of indigenous politics," he claims, "Native communities will occupy a dependent and reactionary position relative to the state" (59; for a similar critique, see Byrd, "Introduction" 131–33; Cobb 115–18; Schulte-Tenckhoff 75). Through the use of Western political and epistemological frameworks and notions of power, he and other scholars insist, Indigenous knowledges, self-articulations, and the pre-contact historiography of Native governance are marginalized, if not discredited altogether.[17]

Since the turn of the century, a growing number of scholars in the field of Native American studies have turned to the concept of peoplehood to avoid Western forms of legal-political recognition such as nation(hood), state, or tribe and to strengthen Indigenous ways of collective identification.[18] They deem peoplehood to be consistent with both tribal self-definition[19] and the status conferred on Native Americans by federal Indian law and international law (Carpenter et al. 1056–57).[20] Drawing on the work of Cherokee anthropologist Robert K. Thomas,[21] Tom Holm (Cherokee), J. Diane Pearson, and Ben Chavis (Lumbee) declare peoplehood to be based on the "interlocking" aspects of language, sacred history, ceremonial cycle, and place/territory (13, 15). They explain their choice of the terms "place" and "territory," rather than "land," as follows: "Every human group maintains some kind of relationship with territory." "Land," they say, suggests the "mechanistic" human–land relationship. "Land, from this point of view, is equal to that which it produces or to what its actual market value might be." "Place," by contrast, gestures toward the "organic" human–land relationship: "a living relationship in which humans use the land and consider it part of their heritage" (14). While Holm and his coauthors claim that "no single factor is more important than the others" (12), other scholars have insisted on the centrality of place in the peoplehood matrix (Stratton and Washburn 68; Tsosie, "Land, Culture" 1306; Carpenter et al. 1061). According to Kristen Carpenter, Sonia Katyal, and Angela Riley, place defines the "histories, languages, cultures, arts, and continuing peoplehood" of Native American collectives. "It holds all the components that define their cultural existence" (1113; see also 1112).

My analysis of Native Removal writings underlines such scholarly assertions about the centrality of place for visions of Native peoplehood. As my interpretation of nineteenth-century Cherokee texts shows, to the forcibly expelled and relocated tribes, the loss of their homeland meant a threat to their cultural and political survival and forced them to imagine alternative ways of living, being, and belonging. What the writings by these and subsequent generations of Removal authors also bring to light, however, is the fact that land loss often led to a reconceptualization of "place" as "land." While the land continued to be held in esteem as part of tribal heritage and as a source of cultural and political sustenance, it was increasingly also viewed as having market value and as producing goods valuable to those working and living on it. These texts thus challenge the idea of Holm and his coauthors that there exist two sets of discursively stable and fundamentally antagonistic conceptualizations of land: land as place versus land as property. In the Native Removal narratives I discuss, land continues to be represented as place but it is also conceptualized as "real property," vulnerable to continuing appropriation yet essential to Native survival as a people (see Carpenter, "Real Property and Peoplehood").[22]

The major asset of the peoplehood concept, Holm and his coauthors claim, is its rootedness in Indigenous knowledge, relations, traditions, and cultural practices and its suggestion of permanency (16–17). Allowing for a capacious and contingent sense of political identity not constrained by nationalist structures, peoplehood reflects a fairly "accurate picture of the ways in which Native Americans act, react, pass along knowledge, and connect with the ordinary as well as supernatural worlds" (15).[23] Holm and his coauthors view it as distinct from settler colonial law with its categories of identification, potentially even as a form of resistance to that law. However, as Rifkin insists, "the emphasis on the persistence and internal coherence of peoplehood" should not "downplay discussion of the mechanisms through which the United States inserts populations into an alien political framework as well as the disruptive efforts of that process" (*Manifesting America* 18). The political power of Native communities has never existed in a vacuum. As US power increased, tribal sovereignty began to rely on "mutual recognition and interdependence" rather than on "autonomy and independence" (Sturm, *Becoming Indian* 182).

The Native Removal narratives I discuss illustrate that Native visions of peoplehood are always inflected by the struggle with the settler nation about territorial, cultural, and political rights and by past and present constructions of subjectivity in US federal Indian law as well as in international law. While I certainly do not mean to imply that Native peoplehood is dependent on the settler state or can only be thought within the latter's epistemological confines, it is true that geopolitical realities have had a considerable impact on forms of Native collective identification. My close readings of selected Removal writings demonstrate that negotiations of Native peoplehood are grounded in Indigenous community life and cultural practices but also "reflect the colonized political and legal contexts in which Indigenous peoples [have been] forced to live and operate" (Alfred and Corntassel 605).

HISTORICAL NARRATIVE, LAW, LEGAL SUBJECTIVITY, AND NATIVE PEOPLEHOOD

The relation between historical narrative and law was explored by Hayden White in what has become one of his most anthologized articles, "The Value of Narrativity in the Representation of Reality." Based on Hegel's *Lectures on the Philosophy of History*, White suggests that historical narratives are typically written within stable sociopolitical formations having a well-established body of law (15–16; see also Paul 112). He even seems to agree with Hegel's claim that the state typically provides such a legal order, which in turn enables historical prose: "The reality which lends itself to narrative representation is the *conflict* between desire, on the one side, and the law, on the other. Where there is no rule of law, there can be neither a subject nor the kind of event which lends itself to narrative representation" (16; italics in original).[24] Based on these premises, White develops two hypotheses. First, he proposes that "historicity" and "narrativity" are only possible with "some notion of the legal subject which can serve as the agent, agency, and subject of historical narrative in all its manifestations." Second, he claims that "narrativity, whether of the fictional or the factual sort, presupposes the existence of a legal system against or on behalf of which the typical agents of a narrative account militate." This second hypothesis, White then states, "raises the suspicion that narrative in general, from the folktale to the novel, from the annals to the fully realized 'history,' has to do with the topics of law, legality, legitimacy, or, more generally, *authority*" (16–17; italics in original).

White's theories on the relation between historicity, form, and law operate within Western epistemological and political frameworks that can and should not be mapped easily onto Native ways of knowing and knowledge production. Therefore the use of White in an analysis of Native Removal writings might appear counterintuitive. Nevertheless, White's hypotheses regarding the complication of narrativity and law and its salience for the modern emergence of historical consciousness are useful for charting the intellectual terrain of this study.

While Native American communities are not nation-states in the Hegelian sense of the term, from the late eighteenth century onward they have been faced with a nation-state whose legal order has turned them—against their will—into legal subjects and has regulated their identities, cultures, and forms of social organization (Rifkin, *Manifesting America* 29). In line with White's understanding that narratives result from an engagement with the rule of law, Native Removal narratives spring from an engagement of the "involuntarily interiorized" collectives with the legal order that incorporates them (Rifkin, *Manifesting America* 6). Native American Removal writers negotiate, and often militate against, the subjectivities—that is, the subject positions—that settler colonial law has produced in what Louis Althusser has defined as a process of interpellation (117–21).[25]

The subjectivities constructed by settler colonial legal discourse (and, as I show in chapter 5, by other discourses of power/knowledge, such as popular culture and anthropology) challenge, or even refute, the identities and forms of social organization Native collectives have chosen for themselves (see Rifkin, *Manifesting America* 8). While they do not succeed at eradicating Native processes of self-definition and self-governance, they certainly influence and shape them. As my textual analysis of Native nonfictional and fictional Removal narratives reveals, the subjectivities created by colonial discourse have provoked complex processes of negotiation on the part of those interpellated. These processes range from resistance to these subjectivities to their (tactical) appropriation and repurposing, with the ultimate objective to secure Native rights to sovereignty and land. The construction and recognition of Native individuals and collectives by the settler nation as legal subjects and hence as bearers of certain rights is often employed by Native writers to protest dispossession and disenfranchisement. Native Americans, as Jennifer Wicke states, "need to deploy a language of the legal subject" to secure "the return of their land" and their "cultural identity" (465, 466). Embracing "legal subject-hood," she says, can help "bend" "the legal arena... to a variety of discursive purposes" (467).

Based on White's suggestion of an essential connection between the narration of history and legal subjecthood, law, and legality, I conceive of Native Removal narratives as implicit or even explicit negotiations of settler colonial law. The narrativization of Indian Removal by Native writers results from the tensions that exist between Native ideas of peoplehood and the subjectivities created by colonial discourse and from the desire (and political need) to question, and contest, the alleged legality and authority of the settler colonial legal order. By counterposing settler colonial constructions of subjectivity with visions of Native peoplehood, Native Removal narratives inevitably negotiate the latter. They shed light on their historical becoming, comment upon and evaluate their present status, and reflect upon their future being. According to White, "historical self-consciousness, the kind of consciousness capable of imagining the need to represent reality as a history, is conceivable only in terms of its interest in law, legality, legitimacy, and so on" (16–17). As critical engagements with the legality and authority of the settler colonial legal order and the subject positions it has created, Native Removal narratives need to be viewed as manifestations of a Native historical consciousness.

The implicit relation between historical narrative, law, legal subjectivity, and Native peoplehood forms the conceptual and critical backdrop for the more specific questions I wish to address in the chapters to follow: First, how do Native writings on Indian Removal negotiate the legal debates about sovereignty, property, and land ownership that were at the heart of the Removal controversy? As I will demonstrate, Native Removal writings juxtapose Native and Anglo-American ideas of sovereignty and (land) ownership and subject court rulings and a variety of other legal documents to critical readings. Moreover, they inquire into the potential of law to create justice and maintain social order, and they offer insights into the position of the "involuntarily interiorized" (Rifkin, *Manifesting America* 6).

Second, what are the legal and political contexts from which these Removal writings emerge and how do these contexts interact with these writings? My analyses reveal that Native narratives on Indian Removal tie the historical legal context of Removal, which they explore retrospectively, to the legal and political issues prevalent in Native America at the time of their emergence. In many of these writings, this contemporary legal context remains unstated and can only be retrieved when placing them in conversation with contemporary legal texts.

Third, what role does Native writing play in what Rifkin describes as Native "communities' internal processes of organization and self-articulation" (*Manifesting America* 27)? My chapters highlight the vital role Native American literature plays in the construction of Native peoplehood. Mediating between Indigenous knowledges and traditions and the imposed settler colonial political and legal categories of subjectification, these historical narratives contribute to making sense, and strategic use, of settler colonial realities; negotiating Native patterns of social, political, and cultural organization; and emphasizing Indigenous persistence. They make use of the past to determine possible paths for Indigenous peoples to move into the future.

CHAPTER OVERVIEW

The chapters to follow present separate case studies, combining extended investigations of legal contexts with close readings of Native textual production. The groups of texts discussed in each chapter offer various articulations of peoplehood, depending on the legal-political contexts in which they were written as well as the social-political and tribal backgrounds of their authors. My chronological arrangement of chapters is not intended to suggest a narrative continuity between Native writings on Indian Removal or a connection between all texts by way of argument. Neither do I claim that peoplehood is a stable discourse in the history of Native American Removal writing.

Chapter 1, "Domestic Dependent Nations," illustrates how Cherokee writers at the time of Removal and in its immediate aftermath navigated Native Americans' tenuous legal position between state and federal jurisdictions. In the political debates about relocating the southeastern tribes, federal and state courts defined and codified the status of Native collectives within US domestic space and the nature of their property rights. In their speeches and writings in response to these courts' rulings, John Ross, Elias Boudinot, and John Ridge advance a conception of Cherokee peoplehood mediating between tribal epistemologies, genealogies, and histories, and the subjectivities imposed by the settler nation. The complex interplay between settler colonial and Native subjectivities also becomes evident in John Rollin Ridge's novel *The Life and Adventures of Joaquín Murieta* (1854) and his journalistic writings, in which he develops an alternative to the existence of his people as "a domestic dependent nation." What unites these early Removal writings is their respective mobilization of the natural law tradition as a locus of resistance, even as the United States was increasingly turning away from those foundations toward legal positivism.

Chapter 2, "Property-Owning Individuals," centers on Native Removal texts that were written after the actual event took place and that invoked the past in order to intervene in the present, in this case the US federal policy of assimilation and allotment. To justify the transformation of Native American collectives into property-owning individuals, the federal government and the "friends of the Indian" conceptualized the Natives in Indian Territory as propertyless savages and the territory itself as a locus of lawlessness, chaos, and discrimination. In *John Ross and the Cherokee Indians* (1914), a historical monograph on Indian Removal, Rachel Caroline Eaton returns to Removal to emphasize Cherokee agency and capacity for crisis management, leadership, civilization, and nation building and thus exposes as false the settler colonial conceptualizations underlying assimilation and allotment. She speaks out in favor of Native sovereign nations owning their land communally and taking responsibility for their own advancement, independent from the damaging interventions of the US government. While Eaton builds her narrative on the idea of racial linear progress, John Milton Oskison's *The Singing Bird: A Cherokee Novel*, published at some point between 1925 and the early 1940s, challenges this idea as well as the concept of civilization itself. In contrast to Eaton's advocacy of the persistence of the Cherokees as a separate people, he envisions the racial and cultural amalgamation of Native Americans and Americans through intermarriage and interracial interaction and collaboration. While such a horizontal process of amalgamation implies the end of Cherokee political autonomy, it would, in his view, guarantee Cherokee cultural survival.

Between the early 1940s and the early 1990s, few Native writings on Indian Removal were produced.[26] This dearth of Native American Removal literature might be related to the termination policy of the federal government. Between the early 1950s and the early 1970s, the government "terminated" federal aid and recognition of tribal communities and relocated tribal citizens from reservations to cities (Bruyneel 125, 127). Not surprisingly, in those years, as Arnold Krupat points out, Native literature was intensely concerned "with the subject of *identity*," in particular with the individual identities of "mixedblood protagonists" (rather than with the collective identities of peoples) (*Red Matters* 109, 113; italics in original).[27] The US government's subsequent shift to the policy of self-determination, which sought to increase Native administrative participation and to strengthen tribal governments, seems to have encouraged a new generation of Native writers to (again) return to Indian Removal to negotiate forms of Native social organization and collective identity in their works (Cornell 208). These writers' engagement with Removal may also have been encouraged by the impressive amount of scholarship that appeared in the 1980s and 1990s on the legal situation of Native Americans in the United States in general and on Indian Removal in particular, with Native scholarly voices taking a leading role in this upsurge in legal (Removal) historiography.[28] Finally, Native writers' renewed concern with Indian Removal may also have been spurred by the US Congress's designation of the Trail of Tears National Historic Trail in 1987, which turned the Cherokee Trail of Tears into "one of the most heavily commemorated episodes from American Indian history" (Denson, *Monuments to Absence* 10).[29]

Chapter 3, "Indigenous Rights Subjects," focuses on Native Removal novels from the 1990s. While the first two chapters feature Native writers who focus on the role of the subjectifying apparatus of the settler state in their visions of peoplehood, this chapter turns to texts also considering an alternative source of recognition: international law. These novels suggest that international law, with its increasing attention to and advancement of Indigenous rights, might prove a framework of resistance to dispossession. Written in 1992, at the height of "the new subjectivism" of the US Supreme Court, Cherokee writer Robert Conley's *Mountain Windsong: A Novel of the Trail of Tears* emphasizes the limits of restoring justice from within the domestic legal framework and introduces the language of human rights as an alternative discourse with potential for securing Native rights in the domestic arena. Cherokee writer Diane Glancy's *Pushing the Bear: A Novel of the Trail of Tears* (1996) picks up the conversation where Conley left it by adding Indigenous praxis to the international law debates and scholarly theories about the relationship of individual and collective interests.

By advancing a conception of Cherokee peoplehood in which individual and collective interests are in harmony with and mutually constitutive of each other, Glancy's novel emphasizes their compatibility and complementarity. Conley's and Glancy's novels suggest that recognizing themselves as human/Indigenous rights subjects before the international community might help Native peoples challenge the Native subjectivities created by federal Indian law and US politics, and have their political and cultural autonomy and rights to land recognized by the US government.

The Removal novels of Sharon Ewell Foster (African-Cherokee) and Zelda Lockhart (African-Choctaw) treated in Chapter 4, "'Cherokee by Blood'?," reflect extensively on the long-term impact of Native subjectivities, as defined by the settler state, on tribal forms of governance, tribal law, and intratribal relations. In particular, they position themselves with respect to the struggle of the freedmen to secure citizenship in the Cherokee and Choctaw Nations that was in full swing at the time of their writing. The debates about citizenship within these and other former slaveholding tribes have resulted from the racialization of tribal notions of belonging and reflect the deep legacy of federal ideologies of blood and race in Indian country. Foster's *Abraham's Well: A Novel* (2006) and Lockhart's *Cold Running Creek* (2007) retell Indian Removal from the perspective of a group that was marginalized in a twofold manner (dispossessed and enslaved): the African American and African-Native slaves owned by Native American masters. By narrating the slaves' suffering in the face of Removal, these texts establish a literary claim for the acknowledgment of the freedmen's tribal membership. They retell the history of Removal to promote visions of peoplehood grounded in a shared history of suffering, lived kinship relations, and an ongoing commitment to cultural practices. Native peoplehood, they suggest, should be based on Indigenous epistemologies rather than on a settler colonial normative order structured along the lines of property and race. Foster and Lockhart thus pave the way for more inclusive forms of Native Removal writing that also pay attention to and honor the experiences of those walking the trail who were of African American and Afro-Native heritage.

Chapter 5, "'Museumized' *indians*," considers contemporary Native Removal texts that argumentatively follow Foster and Lockhart in that they envision how Native individuals' and collectives' continued reliance on and internalization of settler colonial notions of *indianness* will affect

Native forms of being and belonging. Blake Hausman's and Stephen Graham Jones's speculative Removal novels, *Riding the Trail of Tears: A Novel* (2011) and *The Bird Is Gone: A ~~Monograph~~ Manifesto* (2003), respectively, draw parallels between the historical deprivation of Native Americans of their "real" property and the ongoing appropriation of Indigenous intellectual property. They thus respond to legal debates about what has become known as Native cultural appropriation—that is, the use of Indigenous names, imagery, history, iconography, and other symbols by non-Native corporations, the tourist industry, popular culture, and science without Native permission. By narratively linking the taking of Native land in the context of Removal with ongoing and future forms of Native cultural appropriation, Hausman and Jones illustrate the dangers this most recent form of appropriation poses to Native peoplehood: it renders Native individuals and collectives voiceless, unravels Native forms of belonging, and replaces Native cultural practices with non-Native notions of cultural authenticity. In short, it museumizes Native lives and cultures. Through their novels, Hausman and Jones appeal to Native Americans to disentangle the parameters of Native peoplehood from settler colonial representations and to define themselves on the basis of their own, contemporary values and their shared history of colonization.

The epilogue creates a dialogue between the visions of Native peoplehood and Indigenous futurity that the Native Removal writings discussed in this book develop. It also engages in a final meditation on why Native authors across the tribal spectrum have been returning in their writings to this particular historical act of settler colonial violence and on the particular role of Removal fiction in Native struggles against dispossession. Gerald Vizenor's *Chair of Tears: A Novel* (2012), one of the most recent Native Removal writings and a highly ironic and self-reflexive fictionalization of Indian Removal, will be a source of insight and inspiration for perspectivizing Native Removal literature as a critical practice for imagining and enacting Indigenous futures.

I hope that my comparative, contextualized analysis of Native Removal literature across the centuries contributes to a fuller experience of the dimensions of law that bear upon Indigenous polities and individuals and to a better understanding of the significant role that Native literature plays for Native processes of self-articulation and self-definition, and Native practices of resistance. I also hope to highlight the synergies between aesthetics and politics in fictional and nonfictional Native Removal literature and thus to facilitate greater appreciation of this compelling body of texts.

CHAPTER 1

"Domestic Dependent Nations"

NATIVE VISIONS OF BELONGING AND THE
LEGAL IDEOLOGY OF REMOVAL

THE PERIOD OF Indian Removal brought forth a wave of legal documents that constructed subjectivities for Native Americans that would facilitate the production of a coherent imperial geography and the appropriation of Native lands (Rifkin, *Manifesting America* 26, 48). Besides laws passed by Congress and single southern states, as well as treaties negotiated between the US government and Native tribes, the Marshall Trilogy remains the Removal era's most significant and far-reaching set of rulings, determining the geographical, political, and legal contours of Native America until the present day (Wilkinson, *Blood Struggle* 24). In *Johnson v. McIntosh* (1823), *Cherokee Nation v. Georgia* (1831), and *Worcester v. Georgia* (1832), the Supreme Court, headed by Chief Justice John Marshall, defined forms of Indigenous belonging, including the legal status of Native American collectives and their property rights (Rifkin, *Manifesting America* 41).[1]

To fully grasp the complexities of the Marshall Court's juridical constructs and to comprehend the contemporary Indigenous responses to these rulings, it is necessary to shed light on the "interplay between state and federal courts" and not just—as is often done by Indigenous studies scholars—to concentrate on Supreme Court decisions alone (Garrison 6). For Marshall's rulings should not merely be understood as attempts to circumscribe Indigenous sovereignty. By strengthening federal power over "Indian affairs," Marshall sought to counter a competing legal position being advanced by the state legislatures and state supreme courts of Georgia, Tennessee, and Alabama at the time (Garrison 5, 178). Central to this position was the notion of state sovereignty—that is, the states' authority "to extend [their] jurisdiction to the reaches of [their] territorial limits, regardless of federal-Indian treaties or national legislation to the contrary." According to this view, the states had the right to abolish the laws and governments, and extinguish the property claims, of the Native communities living within their territorial borders (Garrison 6; see also 5). The political discussions about Removal unleashed a "controversy for jurisdiction . . . between the states and the general government, as momentous as any arising since we became independent," to use the words of John Catron, chief justice of the Tennessee Supreme Court (qtd. in Garrison 225). The Native communities to be dispossessed were thus "caught in the overlapping institutional projects of rendering domestic space continuous/contiguous" as well as "defining and negotiating the relative spheres of federal and state jurisdiction" (Rifkin, *Manifesting America* 38; see also Garrison 11; Rosen, *American Indians* 39).

The writings of the Cherokee politicians John Ross, Elias Boudinot, and John Ridge in reaction to this jurisdictional tug-of-war in the context of Removal reflect Indigenous awareness of the precariousness of the Native legal position. These Cherokee intellectuals were highly literate in the English language, deeply familiar with theories of natural law and positive law, and hence able to critically engage with the arguments advanced by American jurists. Moreover, they were the political leaders of a tribal community with a long history of negotiation with the settler state.[2] In their memorials to the US Congress, their speeches within the Cherokee Nation, their correspondence, and their newspaper editorials, these Cherokee writers sought to make sense of the American legal system with its different, idiosyncratic, and often opposing sets of arguments, rationalizations, and rhetoric, and the struggles about jurisdiction. They grappled with, challenged, and resisted the subjectivities created by American law, strategically employed arguments from the natural law tradition to assert Indigenous rights and to challenge settler colonial positive law, and articulated their own visions of Cherokee peoplehood and futurity against the complex workings of that law.

The tenuous Native legal position between state and federal jurisdictions and their respective constructions of Indigenous forms of belonging moved west with the settlers and complicated the process of rebuilding the Cherokee Nation in Indian Territory. About two decades after the Trail of Tears, in 1854, John Rollin Ridge published *The Life and Adventures of Joaquín Murieta*—the first novel ever written by a Native American.

The Life and Adventures is a complex allegory of Removal written at a time when some territories in the West had just achieved statehood and, in the fashion of southeastern states, begun to curtail Native rights and deprive Native Americans of their property. Like the generation of Cherokee writers before him, Ridge responded to the controversy of jurisdiction over Native American affairs by mobilizing the natural law tradition as a locus of resistance at a time when the United States was increasingly turning away from those foundations toward legal positivism. Ridge's use of poetry and the literary device of allegory in his novel, however, allowed him to gauge new and far more radical modes of subaltern resistance: challenging the authority of American law through anticolonial insurrection.

However, one would not do justice to the Removal writings by Ross, Boudinot, and both Ridges if one read them as mere responses to the external challenges posed by US Indian law and policy. My close readings of their writings suggest that they were not merely "ironic counternarratives," as Arnold Krupat calls them, rejecting colonial ascriptions and definitions (Krupat, *Ethnocricticism* 160). Neither can they be largely interpreted as the written products of an emergent Cherokee elite that, besides responding to settler colonial law and policy, was intent on "construct[ing] . . . class-specific narratives of collective identity that . . . serve as the basis for institutionalizing capitalist political-economy and delegitimizing tradition," as Mark Rifkin writes (*Manifesting America* 68, 73). In its use of a "national discourse . . . to increase trade, redefine property ownership and inheritance, and radically curb the authority of town councils," Rifkin states, this elite produced "a large subaltern class still committed to clan and town affiliations" (39, 56). This notion of a "divide between nobly doomed [subaltern] traditionalists and Machiavellian mixed-bloods, wealthy elites, or whatever the Othered group of Cherokees is called" has been critiqued by Cherokee scholar Joshua B. Nelson, who considers this binarism inadequate for grasping the complexity of Cherokee history (153; see also 138).

Underlining Nelson's critique, this chapter argues that the concepts of peoplehood and belonging developed by Ross, Boudinot, and both Ridges in the context of Removal need to be understood as attempts to assert a Cherokee subject position within the US legal system with the object to resist settler colonial incursions and thus to ensure the Cherokees' continued existence on their land as an autonomous cultural-political entity.

Rather than engaging in "assimilationist mimicry," these Cherokee intellectuals pursued "culture-perpetuating strategies"—that is, they thought through possible ways Cherokee traditions and practices could prevail in the face of dispossession (Nelson 149). Rather than merely "talk[ing] back," they articulated visions of peoplehood with what Nelson calls a "peculiarly Cherokee inflection" that were deeply grounded in extant Cherokee epistemologies, customs, and practices (Lyons, "Rhetorical Sovereignty" 458; see also Nelson 151). Produced during a process of intense internal cultural-political changes and negotiations, the writings discussed in this chapter need to be viewed as internal reflections on and negotiations of Cherokee forms and practices of living, belonging, and being.

By the time of Removal, such forms and practices of "Cherokeeness" were far from what is often termed "traditional." In his monograph, Nelson redraws the development of Cherokee culture away from rule based on consensus toward increasing political and governmental centralization, highlighting that Cherokee nationhood proceeded from *"within"* Cherokee culture and was not simply the result of assimilating to or imitating the settler nation (149; italics mine; see also 146). Development toward greater centralization and formalization could also be witnessed in the legal realm. Rather than being ruled by rigid sets of laws, most tribal communities had—prior to contact—been organized by knowledge of precedents and customs, which each generation passed down to the next orally. If the situation required it and consensus prevailed, communities could diverge from precedent. Institutionally, the clan was mainly responsible for exercising legal powers (Deloria and Lytle, *American Indians* 18; Strickland 27). Between 1750 and 1840, the Cherokees adopted a jury system and gradually replaced their law of the blood feud. From 1808 onward, they began to write down and formalize laws, regulating matters such as the inheritance of property, labor contracts, and money lending, and they passed statutes making national officials responsible for punishing crimes, a measure that shifted the task of law enforcement away from the clans. The Cherokees also established a standing legislative committee to manage national affairs when the general legislative council was not in session, introduced courts and a judiciary, and ratified a written constitution modeled after, but not solely based on, the US Constitution. The responsibility for all these efforts toward centralizing and formalizing legal authority and establishing a Cherokee state "belongs with the whole of the [Cherokee] body politic," as Nelson emphasizes, including those with more traditional leanings (153; see also Nelson, 146–47; Denson, *Demanding the Cherokee Nation* 20; Perdue, *Slavery* 56; Daniel 97–98, 106–11).

With their people transitioning from traditional legal principles and practices to a hybrid legal system that combined Anglo-American and Indigenous legal structures, the Cherokee intellectuals discussed in this chapter used Removal and the collective subjectivities for Native Americans constructed in its wake by American law to ponder the forms and sources of law in general and the rule of law within Native communities. John Rollin Ridge's novel, in particular, needs to be read as a critical engagement with the operation of the law within the Cherokee Nation in the West and as a reflection on the forms that law ought to take to guarantee Indigenous perseverance and flourishing in the future.

A PEOPLE WITHOUT LAND? THE WRITINGS OF JOHN ROSS, ELIAS BOUDINOT, AND JOHN RIDGE

Johnson v. McIntosh (1823), the first case of the Marshall Trilogy, "put a final nail in the coffin of the older view of Indian property rights" (Banner 179).[3] By codifying the so-called discovery doctrine, that is, the idea that "discovery gave exclusive title to those who made it," Marshall claimed that Native Americans lost the underlying title to their territory at precisely the moment Europeans set foot on Indigenous lands. While the European powers exercised "ultimate dominion," "a power to grant the soil, while yet in possession of the natives," Native Americans retained merely "the right of occupancy," with "their rights to complete sovereignty . . . necessarily diminished, and their power to dispose of the soil at their own will, to whomsoever they pleased . . . denied" (*Johnson v. McIntosh* 21 U.S. 574; see also Fletcher, "Iron Cold" 631). By sleight of hand and with the help of a legal fiction, Marshall thus turned the Natives from owners into occupants of the soil and opened the door to settler colonial acts of Native dispossession in both the present and future. He remained ambiguous, however, when it came to assigning authority over Native territory: he assigned the preemption right as well as the title to the land to "either the United States or the several states" (*Johnson v. McIntosh* 21 U.S. 585). The alienation of Native lands and the extinguishment of Native title, he further argued, could take place "either by purchase or by conquest" (587).[4] While hinting at the fact that the court did not necessarily approve of the "extravagant . . . pretension of converting the discovery of an inhabited country into conquest," Marshall emphasized that "conquest gives a title which the Courts of the conqueror cannot deny" (591, 588). He conceded that the law of nations clearly regulated relations between the conqueror and the conquered[5] but then proceeded to apply the long-held cultural fiction of Native savagism: due to the savage nature of the Indigenous peoples inhabiting America—their warlike character and their refusal to remove the country from a state of wilderness—the law of nations did not apply, and the European powers had the right to conquer and dispossess them (589–90).

By changing Native proprietary rights from ownership to occupancy, *Johnson* established the legal foundation for the southern states to co-opt Native American lands (Garrison 101). In 1827 Georgia's legislature passed a resolution arguing that Native Americans were mere tenants at will and that the state of Georgia held ultimate title to their lands, could end their tenancy at any moment, and "had the right to extend her authority and laws over her whole territory, and to coerce obedience to them from all descriptions of people . . . who may reside within her limits" (qtd. in Rosen, *American Indians* 39). In the legislative session of December 1828, Georgia's legislators passed a bill extending the criminal and civil jurisdiction of the state over the Cherokee Nation and annexing large tracts of Cherokee land into several state counties (Garrison 104). They also declared that after June 1, 1830, "all laws, usages, customs made, established and enforced in the said territory by the said Cherokee Indians" would be null and void. Georgia's legislature thus decided to abolish the Cherokee Nation, its constitution, its courts, and its laws and determined that those Cherokees who decided to remain in the state after the above date would become subject to Georgia's laws and jurisdiction (qtd. in Garrison 104). In its 1829 session, the state legislature annexed the remaining Cherokee lands, endowed the state militia with the authority to arrest those violating Georgia law on the territory of the Cherokee Nation, and created superior courts to take care of such infringements. The judges in these courts were instructed to treat the entire body of Cherokee law "as if the same had never existed" (qtd. in Garrison 106).

CHAPTER 1

Johnson also became the major point of reference for the southern courts. *Georgia v. Tassel* (1830), for instance, resulted from attempts of Cherokee political leaders to challenge Georgia's extension of its laws over the Cherokee Nation. In its ruling, Georgia's supreme court made use of both the discovery doctrine and the legal fiction of Native savagery to refute Cherokee claims of land ownership, political autonomy, and sovereignty (Garrison 114–15, 118). It diverged from *Johnson,* however, in its unequivocal endorsement of the state's authority to extinguish Native title, arguing that Georgia held the rights previously maintained by the British crown and was "seized in fee of all lands within its chartered limits" (qtd. in Garrison 117; see also 116; Rosen, *American Indians* 65).[6]

The precarious position between state and federal law, as well as Georgia's attempts to eradicate Cherokee sovereignty, forced contemporary Cherokee intellectuals to navigate between the various bodies and institutions of American law. Rather than merely refuting the forms of belonging developed by the Marshall Court, Cherokee leaders carefully weighed the court's reasoning, interpreted it in light of the natural law tradition and Cherokee law, and hence developed complex legal arguments with the aim of strengthening their position between federal and state jurisdictions and ensuring the Cherokees' continued existence as peoples on their land.

The "Constitution of the Cherokee Nation" from 1827 can be considered one of the earliest Cherokee texts that critically engaged with *Johnson* and its construction of Native property rights. The second section of article 1 defines in much detail property relations within the Cherokee Nation and thus challenges Marshall's conceptions of Native occupancy and of Natives as savage strangers to the idea of property:

> The Sovereignty and Jurisdiction of this Government shall extend over the country within the boundaries above described, and the lands therein are, and shall remain the common property of the Nation; but the improvements made thereon, and in the possession of the citizens of the Nation, are the exclusive and indefeasible property of the citizens respectively who made, or may rightfully be in possession of them; Provided, That the citizens of the Nation, possessing exclusive and indefeasible right to their respective improvements, as expressed in this article, shall

possess no right nor power to dispose of their improvements in any manner whatever to the United States, individual states, nor to individual citizens hereof; and that, whenever any such citizen or citizens shall remove with their effects out of the limits of this Nation, and become citizens of any other government, all their rights and privileges as citizens of this nation shall cease. ("Constitution of the Cherokee Nation," art. 1, sec. 2)

The Cherokee Constitution emphasizes that the Cherokees do acknowledge the existence of property. Yet their conception of property has a particularly Cherokee inflection in that notions of collective selfhood are inextricably tied to ancestral tribal lands. As these lands are owned by the nation in common and form the basis of Cherokee collective identity, they are considered inalienable. The "improvements" of these lands are acknowledged to be private property, but their being part of the land makes them inalienable to outsiders. The use of the term "improvement" needs to be read as a reference to the natural law philosophy of land ownership. In his *Second Treatise of Government* (1690), John Locke—himself a colonial administrator responsible for establishing land policy in colonial Virginia—attempted "to secularize the divine foundations of property law," as Brenna Bhandar put it. Grounding the right to property in natural law, he established an inextricable connection between working/improving and owning the land: mixing one's labor with the earth gives someone a right to the land they have improved. While the world had been given to humankind in common by God, human industry justified the private taking of land. And human industry and improvement were defined by Locke narrowly—as making use of the land for agricultural purposes. Unimproved land—that is, land not tilled or planted—was, according to Locke, wasteland, with no value and therefore ready to be taken by anyone willing to make proper use of it (Locke 215–19, 221–22; see also Bhandar, *Colonial Lives of Property* 47–48). According to Locke, however, this labor theory of property did not apply to Native Americans, who did not have natural law rights, he believed, and hence could not possess the lands upon which they lived. His employment of natural law arguments to demonstrate Native lack of possession made Locke very popular among Anglo-American lawyers and justices, such as Marshall, who resorted to his theories to justify their legal doctrines of discovery and *terra nullius* and hence the English colonization and dispossession of Native Americans (Fitzmaurice 384, 387, 407; Bhandar, *Colonial Lives of Property* 49).

In the context of Removal, the Cherokees used Locke's labor theory of property to argue in favor of, rather than against, Indigenous peoples. By highlighting their pursuit of agriculture and their improvement of the land, Cherokee leaders strengthened Cherokee rights to and ownership of the land.[7] Even if one accepted the premise that the Cherokees merely occupied the land,[8] one would have to concede that their efforts at improving the land had generated proprietary rights that could not be infringed upon without violating natural law. The Cherokees thus initially turned to Indigenous positive law—their constitution—and to natural law arguments of ownership to challenge American positive law and its conceptualization of Native property rights.

Cherokee politicians responded more explicitly to *Johnson* in 1828, when, encouraged by the presidential election of Removal advocate Andrew Jackson, Georgia's state authorities began annexing Cherokee lands (Denson, *Demanding the Cherokee Nation* 25; Peyer, *The Tutor'd Mind* 190). As Georgia derived the major justification for its actions from its interpretation of *Johnson*, in his annual message to the Cherokees on October 13, 1828, John Ross, the chief of the Cherokee Nation, refutes Marshall's line of argumentation in that ruling. Ross begins his message by questioning the doctrine of discovery and conquest:

> In the first place, the Europeans . . . discovered this vast Continent, and found it inhabited exclusively by Indians of various Tribes, and by a pacific courtesy and designing stratagems, the aboriginal proprietors were induced to permit a people from a foreign clime to plant colonies, and without consent or knowledge of the native Lords, a potentate of England whose eyes never saw, whose purse never purchased, and whose sword never conquered the soil we inhabit, presumed to issue a parchment called a "Charter," to the Colony of Georgia, in which its boundary was set forth, including a great extent of country inhabited by the Cherokees and other Indian Nations. . . . Thus stands the naked claim of Georgia, to a portion of our lands. The claim advanced under the plea of discovery, is preposterous. Our ancestors from time immemorial

possessed the country, not by a "Charter" from the hand of a mortal King, who had no right to grant it, but by the Will of the King of Kings, who created all things and liveth for ever & ever. (qtd. in Moulton 142–43)

This Indigenous narration of what Europeans view as discovery emphasizes Native possession and marks the settler colonial taking of Indigenous land as illegitimate—as theft. By calling the Natives "the aboriginal proprietors" of the land, Ross refutes colonial fictions of propertyless, wandering savages. He considers the charter issued by the British king to Georgia incapable of transferring Native property rights to Europeans, as its issuance involved neither purchase nor conquest—according to Marshall himself, prerequisites for the extinguishment of Indian title. But the Cherokee chief goes one step further. Comparing the temporalities of Native and settler colonial property rights to the land, he illustrates that while European ownership is rooted in time and dependent on a human-made written document granted by a human not authorized to do so, Native ownership has a mystical origin and is situated outside the confines of memorable time. Native Americans received the land as a gift from God. The land was then passed on from generation to generation, through acts of inheritance, Ross explains in more detail in a later memorial. "This right of inheritance we have never ceded, nor ever forfeited" (Memorial of 18 Dec. 1829 rpt. in *Cherokee Phoenix* 20 Jan. 1830, 1). It was this line of argumentation, emphasizing the Cherokee "right of inheritance and immemorial peaceable possession," that would be rehearsed by Cherokee leaders in the years to come. Not only does the act of perpetual inheritance from time immemorial emphasize the divine and ancient nature of Cherokee proprietary rights, but it also constitutes the basis for another significant argument against Removal brought forth by Cherokee leaders: their deep attachment to their land. "To the land of which we are now in possession we are attached—it is our fathers' gift—it contains their ashes," Ross points out in the 1829 memorial. The land, he thus suggests, is not a commodity that can be sold or exchanged; it is rather an integral part of Cherokee forms of living and being.

After attacking the discovery doctrine, Ross deconstructs Marshall's claim that the Revolutionary War was a war of conquest, giving the newly established United States title over Native lands.[9] "The Cherokees took a part in the war, *only* as the allies of Great Britain, and not as her subjects," he highlights, "being an Independent Nation, over whose lands she exercised no rights of jurisdiction; therefore, nothing could be claimed from them, in regard to their lands, by the conqueror over the rights of Great Britain." Ross then cites the Treaty of Hopewell, which the United States concluded with the Cherokees in 1785, and the multiple treaties signed between individual sovereign Native nations and the United States afterward and points out that in none of these agreements can there be found any evidence for the idea "that our title to the soil has been forfeited or claimed . . . but, to the contrary, we discover that the United States solemnly pledged their faith that our title should be guaranteed to our Nation forever" (qtd. in Moulton 143; italics in original). Ross applies the language of nationhood to a time when the Cherokees had not yet adopted a centralized form of government. Nationhood implies sovereignty; sovereignty, in turn, entails authority over a territory and the people within it and underlines Native claims for land ownership. The Cherokees were sovereign allies and not subjects of Great Britain, Ross argues. And as Great Britain did not hold any rights over Cherokee lands, Native lands were not part of the territory transferred from Great Britain to the newly founded United States by right of conquest (Banner 161).

Ross's citing of treaties and his employment of treaty language ("solemnly," "faith," "guarantee") lays bare the argumentative gaps in *Johnson*, which completely excludes the practice of treaty making from its historical narrative. Treaties signify the long history of US–Cherokee engagement between unequal yet sovereign contracting parties in which the Cherokees were considered the unquestionable owners of the land. Termed "supreme law of the land" by the US Constitution's Supremacy Clause and hence legally superior to state laws such as Georgia's extension laws, the treaties would become the Cherokees' most important weapon in the battle against dispossession. The Commerce Clause of the US Constitution and the various Intercourse Acts passed from the 1790s onward further elevated the status of Native tribal communities as independent and sovereign nations and were therefore also frequently cited by Ross and other Cherokee politicians in all their communications, both among themselves and with the federal government (Moulton 155, 226, 427).[10] Read in light of Ross's writings, *Johnson*—and by implication rulings by the southern courts based on *Johnson*—appears as an anomaly in the long history of Native–settler relations. It is inconsistent with practices of treaty making and contradicts the spirit and letter of the US Constitution.

Ross also counters the cultural fiction of Native Americans as "fierce savages," which Marshall advanced in *Johnson* and which was so readily taken up by the southern judiciary. He does so by developing a counter-narrative of civilization firmly grounded in the natural law tradition. In a letter to the Senate and House of Representatives from February 27, 1829, Ross and other tribal leaders claim that "our improvement has been without a parallel in the history of all Indian nations" and enumerate evidence for such improvement:

> Agriculture is every where [*sic*] pursued, and the interests of our citizens are permanent in the soil. We have enjoyed the blessings of Christian instruction, the advantages of education and merit are justly appreciated, a Government of regular law has been adopted. . . . Under the parental protection of the United States, we have arrived at the present degree of improvement, and they are now to decide whether we shall continue as a people, or be abandoned to destruction. (qtd. in Moulton 157)

The rhetoric of improvement the letter writers use here speaks back to the ideology of improvement that found its clearest expression in Locke's theory of private property ownership, which I have already elaborated on above. According to Locke, uncultivated land was considered waste, in need of improvement and hence deemed free for appropriation; those refusing to pursue agriculture and to cultivate the land were equally in need of improvement and hence ready to be assimilated to a civilized way of life (Locke 227, 232; see also Bhandar, *Colonial Lives of Property* 36). The "ideology of improvement," Bhandar claims, thus "bound together the valuation of land with its people." Progressing from a state of nature to one of civilization was inextricably linked to the appropriation and cultivation of land; in short, without land ownership, no civilization (182; see also 48). Locke's theorization of "the true subject of Reason through . . . his capacity for appropriation," as well as Anglo-American convictions of their own racial superiority, provided the rationale that the colonizers needed to justify the dispossession of Indigenous peoples (182).

By emphasizing their engagement in agriculture, the Cherokee letter writers assert their capacity to progress from a state of nature to civilized ways of living and being, and their achievement of this progression. Their counternarrative of civilization also engages the natural law philosophy of José de Acosta, whose writings were no less influential than Locke's among the English promoters of colonization. In his *De procuranda Indorum* (1588), Acosta came up with a progressive theory of civilization. He divided Indigenous peoples into three classes on the basis of certain cultural signs. The Indigenous peoples belonging to the "first class," Acosta explained, "do not depart greatly from true reason and the common way of life." Signs of their civilization were their "stable form of government, legal system, fortified cities, magistrates," commerce, and "use and knowledge of letters." By contrast, those belonging to the "third class" were "savages similar to wild animals, who hardly have human feelings—without law, without agreements, without government, without nationhood, who move from place to place." Acosta also argued that such people could not be dispossessed because they did not possess in the first place, having no concept of *meum* and *tuum*. They had failed to create dominion by exploiting the laws of nature (Acosta qtd. in Fitzmaurice 402–3). From the early seventeenth century onward, to make their taking of Indigenous lands appear legitimate, promoters of Anglo-American colonization described Native Americans as third-class barbarians devoid of society, closer to animals than to humans, and living off nature rather than making use of it (Fitzmaurice 399, 403–9). The Cherokee Removal writers challenge such placement in the third class. Not only do they exemplify the Cherokees' degree of knowledge and education, but they also underline Cherokee humanity and list all the signs of Cherokee civilization—besides agriculture, the adoption of Christianity, a central government, and the rule of law—that speak against settler colonial dispossession and in favor of Indigenous perseverance.

The major promoter of the Cherokee counternarrative of civilization was Elias Boudinot, who in February 1828 became the first editor of the *Cherokee Phoenix*. In the first issue, he announces that one of his foremost objectives as editor is "to correct all misstatements, relating to the present condition of the Cherokees" (qtd. in Perdue, *Cherokee Editor* 94). Using the language of the law, he declares all the so-called facts that the advocates of Native savagism provide to be "nothing but unfounded assertions."

He "appeal[s] to all honest eye-witnesses" to intervene in favor of the Cherokees and offers his own "unbiased testimony." His speech of defense culminates in the following assertion: "Whoever believes that the Cherokees subsist on game, is most wretchedly deceived, and is grossly ignorant of existing facts. *The Cherokees do not live upon the chase,* but upon the fruits of the earth produced by their labour" (qtd. in Perdue, *Cherokee Editor* 114, 115, 116; italics in original). Like Ross, Boudinot turns to Lockean natural law theories of property to refute the idea of Native lack of possession and to challenge concepts of Native land ownership, or the absence thereof, in American federal and state law.[11]

Upon realizing that their invocations of natural law and re-narrations of the history of European settlement from an Indigenous point of view did not remove the threat of Removal, both Ross and Boudinot decided that legal resistance through federal recognition was their only chance to halt Georgia's increasing encroachment on their land and culture. In mid-May 1830, Boudinot writes in an editorial that the Cherokees wish for "the solemn adjudication of a tribunal, whose province is to interpret the treaties, *the supreme law of the land.*" Only there, he argues, can their "injured rights" be "defended and protected" (qtd. in Perdue, *Cherokee Editor* 118; italics in original). In his message to the Cherokee General Council in July 1830, Ross similarly declares that the only course of action left to the Cherokees is "to consult and employ counsel to defend our cause before the Supreme Court of the United States, in which tribunal, as the conservatory of the Constitution, Treaties, and laws of the Union, we can yet hope for justice, and to which we should fearlessly and firmly appeal" (qtd. in Moulton 191, 192). And such appeal soon followed. *Cherokee Nation,* the second case in the Marshall Trilogy, resulted from the Cherokees' attempt to challenge *Georgia v. Tassel* by appealing to the US Supreme Court.[12] In his lead opinion, Marshall never addressed the question of whether Georgia's extension laws violated treaty agreements or the US Constitution. Instead, he inquired into whether the Cherokee Nation could be considered "a foreign state in the sense of the Constitution" (*Cherokee Nation v. Georgia* 30 U.S. 16). The chief justice concluded that "it may well be doubted whether those tribes which reside within the acknowledged boundaries of the United States can, with strict accuracy, be denominated foreign nations. They may, more correctly, perhaps, be denominated domestic dependent nations," Marshall reasoned. "They occupy a territory to which we assert a title independent of their will, which must take effect in point of possession when their right of possession ceases. Meanwhile they are in a state of pupilage" (17). Marshall hence confirmed the concept of Indian occupancy as outlined in *Johnson*. Moreover, by deciding against conceptualizing the Cherokee Nation as a foreign nation, the Marshall Court declared the Cherokees' inability to sue under the court's doctrine of original jurisdiction. It also extricated itself from the struggles for power over Native affairs between the federal government and the southern states and from the debates about Native rights by concluding that the Supreme Court "is not the tribunal... which can redress the past or prevent the future" (20).

Cherokee Nation, however, also strengthened the Native legal position. Throughout the ruling, Marshall elaborated on the numerous treaties concluded between the Cherokees and the US government and emphasized the "solemn guarantee" to the unceded land that each of the treaties included (*Cherokee Nation v. Georgia* 30 U.S. 15). The chief justice also mused on the anomalous nature of American treaties, which recognized the Cherokees as a "people capable of maintaining the relations of peace and war, and of being responsible in their political character for any violation of their engagements, or for any aggression committed on the citizens of the United States by any individual of their community" (16). At the same time, however, by signing treaties, the Cherokees "subject[ed] [themselves] to many of those restraints which are imposed upon our own citizens." While it certainly existed, Native sovereignty, Marshall claimed, was impaired by the Cherokees' granting the United States "the sole and exclusive right of regulating the trade with them, and managing all their affairs as they think proper" (17). The courts, the ruling conclusively pointed out, were bound by the treaties and the federal laws enacted in the spirit of these treaties. Indian affairs, as Marshall clearly reminded Americans, were under the authority of the federal government, not the states.

Due to its extensive discussion of the nature of Native sovereignty, *Cherokee Nation* was received favorably by Cherokee leaders. Rather than interpreting the ruling as a severe curtailment of Indigenous sovereignty, Ross considers it "a foundation... upon which our injured rights may be reared & made permanent." In light of Georgia's violations of Cherokee rights, Marshall's ruling at least recognized Native sovereignty and rights to the land. "Upon the whole," Ross argues, "I view the opinion of the Court as regards our political character & the relations we sustain towards the United States, as being conclusively adverse to the pretended rights which have been asserted by Georgia over us, under the countenance of the President" (qtd. in Moulton 216–17). Boudinot similarly claims that through the Supreme Court decision, the Cherokees "stand upon a perfectly safe ground as regards themselves—if they will suffer, they will suffer unrighteously—if their rights and their property are forcibly taken away from them the responsibility will not be upon them, but upon their treacherous 'guardians'" (qtd. in Perdue, *Cherokee Editor* 126–27).

Even in political speeches within the Cherokee Nation, Ross rhetorically embraces the settler colonial concept of domestic dependency in order to make a strong claim for Cherokee political rights. He characterizes the Cherokee Nation as a "weak defenceless community . . . forming an alliance with, and placed in the heart of so powerful a Nation as the United States" and as "having surrendered a portion of our sovereignty, as a security for our protection" (qtd. in Moulton 229). Ross hence emphasizes that, irrespective of Georgia's claims to the contrary, the Cherokee community is a sovereign nation (even if this sovereignty is only an impaired sovereignty). By representing the surrender of "a portion of" Cherokee sovereignty as a voluntary act on the part of the Cherokee Nation (rather than a settler colonial legal maneuver) and by highlighting the unequal power relations between the Cherokees and the United States, Ross tries to evoke a sense of obligation on the part of the US government. Overall, *Cherokee Nation* leads to a sense of guarded optimism within the Cherokee community: Ross perceives the possibility that "our unfeeling persecutors may be met and bayed at the bar of justice" and that "our cause will ultimately triumph. It is the cause of humanity and justice" (qtd. in Moulton 217, 218). His mention of the "bar of justice" indicates that he strongly believes in the necessity of continuing to use the weapons offered to the Cherokees by the American legal system itself.

Besides thus employing American positive law for their own political purposes, Cherokee leaders critically engaged in legal-philosophical reflections on the limits of and the potential inherent in law. In an editorial in the *Cherokee Phoenix* from June 17, 1829, Boudinot develops several categories of law. Proceeding from the premise that laws can be categorized either in terms of the lawgivers' degree of civilization or in terms of their moral character, he differentiates between "savage laws," such as the law of retaliation, and "Christian laws & regulations" on the one hand; and tyrannical and nontyrannical laws on the other (qtd. in Perdue, *Cherokee Editor* 108-9; see also 123). While he interprets the treaties, the Intercourse Acts, and the US Constitution as Christian and nontyrannical laws, he considers Georgia's extension laws a tyrannical and unrighteous instrument of colonialism, seeking "to bring the Cherokees to terms": "If this is not the *design* it may possibly be the *tendency* of the law" (qtd. in Perdue, *Cherokee Editor* 122; italics in original). The law, as Boudinot clarifies, can be employed by those in power to achieve their political and economic goals. It can be construed in a self-serving way even if this means it is "contrary to legal right" and "utterly at variance" with international and existing federal law, as Cherokee leaders phrase it elsewhere (Cherokee Memorial 15 Feb. 1830, rpt. in Krupat, *Ethnocriticism* appendix, 2, 4). And even if the law is not explicitly designed to deprive the Cherokees of their rights, law can, through tendentious readings, be construed that way. Boudinot thus deconstructs the idea of American law as just, securing freedom and equality, and of the United States as a nation under the rule of law. He presents settler colonial law as the ideal vehicle for those in power to justify and realize their interests.

Notwithstanding such critique, Cherokee leaders acknowledged law's potential to create social order and justice and to create legal subjects endowed with specific rights. According to Ross, a body of law and a constitution are vital for securing the Cherokees' "common welfare" and for protecting their "rights and happiness" (*Cherokee Phoenix*, 21 Oct. 1829: 2). Ross's encouragement of his fellow Cherokees in February 1830 to "patiently wait for justice through the proper tribunal" suggests that Cherokee leaders saw a connection between law and justice—at least in the case of Christian and nontyrannical laws (qtd. in Moulton 187; see also Cherokee Memorial Feb. 15, 1830 rpt. in Krupat, *Ethnocriticism* appendix, 5).

Ross's call for patience posed a challenge in light of the ongoing disenfranchisement of the Cherokees. Marshall's ambiguous conceptualization of Native tribes as "domestic dependent nations" was readily exploited by the southern judiciary in its efforts to rationalize the extension of jurisdiction over the Creeks and Cherokees. In *Caldwell v. Alabama* (1831), the Alabama Supreme Court characterized the concept of "domestic dependent nation" as "le[aving] the relation of the Indian tribes to the United

States in an awkward dilemma" and felt justified to emphasize state authority (qtd. in Garrison 165). Georgia also continued to abrogate Cherokee rights. In late 1830, for instance, the state legislature implemented a bill prohibiting the passage of any white person onto the territory of the Cherokee Nation without state permission. The question as to whether this state law violated the US Constitution's Commerce Clause led to *Worcester v. Georgia*, in which the Marshall Court was to decide if the Cherokee Republic was a sovereign nation recognized by treaties and outside the jurisdiction of single states (Norgren 112–15).

At first sight, *Worcester*, the Marshall Trilogy's third ruling, reads like a paraphrase of all the arguments Ross, Boudinot, and their Anglo-American supporters had brought forth against Georgia's extension laws.[13] Marshall declared the state law in question to be "repugnant to the Constitution, treaties or laws of the United States." He also modified the argumentation of his previous rulings, in particular *Johnson*. While in *Johnson* he had adopted the "limited possessor" notion of Native land rights, claiming that "exclusive title" rested with the discoverer, in *Worcester* the chief justice shifted to the "limited owner" view of Native title, arguing that discovery conferred only the "exclusive right to purchase"—that is, it merely conferred a right of preemption (*Worcester v. Georgia* 31 U.S. 516; B. Watson 999). In *Worcester*, Marshall also dismissed the idea of the extinguishment of Native title through conquest and considered the colonial charters "blank paper so far as the rights of the natives were concerned" (*Worcester v. Georgia* 31 U.S. 519). While treaties were absent from *Johnson*, *Worcester* included the history of treaty making from 1778 until 1832 and emphasized the treaties' "language of equality." Marshall conceded that those treaties were largely the creation of the colonizers due to the Natives' difficulties with the English language and their illiteracy, and therefore the treaties had to be understood as the former's express will. The chief justice paid particular attention to the Treaty of Hopewell, from which he quoted extensively to demonstrate that it "explicitly recogniz[ed] the national character of the Cherokees and their right to self-government, thus guarantying their lands, assuming the duty of protection, and of course pledging the faith of the United States for that protection" (546, 549, 556).

In contrast to the cultural fiction of Native savagism he had propagated in *Johnson*, in *Worcester* Marshall explicitly referred to the civilizational progress the Cherokees had made. He also emphasized the role of the United States in, and its commitment to, the process of Native civilization. The chief justice finally also elaborated on, and attenuated, the concept of "domestic dependent nation" he had developed in *Cherokee Nation*, this time, however, emphasizing the tribes' political independence. Indian nations, the ruling insists, "had always been considered as distinct, independent political communities, retaining their original natural rights as the undisputed possessors of the soil from time immemorial, with the single exception of that imposed by irresistible power, which excluded them from intercourse with any other European potentate than the first discoverer of the coast of the particular region claimed" (*Worcester v. Georgia* 31 U.S. 559–60). The fact that they had long been considered "nations" capable of concluding "treaties"—terms used in American diplomatic discourse with other nations as well—suggests that the existence of a distinct Indigenous peoplehood could not be denied (559–60). In his conclusory remarks, Marshall again emphasized that state law did not apply on tribal lands and that the intercourse between Natives and the United States was the legal prerogative of the federal government (520).

Legal studies scholars such as Lindsay Robertson and Tim Alan Garrison interpret *Worcester* as "*Johnson*'s undoing" and as a repudiation of the states' rights interpretation of the Commerce Clause, which was geared toward keeping the federal government out of almost every aspect of Indigenous–white relations beyond economic exchange (Robertson, *Conquest by Law* 133; see also Garrison 8). Scholars in Indigenous studies, such as Rifkin, have been more critical of the decision. Rather than repudiating state claims to Native land, Rifkin argues, *Worcester* sought to "fine-tune, and consolidate, a federalist system" that "mediate[d] access to [Indigenous land] through treaties, limiting the official expression of Indians to the signing of such agreements" (*Manifesting America* 51, 53). In Cherokee country at the time, the third ruling was celebrated as a declaration of Cherokee rights (Dale and Litton 5, 6).[14] Boudinot rejoices that *Worcester* places the legal controversy over jurisdiction "exactly where it ought to be, and where we have all along been desirous it should be . . . between the U.S. and the State of Georgia, or between the friends of the judiciary and the enemies of the judiciary" (qtd. in Dale and Litton 5). The controversy is "now set in array between Georgia and the laws, between Georgia and the Constitution," John Ridge, Boudinot's cousin, a skillful lawyer, argues in a similar vein (J. Ridge). And Ross celebrates the Supreme Court as the "strong shield" protecting Cherokee rights but concedes that under the Jackson administration, even such a shield might be of no use (qtd. in Moulton 243).

Ross's apprehensions were not unfounded. As Garrison rightly states, "*Worcester* simply went beyond what Georgia, the president, and a majority of Congress were willing to accept. Consequently, a vacuum now existed in American law" (197; see also 196). This legal vacuum would soon be filled by the Tennessee Supreme Court, which in its 1835 ruling *Tennessee v. Forman* decided on the question of whether the Cherokee Nation was a sovereign state. Chief Justice John Catron, whose opinion was presented as the official ruling of the court, voted to uphold the southern extension laws, spoke out against the idea of Cherokee national sovereignty, considered treaties unconstitutional federal infringements on state sovereignty, and declared *Johnson*, rather than *Worcester*, to be the standard-setting authority (Garrison 198, 207, 208, 211, 217).[15]

Upon realizing that the federal government continued to refuse to intervene on behalf of the Cherokees, a faction of Cherokees, led by Boudinot and Ridge, began to advocate the conclusion of a treaty ceding eastern Cherokee lands in exchange for land in the West. Boudinot's writings reveal that this federal refusal of intervention after *Worcester* was directly responsible for his shift in opinion. The decision of the Supreme Court, Boudinot argues in his letter resigning editorship of the *Cherokee Phoenix* in August 1832, "has forever closed the question of our conventional rights" (qtd. in Perdue, *Cherokee Editor* 163). There is nothing to be hoped for when dealing with a president "who feels himself under no obligation to *execute*, but has an inclination to *disregard* the laws and treaties, as interpreted by a proper branch of the Government" (qtd. in Perdue, *Cherokee Editor* 167; italics in original). To Boudinot, a Removal treaty appears the only legal instrument left to the Cherokees to uphold their sovereignty and to secure their survival as a nation. In a letter to the new editor of the *Cherokee Phoenix*, Elijah Hicks, he defends himself against accusations of a lack of patriotism by reconceptualizing the Cherokee relationship to the land:

> In one word, I may say that my patriotism consists in the *love of the country*, and *the love of the People*. These are intimately connected,

yet they are not altogether inseparable. They are inseparable if the people are made the first victim, for in that case the country must go also, and there must be an end of the objects of our patriotism. But if the country is lost, or is likely to be lost to all human appearance, and the people still exist, may I not, with a patriotism true and commendable, make a *question* for the safety of the remaining object of my affection? (qtd. in Perdue, *Cherokee Editor* 172; italics in original)

In this remarkable passage, Boudinot constructs Cherokee peoplehood as separate from Cherokee ancestral lands. While he admits that the two are "intimately connected," he grants that under certain circumstances they can be separated. Removal is such a circumstance. While Ross and other Cherokee leaders equate the loss of their homeland with the loss of peoplehood and hence fight against Removal, Jackson's intention to "remove" the tribe in spite of *Worcester* encourages Boudinot to envision the endurance of Cherokee peoplehood despite the loss of land. In his vision of a Cherokee collective identity separate from the land, the land ceases to be inalienable. Instead it becomes an object that can be exchanged for other land or goods. He combines this new conception of Cherokee land with a narrative of Cherokee cultural decline. Without the prospect of Removal, he reasons, vice and immorality will spread and hasten "the rapid tendency to a general immorality and debasement" (qtd. in Perdue, *Cherokee Editor* 223–24). Signing the Treaty of New Echota in October 1835 and hence agreeing to alienate what he until then considered inalienable seems to Boudinot the only way left to prevent the eradication of Cherokee political and cultural distinctness, even if his signature meant a breach of Cherokee law.[16]

Ross felt similarly despairing when realizing that *Worcester* did not effect any change. In a memorial to the Senate and House of Representatives from May 1834, Ross and other Cherokee political leaders describe the Cherokees' situation as follows: Since Georgia has assumed jurisdiction over the Cherokees, "the nation is stripped of its territory, and individuals of their property, without the least color of right, and in open violation of the guarantee of treaties." They continue, "at the same time the Cherokees, deprived of the protection of their own government and laws, are left without the protection of any other laws, outlawed as it were, and exposed to indignities, imprisonment, persecution, and even to death" (qtd. in Moulton 291). To express the extent of their vulnerability, the memorialists thus draw upon the concept of outlawry, a staple in both Cherokee and Western legal culture. For a long time, outlawry was an integral part of Cherokee criminal law. If a Cherokee individual caused trouble within clan structures and refused to amend his behavior, the clan could relieve itself from future responsibility for the member's acts by declaring him an outlaw. Outlawry both made the offender a social outcast and divested him of his rights under the blood feud. If the outlaw was killed, none of his clan members would avenge his death. Outlawry also had severe spiritual consequences: the soul of the Cherokee whose murder or accidental death had gone unavenged could not pass into the nightland (Daniel 99, 102). As in Cherokee society, in archaic and medieval Europe, outlawry was one of the harshest legal penalties. Through a performative proclamation, the lawbreaker who failed to stand trial was deprived of his civil rights and his property and was placed beyond the protection of the law. In contrast to the criminal, who stayed in the community and paid retribution for his transgressions, the outlaw was temporarily or permanently banished, was divested of his property, and suffered civic and social death. Presumed to be evil creatures living in forests like wolves, posing a danger to society, outlaws were considered wild beasts rather than human beings; hence they could be arrested and killed with impunity (Bunch 1–2; Seal 20; Rosen, "Slavery, Race, and Outlawry" 127, 129). Deborah Rosen's work demonstrates that in America, outlawry legislation and practices involving white Americans became obsolete after the American Revolution, while "fugitive slaves" continued to be subject to outlawry laws throughout the antebellum period. Especially southern states had statutes containing elements of outlawry—sometimes without using the term ("Slavery, Race, and Outlawry" 127). Hence in both Cherokee and Western cultures, outlawry was a familiar concept; it signified a withdrawal of legal rights and protections and a state of utmost personal and spiritual vulnerability. Ross used outlawry rhetoric to highlight the inhumanity and cruelty experienced by the Cherokees and to denounce the ways in which American law denied to them fundamental rights and equal protection against violence.

Despite pointing their fingers at the failure of the rule of law, neither Boudinot nor Ross and his fellow memorialists went so far as to challenge the ultimate authority of the law or to suggest resistance or noncompliance. They considered the rule of law and recognition by the law to be prerequisites of Cherokee peoplehood. Being placed beyond the shield of tribal law and federal Indian law and being exposed to the tyranny of Georgia's jurisdictional extension was seen as posing a severe danger to the political sovereignty of the Cherokee Nation and the physical and spiritual well-being of its members. While Boudinot and Ross hence agreed on the significance of fundamental legal principles for human thriving, they developed profoundly different visions of Cherokee peoplehood. By positioning himself in favor of Removal, Boudinot prioritized Cherokee political distinctiveness, which he deemed the basis for cultural perseverance. Thus the first of the Treaty Party's resolutions, drafted by Boudinot and Ridge and signed by their supporters in November 1834, stated "that our people cannot exist amidst a white population, subject to laws which they have no hand in making . . . that the suppression of Cherokee Government, which connected this people in a distinct community . . . will completely destroy every thing like civilization among them, and ultimately reduce them to poverty, misery and wretchedness" (qtd. in Peyer, *American Indian Nonfiction* 132). The preservation of political distinctiveness, however, inevitably meant giving up ancestral lands, as Boudinot's resignation letter from 1832 suggests.

Ross, by contrast, prioritized the preservation of Cherokee lands in the East. In a letter to Lewis Cass from February 14, 1835, Ross, along with other Cherokee politicians, expresses his conviction that Georgia's exercise of state jurisdiction and the federal government's unwillingness to protect Native rights made it "impossible for the Indian tribes to be perpetuated as distinct independent communities within the limits of the United States." He proposes to the president that the Cherokee Nation cede to Georgia "an extensive portion of" the lands lying within its charter limits, "reserving to the nation only a fractional part bordering on Tennessee and Alabama." These reserved lands should be granted to the Cherokees in fee simple, he says. To achieve such permanent rights in the soil, however, Ross considers it necessary to sacrifice Cherokee political distinctness: the Cherokees, he suggests, would have to become free citizens of the states they live in, be organized in counties, and be subject to state laws (qtd. in Moulton 321–23). When this offer is rejected, Ross compromises even further, proposing that a gross sum of $20 million be paid to the Cherokee Nation "for its title to all the lands lying within the charter limits of Georgia, No. Ca. Tennessee and Alabama," that all white settlers be removed, and that the Cherokees be protected from the extension of state laws for five years (qtd. in Mouton 325–26). Clearly, Ross was trying to buy time, setting his hopes on the fact that within five years another president would take office and negotiations could be resumed. However, he concedes in the same letter that within this period of time, "love of freedom"—rather than a financial offer from the United States—might induce the Cherokees to purchase another territory and resettle (326).

Ross considers the Treaty of New Echota, concluded in December 1835, to be an "unhallowed and unauthorized and unacknowledged compact" because it was signed without the approval of the National Council, which Ross had, he claims, painstakingly involved in all his negotiations (qtd. in Moulton 325, 472). In a petition to the Senate and House of Representatives from September 28, 1836, Ross, in the name of two thousand Cherokees, describes how this treaty aggravates the Cherokees' vulnerability and outlawry, "despoil[ing]" them of their private property, "stripp[ing] them of every attribute of freedom and eligibility for legal self-defence," and exposing them to violence and death. "We are denationalized," the petition continues, "we are disenfranchised. We are deprived of membership in the human family! We have neither land nor home, nor resting place that can be called our own" (qtd. in Moulton 459). The treaty, Ross points out, considered binding by the settler nation, closes off all avenues for further legal negotiation. It deprives the Cherokees of their native lands and hence denationalizes them. Ross thus alludes to the Cherokee Constitution, which binds the existence of the Cherokee Nation to a clearly defined territory in the East ("Constitution of the Cherokee Nation" art. 1, sec. 1). Once the land is gone, the Cherokee Nation ceases to exist.[17] Ceasing to be a body politic and being unable to fight back leads to a loss of humanity and dooms the Cherokees to a perpetual state of outlawry.

Ross also harshly criticizes the form of land rights that the Treaty of New Echota grants to the Cherokees. In the treaty's third article, the United States promises to grant the Cherokees a patent for the ceded territory but ties this patent to a provision of the Indian Removal Act—"that such land shall revert to the United States, if the Indians become extinct, or abandon the same." It is this provision that Ross refers to when claiming that the treaty assigns lands to the Cherokees "without a real title."

"Now, the use of this very phrase, *revert*, is an evidence that the United States do not consider that there is an absolute property given in the soil allotted to the Indians, in payment for their valuable country." Rather than conferring ownership in fee simple, the United States "only [allow] to the Indians an inferior right of occupancy" (qtd. in Moulton 446; italics in original). Whereas Boudinot contradicts Ross's skepticism concerning this property provision, Ross seems to have become convinced that *"this policy will legislate the Indians off the land!"* (qtd. in Moulton 447; italics in original; see also Perdue, *Cherokee Editor* 218).

Ross finally considers the treaty's proposed sum of $5 million paid by the United States to the Cherokees to be ridiculously low. In the tradition of American travel and landscape writings, he and his supporters celebrate the natural beauty and riches of Cherokee country, the "salubrity of climate," and the immense value of Cherokee improvements to the land (qtd. in Moulton 441–43). While the Cherokee chief had so far insisted on the poverty of these lands and their uselessness to US citizens (322), by 1836, after the Treaty of New Echota was ratified by the Senate and signed into law by the president, he felt compelled to bargain for the best conditions possible for his tribe. Therefore, all his writings around that time deemphasize Cherokee communal ownership of and deep attachment to the land and focus on Cherokee individual possessions and the economic value of the real estate in order to negotiate a higher payment in case Removal could not be averted.[18] Ross was thus eventually forced to implement what Boudinot had dared to imagine first: the separation of people and land. Ross continued his campaign until 1838, when federal troops began to round up Cherokees and force them into stockades. At that moment, he had to admit defeat and asked that the Cherokees be allowed to conduct their own relocation. Removal began shortly thereafter, leading to massive suffering and death (Denson, *Demanding the Cherokee Nation* 41; Nelson 163).

For both Boudinot and Ross, the Cherokees' state of outlawry made a reconceptualization of Cherokee peoplehood as separate from the land and of the land as a fungible commodity a matter of survival for their tribe. The conflict over state versus federal authority was resolved in favor of the states, and the southern removal ideology finally triumphed, as Garrison phrases it (234). As a consequence, Cherokee leaders tried to make the best deal possible for their tribe and to secure physical and cultural perseverance. Ross's meandering between a strong stance against Removal and his taking into account Removal as survival strategy reveals that to call him a traditionalist (as opposed to alleged progressives such as Boudinot and Ridge) means to oversimplify Cherokee politics at the time. Settler colonial political maneuvers induced Cherokee leaders such as Boudinot, Ridge, and Ross to continuously reflect on potential forms that Cherokee peoplehood could take. While the outcome of such reflections often differed, they shared an underlying premise: the perpetuation of Cherokee culture.

The only hope that remained for the Cherokees was that once they were in the unsettled West, they would have to deal with only the federal government, a task far easier than being embroiled between various jurisdictions. Two decades later, however, John Rollin Ridge goes back to Indian Removal to illustrate that in the West, the Cherokees' embroilment in controversies over jurisdiction, and hence their state of outlawry, continued. Examining *The Life and Adventures of Joaquín Murieta* in light of the early Cherokee responses to Indian Removal makes visible argumentative continuities. Like the Removal writers preceding him, Ridge turns to the language of natural law and the concept of outlawry to expose the inhumanity, cruelty, and violence of settler colonial law. In contrast to Boudinot and Ross, whose Removal writings were contemporaneous with and hence immediate interventions in legal and political negotiations about Removal, geared toward averting dispossession and forced relocation, Ridge approaches Indian Removal after the fact and through the lens of fiction. This allows him to reflect on the long-term impact of the kinds of subjectivity created by the settler state in the context of Removal on Cherokee relations and forms of governance. It also enables him to imagine alternative modes of subaltern resistance to dispossession—modes that altogether rejected the authority of settler colonial legal discourse and disrupted the settler colonial legal order: anticolonial disobedience, insurrection, and violence.

PROTESTING AGAINST "NOMINAL SOVEREIGNTY": JOHN ROLLIN RIDGE'S *THE LIFE AND ADVENTURES OF JOAQUÍN MURIETA* (1854)

The Life and Adventures of Joaquín Murieta is a sensational romance about a Mexican outlaw who, with his lawless band, terrorizes the population of California through acts of theft and incredible amounts of killing; it abounds in crime, violence, and gore. As the legal discrimination against Mexicans in California in the 1850s represented in the novel clearly evokes that against the Cherokees by the Georgians in the years prior to Removal, *The Life and Adventures* has generally been considered an allegory of Indian Removal and hence can be viewed as the first Native literary engagement with that policy.[19] While I also read Ridge's novel as a negotiation of Indian Removal, I simultaneously view it as a comment on the situation of Native Americans in the West in the 1850s. Scholars have argued that outlaws and narratives about outlaws reflect dissatisfaction and disruption—"the resistance of entire communities or people against the destruction of its way of life," to cite Eric Hobsbawm (13; see also T. Jones 4). Ridge employs the figure of the outlaw, who changes from good to bad in the face of oppression and who responds to oppression with force and violence, to protest against the curtailment of Native American sovereignty and land rights by the western states, which, in the fashion of southeastern states, deliberately ignored federal arguments against states' rights and those aspects of federal Indian law that did not fit their political ends. The novel thus picks up the conversation where Ross, Boudinot, and John Ridge left it: it reflects on the Native Americans' unsatisfactory position between federal and state law and on the inability, or unwillingness, of federal authorities to intervene in discriminatory and oppressive acts of the state. Drawing a disastrous picture of legal practices and the rule of law in nineteenth-century California, the novel illustrates that, at least with respect to Native Americans, law is mostly not what the US Supreme Court, treaties, or the US Constitution declare it to be; rather it is what American settlers on the ground accept and decide to enforce. It is, as Cherokee politicians argued earlier, "contrary to legal right" and disjoint from the ethical principle of justice. The fictional and allegorical nature of *The Life and Adventures*, however, allows its author to envision forms of Native resistance to settler colonial law going far beyond what Boudinot and Ross dared to write down in their addresses, essays, and memorials (or even to think). By making readers aware of settler colonial law's limited ability to create conditions for Native collectivities to flourish and by thinking through alternate modes of subaltern resistance, Ridge transforms the romance from a genre known for its reification of empire building to one inaugurating its critique.[20]

That *The Life and Adventures* needs to be read as an allegory is already suggested in its paratext. The "Publisher's Preface"—which might have been written by Ridge himself—indicates that the novel is far more than an adventurous and sensational tale about a Mexican outlaw. The novel's author, the preface asserts, is "a 'Cherokee Indian,' born in the woods—reared in the midst of the wildest scenery—and familiar with all that is thrilling, fearful and tragical in a forest-life" (Ridge, *Life and Adventures* 2).[21] While this characterization of Ridge as a (formerly) uncivilized "noble savage" could not have been further from the truth, the preface's emphasis on his ethnic identity establishes a link between the fictional world of the novel and the writer's own life. This link is further strengthened by the consecutive mentioning of Ridge's involvement in the "tragical events" in Cherokee country. The preface here alludes to the stabbing of his father, John Ridge, by members of the Anti-Treaty Party in 1839 as a punishment for his signing the Treaty of New Echota—a murder Ridge witnessed at the age of twelve (Jackson 13).

In the novel's first ten pages, these prefatory connections are more fully spelled out when the heterodiegetic narrator describes the protagonist Murieta's transformation from a Mexican immigrant fed up with his own country and anxious to Americanize into a dreaded outlaw full of hatred for Americans and with a strong desire for revenge. Responsible for this transformation, the narrator does not hesitate to state, is "the social and moral condition" of the United States (*JM* 7). This "condition" is elaborated on further on the next pages. In a first instance of violence, Murieta is forced by "a band of lawless men"—all Americans—to leave his house and his land and to witness the rape of his beloved Rosita. After relocating and getting himself "a little farm on the banks of a beautiful stream that watered a fertile valley," a "company of unprincipled Americans . . . saw his retreat, coveted his little home surrounded by its fertile tract of land, and drove him from it with no other excuse than that he was 'an infernal Mexican intruder'!" (*JM* 10). Still not morally broken, Murieta becomes a professional gambler; he is then falsely accused by a mob of Americans of having stolen the horse he is riding. Without due process of law, Murieta is lashed and his half brother is hanged. "It was then that the character of Murieta changed, suddenly and irrevocably. Wanton cruelty and the tyranny of prejudice had reached their climax" (*JM* 12). Murieta mourns his own transformation from a good man into a villain. Like the narrator, he holds not himself but settler colonial oppression responsible for his change. He tells a friend, "brush[ing] a tear away from his eyes": "I am not the man that I was; I am a deep-dyed scoundrel, but so help me God! I was driven to it by oppression and wrong. I hate my enemies, who are almost all of the Americans." (*JM* 50).

Murieta's fate is a barely veiled narration of the treatment Native Americans faced at the hands of Anglo-American settlers, which Ridge describes in similar terms in the preface to his 1868 collection of poems, *The Poems of John Rollin Ridge:*

> The white man had become covetous of the soil. The unhappy Indian was driven from his house . . . and the white man's ploughshare turned up the acres which he had called his own. Wherever the Indian built his cabin, and planted his corn, there was the spot which the white man craved. Convicted on suspicion, they were sentenced to death by laws whose authority they could not acknowledge, and hanged on the white man's gallows. (Parins and Ward)

Ridge here clearly alludes to the extension laws, through which the southern states gained access to Cherokee lands and assumed criminal jurisdiction over the Cherokees. While Murieta stands for the Cherokees, Rosita's body, ravished by the lawless Americans, stands for the body politic of the Cherokee Nation, which, through the doings of Georgia's citizens, was desecrated and harmed. It may also be read as an allusion to the gradual subjugation of Cherokee women's political and economic power in the course of the Cherokees' centralization of government and the increasing adoption of a political system undergirded by Anglo-American social and gender norms. It was such norms that largely marginalized Cherokee women from the life of the Cherokee Nation (Streeby 32; Brown 98).[22]

However, the character of Murieta can also be read as a comment on the continued discrimination against and oppression of Native Americans through law that took place in California at the time of the novel's publication. By linking the historical discrimination against Native Americans in Georgia to the oppressive workings of the law in California, the novel implicitly raises the question as to why law, which is commonly equated with morality and justice, continuously violates the rights of particular groups. This conundrum prompts him to engage in an extensive legal-philosophical reflection on the nature of law.

Central to Ridge's conceptualization of law is his Romantic poem "Mount Shasta, Seen from a Distance," which he places—in an apparently random position—near the beginning of the novel (*JM* 23–25). Cheryl Walker interprets Mount Shasta as a symbol of cold, unfeeling law and the ideology of Manifest Destiny and reads the poem as a critique of law (124; see also 123, 125, 192). Expanding on Timothy Sweet's brief yet insightful interpretation of the poem's "perceptual linkage of natural with social law" (147), this chapter approaches the poem from the perspective of legal philosophy and interprets the mountain as Ridge's own vision of law. Through the mountain he develops a conception of law based on reason and entirely disconnected from emotions.

Stanzas 1 and 2 characterize the mountain and, by implication, law as Ridge envisions it. It is "unpolluted" by human beings, even aloof from them. (No human has ever reached its top.) It is pure, "hoary," and "def[ies] each stroke of time"—that is, it has existed from time immemorial—to use the Blackstonian term also employed by Boudinot and Ross. By introducing the notion of "monarch mountain" in stanza 3, the speaker links law to a monarch and thus, implicitly, to God, who—as the last stanza indicates—made the mountain. According to early modern European beliefs, monarchs were the greatest power on earth, as they derived their right to rule from God. This is how Ridge views law: divine and ancient in origin, above humanity, having an unassailable authority on earth, and based on pure reason. Such law has a "gaze supreme" encircling "the broad Dominions of the West"—that is, it is capable of ordering newly settled spaces. Under its authority, society flourishes. This is embodied in the poem by the grass that grows greener, by the flowers that bloom sweeter, and by the communities that admire the mountain as the guarantor of "health and happiness." Community members inhale "its calm sublimity" and are thereby elevated to nobler thoughts (*JM*, stanza 4).

The omnipotence of law, embodied by the mountain, and its ability to transform newly settled terrain into a civilized, agrarian landscape (compare references to the plowman and herdsman) are celebrated in the poem's last nine lines:

> And well this Golden State shall thrive, if like
> Its own Mt. Shasta, Sovereign Law shall lift
> Itself in purer atmosphere—so high
> That human feeling, human passion at its base
> Shall lie subdued; e'en pity's tears shall on
> Its summit freeze; to warm it e'en the sunlight
> Of deep sympathy shall fail:
> Its pure administration shall be like
> The snow immaculate upon that mountain's brow. (*JM* 25)

In these lines, the speaker explicitly equates Mount Shasta with "sovereign"—supreme—law and encourages the reader to understand the poem as an allegory of law. He emphasizes the essential role that law plays for the thriving of California. Unlike Walker, I would argue that Ridge does not see the detachedness of law from "human feeling, human passion" as a negative trait. On the contrary, he seems to argue that only if law is aloof from the malleable and unstable emotions of human beings can it be administered purely and unfold its true civilizatory power. The poem is an appeal to disentangle law from the quagmire of human passions and to elevate it to a "purer atmosphere."

Ridge's idea of law corresponds to conceptions of *lex* (as distinguished from *ius*) as we find them in Cicero's *De Legibus* and Saint Thomas Aquinas's *Summae Theologicae*, which he, a trained lawyer with a sound education in Greek, Latin, literature, and law, was likely to have known (Parins 42). Cicero characterizes *lex* as "the highest reason, inherent in nature, which orders what ought to be done and forbids the contrary" (*De Legibus* 1.18–19, translated in M. White, "On the Use" 4). For Cicero, *lex* is "a principle of practical rationality" and "a primary element, principle or 'force' of nature" (White, "On the Use" 4–5). Aquinas, in his *Treatise on Law*, draws a distinction between *lex aeterna*, *lex naturalis*, *lex divina*, and *lex humana*. His understanding of *lex aeterna* closely resembles the Ciceronian definition of *lex* and sounds very similar to the "sovereign law" of divine origin described in the Mount Shasta poem. *Lex aeterna*, Aquinas argues, "is the *summa ratio*, existing in God": "since the *ratio* of divine wisdom . . . has the nature of art or exemplar or idea, so the *ratio* of divine wisdom, which moves all things to their due end, becomes the *ratio* of law. And, according to this, *lex aeterna* is nothing other than the ratio of divine wisdom, considered as that which directs all motions" (qtd. in White, "On the Use" 13). *Lex aeterna* is thus an eternal norm—it is God's own reason presiding over the whole universe and including the norm of nature (Pattaro 252). The term *summa ratio* was often rendered in old-fashioned English as "sovereign type" in the translation of the *Summa Theologicae* by Dominican fathers, which strengthens the link between Aquinas's *lex aeterna* and Ridge's idea of "sovereign law" (White, "On the Use" 13).

The conception of law developed by the poem is distinct from, and even stands in stark opposition to, the various forms of law appearing in the novel. While Aquinas's idea of *lex divina*—divine law as appearing in the Holy Scripture—is not dealt with in the text, *lex naturalis* and *lex humana* are. According to Aquinas, the former is the "human participation in the *summa ratio* that is *lex aeterna*" (White, "On the Use" 15–16). It is the norm of nature: "that part of divine providence and of the eternal norm that humans participate in, whereby a human being is provident for himself, or herself, and for others, and has a natural inclination to the due action and to his or her ends" (Pattaro 253). The latter, *lex humana*, is understood by Aquinas as "the norm posited by human will. It is human will as set out by a sovereign who takes care of the common good of earthly society. *Lex aeterna, lex divina,* and *lex naturalis* require no matrixes. And *lex naturalis*, as part of *lex aeterna*, is itself the matrix of the normativeness of *lex humana*" (Pattaro 254).

In *The Life and Adventures*, *lex naturalis*—natural law—manifests itself in the figure of Murieta.[23] In the editor's preface, Murieta is described as "a man who, bad though he was, possessed a soul as full of unconquerable courage as ever belonged to a human being" (*JM* 4). The rational creature, if we go back to Aquinas, "has a natural inclination to its proper act and end" (Aquinas, translated in Pattaro 253). As a human being, Murieta is inclined to do good and not to offend others. He has, as Ridge has the narrator emphasize, "the innate sensitiveness to honor and right which reigned in his bosom," a pure heart, and a "proud nobility of the soul" (*JM* 11, 14). Despite the harm done to him and despite the multiple crimes he commits, he asserts his humanity, his participation in *lex aeterna*: "I *am* a man, I was once as noble a man as ever breathed, and if I am not so now, it is because men would not allow me to be as I wished" (*JM* 106; italics in original). So if, as the novel asserts, Murieta is still innately good and inextricably bound to *lex aeterna*, how can he in fact be an outlaw? To understand Ridge's complex literary contemplations on the law, it is necessary to take a closer look at the novel's representation of *lex humana*.

As part of *lex aeterna, lex naturalis*, as Enrico Pattaro has interpreted Aquinas's *Treatise on Law*, "is itself the matrix of the normativeness of *lex humana*. A *lex humana* that should come to be at variance with *lex naturalis* . . . will not be a norm . . . but rather the forgery of a norm, of a rule or standard" (254). And this is exactly how human law is portrayed throughout *The Life and Adventures*. It contradicts natural law, is partisan and corrupt, and hence is not a norm to which humanity—in the novel's case Murieta—is bound. Murieta becomes an outlaw because of the utter detachedness of *lex humana* from "sovereign law." The narrator's comment that "he had committed deeds that made him no longer amenable to the law"[24] needs to be read as Murieta's refusal to become amenable to the flawed *lex humana* in California, but not to the *lex naturalis*, to which he feels obliged. To make the violence and oppression of settler colonial law visible, Ridge bends the genre conventions of the sensational romance. Rather than upholding a clear distinction between good and bad characters throughout the story, Ridge turns Murieta, the novel's outlaw and hence ostensible villain, into its noble hero. Murieta's nobility is being depicted as having clear limits, however. In his insurrection against unjust laws, Murieta collaborates with Three-Fingered Jack, one of the most brutal and racist figures in the novel, described by the narrator as a "sanguinary monster" when literally slaughtering helpless Chinese miners for no reason (*JM* 48). While Murieta does not approve of such cruelty, he remains passive and does not criticize it, as he needs Three-Fingered Jack for his own insurrectionist campaign.

The various forms of *lex humana* that appear in the novel are all steeped in human prejudice and remind the reader of "the crownless peaks" in the mountain's shadow "that, like inferior minds to some great Spirit, stand in strong contrasted littleness!" (*JM*, stanza 3, 24). Human law as it is represented in *The Life and Adventures* is not related to the "sovereign law" embodied by the mountain but is described as utterly inferior and tainted by human passions and hence as in contradiction with natural law's principle of human equality. At the beginning of the novel, the reader is presented with a view of California that evokes the situation in Georgia prior to Removal. The "unsettled condition of things" and the presence of "lawless and desperate men" bearing the name of Americans lead to a massive "prejudice of color" and an "antipathy of races." The Mexicans and Chinese are relentlessly suppressed, as they are perceived as racially inferior "conquered subjects" without rights. In this deeply racist Californian society, human law cannot but become a self-serving rhetoric and hence a farce—a theme winding its way through the novel (*JM* 9, 10, 18). Time and again, *The Life and Adventures* exposes, often with much irony, the injustice of the law or the injustice of those claiming to operate within its boundaries.

The novel's trial scenes outline the character and the workings of the law in California and stand in stark contrast to the conception of law developed in the poem. Luis Vulvia, one of Murieta's men and a "dark-skinned" Mexican, as the narrator emphasizes, is captured by the mob of a mining town (*JM* 91). The emphasis on the captive's skin color is to highlight the racial prejudice prevalent in the state: Vulvia is suspected because he is nonwhite. Even though the mob lacks any evidence that he committed the murder they accuse him of, they proceed to hang him without a trial. However, the justice of the peace, embodying the town's supposed civilizatory progress, convinces the crowd "to proceed with him legally, as there was but little doubt of his being found guilty as one of the murderers, in which case he would deliver him over to their just vengeance" (*JM* 93). Far more remarkable than the fact that the mob wants to hang Vulvia on the basis of his racial identity without a fair trial are the justice's arguments in favor of a legal procedure. He considers such a procedure reasonable, as he does not doubt the guilt of the accused. If he were doubtful of Vulvia's guilt, a legal procedure would be too insecure, as it might end with the freedom of the accused due to a lack of evidence. The justice thus considers the legal apparatus, embodied by the law books and papers he is surrounded by, a handmaid in the realization of his personal ideas of justice: he deems it just to punish dark-skinned Mexicans by default, as they have no right to be in the state in the first place. The justice's oxymoronic idea of "just vengeance" expresses his concept of law: law helps to clad human emotions, such as vengeance, into a pseudo-legal garb and to deprive racial others of their rights (see also Rifkin, "'For the Wrongs'" 33). And all of this is done—as Alexis de Tocqueville put it in 1831 when commenting on settler colonial violence against Native Americans—with "singular felicity, tranquility, legally, philanthropically, without shedding blood, and without violating a single great principle of morality in the eyes of the world." "It is impossible to destroy men with more respect for the laws of humanity," Tocqueville concluded sarcastically (369). This is the message the novel's trial scene conveys as well. Human-made law helps the justice order the newly domesticated frontier town according to settler colonial regimes of knowledge and helps elevate the exertion of vengeance to an ethically and morally acceptable practice.

Despite the lack of sound evidence against Vulvia, the justice would probably have found him guilty if it had not been for Murieta's physical appearance during the trial. The latter's performance and the impression he leaves on the justice are yet more proof that law in this mining town is far from just, purely administered, or impartial. Due to his light skin color and his expensive attire, Murieta passes as white. Claiming to be an Anglo-American man named Samuel Harrington, he openly addresses the racism of law: he argues that it suffices to be Mexican to be "hung by the infuriated populace" without "positive proof" (*JM* 94). Besides pointing his finger at the racial bias underlying the town's "legal" proceedings, Murieta demonstrates how easy it is to manipulate law. Spoofing Western law's infatuation with the written word, he produces several letters, written in different hands, which attest to the good character of the prisoner. The justice, "who was already favorably impressed" by Murieta's appearance, readily accepts these letters as evidence "without a moment's scruple" (95). The prisoner is immediately released, and Murieta and Vulvia joke about the ease with which the former tricked the justice. Law is as biased as the people who administer and enforce it—and those administering law at the frontier, the novel explicitly points out, are prejudiced, narrow-minded racists intent on ridding the country of all nonwhites.

The treatment of Vulvia is not an exception but rather the rule. Compared to the standard legal proceedings in California, the work of the vigilance committees and the "California trials" (*JM* 22, 121, 137), Vulvia's trial almost appears like the embodiment of justice. Vigilance committees, which consist of individual white citizens acting in concert, simply hang the alleged culprit without due process (*JM* 22). California trials—a highly ironic term—are characterized by the narrator as taking place right at the scene of a crime. They do not involve the hearing of witnesses and do not require the presence of a judge. If the captured confesses, he is hanged immediately. If he does not confess, the following procedure is applied: "To bring him to his senses, hemp was suggested as a very efficacious thing in such cases, and he was, accordingly, elevated into the top of a tree to take a view of the surrounding country." Not surprisingly, "he confessed without hesitation" (*JM* 127–28). If occasionally, as the narrator states, some people lacked decision of character and doubted whether this procedure was just, the task of administering "justice" was delegated to the supposedly uncivilized, the Cherokees, who are made complicit in the extralegal racial violence. For instance, Murieta's pursuer, Captain Charles H. Ellas, leaves a prisoner in the charge of "two Cherokee half-breeds with the request that they would give a good account of him." Later the Cherokees inform him that "they were ready to give 'a good account' of the Mexican. Nothing more was said on the subject, and the next day, he was found hanging on a tree by the side of the road" (*JM* 128). The narrative is punctuated with irony here, and one clearly recognizes the moral distance at which the narrator places himself concerning such proceedings. Below the humorous surface, the narrator's critique is harsh. He describes the West, imagined by the architect of the policy of Indian Removal, Thomas Jefferson, as a vast tract of land where Natives could live independently from the influence of whites, as a hotbed of rights violations, extrajudicial violence, discrimination, and dispossession (Garrison 240–41).

Brendan C. Lindsay's historical analysis of the workings of the law in California substantiates Ridge's novelistic critique. Californian settlers implemented "a self-interested legal system that favored whites" and "that legalized and naturalized . . . atrocities" against Native Americans (27, 31; see also 3, 11, 23).[25] Legally organized volunteer units murdered thousands of Natives and were remunerated by the state or federal government (25–26, 243). In what Lindsay calls the "legal dehumanization" of California's Natives, the state government passed anti-Indian legislation violating various federal treaties and the US Constitution. Commissioner of Indian Affairs Charles E. Mix's 1858 appeal to California to allow federal trade and intercourse laws to apply to Indian reservations in the state instead of retaining state jurisdiction over those reservations evidences the extent of state violations of federal authority (Rosen, *American Indians* 53). And even if a Californian law did serve to protect Native Americans, the state government, courts, and citizens ignored it whenever it collided with their own interests.[26] Instead of intervening and practicing judicial review, the state judiciary supported discrimination against Native Americans. What is more, Native Americans were prohibited from seeking justice in Californian courts and could only appeal to local justices of the peace, who often did not care to investigate the crimes at hand (Lindsay 27, 28, 227, 246; see also Rosen, *American Indians* 56). California's discriminatory acts against Native Americans, as Rosen argues, "usually met with little federal resistance because their actions furthered the development of a strong national economy, helped strengthen the security of U.S. borders, and increased white control of Native peoples" (*American Indians* 76). As with Georgia's extension laws, federal authorities did not bother to intervene, "acting rather as impotent bystanders to the power of the state and its white citizenry." Hence the Californian tribes were without protection under the laws of the United States (Lindsay 312).

Ridge's critique of human law in California also manifests itself in the novel's increasing intertwinement of law and outlawry, which makes it difficult for readers to distinguish between the two. Not only is racism rampant among the outlaws as well as those purporting to represent the law, but both groups also kill people in great numbers and randomly, without even the slightest attempt to procure evidence: "Arrests were continually being made; popular tribunals established in the woods, Judge Lynch installed upon the bench, criminals arraigned, tried, and executed upon the limb of a tree; pursuits, flights, skirmishes, and a topsy-turvy, hurly-burly mass of events that set narration at defiance" (*JM* 135–36). It is significant that narration collapses at precisely the moment when it tries to trace the workings of the law in California. The narrator seems to be overwhelmed by the amount of violence resulting from the work of vigilante committees. Like "just vengeance," the oxymoron "Judge Lynch"[27] embodies the inextricable connection between law and violence that is criticized throughout the novel. Rather than providing for justice and equality in California, *lex humana* creates an amount of disorder and chaos that narration is not able to render. This is significant when one considers the modes employed in the novel. On the very first page, the narrator characterizes his work as a contribution to the early history of California (*JM* 7). This strategic claim for veracity and authenticity is to mark the novel as a work of realism and to endow it with literary respectability (Streeby 263). It is underlined by the narrator's repeated insistence that what he delivers is "a simple narration of facts" (*JM* 53).

It is not surprising that realism, the mode of "the seemingly ordinary and everyday world," is unable to capture the "topsy-turvy, hurly-burly mass of events" taking place in the novel (Hebard 33). However, this is also true for the second mode Ridge uses alongside realism: romance, the mode known to depict "the world of the extraordinary, a world of adventure where the expectations of everyday conventions have been suspended" (12). While neither of these modes is able to retell the outrageous workings and the violence of *lex humana*, they are able to capture Murieta's actions in much detail. And even when the narrator mentions that it is not "necessary to recount" yet another of Murieta's campaigns, as "it would only be a repetition," he implies that he would be capable of doing so but refrains from it in order not to bore the reader (*JM* 139). On the level of narration, outlawry is presented as much more orderly than human law.

The difference between human law and outlawry is also deconstructed through the novel's destabilization of the binary opposition between civilization and savagery, a strategy that is also present in Boudinot and Ross. A great number of those who are portrayed as being on the side of law and who are hence members of "civilization" are represented in the novel as ignorant and uncivilized. At the same time, the Mexican outlaw Murieta—viewed by Americans as belonging to a "savage" race—is depicted as educated and civilized. His appearance, attire, and behavior regularly confuse Americans as to his true identity (see, e.g., *JM* 41). While he is able to write grammatically correct English, Anglo-Americans throughout the novel suffer from a lack of spelling skills, so that written communication breaks down (*JM* 68, 130–31). The Americans' lack of civilization also comes to the fore in their practices of punishment. Thus, the narrator tells us, "the time-honored custom of choking a man to death was soon put into practice, and the robber stood on nothing, kicking at empty space. Bah! It is a sight that I never like to see, although I have been civilized for a good many years" (*JM* 137). This passage works against the reader's expectations and is saturated with irony. The reader would expect the narrator to dislike the practice of choking someone to death *because* he has been civilized for many years and hence is far removed from such acts of savagery. The concessive clause that Ridge uses implies instead that choking someone to death is in line with so-called civilization. In contrast to Boudinot and Ross, who equate settler colonial ideas of civilization with progress and who embrace the discourse of civilization for their own purposes, Ridge uses *The Life and Adventures* to question Western concepts of civilization. He represents Western civilizatory discourse as nothing more than empty rhetoric employed to legitimate settler colonial violence against racial others—the savages of their imagination.

Besides erasing the fault lines between civilization and savagery and between law and outlawry, Ridge portrays outlawry in the novel as a space of Native opportunity, freedom, and resistance. Reading the earlier Cherokee conceptualizations of outlawry alongside Ridge's novel throws into relief their diverging politics. Ross and his fellow memorialists employed the concept of outlawry to highlight American law's failure to secure the Cherokees' fundamental rights and equal protection against violence, and to describe the extent of their vulnerability and loss of humanity. They did not use it to challenge the authority of enacted law as such. In *The Life and Adventures*, by contrast, outlawry opens up a space for anticolonial insurrection and resistance to unjust law and is a source of empowerment. While, due to his racial status, the laws do not protect Murieta, he finds safety in an "unlawful course" and thus "becomes"—rather than being pronounced—an outlaw (*JM* 14). This self-chosen path, characterized by the narrator as "an act of self-preservation," endows Murieta with freedom from unjust law (49). *Lex humana*'s inequality, in fact, makes Murieta's becoming an outlaw appear as a noble act, because he dissociates himself from corrupt human law and ceases to feel obliged to act according to that law. By placing himself outside human law, Murieta reassumes control over his life, sheds his state of victimhood, and regains, rather than loses, his humanity.

As a nonnational in a newly domesticated space, Murieta uses this newly gained freedom to challenge the boundaries of the legal space he lives in. By randomly committing crimes across the entire territory of California, he defies the US territorialization of heretofore Mexican land and the subsumption of nonnationals under American law (see, e.g., *JM* 109–10). Even though Murieta is, according to the moral universe of sensational romance, the stock villain committing crimes and spreading terror, Ridge constructs his narrative to evoke the reader's sympathy, even admiration, for this villain.[28] Murieta's deeds are unlawful and heinous, yet they are presented as predictable acts of revolt by the oppressed, dispossessed, and disenfranchised. His outlawry is a parable of what happens when human law violates the natural law tenet of equality.[29] Murieta breaks the law in order to be safe from its totalizing power and from its racial violence and to expose its flawed nature and its disjunction from *lex aeterna* and *lex naturalis*. Murieta's own violence functions as a critique of law's violence. While the use of force and violence was not a position that either Boudinot or Ross could have advanced for realpolitikal reasons, the fictional world of *The Life and Adventures* allows Ridge to think through disobedience, defiance of law, force, and extralegal violence as forms of Native resistance. And it is well possible that such thoughts and reflections, which were to Ridge—a trained lawyer—a new mental terrain, led to the novel's ambivalences that scholars have repeatedly pointed out.[30]

However, *The Life and Adventures* does not content itself with questioning the efficacy and justice of Anglo-American law. It also engages critically with the partial administration of law in the Cherokee Nation, which leads to the violation of natural rights and the unraveling of Cherokee peoplehood. After their forced relocation westward, the Cherokees suffered from social strife and fragmentation, and political murder and acts of revenge became an integral part of the life in the nation. The warfare between factions became so intense that some federal agents argued in favor of extending the laws of the United States over Cherokee territory (Denson, *Demanding the Cherokee Nation* 42, 43).[31] Hence Murieta could also be interpreted as embodying the Cherokee outlaw Tom Starr, who began to seek revenge after his father, James Starr—one of the signers of the Treaty of New Echota—was killed by members of the Ross Party in 1845 and thus suffered the same fate as Boudinot, the elder Ridge, and Stand Watie a few years earlier.[32] The novel's preface substantiates such an interpretation by characterizing the forcibly relocated Cherokee Nation as "a place of blood" and by connecting the ensuing narrative to the situation in post-Removal Cherokee country: "the rising of factions, the stormy controversies with the whites, the fall of distinguished chiefs, family feuds, individual retaliation and revenge, and all the consequences of that terrible civil commotion" (*JM* 2, 3). And the fact that Ridge, with a hint of fascination, writes about the "romantic deeds" of Tom Starr in one of his letters to Stand Watie, calling him "a second Rinaldo Rinaldina [*sic*]," similarly suggests that his novel could be understood as a negotiation of the internal conflicts, lawlessness, and violence that characterized the life of the recently expelled Cherokees (letter from 17 Apr. 1846, qtd. in Dale and Litton 38–39).

Ridge's journalistic writings reveal him to be an outspoken critic of post-Removal Cherokee politics and law. The Ross faction, he claims, is so dominant "that it is impossible for the laws, either civil or criminal, to be impartially administered. It almost necessarily happens that juries for the trial of any case are composed of Ross men—frequently the lawyers are of the same party, and judges always, for none other can be appointed." "What chance then," Ridge asks with embitterment, "has a Treaty man or an Old Settler who is obnoxious to the other party, for his life, or his property, tried as he is in a Court of his enemies, where Prejudice and Hatred, instead of Justice, hold the scales?" (*Trumpet* 51).[33] The *lex humana* that *The Life and Adventures* critiques is hence also the *lex humana* in Cherokee country, which is not racist but, from the perspective of a member of the Treaty Party, is utterly biased, prejudiced, and responsible for the violation of natural rights (life and property). Unlike the "pure" administration of "sovereign law" in the Mount Shasta poem, the administration of law in the Cherokee Nation is entrenched in "the deadly difference of opinion." The root of such "discord and contention" was, according to Ridge, "the stern denial of justice by the Supreme Court of the United States in 1831." Ridge here refers to Marshall's notion of domestic dependency, which made the Cherokees easy prey to "the iron arm of cold State policy" (49, 50).

In the figure of the outlaw Murieta, Ridge thus embeds a critique of both American law and the state of affairs in the Cherokee Nation. What does such criticism mean when read in conjunction with Cherokee visions of peoplehood at the time of Removal? While two decades earlier Ross and Boudinot had celebrated the potential they saw in the *Cherokee Nation* ruling, by the time Ridge started writing *The Life and Adventures*, the long-term impact of the decision on the lives of the forcibly relocated Cherokees had become all too visible. In Ridge's view, the idea of domestic dependency that Chief Justice Marshall had concocted had produced a situation of uncertainty and dependence, which *Worcester* could not alleviate and which undermined the project of Cherokee nation building in the West. The sovereignty that Marshall had granted the Cherokees, Ridge argues, is just "nominal" rather than "real" and hence a "useless peculiarity" (*Trumpet* 53). While the Cherokee Nation "pretends" to have sovereignty, this sovereignty is, in Ridge's view, impaired by the surrender of some rights that are staples of sovereignty: the possession of territory in fee simple and the right to dispose of it to whomever one pleases. Ridge's position echoes that of Ross, who argued two decades earlier that an "absolute property given in the soil" is the prerequisite for the persistence of the Cherokees as a people.

Ridge's remedy to this "nominal sovereignty," however, differs greatly from what Ross and other Cherokee leaders envisioned. He believes that confusion will prevail among the Cherokees "until a strong arm is extended over them—I mean the laws of the United States." Ridge, however, knew from experience—his own as well as that of his ancestors—that US law was notoriously unable to protect Indigenous geopolitical formations within colonized national territory. To come under the protective shield of American law, Ridge suggests, the Cherokee Nation needs to become "an integral part of the United States, having Senators and Representatives in Congress, and possessing all the attributes, first of a territorial government, and then of a sovereign State" (*Trumpet* 52; see also letter from Ridge to S. B. N. Ridge, 5 Oct. 1855, qtd. in Dale and Litton 86–87). Entering the Union as a separate state, Ridge claims, would end the harassment of Native communities by state laws and endow the Cherokee Nation with the legislative power to regulate, control, and govern real and tangible property, as well as Native individuals and enterprises within fixed and secure territorial boundaries. In short, it would end the Cherokees' vulnerable position between state and federal jurisdictions and secure their persistence as a people. Thus, as Rifkin points out, Ridge does not seek to dissolve Cherokee nationality but to "insulate" it against those American legal traditions seeking the erosion of Native sovereignty ("'For the Wrongs'" 40–41). The sovereignty he envisions, however, is grounded in the continued progress of Cherokee civilization. To him, "sovereign law" as embodied by Mount Shasta and the rule of law flowing from it are prerequisites for the flourishing of Native America.

In the colony, "sovereignty," as Achille Mbembe claims, "consists fundamentally in the exercise of a power outside the law (*ab legibus solutus*)" (23). The ending of *The Life and Adventures* suggests, however, that operating outside of and defying American law is unable to secure the Cherokees' long-term sovereignty. Murieta's severed head, drowned in alcohol and placed into a jar, signifies the state's successful containment of subaltern resistance through outlawry. Its exhibition all over California serves to undo Murieta's acts of defiance against American law and the

US territorialization of heretofore Mexican land. "The dismembering and exhibition of the outlaw, then," as David J. Drysdale has succinctly put it, "is part of a vocabulary of domination through which the United States established its sovereignty over its new territorial acquisitions" (101). The state's successful extermination of the outlaw thus questions the feasibility of anticolonial resistance and subaltern disobedience to the law. The novel's ending seems to suggest that dismemberment—that is, political extinction—might also be the fate of Native Americans in the West if they resist American acts of territorialization and colonization. Like Murieta's head, they might end up as specimens of the past, preserved in alcohol and ready to be exhibited all over the nation. The narrator's comment that Murieta was only captured because he carelessly separated himself from the main body of his men can be understood as an appeal directed at members of the Cherokee Nation: they should end their fragmentation and separation, and establish a just rule of law in order not to become easy prey to an American legal system eager to rationalize in favor of the curtailment of their rights (*JM* 153). In Ridge's view, communities, Native and non-Native, can only "thrive," to return to the Mount Shasta poem, if the administration of the law is as pure as the immaculate snow on the mountaintop. Legal discrimination and dismemberment can only be prevented by the full incorporation of the Cherokee Nation into the Union as a separate state. Being continuously trapped between state and federal jurisdictions as "domestic dependent nation" with impaired sovereignty and truncated property rights, and facing ongoing discrimination and oppression by American law, was certainly not an option for Ridge.

Indian Removal turned Natives into subjects without rights and forced migrants, and it posed a severe threat to Native social and political formations. Due to its impact on Native forms of living, Removal led to the first large-scale immersion of Indigenous intellectuals into the legal-political debates of the settler nation, as lawyers, writers, editors, and politicians. In the context of Removal, the Native communities concerned, first and foremost the Cherokee Nation, began to employ the law—Indigenous law, federal law, and natural law—as a medium of resistance to the curtailment of their political and property rights. Recourse to the language and concepts of the law in various forms of Cherokee writing, ranging from speeches, memorials, and newspaper editorials to novelistic writing, became both a political and an aesthetic practice. Through their texts, the Cherokee writers explored in this chapter tried "to make the discourse of law, in some sense, work for (and not against) them" (Carlson, *Sovereign Selves* 38). The visions of peoplehood they developed in their writings were based in Cherokee knowledge and traditions yet also critically engaged with the subjectivities produced by both federal and state courts. They constantly meandered, as Nelson has so succinctly put it, "between adaptation and perseverance" (175).

The Cherokees' relationship to law was thus a highly complex one. Their precarious position between state and federal laws forced Cherokee intellectuals to carefully engage with the various bodies of American law and the institutions that represented it. Rather than merely protesting against subjectivities developed by the Marshall Court and state courts that, more often than not, flatly contradicted Native social and political-legal forms of collective organization, they acknowledged federal law's potential to secure Cherokee political rights and land ownership and Cherokee political distinctness. Besides engaging with federal law, the Cherokee writers I have discussed also reinvigorated a tradition of natural law defense of Indigenous rights preceding English colonization to resolve their vulnerable position between the jurisdictions to their advantage.[34] Their deep engagement with natural law also prompted these writers to intensely meditate on the function of the law in the Cherokee Nation. The governing of the Cherokee Nation according to the rule of law is identified by all these writers as a prerequisite for the Cherokees' continued existence as peoples.

In the context of Indian Removal, writing became a vehicle for Native intellectuals to argue for their ownership of the land and to mediate between the classical forms of Western legality—personhood and statehood—and Indigenous political, legal, and cultural traditions and epistemologies. The forms of legal resistance established by the Cherokees in the context of Removal became a blueprint for Native communities across the United States forced to deal with "removals"—settler colonial incursions on Native forms of living, being, and belonging—across the centuries until the present day.[35]

CHAPTER 2

Property-Owning Individuals
Early-Twentieth-Century Removal Writing and the US Federal Indian Policy of Assimilation and Allotment

THIS CHAPTER CREATES A dialogue between two Cherokee Removal texts from the early twentieth century—one nonfictional, the other fictional—and an array of legal-political writings negotiating the contours of federal Indian legislation from the 1870s to the 1930s, most notably the federal policy of assimilation.[1] The assimilation policy, in all its multiple facets, strove to Americanize Native Americans by indoctrinating them with the contents of "civilization" and by destroying tribal culture, which was devalued as premodern. While Native Americans might survive as individuals and as such be absorbed into the American populace, their existence as Indigenous peoples was to come to an end (Prucha, Introduction 7; Denson, *Monuments to Absence* 6). Assimilation purported to be radically different from the policy of Removal, whose goal had been displacement and isolation rather than absorption. The linchpin of assimilation was the Dawes Severalty Act from 1887, also known as the General Allotment Act, which authorized the US president to survey Native tribal lands—except those of the "removed" tribes in Indian Territory—and to divide them into allotments for individual Native Americans. The Dawes Act awarded each head of household 160 acres, persons under age eighteen 40 acres, and each single person or orphan 80 acres. The United States functioned as trustee of the homesteads for twenty-five years. While in this time period those tracts were inalienable, the federal government had the right to sell "surplus" tribal land to non-Natives. Native allottees became subject to the laws of the territory or state in which they resided and received US citizenship. In 1893 Congress entrusted the so-called Dawes Commission with the task of allotting the lands of the Five Civilized

Tribes, either through negotiation or by force. In 1898 Congress passed the Curtis Act, which finally extended the allotment policy over Indian Territory, dissolved tribal governments, and abolished communal lands (Garrison 242; Denson, *Demanding the Cherokee Nation* 238; Holm, *The Great Confusion* 13; Perdue and Green, *North American Indians* 90). The majority of members of Congress were convinced of their right to violate treaties that had established the reservations due to the *United States v. Kagama* decision by the US Supreme Court in 1886. That year the court had ruled that Congress had absolute authority over Native tribes, notwithstanding any treaty rights or claims of Native sovereignty to the contrary. Five years after the passage of the Curtis Act, in *Lone Wolf v. Hitchcock*, the court put the allotment policy on a sound legal basis by attributing to Congress "plenary power," including the ability to break treaties free from judicial review. The plenary power doctrine facilitated large-scale Native dispossession through allotment across the United States: between 1887 and 1934 Native landholdings in the country declined from approximately 138 million acres to 48 million acres (Garrison 242; Riley, "Native American Lands" 375; Holm, *The Great Confusion* 157; Riley and Carpenter 184; Black 98–100; Perdue and Green, *North American Indians* 92).

The transformation of Native Americans into property-owning individuals was viewed by the federal government as the major catalyst of both civilization and Americanization. Forcibly changing forms of Native collective land ownership through the allotment of Native lands, US officials surmised, would alter Native collective identity due to the inextricable connection between Native tribal lands and forms of Native belonging down to the most intimate level, the Native family. Owning lands in common, officials thought, strengthened intratribal relations and Native cultural practices and reduced the incentive to work. As individual proprietors and homesteaders, Native Americans could be integrated into US civilized society as citizens far more easily. Even more important, allotment would make surplus lands available to settlers for economic use. No one expressed the allotment policy's twofold attack on Native forms of belonging—communal property and collective identity—more succinctly than President Theodore Roosevelt in his first annual message on December 3, 1901: "The time has arrived when we should definitely make up our minds to recognize the Indian as an individual and not as a member of the tribe. The General Allotment Act is a mighty pulverizing engine to break up the tribal mass. It acts directly upon the family and the individual" (qtd. in Riley, "Native American Lands" 375).

The formerly expelled Native nations were by no means passive in this settler colonial assault on their territory and sovereignty. They strongly opposed the federal government's policy of allotment, defended Native sovereignty in journalistic and political writings and hearings, and disrupted allotment proceedings. After passage of the Curtis Act, delegates from the Five Civilized Tribes worked together across tribal lines toward the founding of a Native-governed state of Sequoyah, which was to be separate and distinct from Oklahoma Territory. But none of these counterarguments or -measures had the desired result of stopping the allotment process. On April 26, 1906, Congress passed "An Act to Provide for the Final Disposition of the Affairs of the Five Civilized Tribes in the Indian Territory," which put into place what Robert Conley has characterized as "a regime of bureaucratic imperialism." While the act did not prohibit Native Americans in Indian Territory from electing their chiefs and councils, political power was from then on located in Washington, DC. The Department of the Interior took over tribal schools, educational funds, government buildings, and furniture. The US president had the power to appoint a principal chief for any of the tribes. And if a chief failed to sign a document presented to him by the US authorities, he was to be removed from office, or the secretary of the interior could simply approve the document. In June 1906, Congress passed an enabling act providing for the admission of Indian Territory and Oklahoma Territory into the Union as a single state. Thus, on November 16, 1907, the new state of Oklahoma became officially part of the Union (Conley, *Cherokee Nation* 202). Similar to the Removal years, Native Americans in Indian Territory felt utterly unprotected by their own governments, laws, and courts; suffered from violence and dispossession; and had to take US citizenship and come to terms with the fact that they were now subject to the laws of the newly created state. It was only in 1934 that the Indian Reorganization Act ended the allotment policy and oversaw the creation of tribal governments and the recovery of Indian lands (Brown 10; Garrison 242; Reed 253; Denson, *Demanding the Cherokee Nation* 243).

While formally and functionally different, the Removal texts published by the Cherokee authors Rachel Caroline Eaton and John Milton

Oskison have in common that they return to Indian Removal in order to critically comment on the legal and political disenfranchisement of Native Americans in the context of assimilation and allotment. What is more, both authors go back to Removal to (re)examine, (re)imagine, and play through visions of Cherokee peoplehood at a time when Cherokee nationhood "lay dormant," as Christopher B. Teuton has so aptly phrased it, and when governmental and territorial control was subsumed by the US Department of the Interior (84).

Eaton had been born a citizen into the very nation whose dissolution she had to witness shortly before she began working on her thesis, "John Ross," while doing graduate work in history at the University of Chicago. This thesis provided the foundation of a much expanded manuscript, which was published in 1914 under the title *John Ross and the Cherokee Indians*. Notwithstanding its title, Eaton's book is far more than a political biography of John Ross. In fact, it can be considered the first revisionist history of Indian Removal and the first history of Indian Removal ever written by a Native American.[2] Writing at a time when the effects of assimilation and allotment became increasingly visible, Eaton turns to Removal to put this federal Indian policy into historical perspective and to point out its erroneous and detrimental nature. By going back to the Removal era, Eaton also speaks back to speeches by proponents of allotment, such as Henry L. Dawes and Charles Painter, and to governmental reports, such as the *Report of the Dawes Commission to the Five Civilized Tribes*, which characterized Natives as "savages" and Indian Territory as everything "civilization" was not. Rather than foregrounding the coercive and violent aspects of Removal, her historical monograph traces John Ross's and other Cherokee leaders' diplomatic interventions and efficient crisis management during Removal and their rebuilding of the Cherokee Nation in the West. It portrays Native Americans as responsible and intellectually capable agents of their own fate and progress. Rejecting the rhetoric of assimilation and allotment and representing allotment not as a departure from but as a continuation of Removal, Eaton argues in favor of the continued existence of the Cherokees as a sovereign people residing on communally owned land and improving themselves independently from the damaging influence of the federal government. To her, Cherokee advancement is a gradual and evolutionary process, best achieved under the leadership of the educated, multiracial Cherokee elite on sovereign Native territory.

Also born in Indian Territory, Oskison was educated at Willie Halsell College, Stanford, and Harvard. He pursued a forty-year publishing career, during which he produced both fictional work and journalistic pieces (Brown 12). His recently rediscovered *The Singing Bird: A Cherokee Novel* is written from the perspective of a group of missionaries who accompany Cherokee Removal to the West, witnessing both the hardships of forced relocation and the Cherokees' efforts at rebuilding their community. The novel was written at some point between 1925 and the early 1940s[3] and thus at a time when the assimilation and allotment policy came increasingly under fire for being an inadequate solution to what had become known as "the Indian problem." The Meriam Report, which was published in 1928 with the title *The Problem of Indian Administration*, was much more interested in the workings of government agencies than in Native American lives. However, as the report extensively described the devastating effects of assimilation and allotment on the physical, spiritual, and economic health of Native Americans and demanded a reorientation of US Indian policy, it was of critical significance for Native Americans all over the United States. Writings by John Collier, who was commissioner of Indian affairs between 1933 and 1945 and was responsible for terminating the policy of assimilation and allotment, similarly criticized previous Indian policies and put into place new models of Native–Anglo-American interaction and cooperation. Oskison's *The Singing Bird* needs to be viewed as a Native intellectual response to these writings, whose influence on federal Indian law has been widely asserted.[4] While Eaton builds her narrative on the idea of racial linear progress, Oskison challenges this idea as well as the concept of civilization itself. In contrast to Eaton's advocacy of the persistence of the Cherokees as a separate people, he envisions the racial and cultural amalgamation of Native Americans and Americans (as an alternative to the top-down assimilation of Native Americans), which is to be achieved through intermarriage and interracial collaboration at eye level. Amalgamation under these terms, Oskison speculates, has the potential to produce a new Anglo-Native society based on the fusion of the best traits of both cultures, focusing less on individual than on communal values.

"ADMINISTRATIVE ABILITY" AND "A REAL CAPACITY FOR ANGLO-SAXON CIVILIZATION": RACHEL CAROLINE EATON'S *JOHN ROSS AND THE CHEROKEE INDIANS*

At the time of Eaton's writing, the belief in progress and Anglo-Saxon civilization as the apex of social evolution was not only a staple in US legal-political discourse but was also endorsed by the scientific findings of American anthropologists. Drawing on the work of his academic teacher Lewis Henry Morgan, John Wesley Powell, the first director of the US Bureau of Ethnology, argued in favor of cultural evolutionary stages through which all societies, including Native societies, progressed linearly. To him, the transformation of "Indian life" was inevitable and had to be encouraged and facilitated by settler colonial interventions. In a letter to Senator Henry M. Teller from March 23, 1880, Powell took the opportunity to outline how scientific ideas on civilization should direct federal Indian law and policy. "All of our Indian troubles," he wrote, "have arisen primarily and chiefly from two conditions inherent in savage society," communal land ownership and the idea of land as "the locus of religion." "When an Indian clan or tribe gives up its land," Powell continued, "it not only surrenders its home as understood by civilized people but its gods are abandoned and all its religion connected therewith, and connected with the worship of ancestors buried in the soil; that is, everything most sacred to Indian society is yielded up." Hence he considered "removal," the separation of Native communities from their ancestral lands, to be the "first step to be taken in their civilization." Second, he argued that the allotment of Native lands—that is, the implementation of private property ownership in land—would ultimately settle all existing "troubles." Powell finally also recommended total assimilation and US citizenship as the objectives central to all legislation (Powell qtd. in Worster 270; see also Hoxie 17, 21, 23).

My first chapter demonstrates that discourses of civilization and progress had long been an integral part of Native historical and fictional textual production as well. Cherokees writers, in particular, time and again insisted and prided themselves on the exceptional nature of Cherokee civilizatory progress, using it as an argumentative weapon in their fight for sovereignty and against settler colonial acts of dispossession.[5] Due to such omnipresence of the concept of civilization in both Anglo-American law, policy, and science and the Indigenous/Cherokee narrative tradition, it does not come as a surprise that Eaton, too, positions herself and her work with respect to this concept. In the preface to her historical monograph, she proclaims that her history of Removal seeks "to trace the evolution from barbarism to civilization of one of the most progressive tribes of North American Indians." Eaton's subscription to concepts of human linear development and progress and her assertion of a binary between savagery and civilization suggest her agreement with Anglo-American lawyers, politicians, and scientists on the inevitable progression of the Native. From today's perspective, she appears almost complicit in such chauvinistic colonial rhetoric. Eaton's apparent complicity,[6] however, clearly has its limits when it comes to the role the US government is to play in the social evolution of the Native. In contrast to Powell's interventionist approach, she clarifies in her prefatory remarks that US interference with Native lives and culture, such as economic interaction, "forcible removal," and "the horrors of the Civil War," can do nothing but destroy "the hard-won prosperity" the Natives had achieved so far. Native civilization, she asserts, is inevitable and happens gradually. Because American political and legal intervention is based on a notion of the Native as "lurk[ing] darkly on the outskirts of civilization" and as incapable of "Anglo-Saxon civilization," it is, by its very conception, doomed to failure (Preface).

Eaton hence uses the preface to set herself apart from the discourse of Native savagery prevalent among politicians, lawyers, historians, ethnologists, and the self-proclaimed "friends of the Indian"—in short, the majority of those involved in what was subsumed under the heading of Indian reform (Holm, *The Great Confusion* 7). In his various speeches at the Lake Mohonk Conference of the Friends of the Indian in the 1880s, Henry L. Dawes, chairman of the Senate Committee on Indian Affairs and the architect of allotment, painted a picture of the Native as a "blind, helpless, ignorant" creature not knowing the language of the country, wasting his time on the reservation, and not having a clue about how to produce anything to live on ("Solving" 29; "Defense" 104). He pointed out that throughout hundreds of years of Indian policy, the Native "continued to be just about what he was when we found him—a savage people speaking a strange jargon that we did not understand, ignorant, and depending upon the game of the forest for his subsistence" ("Solving" 28).

According to Dawes, the Native's infantile and primitive state obliged the United States to "[attempt] to make something out of him" ("Solving" 29). Despite being physically and mentally an adult, he needed to be treated like a child and taught "to stand alone first, then to walk, then to dig, then to plant, then to hoe, then to gather, and then to *keep*" ("Solving" 29; italics in original). It was views of "the Indian" such as these, shared by Powell, Dawes, and many others involved in "Indian reform," that laid the conceptual foundations for the kind of federal Indian law and policy that Dawes himself endeavored to implement. The "Indian reformers" worked for the passage of laws that involved, as Lawrence C. Kelly has phrased it, teaching Native Americans "the agricultural arts," "subsidiz[ing]" missionary societies "to bring them [the Natives] the benefits of Christianity and formal education," "weaken[ing] . . . tribal autonomy and the authority of Native leaders," and emphasizing individual property ownership (148).[7]

The dysfunctional Native reservation was another staple in the reformers' and politicians' speeches and reports and was used as an additional argument in favor of breaking up tribal units through allotment and incorporating Natives into the American polity as individuals. Charles Painter, full-time agent of the Indian Rights Association from 1884 to 1895, claimed in his speech at the Fourth Annual Lake Mohonk Conference that the walls of the reservation needed to be broken down immediately in order to let civilization in. To him, the Native reservation was the antithesis of civilization: it excluded "law and social order, and the institutions of organized society" and "[shut] in savagery and lawlessness" (72; see also 73). An even more scathing description of the Indian reservation was submitted to Congress on November 20, 1894, by the Dawes Commission to the Five Civilized Tribes, the three-member commission headed by Dawes himself, which had been created in 1893 to work for the allotment of the lands of the Five Civilized Tribes, either through negotiation or by force (Denson, *Demanding the Cherokee Nation* 232–34). This report, which became widely publicized before congressional committees and reform organizations, declared the creation of Indian Territory—a sovereign and isolated territory in which the Natives would be able to work out their own advancement—to be a failure. In part, it argued that this was due to geopolitical changes, such as the formation of states and territories surrounding Indian Territory and the influx of American citizens into Native lands ("Report of the Dawes Commission" 189–90). Under such circumstances, "isolation [was] an impossibility." But even if isolation existed, the report stated, "it could never result in the elevation or civilization of the Indian" (190). The commission then listed in detail what its members saw as the miserable conditions in Indian Territory that were responsible for producing retrogression and that endangered the lives of both Natives and non-Natives settling there. First and foremost, the Natives were unable to govern themselves. The "so-called governments of these five tribes," the report emphasized, had become "powerless to protect the life or property rights of the citizens." Even the courts were "helpless and paralyzed," so that violence, robbery, and murder abounded and went unpunished. "A reign of terror" existed, and "barbarous outrages, almost impossible of belief, [were] enacted" (190). The commission described tribal governments as utterly corrupt: they had "fallen into the hands of a few able and energetic Indian citizens, nearly all mixed blood and adopted whites, who [had] so administered their affairs and [had] enacted such laws that they [were] enabled to appropriate to their own exclusive use almost the entire property of the Territory of any kind that [could] be rendered profitable and available" (191). According to the report, full-blood Natives were excluded from fertile lands, were dependent on the wealthy class of mixed-bloods, and did whatever the latter requested. They were uneducated, poor, and "making little if any progress in civilization" (191). Under such circumstances, the commission argued, Native claims to hold lands in common rang increasingly hollow. In fact, communal landholding had become a rhetorical device employed by the wealthy political elite in order to continue monopolizing the land (192). The commission hence performed a sly argumentative move. While the advocates of allotment had long complained about the existence of communal property and conceptualized it as the antithesis of civilization, the Dawes Report argued that it was not the presence of communal property that made allotment necessary but its imperfect implementation and its abuse by mixed-blood tribal leaders.

Due to the Natives' incapacity to govern themselves and the deplorable conditions outlined, the commission declared it the right, if not the obligation, of the US government to revoke the rights granted to the Five Civilized Tribes by treaty, in particular the right to self-government (193). It also portrayed allotment as a humanitarian intervention: it was geared toward restoring the rights of full-blood Natives, who were at the mercy of a few mixed-bloods and whites using Native lands and structures of government for their own economic profit. In this view, allotment did not endeavor to destroy Native culture; instead, it sought to wrest it from the hands of a corrupt, mostly white elite. Hence it was directed against whites rather than Natives, as the twisted logic proposed by the Dawes Report had it.

The report of the Dawes Commission had wide repercussions and directly influenced federal Indian law and policy. It supplied Congress with the arguments necessary to inaugurate the allotment process, and it paved the way for congressional statutes such as the Curtis Act. Its depiction of the members of the Five Civilized Tribes as either ignorant and helpless savages or corrupt and selfish mixed-bloods or adopted whites, and of Indian Territory as a place of barbarism, discrimination, corruption, and lawlessness, also entered court rulings, including those of the US Supreme Court, and thus greatly influenced juridical discourse.[8]

It was such ideas of Native individuals and collectives that Eaton found herself confronted with while researching and writing her book. As an Indigenous historian trained in the Western academy, Eaton combined techniques of Western historiography with Indigenous historical practice. As she points out in her preface, her book is based on both published works by Euro-American authors and manuscripts from Western archives, and stories told to her by Lucy Ward Williams, a Cherokee "fireside historian" (Preface).[9] While on the surface her history of Removal might appear as a retelling of well-known events with a particular focus on one individual, John Ross, reading the text in light of the legal-political debates about assimilation and allotment reveals that Eaton writes a counter-history of Removal to demonstrate that the US Indian policy of assimilation and allotment rests on false premises and is driven by the same self-interest, greed, hypocrisy, and ignorance that marked Removal policy.

John Ross and the Cherokee Indians is a eulogy on the Cherokee capacity of advancement, leadership, and rebuilding rather than a tale of Native victimhood, suffering, and decline. Eaton structures her narrative as follows: Chapters 1 to 6 constitute a rising action, describing both John Ross's personal history and the history of the Cherokees from the eighteenth century onward. The climax is reached when the Cherokees adopt a constitution in 1827 and publicly affirm their sovereign status as a nation.

Chapters 7 to 15 are what might be called a peripeteia in the Aristotelian sense: the machinations of Georgia and the federal government in favor of Removal lead to an intratribal crisis that reverses the positive evolution of the Cherokee Nation outlined up to that point. This structure is then repeated in the second part of Eaton's book. Chapters 16 to 18 report—again in the form of a rising action—the successful rebuilding of the Cherokee Nation in Indian Territory, climaxing with the relative prosperity the Cherokees achieved before the Civil War. The Civil War is then the second reversal in the text, undoing all the work accomplished so far. The book ends with the Treaty of 1866 and Ross's death. It is true that in thus structuring her narrative, Eaton firmly relies on, and reinscribes, settler colonial discourses of civilization and progress. What is equally true, however, is that the two groups of chapters describing Cherokee efforts at civilization and advancement before and after Removal outright reject the settler colonial association of civilization and progress with settler culture and challenge colonial depictions of Native Americans as inimical to progress, uncivilized, or unwilling to become civilized in both the Removal and the allotment eras.

In her chapter on the early history of the Cherokees, Eaton argues convincingly that the Cherokees embraced civilization, progress, and modernity for themselves and were the agents of their own advancement.[10] She underlines the Native agency driving this process by multiple active constructions. She points out that the Cherokees "outgrew" certain "ancient customs," such as the blood law, and "were rapidly taking on civilized manners and customs" (Eaton, *John Ross and the Cherokee Indians* 17, 23).[11] She also mentions that Moravian missionaries established a mission station among the Cherokees only because of "a desire on the part of the Cherokees to educate their children" (*JR* 18). This "intellectual vigor," as she terms it, coincided with an increasing interaction with the non-Native world, through missionaries, intermarriage, and trade (*JR* 11; see also 19, 20). The offspring of multiracial unions formed with settlers, the "mixed-population," Eaton insists, soon became the major promoters of "civilized ideas" and have been "the dominant political [force] among the Cherokees" (*JR* 20). As a result of their efforts, the Cherokees were "the most powerful and most civilized of all North American Indians" at the beginning of the nineteenth century (*JR* 7). To prove her point to her non-Indigenous readers, Eaton quotes an American newspaper that openly acknowledges Cherokee leaders to be "men of cultivation and understanding" (*JR* 28). As becomes obvious here and in other passages in her historical monograph, and as Kirby Brown has rightly noted, Eaton presents "Cherokee national emergence as a decidedly modern and masculinist project that was driven primarily by the acculturated Cherokee diplomats and political figures." She thus "minimizes the significance of cultural traditionalism" and elides Cherokee women from tribal history (Brown 113, 114).

Chapter 6, the book's first climax, opens with Eaton's assertion that by the mid-1820s, the Cherokees "were almost as progressive as the white people of the state [of Georgia] of that time," which she backs up by a counternarrative of Cherokee civilized achievement spanning several pages (*JR* 52; see 52–58). Georgia's atrocious attacks on Cherokee territorial sovereignty, she argues, even heightened the Cherokees' desire for civilization: striving for civilization then became far more to the Cherokees than an incentive to improve themselves; it turned into an act of "self-preservation" (*JR* 51). "Adherence to some of their primitive customs in government had given rise to the accusation that they were uncivilized," Eaton says. "In order to disabuse the mind of Georgia and the whole world of this idea, and to establish a firmer political foundation on which to build a greater Cherokee Nation, the Cherokees determined to establish a regular republican form of government based on a written constitution" (*JR* 53). Eaton thus portrays civilization efforts not only as an integral part of Cherokee society and culture but also as a strategic and diligent move on part of the Cherokee leadership to undermine Georgian arguments of Native savagism and to create political structures signifying stability and permanence.

The impression Eaton seeks to create in the second rising action of her monograph is that of a modern Cherokee Nation capable of governing itself, managing its own affairs, and uplifting its citizens after its dispossession by the United States.[12] Her descriptions seek to deconstruct the image of what she terms "the proverbial 'lazy Indian,'" a savage unable to help himself and dependent on the federal government for his advancement. This image, she argues, was used by government officials to put Indian law and policy on a solid ideological basis (*JR* 162). The Cherokees' post-Removal efforts at advancement that Eaton enumerates at length in chapter 18 talk back immediately to the accusations made by the Dawes Commission. One by one, she contradicts the points made by the commissioners. In spite of the traumatic nature of Removal and the tremendous losses it entailed, members of the Cherokee Nation, due to their "ingenuity and energy," managed to build log cabins with maize patches, if not "good farms and comfortable homes with vegetable gardens, and orchards." They firmly established themselves on the land as farmers and settlers, working for rich harvests. Eaton hastens to emphasize that this was true for both "the more thrifty" as well as "the most unprogressive full-bloods" (*JR* 162).[13]

The Cherokees also did everything in their might to keep out white intruders and squatters. Nevertheless, they entered Cherokee country and proved "a demoralizing influence to the Indians" (*JR* 163). Moreover, the Cherokee government dexterously and effectively resolved conflicts with surrounding tribal communities and established a well-functioning public system of both lower and higher education, to which all children and adolescents had access (*JR* 168–69, 171–72). Even though Eaton concedes that Ross's government "grew to be autocratic and imperial" due to his nepotism, and that there might doubtless be "some elements of truth" in the charge that he enriched himself and his friends and relatives through his patronage, "satisfactory proof of the accusation is entirely lacking" (*JR* 165, 172).

Eaton also explicitly addresses the allotment advocates' argument that the Natives, whom they present as purely collectivist societies, need the Western institution of private property as an incentive to work, to prosper economically, and to create stable social structures. By developing a counternarrative of private property, she dissolves the contradiction between collective and private property that constitutes the center of the ideology of allotment. Ever since the early nineteenth century, Eaton stresses, when highways began to be established throughout Indian country, the "accumulation of property" has played a significant role in Cherokee culture (*JR* 20). Enshrined in the Cherokee Constitution, she insists, the Cherokee system of property combined communal and individual ownership in complex ways and to the social and economic benefit of the community. Echoing John Ross and other Cherokee politicians before her, who time and again mentioned the private ownership of improvements in their arguments against Removal, Eaton emphasizes how individual Cherokee citizens developed their privately owned improvements according to their "fancy or business judgment." Encouraging Cherokee individuals to build their own homes and farms and to work in their gardens and orchards, the Cherokee property system fostered as much business acumen and self-interest as the Anglo-American system (*JR* 162). Private property also influenced one's social status within the Cherokee Nation: everybody who could afford to, Eaton states, kept slaves, both before and after Removal, as "it was considered an indication of wealth and standing in the community" (*JR* 165; see also 20). In the Cherokee Nation, private property coexists with communal property, she claims. And it is from this confluence of individual and collective interests that collective Indigenous sovereignty derives its strength.

The Cherokees in Eaton's book are property-owning individuals deeply invested in individual and collective progress, and their advancement is not dependent on any federally instituted program or policy. Even though she does not explicitly cite the Dawes Report, it is constantly present between the lines and repeatedly challenged. As a rule, reports by government agents, Eaton warns her readers, need to be taken with a grain of salt. As an example of how such reports are misrepresentations and fabrications driven by self-interest, she introduces the story of General Matthew Arbuckle. In his report on Indian Territory to the War Department in 1840, Arbuckle included information drawn from "the wildest rumors started by partisans" in order to convince the department of which measures to take and which men to support (*JR* 141–42).

Besides arguing that US interventions in Cherokee life are superfluous because of the Cherokees' capacity to civilize, Eaton portrays such interventions as a detriment to tribal advancement. Each of the book's rising actions is followed by a peripeteia brought about by US policies or domestic conflicts threatening Cherokee sovereignty and leading to what Eaton describes as atavism: a retrogression of the Cherokee Nation (*JR* 135, 174, 192). Such retrogression time and again resulted from the self-interest motivating US interventions and from the degree of mismanagement characterizing them—US policies were "strangely bungled," as Eaton phrases it (*JR* 118).

Eaton provides the reader with multiple examples of the selfishness and greed behind US policies. She points out that "in her determination to cleanse her soil of the aborigines the state [of Georgia] and her citizens were prepared to go to any length, though all the while strenuously disavowing any selfish or sinister motives toward the Indians" (*JR* 79). The federal government, she claims, was no better. Its Indian policy, which she once even calls a "plot," was an outgrowth of "Anglo-Saxon acquisitiveness under the guise of necessary economic development" (*JR* 83, 162; see also 28).[14] The machinations that the federal government contrived to convince a Cherokee faction to sign the Treaty of New Echota were so cunning and intricate that even professional historians have had difficulties bringing them to light (*JR* 96). Such machinations continued after Removal. Eaton points to the secret activities of government agents in Indian Territory seeking to start "a train of events which threatened to blot a nation out of existence and which actually caused its people to retrograde in civilization for three decades" (*JR* 135).

Eaton also draws attention to the great degree of mismanagement she sees as inherent in US interventions in Native affairs. In her description of Removal, she contrasts the "removal" organized by the federal government and that organized by the Cherokee government. Over several pages, she characterizes the forced relocation of the Cherokees by the United States as the epitome of "incompetence" and "inadequacy" (*JR* 117, 118). When the Cherokee Council took over, the situation immediately improved (*JR* 119). "Left to themselves," Eaton writes, "the Cherokees set about organizing their forces and bringing order out of chaos in a logical and businesslike manner." Due to the organizational skills, intellectual acumen, and political vision of multiracial leaders like John Ross, she stresses, the Cherokees survived their gruesome march west as a nation (*JR* 122). Eaton claims that Ross's vision "to make the Cherokees the greatest nation of civilized Indians," which he had held since early manhood, was the primary reason the tribal community did not disintegrate (*JR* 173).

Eaton fashions Indian Removal as "a most important period of Cherokee history," from which one can learn for both present and future (*JR* 209). By the end of her monograph, the reader suspects that just as the pre- and post-Removal phases of Cherokee advancement were interrupted by wrongheaded US interventions, the post–Civil War period of "Reconstruction of the Cherokee Nation" will again be truncated by another misguided US interference with Native lives. Whenever the Cherokees prosper, the narrative's structure suggests, the United States rolls back Native advancement for several decades. "And the end was not yet" (*JR* 120). This ominous foreboding clearly evokes assimilation and allotment, which, as implied by Eaton, again strikes at the heart of Cherokee forms of belonging by allocating Native lands and regulating Native lives. Just like Removal, it hampers Cherokee civilization, as it is equally ill enforced, based on false premises and gross misrepresentations, and solely geared toward incorporating Native lands and lives into the settler nation. In her evaluation of the federal Indian policy of assimilation and allotment, Eaton thus comes to a conclusion similar to that of the Meriam Report in 1928.

Based on her narrative of Cherokee "administrative ability . . . [and] capacity for Anglo Saxon civilization" (*JR* 160), Eaton draws the following conclusion: "tribal salvation" is best achieved if worked out by the "individual efforts" of Cherokees, "untrammeled by state interference" (*JR* 173). Multiracial Cherokee leaders such as Ross are best equipped to advance their tribe, although she concedes that "a number of other strong and able men in some of whose veins ran no drop of white blood" contribute significantly to the work of multiracial leaders (*JR* 173, 209). The thorough education of their children, Eaton argues, will eventually play into the hands of the Cherokees, as it qualifies the next generation to take prominent leadership positions in the Cherokee Nation (*JR* 170). Together with the work of the missionaries, Eaton explains, the Cherokee civilization program, executed within the well-functioning social and political structures of the Cherokee Nation, is the best and most efficient way for the tribal community to move up the ladder of civilization. Instead of further "hindering both civic and economic development" (*JR* 127), the United States should rather reflect on the effects of its past policies, "awake to the enormity of its injustice and inhumanity towards a valiant aboriginal people," and make amends to the Cherokees (*JR* 125).

What precisely these amends could look like Eaton does not address in her book. However, her narrative advances the idea that the flourishing of Cherokee life is dependent on both the continued existence of the Cherokees as a self-determined, politically autonomous people on communally owned land and the noninterference of the US government with tribal culture and forms of governance. As conceptualized by Eaton, Cherokee civilization does not imply the eradication of tribal customs, social structures, and forms of belonging—the subsumption of "Indianness" by whiteness. On the contrary, successful civilization is grounded in

Indigenous cultural preservation. Acknowledging this, as well as realizing the injustice and inhumanity of past and present settler colonial laws and policies, Eaton's monograph appeals, is the least a "recreant nation" should do (*JR* 125).

"WE WERE INDEED ONE BIG FAMILY!" JOHN MILTON OSKISON'S *THE SINGING BIRD: A CHEROKEE NOVEL*

While the United States would certainly not become "recreant" in the ways and to the extent Eaton had hoped for, in the first three decades of the new century, a new generation of Americans began to question earlier convictions that it was best to coerce Native Americans to give up their culture and to "indoctrinate" them with "the competitive and individualized model that was, to them, the American way of life" (Holm, *The Great Confusion* 8). This new generation of Americans rejected the notion of the "vanishing Indian" and instead voiced their appreciation of certain facets of Native culture that they found worth preserving. Even members of the Lake Mohonk Conference, the hotbed of assimilationism, started backing away from the "vanishing" policy (Holm, *The Great Confusion* 130, 132, 136, 193, 143). Such change in thinking about Native Americans, however, did not precipitate an immediate change in Indian policy. Holm points out the "white confusion regarding Native Americans" in those years: while the new reformers were convinced that an identifiable Native presence in American society should be preserved, they continued to cling to a concept of civilization rooted in white values and institutions. What they lacked was a new theoretical basis for "Indian reform" (*The Great Confusion* 147; see also 130, 148, 152).

Oskison's *The Singing Bird* thus appeared in a transitional period, when the underlying premises of federal Indian policy were increasingly questioned and its contours came under scrutiny. Oskison involved himself in this debate on various levels. First, as one of the founding members and executive officers of the Society of American Indians, founded in 1911 as the first Native American rights organization, he worked for the incorporation of Native Americans into white civilization upon an equal footing in order to "contribute materially and spiritually to modern civilization" (Larré, "Assimilation" 9; see also Larré, Introduction 17–18). Second, between 1903 and 1912, he contributed to discussions about "the Indian question" through his journalistic writings, which deal with conditions in

Indian Territory, the effect of past federal policies, and possible political alternatives (Powell and Mullikin xxi). Finally, after giving up his journalistic career, he continued his political interventions in his fictional works, including *The Singing Bird*.

From the multiplicity of government documents discussing contemporary federal Indian policy and its underlying premises, the Meriam Report stands out. Not only was this report a direct result of the new trends in thinking about Native Americans, but—due to its official nature and the caliber of its authors—it also promoted such thinking and provided much of the data used to reform federal Indian policy through new legislation. The report was commissioned by the Institute for Government Research, which appointed one of its members, Lewis Meriam, to be director of the survey team (Holm, *The Great Confusion* 187). In the 847-page report, Meriam's team, after surveying the conditions of Native American tribal communities, came to the conclusion that the policy of assimilation and allotment had been an outright failure. Allotment was a success in the sense that it had facilitated the transfer of Native property to non-Natives and satisfied white greed for Native lands (Institute for Government Research 7). Its downside was that it left the Native utterly dependent on "unearned income," such as the sale and leasing of his lands, "and postponed the day when it would be necessary for him to go to work to support himself" (8). The governmental interventions geared toward the education and advancement of the Native American were even more flawed: they were underfunded, carried out by incompetent staff, and lacked a well-developed training program (8–9). They also sought to estrange Native children from their culture and family life, negatively impacted Native physical and spiritual health, and were therefore harmful rather than beneficial to Native advancement (15). Finally, the report highlighted that the major problem with federal Indian policy was the reformers' attitude toward the Natives and their culture. "Both the government and the missionaries," the report claimed, "have often failed to study, understand, and take a sympathetic attitude toward Indian ways, Indian ethics, and Indian religion. The exceptional government worker and the exceptional missionary have demonstrated what can be done by building on what is sound and good in the Indian's own life" (16). In short, the report criticized assimilation and allotment as Eurocentric approaches, superimposed upon Natives by a white leadership that had in mind Native property rather than Native people themselves (16). The policy of assimilation and allotment had proven a failure, as it ignored Native traditions, systems of ownership, and ways of life; was conducted in a haphazard fashion; was grossly underfunded; and pauperized Native Americans by destroying the economic basis of their culture (6, 7, 8–9). Thus it fostered the exploitation and degradation, rather than the advancement, of Native Americans—a conclusion strongly reminiscent of Eaton (15, 18).

The Meriam Report also made suggestions as to the shape of future Indian policy. It left no doubt that such policy should still aim at "the advancement of a retarded race" and the "simplification" and "expedition" of the Natives' "merger with the population of the states in which they reside" (Institute for Government Research 20, 51; see also 22). The Meriam Report thus expressed a firm belief in the hierarchy of races and the need for Native Americans to adapt to the Anglo-American way of life, under the leadership of non-Native reformers. Moreover, it did not foresee a return to Native political autonomy. Where it differed from previous official articulations, however, was in its proposal of an alternative vision of the role of Native Americans and their culture in this process of civilization. Central to this vision was an "understanding of and sympathy for the Indian point of view." It was necessary, the report argued, to "tak[e] the time to discuss with them [the Indians] in detail their own affairs," "to lead rather than force them to sound conclusions," and to "[give] major consideration" to "the Indian point of view and the Indian interests." It was also vital "to substitute educational leadership for the more dictatorial methods now used in some places" and to give "the Indians themselves . . . a large hand in the preparation of the program." There was "no reason at all" for Native societies to turn into "replicas" of Anglo-American society. They should rather "supplement" their own traditions and activities with those aspects of Anglo-American culture that appealed to them. Hence "the object should not be to stamp out all the native things because a few of them have undesirable accompaniments but to seek to modify them gradually so that the objectionable features will ultimately disappear" (22, 44, 45). Many facets of Native life, the commissioners stressed, were valuable additions to "the dominant civilization." By collaborating with Native individuals and social units (governments, families, and so on), by providing young Native Americans with an education fostering "initiative and independence," and by giving out scholarships to the most promising among them, the Meriam Report opined, the federal government could establish a policy that respected not only the Native's property rights but also "his rights as a human being living in a free country" (22; see also 32, 35, 37).

Even though the publication of the Meriam Report led to an intensified interest in Indian policy reform, it took one individual, John Collier, since 1933 commissioner of Indian affairs, to effect an actual paradigm shift (Genetin-Pilawa 157).[15] In 1922 Collier had published an article titled "The Red Atlantis," about his visit with the Pueblos, in which he evaluated the Indian policy pursued by the federal government since the 1870s. This article can be considered a blueprint for his later reform efforts as a commissioner. "The guiding policy down to the present," Collier reasoned, "has been to deprive the Indian of his land by direct and indirect means, and to trample out his community life—his 'tribal relationships' in which his physical stamina and moral life are implanted and from which flowers his spirit" ("Red Atlantis" 19). It has been "autocratic and lawless" and has had a "crushing effect" on Native Americans (63, 66). To foster "community initiative" and to return to the Native "the status of man," Collier made four suggestions for change with regard to Indian policy. First, "the Indians must be given civil status. Today the non-citizen Indians are 'wards' of Congress and of the Bureau of Indian Affairs of the Department of Interior." Second, "the dwindled reservations which still exist must be conserved; and those Indians on whom individual ownership has been bestowed or forced must be permitted to establish some form of cooperative landholding." Third, "instead of being broken down, the tribal relationships must be conserved, encouraged and helped to make their own adaptations." Fourth, Native "agricultural and industrial communities must be given advantages equal to, and in the main the same as, those claimed by white farming communities all over this country" (19–20). Collier hence spoke out in favor of preserving Native forms of belonging—forms of property as well as forms of social organization—judging them to be essential for the physical and spiritual health and survival of Native communities.

Just like the Meriam Report a few years later, Collier considered the policy of assimilation and allotment to be detrimental to tribal life and the flourishing of Native Americans—"manacles" and a "one-hundred pound drag" tied to their hands and legs, preventing them from "run[ning] well the modern race." However, his efforts to preserve Native American land and culture did not mean that he rejected the idea of assimilation. "*Assimilation*, not into our culture but into modern life, and *preservation and intensification of heritage* are not hostile choices, excluding one another, but are interdependent through and through." While Collier did not consider Native adaptation to American culture mandatory, he insisted on assimilation into "modernity," by no means a less Eurocentric concept (*Zenith* 203; italics in original). In contrast to the advocates of assimilation, Collier was convinced of the compatibility of Native culture and traditions with Western conceptions of modernity. He was also certain that Native Americans would be able to compete with whites once given equal opportunities and once allowed to develop according to their own cultural standards ("Red Atlantis" 20, 66). "Helping the Indian help himself" was only a tool for achieving that "other things follow as they are already following"—that is, Natives' inevitable assimilation into a modernity shaped according to Western standards. While this might not happen in a lifetime, it was, according to Collier, "a probability, and a real one" ("Office" 210, 227; see also Holm, *The Great Confusion* 193).

The thoughts expressed in "The Red Atlantis" influenced the shape of federal legislation passed under the aegis of Collier, such as the Indian Reorganization Act, which was signed into law in June 1934. Even though the final law was a pared-down version of Collier's much more sweeping original bill,[16] it aimed at consolidating Native land allotment back into tribal lands, increasing tribal self-government, and implementing economic development programs. It was the legal centerpiece of what Collier called the Indian New Deal and signified the official end of the federal Indian policy of allotment and assimilation (Denson, *Demanding the Cherokee Nation* 247; Holm, *The Great Confusion* 188; Talbot 555–58). Through the Indian Reorganization Act, Collier wanted "to help the Indians to keep and consolidate what lands they now have and to provide more and better lands upon which they may effectively carry on their lives. Just as important is the task of helping the Indian make such use of his land as will conserve the land, insure Indian self-support, and safeguard or build up the Indian's social life" (Collier, "Office" 210–11). Despite such lofty goals, Collier's administrative vision of Native self-management and self-government remained inextricably tied to his assimilationist agenda.

Ultimately, as Jodi Byrd reminds us, self-governance was for Collier "a tool for assimilative incorporation" (*Transit of Empire* 193).

Oskison's *The Singing Bird* needs to be read as an Indigenous fictional intervention in these debates about federal Indian policy. Similar to Eaton, Oskison narrativizes Indian Removal and its aftermath to emphasize the Cherokee capacity for civilization and nation building in the face of the harm caused by US federal Indian law and policy. His novel, however, develops a far more radical social vision than Eaton's historical monograph. It presents the gradual and egalitarian mixing of cultures as true civilizatory progress and as eventually rendering the specific projection of Indigenous peoplehood superfluous. Realizing such a vision, the novel suggests, requires Anglo-American reformers to cease thinking in hierarchies. Instead they must treat Native Americans, especially Native leaders, as equals and be willing to engage in processes of cultural exchange and mutual adaptation. This can only be accomplished, however, if prejudice gives way to a general openness toward Native cultural and intellectual accomplishments and if firm belief in the linear progression of cultures yields to cultural relativism.[17]

On the surface, as Timothy B. Powell and Melinda Smith Mullikin point out, the story of *The Singing Bird* appears "deceptively simple," tracing the failure and subsequent recovery of the relationship between Dan Wear, an ardent missionary, and Ellen Morin, the spoiled daughter of a wealthy eastern family (xxvi). When the novel does not focus on the two of them, it describes the prospering of the missionary station established by Dan and his nephew Paul and the latter's growing attachment to Miss Eula, the third missionary worker. The narrative situation in the novel—it is told by Paul—might strengthen the impression that *The Singing Bird* centers mainly upon non-Natives and their view of the frontier. However, already the novel's title complicates such a reading. Not only is the idea of a singing bird—a wife unwilling to have children, as the reader learns later in the novel—taken from a Cherokee legend, but the subtitle also announces that Oskison's is a "Cherokee novel." Situating the novel in the debates about federal Indian law and policy of the 1920s and 1930s resolves this seeming paradox and demonstrates that *The Singing Bird* expresses a unique vision of Indigenous peoplehood.

In the novel, each of the missionaries represents a different attitude toward the Cherokees and their capacity to civilize.[18] The discussions taking place between Ellen, Paul, Dan, and Miss Eula embody various strands of opinion in debates about the shape "Indian reform" should take. In this tableau of white viewpoints, Ellen represents an outright racist and pessimistic stance. She is convinced that Dan's missionary project, in fact the entire project of civilizing the Natives, is a waste of time, as the Natives, due to their racial inferiority, are not worth saving and doomed to extinction. In her letters to her father, she describes the Cherokees she encounters as unintelligent, backward savages with little potential (Oskison, *The Singing Bird* 13, 44–45, 47).[19] Paul offers a genealogical explanation for her attitude: her family "had been conquerors, subjugators," and "it had long been in their blood to prevail" (*SB* 16). Ellen's views represent a mind-set that was widespread in the nineteenth century and was supported by scientists such as Charles Caldwell, Samuel George Morton, and George Combe, who deemed it an irreversible fact that Native Americans were inferior to the Caucasian race (Horsmann 155–58, 168).

Oskison sidelines Ellen's position in various ways. In contrast to the other characters, he constructs her as a flat character. Her transformation from an Indian hater into an industrious worker at the missionary station toward the end of the novel has less to do with a change of her convictions than with her desire to win back Dan for a lack of alternatives. What is more, Paul—the novel's narrator—strongly dislikes Ellen and presents her in very negative terms, attributing to her a selfish, manipulative, narcissistic, and unstable personality (e.g., *SB* 4). As a consequence, the reader cannot help but join Paul and the novel's other characters in disliking her and disavowing her ideas. Readers inevitably align themselves with Dan and Paul, who both increasingly distance themselves from Ellen and whose own attitudes toward Native Americans undergo the most dramatic changes. Through this character constellation, (non-Native) readers who might initially have shared some or many of Ellen's prejudices are encouraged to surmount what Powell and Mullikin call "the intellectual barriers" that prevent them from understanding and sympathizing with the novel's Cherokee characters (xxvii).

Miss Eula represents those "friends of the Indian" who considered the Natives to be in a state of barbarism and who deemed them capable of "regeneration" and civilization. Her pet example is the Cherokee girl Catherine Swan, who arrives at the Kingslake missionary station in a state of "rich barbarism" but who soon turns into the epitome of civilization (*SB* 7–8). To advance the Cherokees, Miss Eula learns the Cherokee language and puts great effort into understanding Cherokee culture and the meaning of the land for the tribe (*SB* 13). She maintains her attitude toward the Cherokees throughout the novel. While she takes her task seriously and is very sympathetic toward the Natives, she upholds her belief in the value of Anglo-American civilization and education and, most of the time, sees herself as a teacher passing on knowledge to what she considers a retarded people. While she respects the Cherokees' way of life and their traditions, assimilation is to her, by and large, a unidirectional process, in which Native Americans are encouraged to gradually modify their habits and to adapt to the settler colonial way of life. Preferring educational leadership over dictatorial methods, Miss Eula acts out the civilization program envisioned by reformers such as Dawes.

Paul's presence in Indian country has more to do with his loyalty to and love for his uncle Dan than with a deep desire to proselytize among the Natives. At the beginning of the novel he reveals himself to be a very lukewarm assimilationist, feeling "no martyr's zeal for the task of teaching the Indians the story of Christ crucified and a knowledge of the white man's way of living." He is not convinced that whites have much to offer to Native Americans, thinking often "that the red men lived more sanely than the whites" (*SB* 22). It is also Paul who criticizes federal Indian policy, which he considers to be based on greed and covetousness (*SB* 99, 158–59). In addition, he time and again describes the abominable behavior of the Anglo-Americans he encounters. Oskison uses Paul to destabilize the boundary between "heathens" and "Christians," "savages" and "civilized," a rhetorical strategy he shares with many Native writers before him, including those responding to and writing on Indian Removal, such as Ross, Boudinot, John Rollin Ridge, and Eaton (*SB* 25, 28).

Throughout the novel, Paul functions as a mediator between Dan and the reader. Lacking Dan's lofty ideals and capacity for reflection, Paul is Dan's disciple, eager to be instructed by him in the ways of the world. He accompanies Dan to his meetings with Cherokee leaders and informs the reader about the things he learns there (*SB* 49). Oskison's choice of a young, white, open-minded narrator is certainly strategic: his white readers are likely to trust him and engage with him in a process of intercultural learning. Paul asks Dan questions the reader might want to ask and, inspired by Dan, begins to question all the preconceived, ethnocentric cultural notions he has carried with him to Indian country. The polygamy some of the Native Americans are said to practice, for instance, causes Paul to ponder on the practicality of Dan having two wives—Ellen as a lover and Miss Eula as a "helpmeet." "But that would mean sanctioning immorality! Then, for the first time, I put to myself the question, What is morality? And after that no hope of sleep remained." Paul comes to believe that morality is not universal but varies from culture to culture. And the longer he lives among the Cherokees, the more wise and reasonable their approach to morality appears to him (*SB* 83; cf. 147).

Despite such insights, Paul does not renounce the discursive edifice of civilization. To him, it remains an unchangeable given that all cultures progress linearly. Upon inspecting a well-written letter by a Native scholar at Oak Hill, Paul concedes that "the Cherokees have come a long way on the road to what we call civilization" (*SB* 143). And when touring the cabins of former students to inquire into their living situation, Paul again states his conviction "that we were living and laboring with a people hardly more than a generation removed from the hunter stage. They had come forward with almost incredible swiftness, but were still as capable of wrecking as of building a stable civilization" (*SB* 168).

Paul does not manage to shed settler colonial fantasies about Native Americans either. Despite his awareness of the racial stereotypes prevalent in the East and their power in US legal-political discourse, he himself occasionally fantasizes about exotic savages roaming freely in the wilderness and considers the older Native men surrounding him to be noble savages, whose "primitive" life he perceives as a healthy and satisfying alternative to the competitive spirit of the emerging industrialist-capitalist society (*SB* 10, 147). His conceptualization of the Natives as noble savages uncorrupted by civilization (first and foremost by education) is reminiscent of the Romantic writings of the eighteenth and nineteenth centuries. While, like the Romantic writers, Paul is wary of the effects of civilization on Western societies, this very civilization remains the evolutionary yardstick for him. He holds firm to the idea that everything should be done to speed the Native Americans' adaptation to that very civilization, if only to make them capable of competing with whites.[20] Commissioner of Indian Affairs Collier was convinced that tribal relationships and culture had to be preserved, as they enhanced the Natives' capacity to adapt. In Oskison's novel, Paul holds a very similar view. In order not to "wreck" their civilizational progress, he argues, the Cherokees need "something to symbolize the sustaining strength of the old beliefs" (*SB* 168).

Oskison employs the novel's protagonist, Dan, to develop a vision of Anglo–Native interaction that far transcends the ideas expressed by "progressive" Indian reformers in the 1920s and 1930s. Rather than envisioning a process of Native adaptation grounded in linear progressivism and racial hierarchization, by the end of the novel Dan imagines the formation of an Anglo–Native society emerging from the fusion of Native and Anglo-American cultures.

Dan is the novel's moral center and its hidden narrative voice. Not only does Paul adore him and adopt his opinions readily and, most of the time, unquestioningly, but his narration of events is also mainly based on Dan's journal entries (*SB* 38). Paul's narrative is hence grounded in Dan's view of the world, his ambitions, and his visions. Dan is also the character who undergoes the most striking development throughout the novel. At the beginning, he wholeheartedly believes in civilization; conceptualizes assimilation as a linear, unidirectional process; and patronizes Native Americans. "The Cherokees must learn the ways of the whites, and prepare to meet them as equals at their own game," he explains to Paul (*SB* 33). While he thus signals that he considers Native Americans intellectually as capable as Anglo-Americans, he takes for granted that the American way of life is what the former need to adapt to. His centeredness on his own set of cultural values becomes particularly evident when he says to Paul "with fervor": "However men twist, travesty, or ignore the teachings of Christ, they will prevail. Always remember, Paul, that upon no other foundation can a people live securely" (*SB* 22). At the beginning of the novel, Christianity is for Dan the enduring essence of civilization, which is why civilization is for him without alternative and justifies US interventions in Indian country.

It is his encounter with Cherokee intellectuals and leaders that prompts Dan to embrace a radically different model of interaction with the Natives, one based on appreciation, respect, mutual exchange, and adaptation (see also Powell and Mullikin xxix). His conversation with Ta-ka-to-ka, head war chief of the Western Cherokees, causes the first of multiple cracks in Dan's set of beliefs. Not only does Ta-ka-to-ka see through the machinations of white politicians and remain unimpressed by their threatening gestures, but he also draws Dan's attention to the inconsistencies between federal Indian policy and the United States' supposed objective to civilize the Cherokees: "If that Great Father the President wanted the Cherokees to follow your road, why did he send us to the west with a blanket and a rifle gun instead of with a hoe and a spelling book?" In response, Dan can only shrug, unable to explain this rather obvious hypocrisy. He immediately admits that Ta-ka-to-ka is a "philosopher worth knowing" and confesses his wish that "he were one of us" (*SB* 36–37).

Dan's change in thinking about Cherokee culture manifests itself as "an unholy light" in his eyes, as Paul describes it (*SB* 36). Once kindled, this light translates into an insatiable hunger for knowledge about Cherokee forms of living and being. In the weeks to come, Ta-ka-to-ka and Dan become intellectual sparring partners, exchanging knowledge about astronomy, physics, and the healing power of herbs. Dan realizes that Ta-ka-to-ka is by no means backward and uncivilized but a shrewd politician and a keen and critical observer approaching the world rationally and pragmatically. Their conversations are model intercultural exchanges, in which both discussion partners treat each other with respect and learn from each other (*SB* 37–38, 49).

The second Cherokee who deeply influences Dan is Sequoyah, the creator of the Cherokee syllabary, whom Dan appreciates for his contributions to Cherokee literacy (*SB* 76). His interactions with Sequoyah encourage Dan to question, and then to reject altogether, his earlier position that without adopting Christianity, humans cannot live securely. He instead concedes that when it comes to religious beliefs, "a man follows the light that is in his own heart" (*SB* 76). Dan stops measuring Cherokee culture by the yardstick of Eurocentric notions of civilization. Rather than trying to convince Cherokees to adopt his own set of cultural norms, he begins to value Cherokee culture and traditions in their own right.

Dan thus moves from a fervent belief in the linear progression of all races from barbarism to civilization to a Boasian cultural relativist approach to human diversity. In the early twentieth century, Franz Boas and his disciples began to question the validity of hierarchizing various cultures and the idea that all cultures could be located on a linear evolutionary scale. Differences between cultures, they instead claimed, were not grounded in racial hierarchies but were the product of particular histories and unique adaptations to specific circumstances. Boas's argument for historical particularism challenged the prevalent assumption that universal laws governed humanity and that all cultures inevitably followed these laws (Holm, *The Great Confusion* 191, 192; Crawford and Kelley 3–5).[21]

Halfway through the novel, Dan thus turns into an admirer of both the Cherokee intellectual elite and Cherokee culture in general. Sequoyah is to Dan "the greatest man I shall ever know"; he even compares his wisdom, patience, and calmness to that of Socrates. He confesses to Paul what he surmises might be apostasy: "But I can no longer think of him [Sequoyah] as a heathen destined to fail of salvation. I accept him on his own terms. He is committed as surely to an ideal, as wholly concentrated to a noble purpose, as our Christ was" (*SB* 110). John Ross, in turn, is "loved" by Dan for his "indomitable" spirit and his resistance to Removal. And he considers the Cherokee way of life "as civilized as that of their white neighbors" (*SB* 155, 122). Accepting the Cherokees on their own terms and learning from them has become Dan's creed. Rather than measuring Indigenous cultures against a given frame of reference, Dan sees their individual merits and acknowledges their unique development. His cultural relativist perspective eventually leads to his gradual abandonment of his work at the mission station and his increasing collaboration with Sequoyah,[22] which, as Paul admits, Dan now seems to find more important (*SB* 110–11).

Dan's new approach to Cherokee culture also leads to his reassessment of federal Indian policy, which he criticizes for dividing the Natives among themselves and for destroying them. He suggests that the major motor behind these policies has been the Anglo-American hunger for land, which has persisted ever since Europeans set foot on the American continent, hence emphasizing the *longue durée* of settler colonial aggression and oppression (*SB* 35, 114–15). Dan's critique clearly reverberates beyond the historical setting of Oskison's novel. Assimilation and allotment also divided and destroyed both the Indigenous land and patterns of life.

Dan's changed attitude toward Cherokee culture is best encapsulated in his vision of his new church at the Oak Hill missionary station in the West: "I want it to be Indian, a spiritual home for the Cherokees, familiar and friendly. We will seat the old people near the fireplaces so that as they smoke they may spit in the ashes" (*SB* 69). It is not to be a Christian church but a Native–Christian church. Rather than trying to convince the Cherokees to exchange their cultural beliefs for Christian civilization, he seeks to give Native culture a place within Christianity, a process through which Christianity itself becomes indigenized and altered.

Dan's "Indian church" is one of the most powerful images in the novel. It stands for an Anglo–Native society created through interracial collaboration and intercultural exchange. The emergence of such a society is dependent on a cultural relativist approach to Native America and on a rejection of linear progressivism and racial hierarchization. Oskison narratively constructs the Oak Hill missionary station in Indian Territory as a microcosmic image of such an Anglo–Native society. At Oak Hill, missionaries, Cherokee students, and selected other Cherokee adults live, learn, and work together. Their fates, as the novel emphasizes, are inextricably intertwined with one another. Private property does not play a role at Oak Hill. Instead, the station is a community of property, in which everyone works together and shares the produce of their labor. Community members exchange and discuss knowledge and strategies on how to survive and prosper, and after Ellen's departure there is not one white character at Oak Hill who does not adopt aspects of Cherokee culture. While Paul and Miss Eula occasionally relapse into hierarchical thinking and measure the Cherokees at the station in terms of their "civilization," Dan's desire to incorporate Cherokee traditions, beliefs, and cultural practices into his own apparatus of knowledge, and hence to adjust and enhance it, gains increasing ground, among both non-Natives and Natives. Even Sequoyah finally concedes: "Maybe this Jesus talk is not all lies, and maybe some of the old beliefs of the Cherokees were wrong. The road to the truth ought to be plain, but it is not always that way. We will both look for it" (*SB* 79). Together, the missionaries and the Cherokees at the station try to find the true way of living by pooling their respective intelligence and culturally specific knowledge. Their common search for truth turns them, as Paul puts it, into "one big family!"—more specifically, an "all-New-England-Cherokee family" (*SB* 70, 169–70; see also 122). While the policy of assimilation and allotment worked toward breaking up the most intimate set of Native social relations, the family, Oskison uses his novel to advocate the implementation of new kinds of familial structures, transcending the supposed divides of race and culture. The fusion of Anglo-American and Cherokee cultures in the daily lives of the residents at the mission station suggests that amalgamation is not only possible but highly profitable for both individuals and the community as a whole.

The novel sharply contrasts this harmonious economically, culturally, and socially productive Anglo–Native microcosm of the mission with the fraught interracial relations Ellen describes in her letters from her visit back east (*SB* 65). Despite his excellent education and his impeccable manners, Richard, a former Cherokee student of Dan's who studied in the East, encounters racial hatred when he expresses his love interest in Catherine, the daughter of a wealthy New England family. While previously welcome in the homes of wealthy New Englanders, who pretend to be friends of the Indian, he and Catherine have to fear for their lives upon announcing their intention to get married (*SB* 65). Even Ellen—one of the novel's most prejudiced characters—realizes how "illogical" it is "to civilize, educate, and equip the savage to live as we do, then deny him the only privilege which if exercised would make him and his children one with us" (*SB* 63). Through Ellen, Oskison addresses what he perceives as the hypocritical nature of Anglo-American assimilationism. In *The Singing Bird*, the Anglo-American desire to incorporate Native Americans into white society is revealed to be no more than lip service. To the New Englanders back east, assimilation is a unidirectional process in which Native Americans adopt the essentials of civilization and shed their "Indianness" but do not mingle with Anglo-American society genetically. They seek to create a community of (white) culture rather than a community of blood.

The Singing Bird presents such a community of blood as the prerequisite for the creation of a society that combines the best traits of Native American and Anglo-American cultures. The future of Cherokee culture and Anglo–Native society rests particularly with the fruits of Native–white unions, such as Richard Sr. and Catherine's. Oskison has Catherine emphasize that her and Richard Sr.'s multiracial child, Richard Jr., may be best qualified for interpreting and conserving the Cherokees' old beliefs, which will serve as the foundation of an Anglo–Native society. He, she says, "could do a good job if he will keep his eyes and ears open, go away to Harvard for his English, and come back a Cherokee" (*SB* 156). Catherine's statement reflects the complexity of the novel's identity politics.

Going to Harvard—that is, leaving Indian Territory and immersing himself in Anglo-American knowledge—Catherine muses, will not lessen but rather intensify Richard Jr.'s "Cherokeeness." Living among non-Natives and acquainting himself with their ways of seeing the world makes him conscious of the value of Cherokee culture and makes him realize which aspects of Cherokee living and being need to constitute the heart of the new society. Studying at Harvard provides him with the intellectual tools and the reputation needed for working toward the formation of an Anglo–Native society. Born biracial and spoon-fed both Cherokee and Anglo-American culture throughout his life, Richard Jr. is presented as being much better equipped to assume a leadership position in this new society than monoracial leaders like Sequoyah, Ta-ka-to-ka, Dan, or Richard Sr.[23] Richard Jr. hence embodies the role Oskison must have imagined for himself and other racially mixed Native Americans.[24] He also stands for the movements and migrations that have been an integral part of Cherokee identity formation, as Cherokee scholars have recently asserted.[25] Going away from Indian Territory and immersing oneself in Anglo-American culture and education must not be equated with assimilation into white culture and with loss of "Cherokeeness," the novel suggests. On the contrary, it fosters critical engagement with both Cherokee and Anglo-American culture and equips one to recover and recenter old tribal beliefs and to develop societal visions across cultures.

According to Oskison's fictional world, Native–white unions, such as Richard Sr. and Catherine's, from which future multiracial leaders spring, will gradually cease to evoke the specter of miscegenation. The marriage of Willis Corn, a Cherokee educated at Princeton, and the Anglo-American Miss Every, mentioned at the end of the novel, "caused scarcely a ripple of comment in the New Hampshire village where they were united by her uncle" (*SB* 169). Their "union" stands for the possibility of union of Native and Anglo-American cultures. To Oskison, such union has tremendous potential, especially for white America. He has Catherine confess: "I shudder to think of what I should have missed by submitting to Mama and Uncle Obidiah and renouncing my Cherokee!" (*SB* 155). It is certainly not too far-fetched to read Catherine's statement allegorically, as an expression of *The Singing Bird*'s political vision: renouncing Native American cultures through policies such as assimilation and allotment signifies a tremendous loss to the United States. And an uncritical belief in linear progress, as it has been enshrined in federal Indian law and policy, produces cultural chauvinism and narrow-mindedness and precludes the possibility of intercultural learning.

The genre of the novel thus seems to have inspired Oskison to move beyond the social visions he endorsed in his earlier journalistic writings, which were based on the idea of linear progressivism that Cherokee historian Eaton chose as the theoretical foundation for her study.[26] Like Eaton, Oskison conceptualized the cultural development of Native Americans as a "race" toward "higher civilization" and portrayed Anglo-American civilization as inevitable and without alternative ("Cherokee Migration" 352; see also "President" 355). As a consequence, the amalgamated society Oskison envisioned at that time was explicitly Anglo-American in character and resulted in the "complete absorption of the Indian into the white race." It consisted of competitive, property-owning, self-reliant individuals represented by the American government ("Outlook" 359, 361; "Remaining Causes" 377; "Making an Individual of the Indian" 381, 387, 390; "Friends of the Indian" 363; "Closing Chapter" 431). As a work of fiction, *The Singing Bird* allowed Oskison to think—albeit somewhat tentatively[27]—about the possibilities inherent in an Anglo–Native society that is not solely premised on Western epistemological frameworks and notions of linear progress and in which amalgamation takes the form of transculturation[28] rather than assimilation.

However, the social vision Oskison develops in *The Singing Bird* implicates the end of Cherokee political autonomy and a form of peoplehood based in specifically Cherokee cultural practices and tied to specific tribal lands. While Cherokee cultural values are to contribute to the social foundations and fabric of the Anglo–Native society Oskison envisions, they will, in the long run, not be recognizable as distinctly Cherokee. Through the biological and cultural fusion of Native and Anglo-Americans into a new society, Cherokee lands will cease to be Cherokee, instead becoming part of American territory. Such a vision does not seem surprising given the political realities of the time in which Oskison likely wrote his novel. After all, Congress had already dissolved Cherokee tribal government and placed the Cherokees under the jurisdiction of the newly founded state of Oklahoma. Hence it is possible that Oskison did not believe that a return to a form of Cherokee political autonomy, in which land could be tribally owned and culture could be preserved, was likely to happen.

To him, the amalgamation and absorption of Native Americans seem to have become inevitable, but their precise terms had yet to be determined. *The Singing Bird* constitutes a significant site where Oskison could imagine what amalgamation based in egalitarianism could mean for both the colonized and the colonizers. For the colonized, it would guarantee the perseverance, rather than the extinction, of tribal cultures as part of a new culture. For the colonizers, it would allow for the possibility to stop "choos[ing] the evil way" and to proceed on "the road to the truth," to use Dan's and Sequoyah's words (*SB* 79, 115).

Placing Eaton's and Oskison's writings in conversation with each other and with the debates about federal Indian law and policy around the time of their publication sheds light on the complicated politics of each of these writers and challenges long-dominant scholarly perceptions. Until Lionel Larré's recent recovery of his writings, Oskison was largely treated by scholars of Native American studies as engaging in "fundamentally assimilationist" politics and as writing "novel[s] of assimilation" focusing mainly on whites (Weaver xi; S. Teuton, "The Native Novel" 430; see also Ronnow).[29] In a similar vein, Eaton's *John Ross and the Cherokee Indians* has so far received only marginal scholarly attention[30] due to the text's support of Western notions of civilization, which at first sight runs counter to scholarly expectations of Native writings as acts of resistance to settler colonial policies and practices.[31] Legally contextualizing the authors' Removal writings, however, reveals that rather than acquiescing to assimilation and allotment and the subjectivities this policy imposed on Native Americans, they strategically turn to the history of Removal to suggest alternative social visions and forms of living and belonging. In their writings, both Eaton and Oskison challenge what Brown has called the "grand moral drama of white racial triumphalism," which inevitably ends with the dispossession of Native Americans and the dissolution of their polities (*Stoking the Fire* 63). Support of assimilationism in the form of "the wholesale rejection of Indigenous values and their replacement with Eurowestern values" is certainly not on the agenda of either of these texts (Justice, *Fire* xvi). They rather need to be understood as "cultural sites of resistance that Native people used to fight the encroachment of white cultural practices and beliefs as well as political oppression," as Kiara M. Vigil phrased it when talking about selected Native writers from the Progressive era (15). Native protest writings such as Eaton's and Oskison's could indeed have an impact on federal Indian law and policy, as Jason Edward Black has demonstrated by pointing to Collier's many meetings and discussions with Native leaders (149). Their Removal writings suggest that Eaton and Oskison demanded a new deal for Natives. Given the positions voiced in *John Ross and the Cherokee Indians* and *The Singing Bird*, one can only surmise that the Indian New Deal that the US government finally offered to Native Americans must have been seen as a sign of progress by both writers, but it certainly did not satisfy their demands.[32]

CHAPTER 3

Indigenous Rights Subjects

NATIVE REMOVAL LITERATURE OF THE 1990S
AND THE LIMITS OF DOMESTIC LAW

NATIVE REMOVAL LITERATURE of the 1990s can be situated between two legal-political discourses that both centered on self-determination. One of these discourses was located in the US domestic arena. The federal Indian policy of self-determination emerged in the late 1960s and 1970s and marked a shift away from the antecedent termination policy, through which the federal government had sought to complete the end of reservations and federal services and protections "as rapidly as possible" (House Concurrent Resolution 108, 1953, qtd. in Wilkinson, *Blood Struggle* 57). Self-determination appeared, in some ways, to embody what Rachel Caroline Eaton had envisioned as early as 1914: Native leadership and responsibility rather than federal dependence. In his special message to Congress in 1970, President Richard Nixon defined self-determination as the effort "to strengthen the Indian's sense of autonomy without threatening his sense of community" (qtd. in Rifkin, *The Erotics of Sovereignty* 1; see also Wilkinson, *Blood Struggle* 189–98).

Legal scholar Charles Wilkinson characterizes the policy of self-determination, in retrospect, as "a launching platform for tribal advancement generally," expanding tribal control, tribal infrastructure, and Native leadership opportunities. It also affected the American courts, which, in their rulings on the nature of tribal governmental powers, looked to the policy of self-determination for guidance (*Blood Struggle* 197).[1] Despite its focus on tribal advancement, however, the policy, as Rifkin critically observes, changed "neither the structures for determining who or what gets to count as a tribe nor the perception of tribes as semimunicipal units within the scale structure of U.S. federalism" (*The Erotics of Sovereignty* 5). Self-determination did not prevent the US Supreme Court from taking an increasingly skeptical stance on Native rights either. From the 1990s onward, the Rehnquist Court—as the Supreme Court headed by Chief Justice William H. Rehnquist between 1986 and 2005 has come to be known—displayed a growing interest in the protection of non-Native interests at the expense of Native sovereignty, which legal scholars such as Robert N. Clinton have described as "neo-colonialism" (98; see also Wilkinson, *Blood Struggle* 253, 268).

In 1984 Vine Deloria Jr. and Clifford M. Lytle expressed their disillusionment with the policy, remarking that self-determination—as opposed to self-government—cannot "[exist] at the whim of the controlling federal government" (*The Nations Within* 19). Self-determination, as it came to be defined in the United States, simply implied the replacement of non-Natives by Natives in the bureaucratic state apparatus. Institutional structures and the underlying premises of US Indian policy, however, remained unchanged (217, 223). Increasingly faced with the limits of this new policy, Native Americans longed for, and began to fight for, a broader conception of self-determination, one exceeding the jurisdiction of the settler state (Rifkin, *The Erotics of Sovereignty* 6).

The other discourse of self-determination to which Native Removal literature of the 1990s subscribes is located in the international arena and began to gain traction in the wake of the decolonization movement after World War II (Wiessner 35). In the UN Declaration on the Granting of Independence to Colonial Countries and Peoples (1960), self-determination was defined as belonging to all peoples. At the time, it was interpreted as "strong" or "external" self-determination—that is, as the right to achieve statehood and to secede from the settler nation (Schulte-Tenckhoff 76–77; Engle, *Elusive Promise* 68). This notion of self-determination allowed Indigenous peoples to demand a shift away from the focus of human rights on the relationship between individual and state authority toward the right to administer themselves collectively, as peoples. Indigenous politicians and activists argued that their ongoing existence as distinct peoples depended first and foremost on the acknowledgment of their collective rights, most importantly their right to self-determination (Eide 37; Engle, "On Fragile Architecture" 152; Schulte-Tenckhoff 81; Henriksen 80).

The states, by contrast, found the notion of Indigenous self-determination extremely problematic because, especially in the strong form in which it was initially conceived, it challenged the existing political and legal order and, potentially, their territorial integrity. Hence, in the late 1980s and early 1990s, when an increasing number of Indigenous rights advocates began to turn to international human rights law in their struggles for legal and political rights, self-determination became the collective Indigenous right most controversially and extensively debated.[2] Debates about self-determination came to a head in the tug-of-war about what in 2007 would become the UN Declaration on the Rights of Indigenous Peoples (UNDRIP).[3] Even though states eventually allowed the language of self-determination to be incorporated into UNDRIP, they did so only in the form of "weak" or "internal" self-determination—that is, a people's right to social, economic, and cultural development and the right to determine its political status within a given state (Engle, "On Fragile Architecture" 161).

Native American writers in the 1990s thus found themselves in the midst of domestic and international legal discourses that were identical in terms of terminology yet highly different with regard to the scope of the rights they intended for Indigenous peoples. Realizing the limits of the domestic discourse of self-determination and its rootedness in the jurisdictional authority of the settler nation, Native leaders increasingly looked to the international arena, where Indigenous rights advocates strove to implement a more capacious form of self-determination. Even though they would ultimately fail in this endeavor, throughout the 1990s and early 2000s, Indigenous rights emerged as a new normative framework signifying possibility. Especially in the United States, with the observation of the Columbus Quincentennial in 1992, Indigenous rights rhetoric and arguments gained increasing prominence.[4] Adopting the language of Indigenous rights embodied for Native collectives the potential to make legal inroads into the forms of subjectivity imposed upon them by the settler colonial state.

Robert Conley's *Mountain Windsong: A Novel of the Trail of Tears* and Diane Glancy's *Pushing the Bear: A Novel of the Trail of Tears*, published in 1992 and 1996, respectively, deeply engage with domestic legal developments in the United States as well as the Indigenous rights debates that took place in the United Nations. They are heavily invested in imagining forms of Native collective identity in response to, and by selectively drawing from, the discursive formations of the settler state and the newly emerging international regime of rights. Conley's *Mountain Windsong* critiques the idea that Native American rights can be secured from within the US legal order. Through the jarring juxtaposition of historical legal documents against a romantic plot, the novel deconstructs the idea of domestic law as an agent of change and introduces the language of human rights as an alternative framework of Native resistance. Continuing the conversation that Conley started, Glancy's *Pushing the Bear* engages with a question at the heart of conceptual debates about Indigenous rights: whether and how Indigenous rights—that is, a body of collective rights—can be embedded and realized in a staunchly individualistic human rights regime. Non-Indigenous state representatives have long considered Indigenous rights an anomaly within the system of international law and have been skeptical about, if not outright opposed to, the legal codification of such rights. Indigenous representatives, in turn, have grappled with the tension between the (individual) subject of human rights and the (collective) subject of Indigenous rights and hence with the potential impact of an individual-centered legal regime on tribal governments, communities, and traditions. On closer scrutiny, the novel opens up an alternative way of thinking about the relationship between individual and group rights. It thereby contributes to closing the theoretical gap between these rights, which has stymied Indigenous rights debates considerably and which has bred Indigenous skepticism about the usefulness of international law in the fight for Indigenous rights. Conley and Glancy return to Removal to highlight the continuities between past US Indian policies and the policy of self-determination and to think about what it means for Native Americans to define themselves and to be recognized as Indigenous rights subjects. Each of the texts demonstrates that from the 1990s onward, international law has impacted Native internal processes of self-definition. As Joanne Barker puts it, it has opened the door to Native Americans to "rearticulate themselves to other discourses than those of oppression (as the oppressed), to shift 'the intelligibility of their historical situation' from the legal constraints of federal plenary power to the internationally recognized legal status and rights of *peoples* to sovereignty and self-determination" (*Native Acts* 10; italics in original).

CHAPTER 3

THE "DEATH OF [FEDERAL] INDIAN LAW": ROBERT CONLEY'S *MOUNTAIN WINDSONG* AND THE LIMITS OF DOMESTIC LAW

In his *Handbook of Federal Indian Law* (1941), Felix S. Cohen, who is credited with creating the academic field of federal Indian law, outlines what he considers the "three fundamental principles" generally adhered to by courts when ruling on the nature of Native tribal powers since the Marshall decisions from the 1820s and 1830s:

> (1) An Indian tribe possesses, in the first instance, all the powers of any sovereign state. (2) Conquest renders the tribe subject to the legislative power of the United States and, in substance, terminates the external powers of sovereignty of the tribe, e.g., its power to enter into treaties with foreign nations, but does not by itself affect the internal sovereignty of the tribe, i.e., its powers of local self-government. (3) These powers are subject to qualification by treaties and by express legislation of Congress, but, save as thus expressly qualified, full powers of internal sovereignty are vested in the Indian tribes and in their duly constituted organs of government. (*Handbook* [1941] 123)

Aside from individual Supreme Court rulings curtailing the rights of Natives,[5] this Marshallian framework largely remained in place until the 1980s. When Cohen's *Handbook* was revised in 1982, Rennard H. Strickland did not substantially alter the above formulations (*Handbook* [1982] 241–42).

Beginning in the 1990s, the majority of contributions to federal Indian law scholarship bemoan the "malaise" or even "death" of federal Indian law (Frickey, "Doctrine" 5; Robert A. Williams qtd. in Tsosie and Coffey 194). Disheartened, disappointed, and frustrated by the rulings of the Rehnquist Court pertaining to Native Americans, scholars of federal Indian law began to engage in "withering criticism" of the court's performance and to doubt that it could be redeemed from its anti-Native course (Frickey, "Doctrine" 10, 12).

In a 1996 landmark publication, frequently cited by scholars of federal Indian law to the present day, David H. Getches complains that the Supreme Court "has recently begun to [abandon] entrenched principles of Indian law in favor of an approach that bends tribal sovereignty to fit the Court's perceptions of non-Indian interests." Its decisions are characterized by what Getches calls a "subjectivist trend": a marking out of the boundaries of Native self-government based on the judges' own notions of what is desirable rather than on established rules. Whenever a decision involves non-Native interests, the judges roll back Native sovereignty to avoid cultural conflict. Foundation principles are only cited and acted upon if non-Native interests are not concerned (1573–75; see also 1576, 1594, 1631). Frickey similarly describes the Supreme Court's move away from foundation principles and its emphasis on "non-Indian-law values." "Rather than moving the field [of federal Indian law] toward sounder structural, normative, and practical moorings," he complains, "the Court has left the law in a mess, done little to promote effective solutions to practical problems, and been more normatively concerned about undermining tribal authority to protect nonmembers than about promoting a viable framework for tribal flourishing in the twenty-first century" ("Doctrine" 8, 11).[6] The Supreme Court's ongoing judicial subjectivism has recently prompted Native legal scholar Walter Echo-Hawk to conclude that domestic law is "ill-suited for the task" of protecting Native cultural integrity and sovereignty, as it is "weak" if not "non-existent" (24).

Conley's *Mountain Windsong* needs to be read as a literary negotiation of the "death" of federal Indian law and its limited use in the fight for Native rights. The novel is an adaptation of the Cherokee singer Don Grooms's song "Whippoorwill" about the love between Oconeechee and Whippoorwill (called Waguli in the novel). Its frame narrative is set in present-day North Carolina, where a Cherokee grandfather tells his grandson, LeRoy, about Oconeechee and Waguli, two Cherokee lovers separated through Removal. Waguli is forced to move west to Oklahoma by foot and steamboat, while Oconeechee hides with other Cherokees in the East, where she searches for Waguli for four years. Gun Rod, an old white widower once married to a Cherokee woman, helps Oconeechee locate Waguli, guides him back east, and reunites him with her. Through the help of another Anglo-American, Wil Usdi, the Eastern Cherokees regain selected parcels of land, so the reunited couple ends up settling close to the spot where they initially met.

The plot suggests that *Mountain Windsong* is a rather conventional novel: a standard coming-of-age narrative that serves as a frame for a historical romance. If placed in conversation with the legal developments around the time of its publication, however, *Mountain Windsong* turns out to be a critical and politically highly relevant text. For underneath its conventional plot, the novel engages with the shortcomings of federal Indian law and its complicity with the project of colonial subjugation.

In *Mountain Windsong*, federal Indian law is metonymically embodied through the Treaty of New Echota. Chadwick Allen has shed light on how contemporary Indigenous activists and writers, rather than deconstructing and questioning the authority of treaties, have "re-recognized," "re-centered," and "reified" the discourse of treaties in order "to re-establish treaty documents as powerful and authoritative and as binding on the contemporary settler nation" (61, 62).[7] While especially the early Cherokee Removal writers indeed re-recognized the authority of treaties in their struggle against dispossession, Conley decenters rather than recenters the authority of treaties, highlights their highly fraudulent nature, and deprives the reader of any hope for restorative justice for Native Americans from within the US domestic legal system.

Mountain Windsong is particularly remarkable in that it contains various forms of historical writings, including the entire text of the Treaty of New Echota.[8] The juxtaposition of nonfictional and fictional textual material in Conley has not yet been treated with sufficient analytical depth. Arnold Krupat claims that the documents "are dropped in as efficient if esthetically jarring means of conveying the facts and feel of the period" ("Representing Cherokee Dispossession" 23). While it is true that the historical documents corroborate the grandfather's story, far from being dropped in, they are carefully placed in the narrative and do much more than merely "[convey] the facts and feel of the period." Stretching over eighteen pages, the Treaty of New Echota is the text around which the entire novel gravitates. Due to its sheer length and its highly complicated bureaucratic register, it sits uncomfortably within the easily readable love story between Oconeechee and Waguli. Rather than presenting it as a document of Cherokee sovereignty, Conley's placement of the text suggests that it was not a lawful agreement and that it blatantly contradicted Cherokee structures of political decision making. Preceding the Treaty of New Echota is an excerpt from Anglo-American ethnographer Charles C. Royce's *The Cherokee Nation of Indians* from 1887 that outlines its prehistory.[9] This excerpt argues that Removal went into effect for two reasons: first and foremost, due to the machinations of one American individual,

President Andrew Jackson, whose attitude toward Native rights to the land differed significantly from those of the presidents preceding him; secondly, through the actions of members of what would become known as the Cherokee Treaty Party, who, as Royce has it, in order "to enhance [their] own importance," acted against the majority Cherokee opinion and signed the Treaty of New Echota (Conley, *Mountain Windsong* 44; see also 42, 45).[10] Read against Royce's text, the Treaty of New Echota appears as a thoroughly corrupt, treacherous, and fraudulent colonial document. Its own narration of its prehistory cunningly distorts the fact that the treaty was concluded with a group of people not authorized to do so (*MW* 48, 49, 60).

Throughout the novel, Conley takes great effort to highlight the Cherokees' historic struggles against autocratic oppression and emphasizes that democratic decision-making processes have been an integral part of Cherokee history.[11] Such emphasis makes Boudinot's and Ridge's signing of the treaty appear as an anomaly in Cherokee country—a social elite superimposing its will on the mass of Cherokees.[12] The novel's juxtaposition of the democratic decision-making processes, in which every tribal member is invited to participate, and the way in which the Treaty of New Echota was concluded points the reader's attention to the dishonest and manipulative nature of colonial policy and its methods of creating apparent consent. Rather than emphasizing the Native sovereignty inherent in treaty making, *Mountain Windsong* alleges that, more often than not, treaties are the opposite of sovereignty, as they are concluded with individuals not authorized to do so. They are often also the opposite of justice. When, in Royce's excerpt, President Jackson is cited as wishing to execute the treaty "without modification and with all the dispatch consistent with propriety and justice," the reader realizes that in the context of American settler colonialism, justice has become an empty referent and has been disjoined from its ethical underpinnings (*MW* 46).

The novel's pages following the Treaty of New Echota suggest that the treaty was a document the United States did not consider binding—at least not with respect to the articles that included promises to the Natives. The farther Waguli is forced westward, the more deceptive the treaty's provisions prove to be. Article 8 states that the Cherokees are to be "comfortably removed," with the government providing a sufficient number of steamboats and baggage wagons, "so as not to endanger their [the

Natives'] health, and that a physician well supplied with medicines shall accompany each detachment of emigrants removed by the Government" (*MW* 53). The narrator repeatedly points out the lack of wagons and horses on the Cherokees' forced migration west, so that even many of the sick, old, and very young have to walk. Waguli sees that Cherokees are dying in masses without medical help, very often from the low quality of the food provided by the government (*MW* 95–96, 103, 125, 128).[13] Article 9 claims that agents are appointed by the government to "make a just and fair valuation of all such improvements now in the possession of the Cherokees as add any value to the lands" (*MW* 53–54). The narrative, by contrast, informs the reader about the deprivation of the Cherokees of their lands and goods and the immediate looting of their houses by white settlers (*MW* 87, 106).

Conley has Ralph Waldo Emerson, one of America's celebrated literary geniuses, function as his mouthpiece when passing judgment on the Treaty of New Echota. In his letter to President Martin Van Buren, inserted into the novel about a dozen pages after the treaty, Emerson calls it a "sham treaty," a "needless act of terror," and "an instrument of perfidy" (*MW* 75–76). For Emerson, the entire enterprise called Removal is a "conspiracy" put into action by the American government so fast "that the millions of virtuous citizens, whose agents the government are, have no place to interpose" (*MW* 77). Emerson's letter lends support to the argument developed by Conley throughout his novel: treaties are the outgrowth of a cankerous colonial machinery that cannot be stopped by the protests of civilians and that is self-perpetuating. This machinery is to Emerson the "denial of justice" and "vast an outrage upon the Cherokee Nation and upon human nature" (*MW* 76, 77).[14]

Mountain Windsong also suggests that the American government considers the rulings of the US Supreme Court regarding Native Americans just as nonbinding as the treaties it concluded with Native nations. In a dialogue between Oconeechee's father and Waguli, the former explains to the latter that *Worcester v. Georgia* was not binding to the president. Waguli responds in disbelief, "The great chief of the white men ignores his own law?" The father replies, "Yes. Are you surprised?" In such a political climate, there is no hope for the Cherokees and no chance to reach a just agreement. When Waguli asks Oconeechee's father, "Will we have to move? . . . What will become of us?," the latter can only reply, "I don't know" (*MW* 18–19). The novel's bleak message is that the entire American political system is so infested with the ideology of conquest that the individual interventions of the small number of supportive non-Natives in the novel—Wil Usdi, Gun Rod, and the camp's preacher—are able to alleviate the suffering but incapable of restoring justice.

That the history of Removal is vital for Cherokee politics and processes of collective identity formation up to and beyond the present day is emphasized in *Mountain Windsong*'s frame narrative. LeRoy, who stands for the coming generation of Cherokees, senses that the summer his grandfather introduces him to the Removal history of his ancestors "was more important than all the others. It was more necessary, it seemed, more immediate, more vital"; it was "essential, life-supporting" (*MW* 99). He realizes that the story his grandfather has told him is different from the information that his history schoolbooks provide about Indian Removal. By concentrating on the pain and suffering caused by Removal, by telling (legal) history from the bottom up—that is, from the perspective of ordinary people—and by outlining the impact of the law and politics of Indian Removal on Native forms of belonging down to the most intimate level, the grandfather makes LeRoy understand "what [this story] really meant" (*MW* 130–31). LeRoy intuitively knows that by learning about the past he has learned something vital about the present and the future too.

Conley's choice of the Trail of Tears as the subject of his novel after a decade of rulings by the Rehnquist Court, and right around the time scholars of federal Indian law were, as Frickey describes it, "caught between a frequent sense of hopelessness on the practical level and arguably unduly abstract critique on the conceptual level," thus seems not coincidental ("Doctrine" 12). Conley turns to the history of Indian Removal to present a less abstract form of critique of the workings of federal Indian law. By relating Oconeechee and Waguli's horrendous fate, *Mountain Windsong* reminds its readers of the effects of federal Indian law on the everyday lives of the individuals under its grasp and thus adds an affective dimension to the more abstract intellectual debates. After finishing the novel, readers cannot fail to understand that "people can only advance so far under an unjust legal regime, and [that] any gains remain subject to divestment at the discretion of government," as Walter Echo-Hawk and James S. Anaya have so succinctly phrased it (252).

Mountain Windsong's ending is very ambivalent: the narrative on the fraudulent nature of federal Indian law eclipses its romantic ending. On the surface, Oconeechee and Waguli are happily reunited in the East and even get the chance to settle on their own piece of land. However, the protagonists' individual happiness in the East cannot gloss over the fact that Native collective suffering continues in the West. This escapist ending constructs a fate that the readers perceive to be exceptional and coincidental and hence leaves them unsatisfied. LeRoy expresses exactly this mixture of feelings: "Grandpa leaned back against the big tree. I could tell that the story was over, and even though it had a happy ending, I was kind of sad" (*MW* 217). The ending triggers readers to ask a question similar to that Waguli asked earlier: what will become of the Cherokees in the West who were not lucky enough to go back east? This question is not answered by the novel. However, its exposure of the malaise of federal Indian law and its detachment from justice does not leave any room for optimism. In the West, justice cannot be restored, as the United States will not honor treaty obligations and will continue to cast greedy eyes upon Native lands. The domestic legal system, *Mountain Windsong* suggests, does not foster but rather undermines Cherokee self-determination.

HUMAN RIGHTS AS AN ALTERNATIVE NORMATIVE FRAMEWORK FOR NATIVE RESISTANCE

Contemporaneous with the debates in legal scholarship and Native literature about the limitations of the US domestic legal order, Indigenous politics internationalized and Indigenous people began to "seiz[e] upon the institutional and normative regime of human rights that was brought within the fold of international law in the aftermath of World War II and the adoption of the UN Charter" (Anaya, "Indian Givers" 110). In the 1970s, Indigenous people for the first time took part in a series of international conferences and directly appealed to international intergovernmental institutions. The 1977 International Non-Governmental Organization Conference on Discrimination in Geneva fostered a transnational Indigenous identity and patterns of global coordination—a phenomenon that Ronald Niezen has called "indigenism" (*Origins* 29–31; see also Anaya, *Indigenous Peoples* 57; Engle, "On Fragile Architecture" 142).

In the beginning, Indigenous rights advocates deplored that human rights law foresaw neither strong forms of self-determination nor collective cultural rights. They were also concerned that the normative framework of human rights, once employed for Indigenous ends, could impose on Indigenous peoples new modes of legal subjectivity that would displace tribal cultural values and disrupt tribal relationships (Riley and Carpenter 193). After all, to their Indigenous critics, human rights were "inseparable from the civilizing mission of the colonial days or the globalizing and liberalizing mission of neocolonialism" (Engle, "On Fragile Architecture" 151; see also Pulitano 6).[15] Despite such skepticism about the usefulness of international human rights for their cause, Indigenous rights advocates, from the late 1980s onward, increasingly grounded their demands in generally applicable human rights principles. Two developments in international law are usually cited to explain Indigenous people's increasing turn to human rights despite their initial reservations. On the one hand, after years of Indigenous struggle, in 1989 the International Labor Organization (ILO) agreed upon ILO Convention No. 169, the first international treaty protecting the rights of Indigenous peoples (Anaya, *Indigenous Peoples* 58–61; Engle, "On Fragile Architecture" 142, 152; Williams, *Like a Loaded Weapon* 174). On the other hand, the UN Working Group on Indigenous Populations (UNWGIP), which was established by the UN Human Rights Commission and the UN Economic and Social Council and was entrusted with the task of drafting a declaration on the rights of Indigenous peoples for adoption by the UN General Assembly, completed this task by 1993 with the support of Indigenous representatives from all over the world. Indigenous people's heightened international activism convinced the UN General Assembly to declare 1993 the "International Year of the World's Indigenous People," followed by an "International Decade" carrying the same theme (Eide 34; Wiessner 38–39; Riley and Carpenter 191; Pulitano 15; Anaya, *Indigenous Peoples* 57).

The potential inherent in the normative regime of human rights has not only enthused Indigenous rights activists all over the world but has also been acknowledged by scholars of federal Indian law. While some of them, such as Getches, remain committed to the idea that "traditional doctrine can be redeemed" and that "tribal self-governance and Indian rights are best preserved within the established constitutional and legal order" (1576, 1582),[16] others, such as Anaya, Frickey, and Williams, have advocated consideration of international human rights law as source of legal protection for Native American rights. In the early 1990s, Anaya explained that Indigenous rights norms may also "be invoked in purely domestic adjudicative settings... [and] be used to guide judicial interpretation of domestic rules" ("Indigenous Rights Norms" 38). Building on Frickey, Williams has hailed contemporary international law as an apt tool "for guidance in defining the basic rights of tribal Indians as indigenous peoples" (*Like a Loaded Weapon* 166; see also Frickey, "Domesticating" 74). To him, the discourse of Indigenous rights has the potential to replace the language of racism that has constituted the basis of federal Indian law since the nineteenth century (165).

The moral and ethical clout of human rights has also affected Native American writings on Indian Removal. Conley's *Mountain Windsong* introduces the normative framework of human rights as an alternative to the existing domestic legal order that the novel portrays as so ill-suited to advancing Native claims for sovereignty and land. The novel's climax in terms of cruelty and violence is Waguli's internment in the stockade. These pages abound with figurative language seeking to highlight Native suffering, to indict US imperial violence, and to rouse the reader's empathy. Through internal focalization, Conley has the reader perceive the atmosphere in the stockade—"sights and sounds and smells." The abounding parallel constructions beginning with "he saw" or "he heard" enumerate the assaults of the stockade on the Cherokees' lives and minutely outline the degrading treatment they suffer at the hands of the colonizers. Women are raped, prisoners are made compliant through whiskey, and children die from malnutrition. The crying of children, the wailing of mothers, and the groaning of the elderly are contrasted with "the laughter and the cursing of soldiers" (*MW* 95, 96). Much more than sight or sound, however, the smells in the stockade embody what Waguli considers "white man's hell": "Fetid odors of human waste, the stench of sickness, the scent of death, the rank smell of rotten meat, the general rankness of unwashed bodies crowded together in too close proximity, all combined to produce a suffocating, mephitic assault on his nostrils and lungs and a savage and virulent affront to the dignity of humankind" (*MW* 96). The novel's focus on the assaulted Native body and senses, and the degree of US imperial violence, leads to a destabilization of the binary between savagery and civilization in the tradition of earlier Cherokee Removal writings, in particular John Rollin Ridge's *The Life and Adventures*. While the allegedly civilized colonizers become the actual savages, the "Indian savages" of the white imagination are presented as the civilized victims of a lethal political-military complex that intends to decimate the continent's Native inhabitants.

Central in this passage and paragraph—hence its climactic position at the very end—is the phrase "dignity of humankind." One could argue that Conley's use of the phrase is a vernacular one, implying that every human being possesses an intrinsic worth that should be commonly respected. However, in a text that so deeply engages with the law and its multiple manifestations, it seems not far-fetched to connect his mention of human dignity with the concept's rich legal history. The idea of human dignity is deeply rooted in the history of ideas, with its origin reaching back as far as Roman philosophy, winding its way through the political philosophies of the following centuries (Petersen, par. 3–6; McCrudden 723). In the first part of the twentieth century, it entered constitutional and international legal discourse and became one of the key concepts informing the legal framework of human rights. A glance at the Universal Declaration of Human Rights and its frequent use of "dignity" (in the preamble and in articles 1, 22, and 23) reveals that by 1948, the notion of dignity had "become a central organizing principle in the idea of universal human rights" (McCrudden 675). By 1986 it had become so ingrained in the United Nation's conception of human rights that the UN General Assembly, in its guidelines for new human rights instruments, demanded that such instruments were to be "of fundamental character and derive from the inherent dignity and worth of the human person" (qtd. in McCrudden 679; see also 656, 664, 677).

Conley's insertion of the idea of human dignity in his novel as the climax of a long catalog of human rights violations signifies his awareness of its international legal prominence. By framing the Trail of Tears as a violation of various human rights,[17] he points his readers' attention to the magnitude of the crimes that were committed in violation of the Treaty of New Echota. Once again, federal Indian law is portrayed as utterly incapable of protecting Native American rights. It is in the stockade that Waguli realizes for the first time the hopelessness of the Cherokees' situation: "Slowly, complete realization of the total significance of all these things came into Waguli's mind, and it was cataclysmic, earth shattering. . . . It was like the crack of doom. . . . There was no hope. None. Nothing but defeat, disaster, despair, and death" (*MW* 96–97). By conceptualizing the colonizers' crimes as an assault on his protagonist's human dignity, Conley constructs Waguli as a human rights subject in need of legal protection. He thus introduces in the novel an alternative to the normative framework of federal Indian law, possibly with a greater potential for restoring justice than Indigenous protests or maneuvers from within the American domestic legal system. By emphasizing human dignity, Conley draws attention to the different ontologies of the regime of human rights and federal Indian law. While the former is rooted in the philosophical concept of human dignity and is not primarily dependent on the interests and will of states, the latter originates in the state itself and is hence inextricably tied to the political interests of state actors. Human rights discourse possesses a moral clout that the state cannot diminish (see Anaya, "Superpower Attitudes" 252).

While *Mountain Windsong* does not provide any answers as to how the human rights approach might be repurposed by Native Americans in their fight for rights, its own employment of human rights rhetoric to critique settler colonial practices alludes to the potentialities inherent in this alternative legal discourse. By using the language of human rights, the novel confronts Indigenous skepticism concerning the value of the normative and institutional regime of human rights for Indigenous struggles for self-determination. It suggests that Native Americans constituting themselves as Indigenous rights subjects—that is, trying to obtain recognition and rights as "Indigenous peoples"—might prove a reformative inroad into the morally tainted, self-justificatory, and self-serving domestic legal regime. It might be a powerful tool for them in the future to push the boundaries of Native sovereignty and property rights and to exchange self-government for what Deloria and Lytle have called "true self-determination" (226).

"KERNELS ON A COB OF CORN": INTERNATIONAL DEBATES ABOUT INDIGENOUS RIGHTS AND DIANE GLANCY'S *PUSHING THE BEAR*

International debates about Indigenous human rights became particularly fervent in 1994, when the Sub-Commission on Prevention of Discrimination and Protection of Minorities adopted the UNWGIP's proposed draft declaration, submitted it to the Commission on Human Rights, which in turn established its own working group to prepare the declaration. Between 1995 and 2006, this working group met eleven times with state delegations and Indigenous representatives and thereby encouraged "an extended multilateral dialogue on the specific content of norms concerning indigenous peoples and their rights." It became an important forum for Indigenous peoples to conceptualize their rights and to promote these rights within the international arena (Anaya, *Indigenous Peoples* 63–64; see also Henriksen 78).

The long time span of discussions among members of the working group, governments, and Indigenous peoples points to the wide gulf that existed between their respective ideas of Indigenous rights. By the turn of the century, only two of forty-five draft articles had been adopted by the working group: one on the right to nationality for Indigenous individuals (article 6) and the other on gender equality (article 44). Both provisions were noncontroversial, as they reaffirmed existing individual human rights. All the other articles were still on the table, and the Indigenous representatives resented the changes that the state delegates demanded. In those years, it appeared as if the process of elaborating a draft declaration was doomed to failure (Henriksen 82; Chávez 97–101).

The adoption of the declaration was hampered by a number of conceptual debates. At the forefront of these debates was the question of how Indigenous rights—that is, a body of collective rights—could be integrated into a human rights regime that, according to Siegfried Wiessner, is staunchly "individualistic" and "inhospitable to claims of collectives" (qtd. in Parrish 302; see also Daes 261). "To many people," Will Kymlicka argues, "the idea of group-differentiated rights seems to rest on a philosophy or world-view opposite to that of liberalism. . . . Group-differentiated rights . . . seem to reflect a collectivist or communitarian outlook, rather than the liberal belief in individual freedom and equality." Collective rights are hence often framed as inimical to individual rights and as leading toward the suppression of individuals in the name of group solidarity (*Multicultural Citizenship* 34; see also 39; Xanthaki 16).[18]

It was such perceptions of collective rights that made their recognition "one of the most contested issues" in international law and politics (Xanthaki 13). Acknowledging collective rights would mean to fundamentally challenge, as Allen Buchanan phrases it, "the core normative assumption of post–Second World War international law: that a regime of individual human rights [was] sufficient for achieving an acceptable international legal order" (91). With the increasing clout of the Indigenous rights movement, however, even leading opponents of collective rights had to admit that Indigenous rights were an "emerging exception" to their critique of collective rights, because Indigenous ways of life were vulnerable, under constant attack, and profoundly incompatible with Western legal and social institutions (Jack Donnelly qtd. in Xanthaki 31). Therefore, since the late 1980s, there has developed a consensus that Indigenous peoples do possess distinct collective rights, such as rights to cultural integrity, land and natural resources, environmental security, and control over their own development (Barsh, "From Object" 44).

When it came to legally codifying such rights in the form of an Indigenous rights declaration, however, representatives from the various states, first and foremost the United States, voiced their skepticism if not outright opposition. In the "Report of the Working Group on Indigenous Populations" from August 1993, the representative from the United States expressed her concern about the extent of collective rights that the proposed declaration assigned to Indigenous groups. She was afraid that such group rights could lead to the submergence of the rights of individuals. The representative from Sweden similarly remarked that the inherent rights of each individual should not be weakened. "Therefore," state representatives concluded, "indigenous rights, even when exercised collectively, should be based on the nondiscriminatory application of individual rights" ("Report of the Working Group" 20).

When two years later the United Nations collected comments from governments about the draft declaration recently adopted by the subcommission, it was again the United States that contended that the text referred to "'rights' which do not currently exist under international law" ("Consideration of a Draft" 7; see also 8). The United States reasoned that based on "its domestic experience," it held the "general view . . . that the rights of all people are best assured when the rights of each person are effectively protected" (qtd. in Xanthaki 32). Anaya has claimed that the US opposition to collective rights was a remnant of the Cold War, when "the struggle for the primacy of individual rights over collective rights was part of the ideological struggle for the primacy of the U.S. model of the state over the Soviet model." If such an ideological aversion existed, it went hand in hand with the fear of what the empowerment of formerly colonized groups through the regime of human rights might mean for the sovereignty and territorial integrity of the settler states (Anaya, "Superpower Attitudes" 257).[19] And even among those states endorsing Indigenous collective rights in principle,[20] there were disagreements about the relationship between collective and individual rights. Some delegates claimed that collective rights could be granted but had to be forever subordinated to individual rights, or at least never "undermine" them. Others argued that collective and individual rights should be balanced without establishing a fixed hierarchy (qtd. in Barsh, "From Object" 796).

Through its narrative reconstruction of Cherokee peoplehood at a historical moment of both individual and collective despair and disenfranchisement, Glancy's *Pushing the Bear* adds Indigenous praxis to the international law debates and scholarly theories about the relationship between individual and collective interests. First, through its narrative technique and its emphasis on the historical presence of individual property rights within the Cherokee Nation, the novel challenges the widely held belief that Native societies, through their focus on the collective rather than the individual, neglect the interests of individual members (see, e.g., Xanthaki 16). By suggesting that in Native communities individualism as well as individual rights do exist, it questions the oft-repeated claim that Indigenous collectivism cancels out individualism or hampers individual development. Second, by developing a vision of Cherokee peoplehood in which individualism and collectivism are in harmonious balance, *Pushing the Bear* speaks back to the United States' celebration of unfettered individualism and its view of collective and individual rights as incompatible and mutually exclusive. Emphasizing the adaptability of Native cultures and their ability to indigenize Western practices and knowledge frameworks for their own purposes, the novel also gestures toward the potential inherent in the subjectivities produced by international law.

Most conspicuously, it is through her choice of narrative technique that Glancy draws attention to the presence of individualism in Cherokee culture. The novel tells the story of the Trail of Tears from the perspective of a multitude of characters, first and foremost Maritole, a mother, wife, daughter, and aunt, and her husband, Knobowtee. The novel travels chronologically through each month and location along the trail. Glancy includes the voices of more than forty narrators, the majority of whom are Cherokees. There is no hierarchy of voices; each voice is separately identifiable, telling its experiences and its own version of events. From the individual voices emerges the communal story of Cherokee Removal; the individual narrators tell their stories as members of a collective, more precisely a nation. While American historical novels tend to individualize the experience of collectives, *Pushing the Bear* fashions the Trail of Tears as both a collective and an individual experience. The novel's narrative style, which has been called "communal first-person," embodies a simultaneous presence of collectivism and individualism in Cherokee culture (Glancy, Afterword 188). The existence of many, clearly identifiable voices demonstrates that the individual—their identity, emotions, and personal desires—is not submerged by being part of a collective. Nevertheless, the individual narrators' frequent use of the first-person plural personal pronoun "we"—that is, their conceptualization of themselves as members of a group—demonstrates that their existence and well-being are inextricably tied to and dependent on the continuation of that collective.

On the level of story, Glancy places a similar emphasis on the existence of individualism within the Cherokee Nation by having her narrative in part revolve around individual property rights. Kenneth H. Bobroff points toward the "myth of common ownership" that has dominated Anglo-American thinking about Native Americans ever since the seventeenth century. According to this myth, Native societies are "communist," hold all their lands in common, and do not recognize individual property rights, which confines them to a state of uncivilized savagery (1565, 1567). As my previous chapters have shown, this myth of common ownership shaped federal Indian policy and law throughout the nineteenth century. It also corroborated the Rehnquist Court's subjectivist tendency to subordinate tribal interests in land to the non-Indian owners of fee land within the reservation. "The Court," Rebecca Tsosie states, gave "stringent protection to non-Indian owners of fee land on the reservation, while it treat[ed] the group rights of Indian nations to their trust lands as a social anachronism of 'communal property,' that [could] be made secondary to non-Indian interests" ("Land" 1298; see also 97; Singer 7, 43). This myth also haunted debates about the draft declaration. Indigenous collective property rights, in particular collective land rights, were among the earliest and "most insistent demands of indigenous peoples" within the human rights framework. Besides being perceived as a threat to the existence of states, Indigenous collective property rights were—in historical fashion—viewed by state representatives as incompatible with, if not to the detriment of, individual property rights (Buchanan 95; Tsosie, "Land" 1303; Engle, "On Fragile Architecture" 161).

Pushing the Bear hones in on the idea that by the time of the Trail of Tears, individualistic conceptions of ownership had long held a firm place in Cherokee culture. Rather than as strangers to the idea of private property, the protagonists are presented as desiring personal property and as defining themselves, at least in part, through what they own. Maritole in particular is deeply attached to all the commodities that she has accumulated throughout her life and that are stored in the cabin she is forced to leave. When the soldiers allow her to head back and retrieve some of her belongings, she encounters a family of white settlers that has already occupied her home:

> I pulled the cooking pot out of the hearth with my hands, and it spilled on the floor: *"Mine!"* I screamed at them in Cherokee. My plates and forks. I turned the table over.... I kicked over a chair in my rage.... "This cabin is mine!" The words spit from my mouth. My body was stiff as a beam...."My forks and ladles. The quilts my grandmother made. Our corn!" ... It was my farm! We had not even cleared all the fields yet. Who is the white man to drive us from our land? (*Pushing the Bear* 14–15; italics in original)[21]

What is most striking in this passage is Glancy's frequent use of first-person singular possessive adjectives and pronouns. "My" and "mine" immediately evoke classic property theory, which rests on a monopolistic conception of the owner and the notion of an autonomous individual whose rights supersede those of all other actors (Carpenter et al. 1088). Albert Gallatin's notes on the Cherokee language—written down with the help of missionary Samuel Worcester—demonstrate that by 1836 there were Cherokee equivalents to all possessive pronouns (243). Such linguistic findings underline Bobroff's claim that at least by the time of Removal, "Cherokee farmers had a well-developed sense of ownership in their improved lands." And even long before Removal, he argues, "Cherokees recognized extensive and well-developed rights in personal property" (1583). Martitole's indignant and emotional reaction to the loss of her property highlights the presence of concepts of private property within Cherokee culture and their significance for Cherokee self-identification.

She challenges the myth of common ownership and refutes Anglo-American views of Native communities as "communist" societies neglecting, or even suppressing, the individual and their rights. The quotation also demonstrates the complex nature of Cherokee property systems. While the cabin and the items in the cabin are marked as Maritole's personal property, the land is conceptualized as "our land" and the proceeds from the land as "our corn," owned by all tribal members in common. In the tradition of earlier Cherokee Removal writings, *Pushing the Bear* thus emphasizes that individual and communal property coexist in Cherokee culture. It reminds the reader of Stuart Banner's pithy statement: "The Indians had property just as much as the settlers did; they just organized it differently" (9). Through her use of possessive adjectives and pronouns signifying Native concepts of ownership, Glancy marks the settler colonial policy of Indian Removal as an illegitimate appropriation of Native belongings—as theft.[22]

Indigenous notions of individual property, *Pushing the Bear* suggests, are inextricably tied to settler colonial conquest and dispossession. The word "mine" is used in the novel again when Maritole's brother Tanner muses upon the discovery of America, the time the white men "dragg[ed] their ships across the ocean. '*Mine*,' they say" (*PB* 181; italics in original). The reader links these two italicized possessive pronouns: the colonizers' "mine" voiced at the moment of discovery and the motor of colonial expansion over the next centuries, and Maritole's "mine"—her desire to keep what the Cherokees have increasingly come to value ever since the first contact. Intermarriage and intense participation in the Anglo-American capitalist economy have promoted the acquisitive and accumulative spirit among the Cherokees and have led to a change in tribal leadership over time. As Maritole states, "Once our leaders were holy men and chiefs. Now I heard the voices of traders and landowners, especially half-breeds who sold deerskins to the Panton & Leslie Company" (*PB* 64). Lacey Woodard, another Cherokee character in the novel, similarly ponders the impact of settler notions of property on Cherokee forms of ownership (*PB* 95). While Anglo-American concepts of land as an alienable commodity seem absurd to her, she realizes that the wealthy within the Cherokee Nation, in order to heighten their economic success, have begun to view not only land as alienable but also human beings. All these passages imply that Cherokee notions of alienability and inalienability have been inflected by Anglo-American concepts of property, and the Cherokees' desire for personal property has been awakened and intensified through the colonizers' attempts to deprive Native communities of their lands throughout the centuries.

Maritole's identification with her personal property is so intense that its loss impacts her physical well-being. As she considers the cabin, as well as the corn she planted, as the heart and ribs of her own physical self, dispossession makes her body stiffen and collapse (*PB* 13). During the trail, her physical suffering in the wake of dispossession becomes even more pronounced: "The cold sat upon my bones. It was as though I had no clothing. It was as though I had no skin. I was nothing but a bare skeleton walking the path. I felt anger at the soldiers. I felt anger at the people in my cabin. They were using my plates and bowls. Sleeping under my quilts!" (*PB* 58). Through dispossession, Maritole's body is stripped of its clothes, even its skin, which highlights the intimate connection between her identity and her belongings. Being reduced to a "bare skeleton," she is not recognizable any more as a Cherokee, not even as a human being. The close connection that the novel establishes between property and personhood calls to mind the "personhood perspective" that Margaret Jane Radin proposes in her oft-quoted contribution "Property and Personhood." In order "to achieve proper self-development—to be a *person*," she hypothesizes, "an individual needs some control over resources in the external environment" (957; italics in original). Since personhood is inextricably tied to personal property (which she contrasts with purely fungible property), Radin continues, the loss, or in the case of Removal theft, of such personal objects occasions pain (959, 960). From the numerous kinds of personal property, she singles out the home as being "affirmatively part of oneself" (992, 1013). Radin's theory is, of course, based on Western ideas of personhood and property. However, the fact that by the time of Removal, Cherokees participated in the Anglo-American capitalist economy and recognized rights in personal property may justify using her thoughts on the significance of personal property for self-identification and self-development as an interpretive avenue to Glancy's novel. Maritole's sense of self is bound to her cabin and other personal belongings. By depriving her of the farm and the improvements that signify Native permanence on the land and that constitute her sense of self, the colonizers deprive her of her identity. In her own view, by losing her property she has also lost personhood and what the colonizers construe as civilization. She has finally turned into the propertyless, unsettled, rootless, uncivilized "savage" of settler colonial discourse, who could, according to Western theorizations of property, be rightfully dispossessed of her land (see Wolfe 396).

Maritole's self-identification through what she owns is presented in *Pushing the Bear* as the rule rather than as an exception in the Cherokee community. For instance, her husband, Knobowtee, is intensely driven by the desire to own. Proprietary interests have long structured his life choices and social relations. He confesses to having married Maritole and his previous wives because of their possessions (*PB* 151; see also 60, 61, 72). The historical property lists of three Cherokees[23]—Wauskulta, Sally Bee Hunter, and Chief John Ross—included by Glancy in her novel strengthen the argument that by the time of Removal, private ownership had a firm place in tribal life and had created social classes and hierarchies in Cherokee society. The lists also visualize the complex nature of Cherokee property systems: while the land is owned in common (acreage is not part of the lists), improvements made to the land, encapsulated by the term "field" (that is, cleared and cultivated lands), are the personal property of individuals. Improvements also include houses, fruit trees, wells, fish traps, stables, workhouses, and slaves, as the presence of "negro houses" on Ross's list indicates. The repeated mention of fences on all lists conveys the significance that Cherokees attribute to marking off such improvements in order to make visible and protect their individual property. The property lists also support the novel's argument that the Cherokees' increasing sense of private ownership results from their interaction with the colonizers and develops in response to the colonizers' efforts to appraise and eventually appropriate Indigenous improvements and lands. Produced by agents appointed by the government after the conclusion of the Treaty of New Echota, who canvased Cherokee country in an attempt to valuate Cherokee improvements, the lists signify the impact of settler colonial policy of dispossession and regimes of property on Indigenous social orders and forms of belonging.[24] Their confrontation with settler colonial incursions on and appraisals of their lands and lives prompts individual Cherokees to present themselves as property owners. Emphasis on private property ownership is increasingly viewed as the only way to counter dispossession or to, at least, secure monetary retribution as the Treaty of New Echota provided. Hence notions of private ownership take on greater meaning and become inscribed in tribal structures and identities (*PB* 77–79).

Pushing the Bear also establishes an inextricable link between settler colonial policies of dispossession and the unraveling of Cherokee forms of collective identification. The marriage of Maritole and Knobowtee signifies how the Cherokee sense of belonging suffers once the tribal homeland is lost and the desire to save one's property becomes all-consuming. Seeing in each other merely the personal property that they have failed to retain when being forcefully relocated, Maritole and Knobowtee increasingly lose touch with each other on the trail. With the land and improvements gone, the bond between them dissolves. Knobowtee can embrace Maritole only when he imagines her to be the farm. What he loves is the farm but not his wife, whom he considers a means to a proprietary end (*PB* 177; see also 18, 40). Maritole's affair with Sergeant Williams also illustrates the destructive impact of Removal on the most intimate Indigenous relations. For Maritole, a sexual affair with an American soldier—that is, complicity with the colonizer—appears to be the only way to get her property back, even if this unweaves her relationship with Knobowtee. She demands from the soldier: "'Take me back to my land. . . . Get that white man and woman out of my cabin. . . . Give us back what is ours'" (*PB* 169). Glancy presents her protagonist's illicit affair as emblematic of the condition of the entire Cherokee Nation. At several points in the novel, she links Maritole's affair to the signing of the Treaty of New Echota by a Cherokee faction.[25] Just as the loss of Cherokee land and her improvements drives Maritole into the soldier's arms and makes her violate her marital vow to Knobowtee, the imminent threat of dispossession and forceful Removal drives one faction of the Cherokee Nation into the arms of the US government, deciding to alienate what is not alienable and thus to act against the legal principles and will of the collective. Just as Maritole's desire to regain via the soldier what she has lost severs the ties to her husband, the Treaty Party members' signing of the Treaty of New Echota, and thus their collaboration with the US government, produces communal dissension and collective fragmentation.

Pushing the Bear emphasizes that the longing for private property in the context of Indian Removal leads to social envy and further stratification of Cherokee society according to economic wealth. Walking the

Trail of Tears, the Cherokee characters repeatedly address the social hierarchies within the tribe. Maritole envies those Cherokees carrying more belongings with them than she does and wonders "why they [had] so much while I had nothing but a cooking pot and blankets?" (*PB* 31). Among the wealthy tribal leaders, Chief John Ross, in particular, arouses the envy and ire of his tribal members and is harshly criticized for riding on a steamboat instead of walking the trail (*PB* 37). Tanner complains about Ross's infatuation with private property, which he deems the reason for the chief's decision not to walk with the rest: "Look at Ross. How he listed all his property. How he kept count. Now he rides on a steamboat to the New Territory" (*PB* 75). Inordinate attachment to private property is associated with a lack of tribal solidarity and with an emphasis on individual rather than collective well-being and comfort.

"Certain forms of property," Kristen Carpenter, Sonia Katyal, and Angela Riley argue, "are integral to human individuation: they are tied to the development of a sense of self that is separate from other people" (1050). The intense fragmentation during the trail causes Maritole to feel for the first time what it means to be individual: "I felt separate. On my own. Individual. I'd heard that word. Now I knew what it meant" (*PB* 201). The individualism she describes is not the celebratory classical liberal individualism outlined by John Locke. Lockean individualism is premised on a foundational myth of the state of nature that guarantees individuals utmost liberty. It views society as "a 'contract' into which these ontologically free individuals enter on a rational calculation of self-interest, as a regrettably necessary compromise in which they submit to the 'artificial' constraints of society in order to preserve, as far as possible, their 'natural' individual liberties" (Albrecht 6). By contrast, the individualism in *Pushing the Bear* results from the breakdown of the collective due to its members' exceeding materialism in the face of settler colonial dispossession. It is a form of social isolation and loneliness, and it is harmful, rather than beneficial, to the individual human being. While in Locke's conception, the individual, with their liberties, is ontologically prior to society, in *Pushing the Bear*, the individual is portrayed as flourishing best within a functioning collective. Human individuation and the individual's development of a sense of self separate from the collective through an overly intense desire for private property are presented in the novel as problematic for the continued flourishing of the Cherokees as a group.

The inextricable connection between individual well-being and the well-being of the group is expressed various times throughout *Pushing the Bear*. Group practices, such as storytelling, are vital for the survival of the group as well as its members, as they help them preserve communal life and give consolation. Maritole's father reflects on the significance of the basket maker's stories for individual and group welfare (*PB* 158). Knobowtee explains how the sound of interacting voices in the process of storytelling sustains him through difficult times: "I remembered . . . our voices and the meaning of our stories. The feeling of wholeness that held back the cold. To heat me. To be my fire. To be my means to survive the night. Voices interacting. The sound with the thought behind them, just like Maritole's father said. Connecting with others. That was the spark that made the fire" (*PB* 155; for similar passages see 144, 153, 156, 233). That connections with each other are created via language is also illustrated by Glancy's insertion of words and phrases from the Cherokee language throughout the novel. Common language praxis is essential for both Cherokee individual thriving and for their persistence as a people. Finally, the individual Cherokee's economic success is grounded in a system of collective/community labor, mutual help, and sharing. While walking, unidentified Cherokee voices remember how, in Cherokee society, the individual (owner) benefits economically from the collective practice of planting and harvesting corn: "The people work together. . . . All of us move from field to field until the seed is sown. . . . Everyone works together in our individually owned fields. . . . Our goods are shared. Distributed among us" (*PB* 189).[26] Throughout the novel, the group is portrayed as the bedrock of the individual Cherokee's psychological and material welfare. Therefore all its Cherokee characters are convinced that the Cherokees will eventually overcome their fragmentation along the trail and rebuild their community (e.g., *PB* 217).

The intense feelings of separation from the community and its internal fragmentation cause Maritole and the other characters to question their emulation of Anglo-American values, in particular their embrace of Western notions of private property. While walking to Indian Territory, Knobowtee critically reflects on his infatuation with his cabin and belongings. "Maybe that was the Great Spirit's lesson. Nothing was mine. I could receive and lose in the same breath. The burden the white man carried was that he didn't know the lesson yet" (*PB* 207). An intense desire for belongings, he concludes, unravels human forms of belonging and leads to the fragmentation of the tribal collectivity into an agglomerate of individuals.

It is against the backdrop of such discussions about individual property and its effect on the community that the book's central metaphor, the bear, needs to be read. Scholars have interpreted the bear as Maritole's way of imagining her oppression on the trail and as a symbol of transculturation itself (Krupat, "Representing Cherokee Dispossession" 33; Fitz 79–80). This chapter draws on Amy J. Elias's interpretation of the bear as "the animalistic state into which they [the Cherokees] are thrown once they adopt the individualism that defines western European values" (201–2). Elias's interpretation is corroborated by Glancy's reformulation of the traditional Cherokee story about the origin of the bear[27] into a story about a fall from community and the dominance of individual desires over collective welfare: "*A long time ago the Cherokee forgot we were a tribe. We thought only of ourselves apart from the others. Without any connections. Our hair grew long on our bodies. We crawled on our hands and knees. We forgot we had a language. We forgot how to speak. That's how the bear was formed. From a part of ourselves when we were in trouble*" (*PB* 176; italics in original). And Maritole and Knobowtee interpret the bear as a metaphor for individual greed. They understand that greed is "in the heart of men," including their own hearts. "No one was free of the bear" (*PB* 183, 221).

Glancy's strong emphasis on Maritole's sense of ownership at the beginning of the novel may initially prompt readers to relate *Pushing the Bear* to nineteenth-century Cherokee political writings that interpreted Cherokee conceptions of *meum* and *tuum* in light of natural law philosophy and presented them as sure signs of civilizatory accomplishment and progress (see chapter 1). However, her increasing focus on the destructive nature of the Cherokees' desire for individual property and its rootedness in settler colonial culture reveals *Pushing the Bear* to be a critique of Western civilization, in particular of what C. B. Macpherson has described as possessive individualism. Based on his study of seventeenth-century Western liberal theorists such as Thomas Hobbes and Locke, he identifies a form of individualism that sees "the individual as essentially the proprietor of his own person or capacities, owing nothing to society for them. The individual was seen neither as a moral whole, nor as part of a larger social whole, but as an owner of himself." In this conception, "society becomes a lot of free equal individuals related to each other as proprietors of their own capacities and of what they have acquired by exercise. Society consists of relations of exchange between proprietors. Political society becomes a calculated device for the protection of this property and for the maintenance of an orderly relation of exchange" (3). Glancy has herself argued that her novel poses an alternative "to Western culture's emphasis on the individual," what she calls "the one-as-all" perspective (Afterword 188). In *Pushing the Bear*, the collective does far more than protect the individual's property and structure economic relations. Walking the trail as a people, as well as remembering past and thinking of future collective practices, such as storytelling, games, ceremonies, and planting, ensures the characters' psychological and physical survival.

The vision of peoplehood that Glancy develops in her novel is deeply grounded in her critique of Western culture, its presumption in favor of the individual rather than the group, and its emphasis of individual rights over group rights. As a state of utter dispossession and political and social breakdown of community, the Trail of Tears opens up a space for reflection on the ways in which Cherokee peoplehood can be reconstructed in the West. These reflections center in particular on the relationship between individual and collective interests. Several characters, including Knobowtee, envision the Trail of Tears as a potential site for overcoming rampant individualism and for bringing individualism and collectivism into a meaningful relation: "We're moving west of the Mississippi now. . . . The small corn farmers as well as the rich landowners. . . . And so we would march. A mix of diverse peoples. Agreeing on little. Our seven clans divided between three white peace clans and three red war clans, with the neutral Long Hair clan to break up disagreements. Small farmers, many of us illiterate. Plantation owners. Slaves. Half-breeds. Whites who'd intermarried. Conjurers. Christians" (*PB* 47). While on the surface this passage bespeaks fragmentation, beneath this surface is egalitarianism: "And so we would march." When Maritole observes that "a rich woman, a trader's wife, with her baby . . . sobbed just like the others," she realizes the incapability of personal belongings to avert settler colonial aggression (*PB* 65). The federal Indian policy of Removal forces all classes of Cherokees to walk across the country. Wealth in material goods becomes meaningless. Knobowtee conveys this insight when asking Tanner, "Does it make any difference now who the fields belonged to?" (*PB* 62). Knobowtee, the character most fixated on private property at the beginning of the novel, develops on the trail into a tribal visionary who seeks to heighten communal spirit and to motivate tribal members not to give up. Walking the trail, he muses, flattens social hierarchies, heightens communitarian feelings, and glues back together the units that have broken apart, such as that of husband and wife (*PB* 219). O-ga-na-ya agrees with Knobowtee about the potential of the trail to encourage self-reflection and renewal: "'We're all torn and hurt,' O-ga-na-ya said. 'But we're nearing a place where we have to start over. Maybe what Maritole did doesn't matter'" (*PB* 217). Walking the trail together helps the Cherokees "push the bear"—that is, overcome their destructive desire for private property and reemphasize Cherokee modalities of relating to each other and the land. And "starting over" is presented as a chance for the Cherokees to reorder their community and, in particular, to negotiate the relation between individualism and collectivism.

Rather than presenting collectivism and individualism as contrasting approaches that cannot be brought into a meaningful relation, the novel presents them as complementary and portrays their careful balancing as the prerequisite for the endurance of Cherokee peoplehood. This vision of complementarity is encapsulated in the powerful image of the kernel and the cob of corn that she has Knobowtee express while looking at the Cherokees walking the trail:

> I looked at the long line of walking people behind me like kernels on a cob of corn. For a moment, I could almost believe we were walking a holy walk. As a unit. As a people. One kernel following another. Our voices united. If we could be one in our walking, we would make it to the new territory. All of us had a part. And if some were silent, it would be like a cob with kernels missing. (*PB* 62)

In Knobowtee's vision of Cherokee peoplehood, the individual and the collective are by no means incompatible but are interdependent. Each kernel is important in and by itself, but it is also part of the cob, the people. A cob without kernels is not a cob. And kernels cannot survive for long without being attached to a cob. Personhood and peoplehood are inextricably intertwined; they are mutually constitutive.

The complementary of individualism and collectivism that the novel espouses in its vision of Cherokee peoplehood has universal ramifications when read in conjunction with the debates about Indigenous collective rights in international law. On the one hand, it challenges the opponents of Indigenous collective rights, who view these rights as incompatible with the liberal-individualist political philosophy that most states subscribe to and that is considered to underlie the Universal Declaration of Human Rights (Buchanan 85). On the other hand, it contributes fruitfully to scholarly inquiries into "whether group rights are in sympathy with, and perhaps form part of, the morality of human rights, or whether they belong to quite a different and potentially conflicting morality." And it adds to scholarly attempts to bridge the theoretical gap between corporatist and liberal-individualist approaches to interests in response to the debates about Indigenous rights in international law (P. Jones 107).[28]

The model of complementarity and interdependence between individual and collective rights that *Pushing the Bear* develops feeds into the argument made by Cindy L. Holder and Jeff J. Corntassel in 2002.[29] Both scholars criticize the prevalent liberal-individualist and corporatist approaches to collective rights for dichotomizing between individual and collective interests, for assuming "that in the final analysis, one type of interest—either the individual or the collective—must be given priority," and for "describ[ing] the significance of group membership for individual well-being in primarily psychological terms" (135, 150). Both approaches, they further claim, tend to frame "the collective/individual rights debate in terms of the individual's 'psychic health' as being contingent on group affiliation" (149). In contrast to this, they argue, "the real-world demands of indigenous groups place a great deal of emphasis on concrete ways in which the preserving of communal life can be important to individuals' well-being.... These practical aspects of communal life make individuals' group interests a lot like their individualized ones, and so suggest that such rights [collective rights] do not introduce new or distinctive theoretical questions" (130).

What Corntassel and Holder think through in theory, Glancy's Cherokee characters act out: the significance of peoplehood—the cob—for the psychological and material welfare of individuals—the kernels. *Pushing the Bear* illustrates that individual Native psychic health, material benefit, and physical survival are not contingent upon group affiliation and tribally specific group practices, such as Cherokee language praxis, storytelling, and collective labor, but they depend on them. If individual interests are embedded into collective pursuits, Maritole and Knobowtee learn on the trail, individual–collective relations become balanced and mutually constitutive, so that the collective gains strength and can survive the settler colonial politics of dispossession. By turning to the Cherokees' experience of dispossession and forced relocation, *Pushing the Bear* helps flesh out scholarly theories about the relationship of individual and collective interests in Indigenous communities. It contributes concreteness and depth to discussions of what it means for Indigenous individuals to live within a collective and to persist as distinct peoples.

Pushing the Bear also speaks back to the oft-repeated claim of state representatives in the debates about Indigenous collective rights that group rights come particularly at the expense of women's rights (Xanthaki 33). At the time of its publication, Glancy's novel was the first Native Removal writing that so consequently took into consideration Native women's perspective on Removal and that gave Native women the same amount of narrative space as men. In the "Author's Note" attached to the novel, Glancy likens the written archive of Indian Removal to a "pottery bowl, broken and glued together with some parts missing and the cracks still showing" (*PB* 236). Some of the major cracks and missing pieces have been Native women's roles during the Removal period and their active contributions to rebuilding Native nations in the West. As a result of Cherokee women's marginalization from the political life of the Cherokee Nation in the nineteenth century,[30] "their voices and influence were either minimized or erased entirely," as Kirby Brown points out with respect to historical and scholarly writings on Cherokee history and culture (98).[31] Cherokee Removal writings until the publication of *Pushing the Bear* reflect this trend. First of all, most surviving accounts of Indian Removal were written by (white) men, with Rachel Caroline Eaton being a notable exception (see also Rozema xv). What is more, as the previous chapters have demonstrated, if women appear at all in these writings, it is as supportive lovers, helpmeets, and maternal figures. Unlike Native Removal writers before her, Glancy fills the cracks of the male-dominated historical archive by seeking to trace through female characters such as Maritole and Quaty Lewis what Removal was like for Cherokee women and how it affected their social, economic, and psychic lives. In particular,

Glancy suggests in her novel a connection between the increasing significance of individual property rights within the Cherokee Nation and the growing curtailment of Cherokee women's rights. Cherokee female character Lacey Woodard, for instance, links Cherokee women's loss of power to Cherokee men's alienation of tribal land. The idea of individual ownership, manifesting itself in particular in the Cherokee ownership of slaves, the novel implies, made Cherokee men receptive to the notion that land, too, was a commodity to be bought and sold, and made them violate Cherokee collective rights to land. And Quaty Lewis lost both her belongings and her husband because the latter—a white settler—responded to impending Removal by claiming his wife's farm as his own property and by allowing her to be expelled to Indian Territory "with nothing" (*PB* 95–96, 24). *Pushing the Bear* hence suggests that it was the curtailment of Cherokee group rights in favor of individual rights (and not the other way around!) that ushered in Cherokee women's disempowerment and disenfranchisement. The vision of Cherokee peoplehood as the perfect balance of individual and collective rights that the novel develops puts an end to Cherokee women's disenfranchisement and re-recognizes matriarchal forms of power, such as the power of assigning farmland in the new territory (*PB* 196). By emphasizing the complementarity and interdependence of individual and collective rights in Cherokee peoplehood, the novel challenges the widely held non-Indigenous view that individual rights inevitably suffer in the presence of Indigenous collective rights.

Significantly, Glancy ends her novel with a key document from Cherokee history: the Act of Union between Eastern and Western Cherokees from July 12, 1839, which she has Knobowtee recite in an interior monologue (*PB* 231–32).[32] Through the Act of Union, the Cherokees form a political collectivity, a "*body politic*," not only to reunite Eastern and Western Cherokees but also to "*provid[e] equally for the protection of each individual in the enjoyment of his rights*" (*PB* 232; italics in original). In its wording, the document calls to mind Anglo-American political documents such as the Constitution of Massachusetts from 1780, which served as a model for the later US Constitution.[33] *Pushing the Bear* capitalizes on such similarities, which the reader familiar with American history perceives. To the non-Native reader, they once more suggest that as early as the nineteenth century, individual rights played as central a role in the reconstruction of the Cherokee Nation in the West as they had played in the process of US nation building. To the Native reader, they convey that individual rights have historically been an integral part of the Cherokees' collective self-conceptualization and that individualism as such is not in conflict with Native tribal life and thought. The novel thus engages with Indigenous skepticism voiced around the time of its publication about conceptualizing Native Americans as Indigenous rights subjects, a legal subjectivity grounded in "the normalizing and even civilizing impulses of Western individualism." It was controversially debated within Indigenous communities whether the human rights framework was not "a threat to indigenous culture" and "a form of cultural imperialism" by superimposing Western concepts of individual and political rights onto Indigenous communities (Engle, *The Elusive Promise* 100; see also Engle, "On Fragile Architecture" 152; Kymlicka, *Politics in the Vernacular* 131). The Act of Union is presented as historical evidence that Cherokee conceptions of nationhood have been grounded in both individual and collective rights and that harmonization of individual and collective rights has hence long been practiced in the Cherokee Nation. It underlines Glancy's literary argument about the significance of the individual in Indigenous political and social praxis and the dependence of group survival and flourishing on the interaction of individual and collective rights. The Act of Union also emphasizes that the Cherokees' rights to sovereignty are solely grounded in their prior existence on the land as distinct polities from time immemorial, "*beyond the record and memory of man*" (*PB* 231–32; italics in original). Significantly, the act appears in the text shortly after Knobowtee's decision to forgive Maritole her affair with the soldier and to build a new life with her (*PB* 222–23). As Karsten Fitz has convincingly argued, "the potential of a functioning relationship between the two young Cherokee people is a metaphor of hope for the whole Cherokee nation" (83). Just as Knobowtee has overcome his excessive individualism and selfishness and reunites with Maritole, the Cherokee Nation will overcome its internal fragmentation, rebalance individual and collective interests, and move into the future as a people.

Pushing the Bear may also be read as an intervention in Indigenous discussions about the feasibility of yet another written document (UNDRIP) emanating from a legal regime (international law) whose development has been inextricably intertwined with the history of colonialism. Despite acknowledging the tainted nature of the written word (see, e.g., *PB* 20–21,

121, 224, 228), the novel makes a strong argument in favor of strategically employing writing—particularly legal writing—in the struggle for Native rights and as a tactic of resistance to disenfranchisement and dispossession. Written words in the form of laws and treaties, Tanner states, were used by the colonial power to curtail Native rights and to appropriate Native lands. Written words, he muses, inhere such a tremendous amount of power that the Cherokees cannot afford not to employ them for their own benefit. Tanner is convinced that by using them the right way, the Cherokees "could do anything with written words" (*PB* 224). The Act of Union stands as proof that the Cherokees eventually decide in favor of making use of writing to assert their peoplehood in the West.

The novel's positioning itself in favor of the usefulness of (legal) writing could be interpreted as an attempt to alleviate Indigenous doubts regarding international law documents such as UNDRIP, with their production and construction of indigeneity. Especially in the last decade, UNDRIP has been harshly criticized from within the Indigenous community for its avoidance of defining "Indigenous peoples" and hence its bypassing of Indigenous peoples' claims to territory and political and cultural autonomy. For instance, in his 2012 presidential address to the annual conference of the American Indian Studies Association, Duane Champagne accused UNDRIP of reducing Indigenous peoples' claims to rights of citizens of nation-states or ethnic groups of citizens. From his view, UNDRIP "presents a comprehensive plan for incorporation of indigenous peoples into nation-state institutions and community" and fails to recognize "the extra-national-legal character of indigenous nations." "In many ways," he states, it is "a summary of existing collective and individual human rights, and deliberately avoids investigating or introducing an indigenous rights perspective." To Champagne, UNDRIP can be seen as only "a partial solution at best" (11, 15, 19–21). To other Indigenous scholars it "reflects a radical disjuncture from previous codifications of the right to self-determination in international law" and is thus "a travesty of a mockery of a sham" (Churchill 526).[34]

In the 1990s, when Glancy wrote *Pushing the Bear*, the concept of indigeneity was seen by many as a novel argumentative framework with which to resist dispossession. Accordingly, an international declaration on the rights of Indigenous peoples was still largely viewed as a potential platform for acknowledging, negotiating, and securing Indigenous rights nationally and internationally. It was believed that, if phrased and used the right way, UNDRIP's words might pave the way for self-determination, the linchpin of the transnational Indigenous struggle for human rights. Even if the declaration would not be recognized by some states, it might revitalize Indigenous rights activism within Native communities and strengthen pan-Indigenous political mobilization. The potential of such pan-Indigenous mobilization is also addressed in *Pushing the Bear*, albeit tentatively. Glancy has several of the novel's characters express their doubts about whether it was the right decision of the Cherokees in 1811 not to join Tecumseh, who wanted to form an alliance with the southeastern tribes to fight against the US government (*PB* 97, 186, 223). Evocations of Tecumseh have a long history. The Society of American Indians (SAI) lauded Tecumseh as the first Native American driven by "the idea of uniting the entire race or a considerable portion of it within a large geographical area." Oskison, who helped found the SAI, even wrote a biography about the Shawnee leader; he dedicated it "to all Dreamers and Strivers for the integrity of the Indian race" (qtd. in Larré, "Assimilation" 8, 9). *Pushing the Bear* is the first Native literary text on Indian Removal that, by evoking Tecumseh, alludes to the benefits accruing from pan-tribal collaborations. One should certainly not place too much evidentiary weight on these passages. However, considering that Glancy wrote her Removal novel in the midst of the UN International Decade of the World's Indigenous People and during the negotiation of UNDRIP, they might not be coincidental but rather expressive of a general trend toward greater pan-tribal collaboration and self-identification as Indigenous peoples.

Reading Conley's *Mountain Windsong* and Glancy's *Pushing the Bear* in light of domestic and international legal developments demonstrates that from the late twentieth century onward, Native American Removal literature begins to engage with international law because of its potential to challenge the Native subjectivities created by federal Indian law and US American politics. With its more capacious notion of self-determination, the normative framework of Indigenous rights, as well as emerging concepts of indigeneity, appeared to offer Native communities a language and grammar with which to expand the federal government's more limited understanding of self-determination as self-government and to resist continuous dispossession. Writing their Removal novels in the midst of debates about Indigenous rights prompted Conley and Glancy to reflect on the significance of indigeneity in the struggle for Native perseverance and futurity. It may also have led them to present their Cherokee characters' claims for political and cultural autonomy on the sole basis of their indigeneity, their prior existence as culturally and politically distinct Indigenous nations from time immemorial. Unlike most Native Removal writers before them, Conley and Glancy thus disconnect claims for Cherokee peoplehood from the Native capacity to "civilize"—that is, to adapt to settler colonial cultural, legal, and political norms. Glancy in particular criticizes Cherokee civilization efforts. She draws a connection between the Cherokees' adoption of Western concepts of private property and the fragmentation of Cherokee collective identity and argues in favor of a very selective and careful adaptation of Western values and norms to Indigenous practices of living and being. "Pushing the bear" is for Glancy a continuous task of Native communities, extending from the past through the present into the future.

CHAPTER 4
"CHEROKEE BY BLOOD"?
CONTEMPORARY AFRO-NATIVE REMOVAL
LITERATURE AND THE FREEDMAN DEBATE

MARCH 7, 2006, was a momentous day in the lives of the Cherokee freedmen.[1] On that day, the Judicial Appeals Tribunal, the Cherokee Nation's highest court, issued its ruling in *Allen v. Cherokee Nation Tribal Council, et al.*, which declared unconstitutional the blood requirement adopted and then added to the Cherokee National Code by the Cherokee Tribal Council in 1993. This blood requirement had held that "tribal membership is derived only through proof of Cherokee blood based on the Final Rolls" (Cherokee Nation Tribal Council Legislative Act 6-92, later codified as 11 CNCA §12, qtd. in Sturm, "Race" 577). The code's reference to blood as the marker of Cherokee citizenship and its mentioning of the Final Rolls both testify to the deep legacy of federal Indian policy in Indian country. The Final Rolls originated in the allotment era. To determine who was eligible for land allotment, the Dawes Act required federal agents to create lists of individuals who applied and were approved for membership in the Five Civilized Tribes. Via this requirement the US government became immediately involved in determining whether or not a person qualified as a tribal citizen. Unsurprisingly, the federal agents' decisions of tribal citizenship status were grounded in their own ideas about race and blood. Abiding by the so-called one-drop rule, they placed all freedmen exclusively on the Freedmen Rolls rather than the Cherokee by Blood Rolls, irrespective of how much Cherokee blood they actually had. The freedmen's absence from the Cherokee by Blood Rolls made it eventually impossible for their descendants to satisfy the blood requirement and thus excluded them from tribal membership in the Cherokee Nation. Being deprived of tribal membership had political, economic, and personal consequences; the freedmen were denied both legal-political rights and tribal ethnic identity, access to the nation's resources, and, most important to many, cultural authenticity. By excluding the freedmen, Jodi Byrd claims, the Cherokee Nation turned them "into refugees of their own histories and identities" ("'Been to the Nation'" 48; see also Adams 105–6; Barker, *Native Acts* 4, 82–83; Sturm, "Race" 575, 577, *Blood Politics* 81).

The Dawes Act and the Dawes Rolls created in its wake thus "helped cement the various racial ideologies from earlier in the century," to use Circe Sturm's words. Using blood quantum to determine the trust status of the allotments—that is, to regulate who was in control of the land—(further) racialized property rights: the less "Indian blood" allottees possessed, the more capable of handling property they were deemed to be.[2] The Dawes Act also delimited the number of those who counted as "Indian" and established "blood degree" as a major legal-political instrument for measuring Native authenticity (Sturm, *Blood Politics* 81; see also 79–80; Barker, *Native Acts* 82). Through the Dawes Act, Joanna Barker states, the idiom of blood became an integral part of "a whole host of subject-making practices that have brought 'Indians' into and under the routine administrative control of the United States" (*Native Acts* 82).[3]

Yet equally important has been the impact of blood degree on tribal constitutional and common law. Many Native nations have incorporated the federal politics of blood into their political structures and have used it to determine tribal membership status.[4] Since the 1970s in particular, managing one's own membership criteria by means of blood quantum rules has become viewed as central to the exercise of tribal sovereignty and as a key aspect of tribal self-determination.[5] Blood rules, Kirsty Gover argues, "can . . . be seen as part of a tribal response to the disruptions caused by shifts in federal policy and changes in tribal demography." They have been the result of strategic choices tribes have made to "[repair] the historic continuity of the communities" and to protect their economic resources and political status (248; see also TallBear 58; Adams 3). But critics of blood rules, such as Hannibal B. Johnson and Robert Warrior, also consider them evidence of the racism prevalent in many Native communities (Johnson 166; Warrior).[6]

In 2006 the judges of the Judicial Appeals Tribunal of the Cherokee Nation argued that the blood requirement contradicted the language of the 1975 Cherokee Constitution and thus dissented from an earlier ruling that had made the exact opposite claim.[7] The tribunal's argumentative turnabout may have obliged the judges to include in their ruling reflections on the nature and value of settler colonial subjectivities for Native sociopolitical organization and for determining the question of what constitutes "Cherokeeness":

> The Dawes Commission had their own federal purposes for including a blood degree in their documents. The federal government continues to use these blood degrees for their own purposes today. . . . The "blood" degrees of the Dawes Commission are absolutely irrelevant for the purposes of determining who is a legal citizen of the Cherokee Nation of Oklahoma. . . . The Cherokee Nation is a Sovereign. The Cherokee Nation is much more than just a group of families with a common ancestry. For almost 150 years, the Cherokee Nation has included not only citizens that are Cherokee by blood, but also citizens who have origins in other Indian nations and/or African and/or European ancestry. Many of these citizens are mixed race and a small minority of these citizens possess no Cherokee blood at all.
>
> People will always disagree on who is culturally Cherokee and who possesses enough Cherokee blood to be "racially" Indian. It is not the role of the Court to engage in these debates. This Court must interpret the law as it is plainly written in our Constitution. (*Allen v. Cherokee Nation Tribal Council, et al.* 8–10; see also 3)

The tribunal expresses its disapproval of the Cherokee Nation's reliance on the "absolutely irrelevant" blood criteria established by federal agents during the allotment era and its definition of membership on the basis of blood (see also Sturm, "Race" 575, 584, *Blood Politics* 74). It rejects the idea of a Cherokee national identity grounded in "'racial' Indianness" and emphasizes the historical significance of multiculturalism for forms of Cherokee belonging. While the judges voice their unwillingness to engage in the debates about "Cherokeeness" that have plagued the Cherokee Nation since its 1866 treaty with the US government, which granted freedmen and their descendants full tribal membership,[8] they spell out the danger of linking tribal political identity to a biological category: by defining itself on the basis of blood, the Cherokee Nation runs the risk of racializing itself and hence endangers its status as a politically sovereign entity.[9] In a similar vein, Marilyn Vann, president of the Descendants of Freedmen Association and hence at the forefront of pro-freedmen activism, provokingly asked, "Is the Cherokee nation a race or a nation?" ("Cherokee Chief"; see also Ray 387).

The tribunal's ruling provoked heated controversies within the Cherokee Nation. In its aftermath, Chad Smith, then Cherokee principal chief, began to work for a constitutional amendment defining the Cherokee Nation in terms of blood. In a special election held on March 3, 2007, 76 percent of those voting favored the proposed amendment and—yet again—excluded the freedmen from citizenship. The freedmen filed a temporary injunction in the District Court of the Cherokee Nation, in which they asked for their citizenship to be reinstated so they could vote in the upcoming general election (*Nash, et al., vs. Cherokee Nation Registrar*). In May 2007, Cherokee Nation District Court judge John Cripps temporarily reinstated the Cherokee freedmen to citizenship until the court could reach a decision regarding the merits of their case, but the freedmen could not get the pro-freedmen candidate elected. Instead, Chad Smith was reelected by a large margin. The Cherokee freedmen had now been twice rejected by their tribe. This rejection, as historian Gregory Smithers emphasizes, reverberated far beyond the legal-political arena: the denial of African-Cherokee identity went hand in hand with "a concerted institutional attempt to erase it from the collective life and memory of the Cherokee diaspora" (225; see also Sturm, "Race" 585, 590).

The Cherokee Nation's rejection of freedmen and denial of their existence were, unfortunately, not exceptions in Native America. A great number of the approximately 160,000 descendants of those formerly enslaved by the Cherokee, Choctaw, Muscogee (Creek), Chickasaw, and Seminole Nations still live in Oklahoma and have had to face ongoing discrimination and a denial of citizenship rights. Thus, in 1979 and 1983, respectively, the Muscogee (Creek) Nation and the Choctaw Nation each adopted new constitutions expelling the freedmen by limiting citizenship to Creek and Choctaw Indians by blood—that is, to all those related to someone on the Creek/Choctaw by Blood Rolls. The freedmen of these and other tribes therefore have seen their own disenfranchisement and ensuing identity dilemma reflected in the struggle of the Cherokee freedmen for the reinstatement of their citizenship rights and an acknowledgement of their history and existence (Somvichian-Clausen; Healy; Johnson 246, 247).

CHAPTER 4

It was in the midst of these legal-political skirmishes that Sharon Ewell Foster and Zelda Lockhart—both of African-Native ancestry—each published a novel negotiating the experience of African-Native slaves shortly before, during, and after the period of Indian Removal: *Abraham's Well: A Novel* (2006) and *Cold Running Creek* (2007). They are the first novels on Indian Removal to focus on the twice marginalized: the slaves owned by the Cherokees and Choctaws who were, together with their Native masters, forcibly relocated by the federal government.[10] *Abraham's Well*, a neo–slave narrative,[11] tells the life story of Armentia, a Black-Cherokee slave, from her childhood as a domestic slave in a Cherokee family in the East in the years prior to Removal, her family's walking the Trail of Tears to Indian country, and her experiences with plantation slavery and the "breeding" of slaves in Indian Territory until the Civil War to her post–Civil War emancipation and reunification with her grandchildren and great-grandchildren on their own land in Oklahoma in the late 1880s. In *Cold Running Creek*, the federal government's Removal of the Choctaws serves as a backdrop against which the rest of the narrative unfolds. The novel's first part, covering the years between 1834 and 1861, centers on Raven, a Choctaw girl whose clan is massacred by white soldiers because they escaped the official "removal" of the tribe after the Treaty of Dancing Rabbit Creek. When the reader meets Raven again, she is the wife of the Choctaw-French plantation owner and slaveholder Grey Fox LeFlore, who does everything he can to maintain his land in their Mississippi home against white attempts to force him west.[12] Raven soon claims Lilly, a Choctaw-looking baby born in the slave quarters, as her own. The approaching Civil War finally gives Grey Fox's white neighbors the chance to deprive him of his land. They also force Lilly into slavery. Part 2 (1861–1863) traces Lilly's life as a slave on the white Bartlette plantation and describes the bodily harm she faces and her unwillingness to consider herself part of the slave community. Part 3 (1863–1881) focuses on Lilly's life after emancipation: her existence as the wife (and peon) of the free Black Willie Kellem and as the mother of two dark-skinned girls, to whom she feels little attachment due to their skin color. After her final escape from her unhappy marriage, she finds out that she is the daughter of Grey Fox and the slave Josephine and that Willie was paid for many years by her French-Choctaw grandfather Jacques LeFlore to keep her away from her Native family due to her African heritage. This knowledge, and the experience of being rejected by what she has considered her (only) family, finally enables Lilly to reject blood discourse, to recognize her children as her own, and to escape with her children and Willie from a Mississippi that is dominated by men as racist as her own grandfather.

Through their choice of Indian Removal as the central topic (Foster) or historical backdrop (Lockhart) of their novels, both authors situate themselves within a scholarly and activist pro-freedmen discourse in which Removal in general and the Trail of Tears in particular have functioned as a pars pro toto for the entire African-Native lived history of shared suffering in the face of colonization.[13] For the advocates of freedmen citizenship, the forced relocation and shared suffering of the enslaved and their Native owners on the Trail of Tears signifies the freedmen's belonging to the so-called Five Civilized Tribes. Lived history is for them more significant for the determination of tribal membership practices than the abstract notion of "historical continuity" evoked by those relying on the Final Rolls to argue in favor of the freedmen's exclusion.[14] Foster's and Lockhart's Removal novels also make a strong plea for the freedmen's lived historic connections to the Cherokee and Choctaw Nations and their intense identification with these communities in the face of settler colonial acts of dispossession and disenfranchisement.

Through fictionalizing the US politics of dispossession and the Native politics of enslavement and racial exclusion as overlapping histories—as in fact informing one another—Foster and Lockhart establish a causal connection between the Natives' dispossession—their loss of communal property—and the growth of chattel slavery—the accumulation of private property within the so-called Five Civilized Tribes. Both authors thus move far beyond earlier Native Removal writings, which either did not explore the adjacent historical relationships between dispossession and enslavement in nineteenth-century Native America at all or, as in Diane Glancy's *Pushing the Bear*, did so only very tentatively.[15] By expounding these relationships and by highlighting their complex dynamics, Foster and Lockhart contribute to an understanding of colonization and racialization as "work[ing] simultaneously . . . in the name of progress and capitalism," as "concomitant global systems that secure white dominance through time, property, and notions of self." Rather than limiting themselves to the vertical relations between colonizer and colonized, they shed light on what Byrd has called "the horizontal struggles among peoples with competing claims to historical oppressions" (*Transit* xxiii; see also xxxiv). Retelling Indian Removal with a focus on both horizontal and vertical interactions allows them to highlight the complicity of settler colonialism with Indigenous regimes of race and hence to shed light on the historical evolution and complexities of contemporary legal, political, and cultural debates about freedmen tribal membership.

Marilyn Vann asked whether the Cherokee Nation is a race or a nation. Foster and Lockhart develop a far more complex picture in their novels. In both texts, race is represented as a social invention, an arbitrary category introduced and naturalized by the settler nation to colonize and take possession of the land. It is portrayed as fundamentally incompatible with Native epistemologies and forms of living. In contrast to Vann, *Abraham's Well* and *Cold Running Creek* do not present "nationhood" as an alternative to "race," with nation signifying culture and race biology. They instead highlight the imbrication of nationhood and race and portray the Western concept of nation adopted by Indigenous peoples in response to settler colonialism as actually enabling the politics of racial exclusion. As an alternative to the discourse of racialized nationhood, both novels advocate the revitalization of pre-Removal conceptions of tribal belonging. They envision forms of peoplehood grounded in traditional notions of kinship, lived history, and ongoing cultural practices. Likely familiar with the debates about identity politics and essentialism in the African American community, Foster and Lockhart employ their novels to gesture toward ways to escape, to use bell hooks's words, "colonial imperialist paradigms" of identity that were imposed upon tribal communities from the outside yet that tribal members have become deeply attached to ("Postmodern Blackness"; *Yearning* 19, 20).

THE INCLUSIVE PAST:
PRE-REMOVAL FORMS OF PEOPLEHOOD

Foster's *Abraham's Well* is told by Armentia, an old woman looking back on her life's progression from slavery to freedom. At the beginning of the first chapter, in a short frame narrative, Armentia introduces herself to the reader: "I am Armentia. I am Cherokee, *Aniyunwiya*, one of The Principal People, and I am Black." She also adds that she still "speak[s] the language of the People, *Tsalagi*," that her "thoughts are still Cherokee," and that "their ways are still [her] ways." In addition, Armentia highlights that she "ha[s] walked the Trail of Tears—*Nunna daul Isunyi*—The Trail Where We Cried" (Foster, *Abraham's Well* 14).[16] Foster thus chooses a programmatic beginning for her narrative. Armentia states succinctly the basic assumption underlying the story she is about to tell: she identifies as African-Cherokee, which has become an "impossible identity" ever since the federal government's segregation of the Dawes Rolls by blood (Gross 141). From her mixed heritage, Armentia declares her Cherokee identity to be salient. While she acknowledges that some of her ancestors came from Africa, she admits to knowing neither their language nor their clan. Her clan, as she highlights throughout the book, is the Deer Clan, to whose multiracial members she feels closely related. They are her kin. And it is through her clan membership that she defines herself. The clan, she also emphasizes, is organized matrilineally, with the women passing on knowledge, land, and life.[17] Hence, for Armentia, lived kinship relations, her Cherokee language praxis, and her participation in Cherokee culture and shared historical oppression provide the basis for her self-identification. For her, these are also the constituents of Cherokee peoplehood. And it is on this vision of peoplehood that her entire story hinges. It is the yardstick against which she measures all her life experiences (*AW* 14, 16–17).

In the frame narrative, Armentia also points to what she considers the driving force of her life story: private property. She begins her tale as follows:

> The day I want to tell you about first, well, it was in the days when there were no fences, when all the land and all the good of the land belonged to all the people in common, and when there were not as many White people as now. The Principal People didn't pay for land to own, water, or fire back then. It was the days when we lived on the land that the Great One gave to us, when we lived on the land that held the dust and the bones of our fathers. (*AW* 15–16)

Armentia highlights the absence of fences and boundaries. Land was owned communally in these days, and private property interests in land did not yet exist. Such absence allowed the Cherokees to live in a geographically dispersed Cherokee community, in which power was decentralized and social coherence was achieved through common cultural practices (*AW* 15, 16–17).

The above passage implies that this harmonious existence would soon be ended by people's increasing desire to own the land individually. This desire to own even manifested itself in children such as herself. Foreshadowing the events to follow, Armentia confesses ruefully, "I would take everything back if I could. I would make everything like it was, I would never have touched the honey" (*AW* 14). She refers to her secret taking of honey from Mama Emma, her mistress, which, she believes, set in motion the chain of negative events befalling her family as well as the Cherokee community. Ascribing such wide-ranging consequences to her own actions belies the narrator's naivety and her inability to connect her individual experiences to the greater historical forces at work. This limited knowledge, however, makes her all the more convincing: Armentia does not belong to the highly educated social elite fighting against marginalization and discrimination by the settler state; on the contrary, Foster constructs her as an ordinary, average woman who has suffered from settler colonial policies and who tries to make sense of her own life. The assumptions Armentia makes about the meaning of property in her life story appear to be intuitive and not bound to any political agenda, which makes her appear all the more trustworthy to the reader. Her plan is to tell, as she repeatedly insists, "the *whole* truth," "the good and the bad of it" (*AW* 14, 121; italics in original). Armentia's is one of the subaltern voices rarely heard in Removal writings. Through her, Foster imagines the impact of settler colonial policies on the "intimate domestic (the Indian home and family)" (Piatote, *Domestic Subjects* 4). Through Armentia's eyes, Foster seeks to spell out the havoc settler colonial interventions wreak on the most intimate levels of Cherokee relations. As Armentia's intuitive remarks suggest, property is the key to understanding the story she is going to tell.

Armentia starts her story by describing the days before the desire for private property destroyed what she presents as an idyllic pastoral state of existence, undisturbed by racial tensions. She describes watching her brother Abraham and his friends play at the nearby stream in harmony with one another and with nature. The three boys, Johnnie Freeman, Golden Bear, and Abraham, represent the racially inclusive nature of Cherokee society at the time. Johnnie has all the physical markers signifying Blackness. His family is not enslaved and is later offered the opportunity to stay on the land. However, as they are part of the Deer Clan and have always resided with their Cherokee brothers and sisters, they cannot imagine not joining them on the Trail of Tears (AW 18, 39, 64). Golden Bear has the copper skin commonly ascribed to Native Americans. He also belongs to the Deer Clan and appears to be a full-blood Cherokee (AW 21). Abraham's skin is described as a mixture of brown, gold, and red and is to reflect his African-Native identity. He is a slave, and just like the rest of his family, deeply immersed in Cherokee culture and social life (AW 19, 20). The three boys represent some of the constituents of what the novel conceptualizes as a multiracial Cherokee community, whose members define their tribal belonging through clan membership, language, and shared cultural practices. Racial differences do not matter within the clan—in fact, all clan members feel they share common blood. As one clan member puts it in the novel, "We are all related. We are the Beloved Community" (AW 44; see also 28, 29, 30). Racial differences are only perceived when occurring outside the tribal world; Armentia admits later in the novel that they sometimes called the African slaves owned by white people "niggers" to highlight her family's own superiority as Cherokee slaves and to emphasize Cherokee patterns of kinship (AW 59).

Armentia portrays her relationship to her Cherokee-white masters as similarly harmonious and as not at all defined along racial categories. Emma Sanders and her husband seem not to belong to the Deer Clan, but Armentia sees them as part of her extended family. They feel so close to each other that Emma insists that Armentia call them Mama and Papa. "Mama Emma" treats Armentia like a daughter, spoiling her, showering her with affection, letting her sleep in her house, even teaching her the Cherokee alphabet. Mama Emma also entertains close relations to Armentia's mother, with both of them working together, sharing goods, and helping each other. Armentia's family and Mama Emma and Papa feel that they are related to one another. Their kinship results in mutual obligations and defines their norms of behavior. Treating their slaves as chattel, as property, and exploiting them for their own profit is clearly outside these norms and hence not even remotely considered by Mama Emma and Papa. The novel thus builds an implicit contrast between pre-Removal Native practices of slavery and white chattel slavery.[18] Slavery in the Cherokee Nation, as Foster has Armentia present it, is not based on coercion and oppression. No one is beaten, and everybody can move around freely. What binds everyone together is their belief that they are related through kinship. "We were a beloved family. We were all Kituwah's children," Armentia explains (*AW* 25; see also 24, 30–31).

Furthermore, the novel establishes a link between group belonging and forms of Indigenous land tenure. Golden Bear's father says, "The Great One gave us this land for all to share alike. . . . It is the way of The Principal People. It is not our way, it is not the Great One's way, to own things that cannot be owned: the sky, the land, or even men" (*AW* 63). He thus gestures toward the complex relations between these two forms of belonging in Indigenous societies. Communal land ownership signals group membership. Western ideas of private ownership, by contrast, run counter to the "way of the Principal People." Thus, despite their familiarity with the category of race, at the beginning of *Abraham's Well*, the Cherokee characters' concept of peoplehood is grounded in kinship ideologies, language, culture, and communal land ownership. Therefore they neither define social boundaries along racial lines nor racialize rights to the land.

Instead of presenting the reader with a harmonious community as yet untroubled by the federal policy of Indian Removal, Lockhart starts her novel in medias res, having a heterodiegetic narrator outline the precarious legal-political situation in which the protagonist Raven's clan finds itself after the official "removal" of the Choctaws to Indian Territory. Despite the Treaty of Dancing Rabbit Creek's provision that some Choctaws could choose to remain in Mississippi, take land allotments, and become state citizens,[19] the US Army kept exerting pressure to relocate everyone west. The novel begins after Raven's clan's successful escape from "removal" and return to its former lands (Lockhart, *Cold Running Creek* 4, 8).[20] Raven's father, whom she calls Inki (Father), negotiates with the whites "to either get what belongs to us or get back onto the journey of being with the others." Deprived of their land and resentful of the "'mixed-blood traders'" politics, the clan members fear the consequences of their escape and are anxious about their future (*CRC* 4, 5; see also 7, 9).

What connects Foster's and Lockhart's novels is their focus on property as the driving force behind their narratives. Just like Foster, Lockhart builds a contrast between Indigenous and Anglo-American forms of ownership. The narrator describes the atmosphere in the settlement of Raven's clan before the massacre as follows: "Against the log cabin, their pots and pans were scattered in a relaxed pattern of belonging" (*CRC* 10). This short sentence serves to characterize the relationship of the Choctaw clan members to their belongings: while moveable goods formally belong to certain individuals, use patterns are presented as inclusive, allowing each clan member to make use of the chattel as they see fit. Such an inclusive use of property shapes Choctaw communal life: the chickens roam freely around the unfenced cabins. And preparing the meals is a collaborative effort of the clan's women, who share the goods rather than making use of their own ingredients (*CRC* 10). The positive relations among the clan's female members, collaborative labor, and the sharing of goods constitute the heart of Choctaw kinship practices. The novel implicitly contrasts such relaxed patterns of belonging and relating to each other with Anglo-American notions of private property rights, which assign to the owner the exclusive authority over the owned item. Such ideas of exclusivity underlie the Choctaw clan's fervent battle with the federal government about the land. The colonizers' unwillingness to share the vacated land with those original Indigenous owners who refuse to move precipitates the massacre and the extinction of the clan.

Similar to Diane Glancy's *Pushing the Bear*, *Abraham's Well* and *Cold Running Creek* both suggest that Native cultural practices and patterns of belonging collapse in the wake of the federal Removal policy. However, the narrative trajectories of these novels differ significantly. *Pushing the Bear* emphasizes the *longue durée* of Cherokee adaptation to settler colonial social and political structures and the social tensions it produced well before Removal. The novel presents the Trail of Tears as a cataclysmic moment exacerbating these tensions yet also enabling a Cherokee national renewal marked by reconciliation and affirmative relationships. By contrast, writing from the position of the twice marginalized, whose rights have been violated in the context of Cherokee and Choctaw nation building, Foster's and Lockhart's novels can neither end with nor celebrate post-Removal Cherokee or Choctaw nationhood. Both authors construct Removal as a moment of disruption, when Indigenous patterns of collective ownership, cultural practices, and long-practiced kinship models come abruptly to an end. Already in the frame narrative, Armentia relates how her desire to possess—her taking of honey from Mama Emma—emerges in the wake of tribal discussions about their impending relocation by the colonizer (*AW* 14). She also comments on how the younger members of the tribe adapt to Anglo-American fashion and cultural practices to convince the colonizers of their progress in terms of civilization and to heighten their chances to remain on the land (*AW* 26–27). And in *Cold Running Creek*, Inki mentions how the biracial heritage of the "mixed-bloods" leads to a revised understanding of Choctaw forms of belonging. They are willing to trade both tribal land and heritage for individual profit (*CRC* 4). Foster and Lockhart represent the federal Removal policy as the moment in which racially inclusive matrilineal kinship systems are permanently replaced by settler colonial regimes of race and property. They depict Removal as sowing the seeds of division and as giving rise to a tribal political and legal order that is grounded in racial difference and the discrimination against, exploitation of, and exclusion of all those of African descent.

CLAIMING WHITENESS: THE ADOPTION OF CHATTEL SLAVERY AND THE STRUGGLE FOR THE LAND

In her influential contribution "Whiteness as Property," Cheryl Harris sheds light on how in early America "rights in property [were] contingent on, intertwined with, and conflated with race." It is through the "entangled relationship between race and property," she argues, that "historical forms of domination have evolved to reproduce subordination in the present." Harris critically observes that in the United States, racial and economic subordination was achieved and maintained through "the *interaction* between conceptions of race and property." "The hyper-exploitation of black labor was accomplished by treating black people themselves as objects of property. Race and property were thus conflated by establishing a form of property contingent on race." "Similarly," she continues, "the conquest, removal, and extermination of Native American life and culture were ratified by conferring and acknowledging the property rights of whites in Native American land. Only white possession and occupation of land was validated and therefore privileged as a basis for property." Both these forms of exploitation contributed to what Harris conceptualizes as the "construction of whiteness as property" (1714, 1716; italics in original). Whiteness became "the property of free human beings" and hence a shield protecting its holder from being enslaved. And whiteness also bestowed on its owners the right to acquire property and to secure it under law. By contrast, nonwhites—that is, African Americans and Native Americans—were excluded from the category of ownership. While the former were propertized, the latter were dispossessed due to their supposed lack of civilization and their making improper use of the land (1721, 1722, 1724).

Reading *Abraham's Well* along with Harris's theory on the construction of whiteness as property creates an understanding of the inextricable link the novel creates between dispossession and taking possession. For it is the threat of land loss in the form of Removal that sets in motion the transformation of traditional kinship structures and family relations into a racialized politics of belonging. In chapter 3, the visit of a white relative of Papa's, who is accompanied by his slave Ephraim, introduces Armentia, Mama Emma, and Papa to the practice of chattel slavery. To her utter disbelief, Armentia is taught by her brother Abraham and his friends that because of their skin color, slaves like Ephraim are conceived of in white society as commodities that can be used and alienated according to their owners' liking (*AW* 30–31). While Johnnie Freeman is aware of the fact that Mama Emma and Papa also own Armentia and her family, Abraham emphasizes the difference between Ephraim and themselves: Ephraim is a "White People's slave"; he is "not family like us. He works for his people" (*AW* 30). It is exactly this treatment of their slaves as kin rather than as chattel or enslaved workers that the white visitor talks about with Mama Emma and Papa and that induces them to change such accustomed practices. Mama Emma later tells her slaves, "The White man says we treat you too good, we treat you too much like family. . . . But you need to know who you are. You are slaves. You have to stay in your place" (*AW* 54). Abandoning Cherokee systems of matrilineal kinship and extended family relations frees Mama Emma from her obligations to her slaves and allows her to reorganize her household hierarchically.

Abraham's Well, however, does not present Mama Emma and Papa's adoption of chattel slavery as an unmotivated imitation of white practices. Instead, it paints a far more complex picture, highlighting the complicated dynamics between their turn toward chattel slavery and the tribe's impending expulsion. The latter is actually the major reason for the white man's visit. He has come to convince Papa to leave the land before the official "removal" (*AW* 46). His critique of Mama Emma and Papa's lenient treatment of their slaves is just a side effect of his visit. In Mama

Emma's mind, however, the information about the impending loss of their land and the critique of their overly lenient treatment of their slaves become two sides of the same coin. Armentia senses her cognitive fusion of both the white man's talk about chattel slavery and the news about the government's Removal plans: "Mama Emma had been acting strange since the white man's visit, since the news that we would have to move. I knew that it was not really her" (*AW* 52). *Abraham's Well* thus establishes a causal connection between Indian Removal—the loss of land—and the Cherokees' adoption of chattel slavery—the propertization of the Black body.[21] Threatened with land loss, Mama Emma ceases to view her slaves as kin; she begins to distance herself from them, does not look at them anymore, and redefines them as property that she can use and treat as she pleases. Her smile becomes, as Armentia deplores, "hard as ice" (*AW* 53, 66, 71).

Being a child, Armentia cannot understand this transformation. She can only imagine that Mama Emma has been befallen by a "sickness" or has been "poisoned" (*AW* 64; see also 53, 54). The novel leaves it to the reader to reflect on what this sickness or poison could be. By constructing a temporal simultaneity between dispossession and taking possession, it suggests that Mama Emma begins to partake in settler colonial structures of domination and subordination for her own Indigenous ends. Through the production of an African-Native other and her implementation of racial difference, she highlights her "civilization"—her adaptation to the cultural practices of white Europeans and her capacity and will to appropriate, to make "proper use" of things. Owning slaves—that is, fashioning oneself as a property-owning individual—also signifies freedom; freedom, in turn, is closely associated with whiteness. By her propertization of human beings, the novel suggests, Mama Emma strives to be identified as both civilized and white. Such identification, she intuits, might turn her from a supposed nonowner into the acknowledged owner of the land in the eyes of the colonizer and thus lead to an acknowledgement of her property rights.

In her argument, Harris draws on Jeremy Bentham's notion of property as "nothing but a basis of expectation." According to Bentham, "the idea of property consists in an established expectation; in the persuasion of being able to draw such or such an advantage from the things possessed, according to the nature of the case" (112, 115). His conception of property is thus "not based on physical possession, occupation, or even use, but the concept of ownership as a relation, based on an *expectation* of being able to use property as one wishes" (Bhandar, "Property, Law, and Race" 209; italics in original). In *Abraham's Well*, Mama Emma and Papa are also convinced to draw certain advantages from the things they possess. Their adoption of chattel slavery is not so much presented as a desire to amass the tangible goods produced by slave labor. Rather, by treating slaves as commodities, they seek to emphasize the white part of their racially mixed heritage, their capacity and will to own, and, by implication, their rights to the land. After selling Abraham to a white man in exchange for a promise to help her stay on the land, Mama Emma starts smiling again, thinking that "it's all over now" (*AW* 73; see also 72, 77). Mama Emma thus views the treatment of slaves as alienable goods, as her possessions, as the only way to ward off Removal, her dispossession.

After meeting Ephraim and having the concept of chattel slavery explained to her, Armentia begins to sense the entanglement between race and property. Her secret eating of Mama Emma's honey needs to be read as a litmus test of kinship relations. Honey, as Armentia explains to the reader, is a very precious item of trade with the white people and is rarely ever consumed by family members. Only she, whom Mama Emma calls her "beautiful, sweet baby," gets treated with a spoonful of honey occasionally (*AW* 28). While Armentia thus understands the use patterns of the honey to be restricted, she considers her occasional consumption of honey as *partaking* in a good that belongs to her family, of which she is an integral part. After seeing that the white visitor is served an entire jar of honey and being confronted with Mama Emma's changed behavior, Armentia's convictions concerning her own position in the family seem to falter (*AW* 37, 46). By "*taking*"—she explicitly does not classify her deed as stealing—six jars of honey, she unconsciously wants to test the nature of her relationship with Mama Emma (*AW* 47; italics mine). Is she kin or chattel? In what way does she belong? Mama Emma's eventual categorization of her act as theft proves to Armentia what she has already felt intuitively: that forms of belonging within the household have changed. Papa's beating of Abraham, who declares responsibility for the theft to protect his sister, leads to Armentia's realization that there "wasn't much difference after that, between us and Ephraim. A slave is a slave is a slave, and a slave master is a slave master is a slave master" (*AW* 58; see also 59).

While before she was confident that "Mama Emma would never beat" them, as "it was not the Cherokee way," she now sees that "the Cherokee way" has given way to white forms of racial subjectivity: she has turned from kin into chattel (*AW* 30–31). The changing form of Cherokee slavery in the course of interaction with the white settlers reflects the transformation of Native kinship relations through white racialized conceptions of property.

In *Cold Running Creek*, Lockhart greatly expands on the entanglement of Native American slaveholding practices and the geopolitical realities they are confronted with. She does so through her choice of narrative technique. While she has a heterodiegetic narrator expound with considerable detail the racial dynamics at work in post-Removal Mississippi and the geopolitical situation of Raven and her French-Choctaw husband, Grey Fox, varied focalization conveys to the reader how their precarious legal-political status impacts the couple's psyches. Thus Lockhart also sheds light on the degree to which settler colonial laws and policies structured Indigenous life choices, cultural practices, and intimate relations.

Already the first paragraph of the chapter following the massacre of Raven's clan encapsulates the geopolitical parameters defining the Choctaw couple's life. It describes Raven and Grey Fox as "[lying] on a bed of sun-crisp linen, in a room decadent with rugs and drapery, held up by white pillars, windows of hand-blown glass that revealed them, vulnerable in their prosperity in a white run Mississippi" (*CRC* 16). The couple's apparent prosperity rests on "white pillars," more precisely on the whiteness that runs in the family. Raven has married a man of considerable wealth—the son of Jacques LeFlore, a white plantation owner of French heritage. He has become one of the Choctaw Nation's leading politicians due to his marriage to a Choctaw woman (*CRC* 24, 25).[22] While Jacques LeFlore had moved to Indian Territory, the new political homeland of the Choctaw Nation, after helping to implement the Treaty of Dancing Rabbit Creek, Grey Fox and Raven had stayed in Mississippi on the four hundred acres of land previously cultivated by Jacques, who could not be dispossessed due to his whiteness. He had instructed his son to hold onto his land and to attempt to reclaim those portions that he had been forced to sell to the English. The aim of Jacques LeFlore, who is portrayed as a highly opportunistic and pragmatic capitalist, has been to live up to his name and to "flourish" in his environment—that is, to amass a fortune by owning land and slaves. To do so, he marginalizes Choctaw culture and traditions and implements racialized modes of governance. For him, marriage to a Choctaw woman and, hence, his son's clan status are access routes to Choctaw kinship networks, politics, and, ultimately, land (*CRC* 24, 25, 34, 99).

Raven and Grey Fox's existence, however, is as fragile as the hand-blown glass windows that reveal them. Mississippi, as the narrator reminds the reader, is run by whites, who are intent on dispossessing the remaining Natives. Raven and Grey Fox's vulnerability derives from their residence on ancestral Choctaw soil, which, through the "removal" of its Native owners, was incorporated into the state of Mississippi. While they are, from a legal perspective, citizens of the state with property rights, they are viewed by the white characters in the novel as members of the Choctaw Nation living in a diaspora[23] and—due to their nonwhite status, their "different blood," as General Thorpe phrases it—as illegitimate occupants of the land. They are considered juridical-political anomalies that need to be "removed" to create a coherent domestic territory (*CRC* 69–70, 37).

Cold Running Creek's portrayal of the geopolitical space the Choctaw characters move in calls to mind what Giorgio Agamben has called a state of exception, "a zone of indistinction between law and nature, outside and inside, violence and law" (41). Mark Rifkin has applied Agamben's ideas on the state of exception to the relationship between Native Americans and the settler state. Through its Indian policy, he claims, the settler state produces a state of exception for Native Americans. While as domestic dependent nations they are excluded from the regular categories of American law, they become part of the sphere of US sovereignty through the very "language of exception" ("Indigenizing Agamben" 90; see also 97). In the state of exception, forms of violence deemed extralegal in US law become legitimate. Agamben considers the person in the state of exception "bare life": life that is the effect of and subject to sovereign violence, that anyone can kill with impunity, and "whose exclusion found[s] sovereign power" (88; see also 47). In *Cold Running Creek*, Native characters are portrayed as inhabiting a state of exception, which reduces them to bare life. Raven's clan is cruelly massacred by the soldiers in response to their resistance to forced relocation. Raven herself is severely mutilated and deprived of the possibility to procreate. And Grey Fox and Raven are eventually dispossessed by General Thorpe and the other southern landowners, and their adopted child Lilly is enslaved. All these acts of violence are either committed with impunity or are sanctioned by recourse to the language of the law—federal Indian law, American property law, or the Choctaw slave codes, the last of which General Thorpe uses for his own purposes despite having no authority to do so (*CRC* 97, 99, 284). They are expressions of sovereign violence geared toward the erasure of Native presence east of the Mississippi and toward "the (re)production and naturalization of national space" (Rifkin, "Indigenizing Agamben" 94).

Their vulnerable status is deeply inscribed in the Choctaw protagonists' psyche and determines their behavioral patterns and social relations. Raven and Grey Fox's marital life is dominated by the stress of holding onto their land in a society in which ownership is seen as a white privilege and that is intent on erasing Native presence on the land. "It is a difficult job to keep up the land, the obligations, the stresses of being the man I am in a white man's society," Grey Fox confesses to his wife (*CRC* 18). He constantly has the feeling of not belonging due to his mixed racial status and, hence, of having no proper rights to the land. His insecurities about belonging(s) are reflected in the paintings of himself and his father above the sitting room mantel. While these paintings function as "a declaration of belonging," serving to assert the family's position in southern society and its rights to the land, Grey Fox's stare—in contrast to his father's confident stare—is merely one of "ambiguous belonging" (*CRC* 24).

Throughout his life, Grey Fox tries to make up for his part-Native heritage by practicing chattel slavery. His father had given him the following advice: "'Own as much of yourself as possible'" and "'say yes . . . to all of them [the slaves] and you will be the richer man for it'" (*CRC* 25, 26). Like Foster, Lockhart establishes an inextricable link between the ownership of slaves, whiteness, and rights to the land. Grey Fox considers "conversations about slavery [to be] conversations concerning the territory he must guard, keep, watch, the land where his home had always been" (*CRC* 50). Like *Abraham's Well*, *Cold Running Creek* presents chattel slavery as a means through which the Native characters seek to claim whiteness and hold onto their land. It is presented primarily as a means to persistence rather than subsistence.

Cold Running Creek repeatedly mentions the Choctaw slave codes that Grey Fox's father, Jacques, helped make an integral part of the body of law of the newly created Choctaw Nation and thus points to the interdependence of Choctaw assertions of sovereignty and the reduction of African Americans and African-Choctaws to bare life (*CRC* 40, 69, 77, 99). Agamben considers the state of exception to be at the center of the state's exertion of sovereignty. He further argues that "the production of bare life is the originary activity of sovereignty" (53; see also 19). Based on Agamben, Rifkin has argued that "the overriding sovereignty of the United States is predicated on the creation of a state of exception ("Indigenizing Agamben" 90)." Reading Lockhart's novel in light of Agamben and Rifkin suggests that the Choctaw Nation's claims for sovereignty and rights to the land are, in a similar vein, predicated on their own creation of a state of exception. To secure their status in the South, the Choctaws avoid associating with African Americans at all cost and strategically use the law to place them outside forms of Choctaw belonging.[24] Jacques's implementation of racialized forms of Choctaw nationhood at the expense of racially inclusive tribal kinship practices appears to him the most efficient way to secure Choctaw sovereignty and to assert territorial rights against settler colonial encroachment. At the same time, this mode of governance serves to increase his own wealth and to enhance his political influence, landholdings, and social status.[25]

Both novels thus present complex arguments in favor of the inextricable connection between the settler colonial geopolitics of Removal and the Native biopolitics of Black enslavement. Rather than aiming to produce large profit margins through slave labor, Mama Emma, Papa, Grey Fox, and Raven are presented as conceptualizing chattel slavery as a way to keep the land. While Foster focuses on how the slaveholding practices of an average, middle-class mixed-blood couple change in the context of Removal, Lockhart also makes a macropolitical argument, through which she critiques Indigenous processes of nation building in the context of settler colonial dispossession. Through her repeated reference to the Choctaw slave codes, she points the reader's attention to the fact that Raven's and Grey Fox's personal choices are part of greater social developments—the increasing significance of race and blood for notions of tribal belonging and the adoption of racialized forms of governance. The novel presents such developments as the result of both settler colonial incursions into Native lands and lives and the machinations of a slaveholding elite that constructs race- and class-specific narratives of Native peoplehood that lay the basis for implementing "a capitalist political-economy and delegitimizing tradition," that is, Native forms of being, living, and relating to each other (Rifkin, *Manifesting America* 68).

PERFORMING WHITENESS: THE SOCIAL CONSTRUCTEDNESS OF RACE

As Ariela Gross has demonstrated, in nineteenth-century America, race was not solely regarded as "a property of blood" but was based on a combination of "appearance, ancestry, performance, reputation, association, science, national citizenship, and cultural practice." Of these, physical appearance and the performance of race stood out in the determination of racial status. Displaying the physical attributes ascribed to whiteness and doing the things the way white people did them, she expounds, "became the law's working definition of what it meant to be white" (8, 9). Gross's insights contribute to a better understanding of the negotiation of race in *Abraham's Well* and *Cold Running Creek*. In both novels, race is presented as a socially powerful yet fabricated and arbitrary social category that fails to grasp the complexity of the Native characters' personal lives, histories, and experiences and that leads to their alienation from themselves and others. Due to the power of race, they struggle to claim whiteness by adapting their physical appearance to white norms and by performing whiteness in their daily lives.

In *Abraham's Well*, race is portrayed as a settler colonial invention geared toward legitimizing stealing from others, particularly land. Foster has Red Bird, a Cherokee preacher, impart this message to Armentia and her clan during the Trail of Tears, when they struggle to understand why they have lost their land: "He [God] does not give [them the land of our fathers]; men steal. Men have stolen long before we were born. Those that steal make up excuses to steal; color, language, dress are just excuses" (*AW* 106). Not only is race presented in the novel as a means to allocate resources and privileges to the colonizers, but it is also revealed to be a highly unstable category of identification. When, once in the West, Armentia is sold by Mama Emma and Papa to work on Master Will Cauley's plantation, the other slaves try to make sense of her racial identity by evaluating her physical appearance and behavioral patterns. Their discussions resemble consultations among jurors in racial identity trials in the United States, which sought to determine individuals' ambiguous racial identities by relying on the evidence at hand (Gross 3, 4, 24, 25):

> "She is an Indian," one would say.
> "No she not. She black like us."
> "She black as some of us, but she shore ain't black as your people," another would mock laughing. . . .
> "Pretty hair," they would say touching me. . . .
> "She got hair like [Miss Lula and Miss Bertha Bell's] children, though she ain't so light skinned as them." . . .
> "You 'most black as me," someone might say to me. "Ain't much difference but your hair. How you know that Indian talk again?"
> "I told you that I'm Cherokee."
> Usually, the person laughed. "You just a nigger, like me."
> (*AW* 131–32)

Her fellow slaves are at a loss to categorize Armentia. Her legal status as a slave is in conflict with her Native tongue, her straight hair, her somewhat lighter skin, and her self-identification as Cherokee. External markers such as skin color, kinky hair, and a certain accent, Gross argues, were in the theory of racial categorization treated as objective markers and scientific evidence of racial identity, "thus reinforcing the notion that race was immediately apparent" (41). The discussions among the slaves in *Abraham's Well* are expressive of the novel's skepticism about the supposedly scientific and objective nature of race and its indictment of race and blood as determinants of belonging.[26] They remind readers of the groundlessness and arbitrariness of all attempts at racial classification, such as those of US federal agents in the context of allotment. Their far-reaching decisions of whether the Indigenous applicant before them was full-blood, half-blood, white, or Black grew out of an unpredictable mixture of criteria, such as phenotypical judgments, behavioral patterns, cultural and linguistic clues, and a substantial portion of personal prejudice. As in Armentia's case, Indigenous self-identification and assertions of tribal belonging were most often ignored in these cross-examinations. Federal definitions of "Cherokeeness," the novel implies, were hence far from accurate, informed by ignorance and racial prejudice, and not to be trusted (see Adams 106–7).

Abraham's Well also reflects on the impact of racial regimes on social organization and relations. Child socialization is presented by Foster as the major tool through which white supremacists ensure that the generations to come view racial difference as an integral part of the God-given social order and hence as immutable. Foster constructs Master Cauley's daughter, Miss Lillian, in opposition to the idea of childhood innocence, which began to dominate American thinking about childhood in the mid-nineteenth century. According to this view, children were, as Robin Bernstein explains, "sinless, absent of sexual feelings, and oblivious to worldly concerns." They were "holy angels leading adults to heaven." Innocent children, she claims, were "raced white": by endowing them with all the phenotypical markers of whiteness, their innocence became inextricably tied to their whiteness. Presented as a white child-angel, Harriet Beecher Stowe's Little Eva is a major example of this notion of childhood. Little Eva performs innocence by transcending and intentionally ignoring social categories such as class, gender, and race—Eva loves everyone; she thus actively rejects knowledge systems from the adult world (Bernstein 4, 6–7). Just like Little Eva, Miss Lillian radiates whiteness. Her name reminds the reader of a blossoming white lily. And her long blond hair and blue eyes prompt Armentia to conclude that "there was no sign that she and I shared any common blood" (*AW* 140; see also 141).[27] Unlike Little Eva, however, Miss Lillian does not perform innocence. Even though she is in a "baby-doll-playing-age," she readily embraces social categories from the adult world, such as race, and allows them to shape her relationship to Armentia. She rehearses common beliefs in white supremacy and rights to the land with a naturalness that makes the reader shudder: "'You know niggers aren't supposed to own land. God doesn't want that. You shouldn't worry your head about that. . . . God made it so White people would own the land. But don't you worry, we are here to take care of you.'" Miss Lillian is also familiar with Anglo-American property law: she knows that she can take the blanket Armentia made from her, as slaves cannot own property and as anything slaves produce belongs to their masters. Armentia points out that "the [racist] words sounded unnatural in [Miss Lillian's] mouth. They sounded rehearsed, like words someone practiced with her" (*AW* 142–43, 147). Armentia thus alludes to the workings of race: racial thinking is instilled into white children by adults; adults familiarize children with their designated roles as masters at an early age, so they learn to accept and perform their racial superiority. Whenever Miss Lillian deviates from the racial script written for her by the adults surrounding her, she is reprimanded. Even though she is permitted to be friends with Armentia, their relationship must conform to the racial hierarchies implemented by the adults: she is the superior to whom Armentia must subordinate herself (*AW* 141, 147). Miss Lillian is Foster's counter-draft to the innocence ascribed to white children in the American popular imagination. By presenting a child in her novel as a major carrier of racial ideology and as a competent performer of whiteness, she seeks to explain how a socially fabricated category such as race could exert such a powerful force in nineteenth-century America, determining everyone's social, political, and legal status, including their right to property.[28]

Cold Running Creek focuses in particular on the performance of whiteness by its nonwhite protagonists, who imitate white manhood and womanhood, even if such conceptions of race and gender stand in stark contrast to their multiracial or Native heritage and Native forms of living. To compensate for his part-Native ancestry, Grey Fox dresses white, comports himself like a slave master, cherishes his property, and socializes with white landowners. By citing his "birthright" to the land in front of General Thorpe, he asserts his legal and political rights as a citizen of Mississippi and his white manhood. Grey Fox's entire behavior is geared toward downplaying, if not suppressing, his Native heritage, symbolized throughout the novel by his constant attempts to hide his long hair underneath his hat (*CRC* 16, 19, 21, 27, 70).

Herself a full-blood Choctaw, Raven feels like a stranger in her own body and home. Her way of dressing and behaving like a white southern lady estranges her from her Choctaw culture and traditions. While she manages to hide her Native heritage during the day, it comes out at night, when no one can see it. She remembers and performs the Choctaw planting dance in the "moonless darkness" dressed in a black cloak that "would keep her safe as the mistress of LeFlore plantation." The ideology of race places her in the position of plantation mistress and constricts her interactions with her slaves. The organization of her household along racial lines is in stark contrast with "the fellowship from the days of her childhood." "The white pillars of the veranda," the narrator tells the reader, "hid her from the dark ones": the white pillars signify the white normative order that divides society along racial lines. Raven longs for both Choctaw cultural practices and racially inclusive kinship networks. She constantly feels drawn to the slave quarters. Notwithstanding such longings, Raven continues to play her part as the racially superior southern mistress and avoids associating with her slaves in order not to risk her family's status in white southern society (*CRC* 21, 23; see also 17, 20, 41). She also meets and socializes with white southern mistresses, even though their conversations do not make sense to her. But her role-play proves to be futile: due to her nonwhite appearance, she is not accepted by the white wives of the other plantation owners, who dismissively label her as "the Indian woman." Raven gradually disappears into "a bell jar of estrangement." She and Grey Fox feel like strangers in their own bodies and home, as they constantly play roles that are out of step with their values and (multi)ethnic upbringing. They are attracted to each other because they "[comfort] each other with belonging"—a belonging that does not extend beyond their bedrooms doors to the outside world (*CRC* 28, 17).

However, by no means does Lockhart present Raven and Grey Fox as innocent victims. Grey Fox abuses his position as a master to sexually exploit his female slaves, including Josephine. He thus not only behaves immorally but also violates the Choctaw slave codes that prohibit such "commingling" with slaves. Raven uses the ideology of race to satisfy her wish for a child. Josephine's (and Grey Fox's) child, Lilly, counts as the LeFlores' property. Thus, when Raven pulls the baby from her mother's arms against her will and raises her as her own child, she acts in line with slave laws, simply making use her own chattel as she wishes. To conceal the baby's origin in the slave quarters and to repress Raven's inhuman act of separating mother and child, she and her husband devise "the lie of the found child" of Choctaw descent, which they try hard to believe themselves. Grey Fox even adopts Lilly, though he knows this is against the Choctaw slave codes. To both of them, Lilly embodies the prospect of finally belonging in ways not grounded in blood lineage: Raven believes herself and Lilly to be united by their ancestors and imagines her to be part of her clan and a future bearer of Choctaw culture. Grey Fox sees in Lilly his Choctaw mother but also vows to teach her his father's and grandfather's values. She will be the heir of the LeFlore empire of property. That Lilly used to be their own property, was ripped from the arms of a Black slave, and is the fruit of Grey Fox's sexually exploitative union the couple attempts to relegate to the realm of forgetting (*CRC* 58–59, 99).

Despite her own qualms with the white racial order, Raven socializes Lilly—whose name also signifies whiteness—according to its norms. Albeit hesitantly, she teaches her that there is a natural distance between herself—as Grey Fox's adopted child—and the slaves (*CRC* 60, 74). When Lilly wants to play with the slave children, Raven refuses, not because she is against it herself but because of her husband's wish to conform to the southern racial order. Grey Fox regularly admonishes Raven not to "dress her like a slave girl and let her run wild with Negro boys" in order not to endanger his standing among the other landowners. That Raven does not believe in racial difference herself also becomes apparent when she reproves Lilly for politically siding with the "Yankees" in the approaching Civil War and not with what the girl calls "the niggers": "'You listen to me, Lilly,'" Raven says. "'You are no better than the slaves. . . . Those are not my teachings, but your father's. I have told you the stories of your ancestry'" (*CRC* 82, 79).

Raven performs whiteness, yet unwillingly so. Alienated from herself and ridden by guilt that she has abused her social position to take Lilly away from Josephine, Raven enters the swamp in the vicinity of the plantation. In *Cold Running Creek,* the swamp is presented as an anticolonial space marked by the absence of the white normative order. It symbolizes an alternative social order in which colors, including skin color, neither matter nor define social status and patterns of ownership. Before Raven enters the swamp, she can still distinguish between the colors green, gray, brown, and black, but once she is inside, all these colors become one. The woman living in the swamp is "mulatto brown" and "redheaded" and thus utterly defies racial categorization (*CRC* 87). Property relations unravel in the swamp. Slave hounds cannot follow the scent of the escaped slaves anymore. White men who have entered the swamp rarely make it out again, as they are incapable of figuring out the swamp's unwritten laws. The swamp forces them "to declare their restless property [their slaves] useless" and to give in to the "challenge" of the swamp (*CRC* 269). Lockhart also constructs the swamp as a decidedly female space. It is dominated by the swamp woman, harboring people for the duration of a moon—a menstrual—cycle. It is a space free from male violence, in which male desire for property and domination falters (*CRC* 41). In the swamp, the male colonizer is not at the center of creation, taming and dominating it, but he shares space with an untamed and untamable flora and fauna. Nonwhite characters who grapple with the ideology of race and the white colonial order all end up in the swamp at some point in the narrative, seeking advice from the swamp woman concerning their multiracial identities and their perceived lack of belonging. The swamp and the swamp woman make all these characters realize the incommensurability of race, notions of white masculinity, and the complex web of identities present in the antebellum South.[29]

Lockhart uses Lilly, in particular, to present a scathing critique of the ideology of race and to throw into relief its persistent ill fit with social reality and the emotional toll it takes on those caught in its apparent logic. Lilly readily embraces white social and racial hierarchies and culture at a young age. She does not show any interest in her mother's Choctaw stories. She starts behaving "like the young heir of the LeFlore plantation" and assuming an air of superiority over the slaves. It is her racial socialization within her family—her self-perception as primarily white instead of Choctaw—that is responsible for her failure to fully know herself and her eventual inability to establish meaningful relations with all those who, according to the ideology of race, are below her in the assumed hierarchy of races (*CRC* 94; see also 59, 65).

Lockhart's shift to first-person narration in the part of the novel dealing with Lilly's life allows the reader to gain insights into the workings of her mind: Lilly defines race primarily along the lines of physical appearance. Her own, lighter, skin color prevents her from making sense of her actual life as a slave on the Bartlette plantation, and she tells the other slaves that she does not belong to them (*CRC* 123, 128, 182). Seeing herself as racially superior, she calls the other slaves "niggers" and works toward establishing a life that she thinks befits her status (*CRC* 136–37). Owning property becomes central in her vision of life, as the ownership of goods and people signifies racial privilege and underlines what she considers her racially superior status. As a free Black man, Willie Kellem has, from Lilly's perspective, the potential to realize her desire for possessions (*CRC* 128, 168, 174). In her dreams, she envisions herself as a property-owning plantation mistress, standing on the porch of her own house, watching her own slaves tending her own crops. She imagines Willie as an African American version of her father, performing whiteness by dressing in "crisp, clean white shirts" (*CRC* 141; see also 160, 162). Such a setting, Lilly believes, would enable her to become as white as a lily; it would restore her social status in white society. It would allow her to be what she imagines herself to be: a part-white southern mistress who claims her whiteness through property and who forms meaningful social relations. Lilly views her current status as the antithesis of such dreams: "I wasn't Lilly LeFlore . . . I was Lilly with no belonging" (*CRC* 163). "No belonging" here suggests both the absence of members of her own family (Lilly does not belong) and the absence of property (Lilly has no belongings).

Lilly is so fixated on her Native–white heritage that she ignores the numerous hints dropped by others that she is the slave Josephine's child and hence Black (e.g., *CRC* 261–62, 271). Refusing to know herself, she leads a miserable existence. Only once in all those long years does she feel "complete," as she herself puts it. This is when she performs southern white womanhood in town and passes as white among the townspeople (*CRC* 276–79). The fact of her passing as white due to her dressing, or rather disguising herself, according to the southern feminine ideal once again reveals the constructedness and arbitrariness of race. *Cold Running Creek* presents race as both a fiction and a fact. As white fabrication imbued with a political purpose (the dispossession of Native Americans and the exploitation of the Black body), race has an enormous impact on the lived experience of the novel's characters. By describing Raven and Lilly as "two generations of Okla Hannali women, not white, not black," *Cold Running Creek* reminds its readers of the failure of "race" to grasp the complex realities of Native lives and the multiracial nature of Native societies, and the emotional havoc it wreaks on social relations (*CRC* 101).

THE EXCLUSIVE PRESENT: FROM KINSHIP TO NATION

Studying the development of Cherokee collective identity from the eighteenth century onward, Circe Sturm has argued that in the early 1800s the Cherokees moved away from a "sense of political community . . . based on ties of culture, kinship, language, and religious worldview" to a racialized conception of nationhood (*Blood Politics* 50; see also 51). Foster and Lockhart use their works of fiction not only to represent this transformation of Native communities from multiracial kin-based communities into nations in the Western sense, structured along the lines of class and race, but also to flesh out what this transformation means for social relations on the most intimate levels of Indigenous interaction. Unlike the Native American Removal writers before them, Foster and Lockhart largely depict Native nation building in response to Removal as a project racialized to its core affecting not merely forms of governance and conceptions of ownership in the Native public sphere but also patterns of social interaction within the Native domestic sphere: the household and the family. This leads to a redefinition of who is in, but not of, the household. People with one drop of African blood—formerly kin and an integral part of Native domesticity—are rejected and degraded to chattel and, finally, erased from tribal memory altogether.

Similar to Diane Glancy in *Pushing the Bear*, Foster constructs the Trail of Tears as the moment when traditional forms of Cherokee peoplehood eventually break down. In contrast to Glancy, who focuses on class and gender, Foster pays close attention the trail's exacerbation of racial differences within the community and the household and thus introduces a new dimension into Native Removal writing. Along the Trail of Tears, racial differences are reinforced among the Cherokees by the soldiers, who divide those walking the trail into three distinct groups: "stinking injuns," "niggers," and "nigger injuns" (*AW* 96). Racial fragmentation of the Cherokee community is also exacerbated by the efforts of the Black Cherokees residing along the route to create a distance between themselves and the slaves on the trail in an attempt to save themselves and their property. Non-Black Cherokees also begin to dissociate or, in Mama Emma's case, further dissociate themselves from what they formerly considered to be their Black family members (*AW* 101). Foster thus portrays the trail as a watershed moment in the relationship between the Cherokees and their Black kin. Armentia says, "The truth is, the Trail didn't just separate us from the land we loved; it split us apart from one another. Though we were all together in that place, the Trail Where We Cried was like a line, some kind of fence between us that separated our people" (*AW* 116–17).[30]

Once in Indian Territory, social fragmentation continues, manifesting itself in the further transformation of Cherokee practices of social interaction and ownership. Like many other non-Black Cherokees, Mama Emma and Papa only "[socialize] with mixed-bloods and pure bloods" and keep "their distance from us, the dark part of their family," Armentia says. She also tells the reader that in Indian Territory, "less and less of the land was owned in common, less and less was shared." Mama Emma and Papa begin to practice plantation slavery, having what they now call the "field hands" pick cotton (*AW* 118–19). The adoption of plantation slavery, as historian David Chang has illustrated with respect to the Creek, "transformed unimproved lands into ownable fields for their owners." Slave labor hence became an important device to "*make* property." "The right to the land," he explains, "was created and retained by labor" (29, 31; italics in original). In the West, Mama Emma and Papa visualize the property they make through the practice of plantation slavery by putting up fences. The novel's emphasis on the omnipresence of fences in Cherokee society after Removal is to highlight the new significance of privately owned land-use rights in Cherokee life. In its depiction of the time before Removal, fences were altogether absent in the Cherokee community and chattel slavery was adopted only to avert Removal. In the West, by contrast, chattel slavery takes on the form of plantation slavery and is pursued for purely capitalist reasons. Mama Emma and Papa seek to accumulate private property to make a profit and to heighten their social status. While back in the East, Abraham was sold with the intention to secure the land, Armentia is sold so that Mama Emma and Papa have the money to buy bricks for their newly built house (*AW* 118, 128).

The fence is thus a central motif in *Abraham's Well*, highlighting the nexus between concepts of property, proprietary practices, group identity, and social organization in the context of Removal. Just as Armentia's mention of the absence of fences in the Cherokee community prior to Removal signifies inclusive use patterns, social inclusivity, and social organization based in kinship, the presence of fences in Indian Territory suggests a decline of such inclusivity and practices of sharing among the Cherokees in favor of private property. The figurative use of "fence" as a barrier "separat[ing] our people" establishes a direct link between changing concepts of property and notions of collective selfhood. The novel relates how in the West, the slaveholding Cherokee elite seek to amass private property. The way they think about property has a decisive impact on their conceptualization of collective identity and terms of belonging. They implement a body of written laws that regulate the lives of the slaves and marginalize them within the Cherokee Nation. Tribal membership becomes dependent on individual property rights. As objects, rather than owners, of property, slaves become excluded from tribal membership (*AW* 167, 184).[31] When Papa tells Armentia's father, "'You work like you are one of The People," he reveals his conviction that slaves no longer belong to the Cherokee community (*AW* 124). "Instead of choosing each other," Armentia relates, "people chose sides, and we—those of us who were slaves—just seemed to be caught in the middle. It was vicious business. Like I said, it was blood business" (*AW* 122–23). The expression "blood business" can be interpreted as bloody business and hence as a reference to the violent conflicts between the signers of the Treaty of New Echota and its opponents. At the same time, through the term "blood business," Foster introduces the idiom of blood into her narrative. Blood has always played an important role in Cherokee culture, as clan membership has traditionally been defined through the mother's blood (Sturm, *Blood Politics* 29). *Abraham's Well*, however, suggests that in Indian Territory a different meaning of blood begins to dominate Cherokee politics. Rather than signifying matrilineal genealogical connection, blood increasingly signifies race; race, in turn, defines the terms of national inclusion and exclusion. Having one drop of African blood and being incapable of ownership, slaves are excluded from the Cherokee Nation, irrespective of their kinship ties.

Foster focuses in her novel on the emotional havoc that such exclusion wreaks on the most intimate levels of social interaction. All of a sudden, Armentia feels threatened by "those who had once been my people." She is "no longer someone Mama Emma [holds] precious" and can "no longer count on her old promises to [her]" (*AW* 168). Possessory desires in tandem with ideas of race have turned affection into separation within her own family: "I looked at my mother, at the sadness she wore each day. But Mama Emma and Papa were sad too. They wore fancy clothes, but it could not cover their trouble. We all had lost each other for land, for bricks, for things that really did not matter" (*AW* 196; see also 194). To alleviate such pain of loss, former kinship traditions begin to be suppressed, to be relegated to the realm of the forgotten. In response to Armentia's attempt to remind Mama Emma that she once was her kin, the latter calls her foolish and repeatedly exclaims, "I remember no such thing!" (*AW* 222). Such amnesia about former kinship ties develops into amnesia about the entire history of slavery after the Civil War. When Armentia returns to

Indian Territory from Texas to claim the land promised to her by the soldiers, Mama Emma and other Cherokees pretend not to know her. Mama Emma even denies having owned slaves at all (*AW* 294–95). In the wake of Removal, the Cherokee elite, *Abraham's Well* suggests, first exclude their slaves from the body of the nation based on their incapacity to own. After the Civil War, when the freedmen are finally able to own land, the Cherokee elite reject their existence altogether. As portrayed in the novel, following Removal, race, land ownership, and nationhood begin to exist in dynamic relationship with each other. Just as Native nationhood becomes defined along the parameters of race and land ownership, Native households are stratified along racial lines. A drop of Black blood turns household members into chattel—disposable and alienable—and thus excludes them from the human category of kin.

Like *Abraham's Well*, *Cold Running Creek* depicts the post-Removal years as witnessing a definition of tribal belonging along racial lines and, accordingly, a restructuring of household relations. The politics of race and property, presented in the novel as "white politics," as Grey Fox calls it, fragments Native kinship networks and turns the LeFlore plantation into a "lifeless" home (*CRC* 46, 50). Due to their alleged racial inferiority, the slaves are considered to be in, but not of, the LeFlore family. Slave breeding, in particular, mars the relations between the Choctaw slaveholders and their slaves (e.g., *CRC* 20, 21, 37, 100–101). Becoming part of the LeFlore family also presupposes an endorsement of such white politics. When the Choctaw Henry Trench arrives at the plantation, Raven knows that Grey Fox and her brother Golden will accept him only if he sides with the southern plantation owners in the Civil War (*CRC* 33, 48, 83). Trench himself is so beset by the idea of accumulating property that he betrays both his future wife, Raven's sister Dove, whom he marries for her property, and his brother-in-law, Grey Fox, whom he eventually turns over to General Thorpe so that the latter will settle Trench's debts (*CRC* 34, 36, 37).

Notwithstanding her own complicity, Raven is deeply embarrassed by and feels guilty about her family's treatment of the slaves and their violation of traditional kinship practices (*CRC* 39, 90–91). She accuses her family members of being "red-skinned puppets who'd just as soon advance the cause of Jefferson Davis as defend a white marauder in Indian Territory. What of our kin who were pushed west against their will? . . .

CHAPTER 4

What of the Chahta who were prisoners, slaves to the Chickasaw? What of the Chahta with Negro blood?" She has thus forgotten neither the racially inclusive patterns of kinship from her childhood days nor the violence that her clan had to endure at the hands of the colonizer. The racial order Raven lives in makes her feel isolated and lonely and causes her to long for "the fellowship from the days of her childhood" (*CRC* 83–84, 23). Raven's desire for traditional Choctaw practices of living and belonging is interpreted by Grey Fox, Golden, and Lilly as a sign of mental instability, if not insanity. On the cusp of dying, she tells Lilly, "'Josephine is your ishki. Josephine is your ishki. Go home.'" Lilly, however, cannot make any meaning of this; neither is the Choctaw word for "mother" part of her repertoire of naming intimates, nor does she have any idea of what might constitute home outside the plantation. Raven's untimely death at the end of the novel's first part thus suggests the ultimate loss of traditional Choctaw forms of naming and relating to each other and their replacement by settler colonial notions of belonging grounded in blood lineage (*CRC* 105; see also 84–85, 103, 105).

Lilly's relationship to the daughters she has with Willie Kellem and her rejection by her grandfather Jacques LeFlore also exemplify that settler colonial forms of belonging infiltrate Choctaw modes of thinking and being down to the most intimate relations. Lilly's sole motivation to have children with Willie is the thought that "family could only be found with family" (*CRC* 196). It turns out, however, that within one generation, the ideology of race has had a devastating effect on Indigenous matrilineal kinship systems, even on the bond between mother and child. While Lilly's birth in the slave quarters did not prevent Raven from loving her as if she were her own child, the presence of African blood in Baby Suddie, manifesting itself as dark skin color, makes it impossible for Lilly to "let the child come into [her] heart." A racial rift runs through the family, with Lilly at the sidelines and Willie and Suddie "mak[ing] kin with each other" (*CRC* 202, 207; see also 198, 203, 223, 229). When her second daughter, Virginia, is born, Lilly's estrangement increases, as this child also looks to her like the slaves on the Bartlette plantation, her skin being "so dark brown beneath my blood." Lilly expresses her preoccupation with skin color metaphorically when floodwater almost kills her family. Searching for her children in the muddy waters, she remarks, "I . . . did not see the girls or Willie, just crests of brown that confused the lines of where the road once was" (*CRC* 212, 226). Brown skin color disables her to see her family and to recognize them as kin. Such a perception stands in stark contrast to the Choctaw "road" of kinship.[32] As Lilly herself admits, she is "engulfed by white darkness." The oxymoron suggests that her subscription to settler colonial racial hierarchies is so all-encompassing that it casts darkness over her network of potential relations: she cannot belong, which leaves her even more isolated and lonely than her mother (*CRC* 236).

Lilly's rejection by her white grandfather, Jacques, on the basis of her African descent constitutes the novel's climax. As soon as Grey Fox informs him through a letter of Lilly's part-African heritage, Jacques disowns his granddaughter and devises an elaborate plan to keep her apart from her Choctaw family. As Jacques does not want people to think that "she's of some kin to [him]," Willie is paid to prevent her from coming into town (*CRC* 281). As Jacques's involvement in the writing of Choctaw slave codes reveals, he has been instrumental in establishing a Choctaw Nation defined not by Indigenous notions of kinship but by racial exclusion. While he favors the inclusion of intermarried whites like himself and white Choctaws like his son, he outright opposes the citizenship of African Americans or Choctaws with African heritage. Lockhart constructs Lilly's rejection of her children and Jacques's rejection of Lilly as emblematic of the Choctaw Nation's rejection of its multiracial history and its inclusive kinship systems in favor of a racialized politics of belonging.

It is Jacques's rejection that eventually prompts Lilly to question her own way of categorizing people. It helps her understand that her stubborn belief in racial categories and hierarchies eclipses other, more inclusive modes of belonging and estranges her from her most intimate relations. These insights eventually cause Lilly to defy white society's racial order and to acknowledge her existence as an Afro-Native woman closely related to both her Native and her African American relatives.

THE INCLUSIVE FUTURE: THE SPECKLED PUP, OR AFRO-NATIVE VISIONS OF PEOPLEHOOD

Foster and Lockhart end their respective novels by offering an alternative to the racialized discourse of nationhood. They develop Afro-Native visions of peoplehood and Indigenous futurity characterized by racial inclusivity and a sense of community grounded in language, cultural practices and beliefs, expanded kinship ties, and a shared history.

In *Abraham's Well*, Armentia functions as Foster's mouthpiece when, on the very first pages of the novel, she expresses her conviction that she, as an Afro-Cherokee woman, belongs to the Cherokee people. Her telling of her own life story—in particular, her account of her shared suffering with her people along the Trail of Tears—is a major legitimation of her initial claim that she is Cherokee, "one of the Principal People" (*AW* 14). Others, she asserts toward the end of her story, "hid away in the mountains" or "watched us as we marched the Trail—their native blood disappearing into White or Black" (*AW* 305).[33] By contrast, Armentia has, throughout her life, *practiced* Cherokee peoplehood. So has her son, Abraham Proof, who could have easily lived the life of a white man due to his looks but who chooses to hold onto his heritage and to pass it on to his children (*AW* 240). In Armentia and Abraham Proof's idea of Cherokee peoplehood, race and property do not play a role. It is rather shared suffering, ongoing cultural practices, and a continued adherence to Cherokee beliefs, passed down from generation to generation, that determine one's belonging. Such ideas are strongly reflective of an ethic that Jace Weaver has termed "communitism," which implies "a search for community . . . the valorization of Native community and values and a commitment to them that may be, in part, politically unconscious" (45).

The image that most powerfully embodies *Abraham's Well*'s vision of Cherokee peoplehood is that of the speckled pup. In 1889 the federal government opened up almost 2 million acres of unassigned land in Indian Territory to settlers, inaugurating the so-called Oklahoma land rush. It is this governmentally instituted land rush that finally enables Armentia and her descendants to claim land and to create a home for themselves. At the time of the land rush, Armentia, by then an old woman living in a shack on the land of the Erwin family, is visited by "a whole group of people . . . all colors, kind of like a speckled pup" (*AW* 307). These people are the children and grandchildren of her son Abraham Proof, who died in the Civil War. He had these children with different women in different places, yet he taught them everything he knew about Cherokee culture and their ancestors and instructed them to find each other and his mother, Armentia. While Armentia is still rejected by the Cherokees and refused access to tribal lands, she now has her own, racially inclusive

Afro-Native-white family, in which money, property, and social status do not play a role (*AW* 308–10). For her, this family fuses past and present. Armentia's great-grandson, named Abraham Proof after her son, looks like Abraham Proof but has the skin color of Johnnie Freeman. He also runs as fast her brother Abraham. Other members of the speckled pup also bear the names of Armentia's clan members (*AW* 309, 312). By passing on knowledge of Cherokee culture and kinship systems, Abraham Proof has secured cultural survival and perseverance in a diasporic community cut off from the Cherokee Nation through the language of law and citizenship. Besides being committed to precolonial modes of relation, the reunited family also acts Cherokee: they own and farm the land collectively and share the resources it offers. The well that they establish on the land they claim and that provides them with water, called "Abraham's well" after Armentia's brother, reconnects Armentia to her life in the East and embodies pre-Removal Cherokee forms of living and being (*AW* 310).

Kathy-Ann Tan criticizes what she considers the novel's "triumphalist ending," along with its "mimetic mode of narration," for "reenact[ing] the dispossession of the Cherokee and the acquisition of their land—to the gain of the black Cherokee freedmen, who have now indirectly 'chosen' being black over being Indigenous" (239, 240, 249). Hence, she argues, the novel "ultimately fails to constitute a harsh critique of slavery and its legacy in the ongoing plight of the descendants of the Cherokee freedmen" (240).[34] Tan's reading, however, does not do justice to *Abraham's Well*'s complex identity politics. At no point in the novel does Armentia choose being Black over being Indigenous. Moreover, her participation in the Oklahoma land rush is represented as her only option to get access to land, after having been rejected by the Cherokee Nation for decades. After all, the novel argues, the land given away in the land rush was part of the lands that had been allotted—"land that was supposed to be ours free," as the novel emphasizes (*AW* 310). The ending thus needs to be read as an account of how the freedmen, due to their rejection, are forced to become complicit in the further dispossession and disenfranchisement of the Native Americans by resorting to the very legal frameworks that have facilitated their own exclusion from the Cherokee Nation. By writing about Indian Removal from the perspective of the twice marginalized, Foster inevitably criticizes both the US politics of Native dispossession and the Cherokee politics of exclusion and its adoption of racialized forms of belonging that fragment interracial tribal relationships and place reconciliation and renewal out of reach. By focusing on the intersection of Native dispossession and Black enslavement, Foster produces an alternative Removal history, one in which slavery plays a central role. In this alternative Removal history, forced relocation and slavery are not framed as separate and finished events that can be safely contained in the past or even forgotten. Rather the novel highlights their mutual imbrication and their implications for Native forms of peoplehood in the past, present, as well as the future.

Armentia's speckled pup, living on land they communally own, represents a microcosm filled with possibility. It embodies an alternative road to the future for the entire Cherokee Nation. This vision clearly transcends the idea of a racialized and territorially fixed nation. Armentia and her multiracial family live outside the Cherokee Nation. Even though this land is not their ancestral homeland, they endow it with ancestral meaning and history by establishing Abraham's well. Their "Cherokeeness" derives from their commitment to and practice of Cherokee culture, their knowledge of traditions and beliefs, and their self-identification as belonging to the Principal People. That this vision transcends the fictional world of the novel becomes apparent in Foster's afterword. There, the author reveals herself to be part of a "speckled pup"—via her paternal grandmother, Emma Erwin, who was Cherokee and whose parents had walked the Trail of Tears (*AW* 327; see also 326). While Foster admits that she does not know yet what it means to be part of such a speckled pup, she endows Armentia with such self-knowledge. Armentia knows that she is, and will remain, a Black-Cherokee, "a hidden part of [her] people." "They may no longer know me," she confides, "I may be in exile, but I know who I am. And I believe that someday they will call me home" (*AW* 316). Foster ends her afterword on a similarly hopeful note: "I have found them. But I still have not been welcomed home. But there is hope." She ends with a reference to the 2006 ruling of the Cherokee Nation Judicial Appeals Tribunal (*AW* 329). The deracialization of Cherokee identity—the transformation from racial exclusivity to inclusivity—is a powerful ray of hope at the end of a highly emotional life story of violence, suffering, loss, and familial reconnection. It is also the vision of an Afro-Native author seeking to come to terms with her own family history.

Cold Running Creek develops a similarly powerful vision of Choctaw peoplehood. At the very moment she is rejected by her grandfather, the scales fall from Lilly's eyes. She becomes aware of the fact that Willie and she married each other to satisfy their respective proprietary desires: she chose him to accumulate goods that she thought she needed to claim whiteness. He took her in to live a secure and comparably wealthy life financed by Jacques LeFlore. Realizing that she does not know herself, Lilly enters the swamp once again. In the swamp woman's cabin, she finds her father's letter containing the truth about her slave mother. She now admits to herself that deep inside she has long known that Raven is not her biological mother. This moment of self-awareness radically alters Lilly's conception of belonging: when she races back to her house to save her daughters from the white mob she sees approaching in her vision, she runs across land that she acknowledges was "trodden by all my escaping ancestors, the golden ones of the sun, the dark ones of the night." For the first time, Lilly sees herself as part of a multiracial kinship network. She openly acknowledges that those with black skin are her ancestors, and hence kin too, and that the history of slavery is her history as well (*CRC* 287; see also 280–82, 284, 285).

The novel ends with the compelling image of Lilly fleeing with her husband and their children to the swamp, the only place in the novel not ordered along racial lines:[35] "When we reached the swamp . . . the sun . . . hummed a deep guttural song about land, wars, reservations, plantations, hummed to summon all the blades of grass, the rivers and streams, the rattling bones in the river bed, summon them . . . to guide Ishki, Inki and Allas home" (*CRC* 289). Lilly, Willie, and the girls are finally a family; Lilly eventually claims her children as kin: she is able to see herself as Ishki, the Choctaw word meaning "mother," and her children as Allas, the Choctaw word meaning "children." She even conceptualizes Willie as Inki, a Choctaw father. By reintroducing the Choctaw terminology for naming intimates that Lilly's mother, Raven, used within her clan prior to Removal, the novel returns to an alternative discourse of belonging, one not grounded in race but in matrilineal kinship relations. Lilly's new self-knowledge and the swamp offer her and her family the chance to reconcile and to live a life away from the racial categorizations and codes of white society. They become agents of their own fate and determine their own lives irrespective of white racial regimes and proprietary practices.

Though geopolitically a part of Mississippi, the swamp is characterized by the absence of colonial epistemologies; it is a space of racial inclusivity, untouched by proprietary desires, and thus it signifies the possibility of home. By having Lilly call the swamp home, Lockhart constructs it as a mental space for Lilly and her multiracial family rather than as a physical home. In this space, Choctaw epistemologies and cultural practices can be reconsidered and familial reconciliation achieved unrestricted by a white normative order that seeks to suppress them. It is a space in which racially inclusive and more flexible forms of Indigenous belonging—forms that operate outside the settler colonial politics of blood—can be revived.

Cherokee scholar Daniel Heath Justice has criticized the "rank ideologies of fragmentation" and the "fragmenting Eurowestern priorities" that lead to "angst and alienation" within Native communities. Kinship, he stresses, is "the foundation of any continuity." "Such kinship isn't a static thing; it's dynamic, ever in motion. It requires attentiveness; kinship is best thought to be a verb rather than a noun, because kinship, in most indigenous contexts, is something that's *done* more than something that simply *is*" ("'Go Away, Water!'" 150; italics in original). By emphasizing the complex and diverse kinship networks that have traditionally made up Choctaw and Cherokee communities and the devastating impact of Removal on Indigenous relations and social formations, *Abraham's Well* and *Cold Running Creek* also promote the idea of Native peoplehood as grounded in kinship, as an ongoing cultural practice rather than a static thing, and as "an active relationship that must be maintained" over time, to use Eva Garroutte's words (185). By reinscribing African Americans and African Natives into tribal histories of Removal, they remind readers of the traditionally inclusive and highly flexible matrilineal kinship networks of Cherokee and Choctaw tribal communities and the long history of African–Native relations and shared suffering, which, as Tiya Miles deplores, has been "a footnote in general narratives of America history, as well as in much of the literature on Native nations as well as on African Americans produced by scholars of American Indian history, African American history, and Ethnohistory" ("All in the Family" 3).[36] Both novels contrast such traditional forms of belonging and relating to each other with the Cherokee Nation's adoption of chattel slavery and, in its wake, the Anglo-American ideology of race. Such "an internal, historical examination" exploring the interstices between Removal and the contemporary freedmen debate, Hannibal B. Johnson has argued, "must be undertaken if we are to understand the foundations of what some see as an identity crisis in Indian Country" (166). The novels provide the historical grounding necessary to put the current legal-political crisis into historical perspective and to call into question a politics privileging biology/ontology over culture, history, and communitism. Foster and Lockhart end their novels with visions of peoplehood not determined by what Jean Dennison has called the federal government's "logic of recognition," which has historically prompted the Cherokee and Choctaw nations to adopt tribal membership criteria satisfying settler colonial subjectivities.[37] They imagine utopian spaces and microcosms beyond the purview of the settler state and hence in opposition to racialized definitions of belonging and exclusion.

Armentia informs her imagined reader that her story will convey the entire truth of her life as a slave, the good and the bad things, as "only the truth will make us free" (*AW* 102). The truth that Armentia seeks to convey to the reader is the interrelatedness of the histories of slavery and settler colonialism, of Black enslavement and Indigenous dispossession. Emphasizing the exceptionalism of both Black racialization and Indigenous dispossession, as Justin Leroy has emphatically argued, has prevented scholars in Indigenous and African American studies from seeing that "the projects of slavery and colonialism have . . . thrived on the slippages and ambiguities of their relationship to one another." Scholars, he has claimed, have so far failed to sufficiently theorize "how to integrate non-indigenous, non-settlers—primarily the enslaved—into a theory of colonialism without subordinating the dispossession they experience to that of indigenous people" (3, 4, 8). *Abraham's Well* and *Cold Running Creek* encourage their readers to (re)turn to the history of Indian Removal to gain knowledge about the intersections and complex dynamics between tribal enslavement and colonialism and the messy terrain of relations between property, race, and Native collective identity. Such knowledge is the prerequisite for resisting colonial ontologies and for imagining decolonial futures. "I'm singing my truth song 'cause someone's going to need to hear it, someone coming behind me is going to need to hear it so she or he can be strong," Armentia says (*AW* 155). Only by listening to the stories of the twice marginalized and by incorporating them into existing tribal knowledge can there be a meaningful present and future for the former slaveholding Native tribal communities.[38]

On Wednesday, August 30, 2017, after having been approached by representatives of the freedmen in their struggle against exclusion, the US district court in Washington, DC, issued the following ruling: while "the Cherokee Nation can continue to define itself as it sees fit," the Treaty of 1866 between the United States and the Cherokee Nation grants the Cherokee freedmen a "right to citizenship in the Cherokee Nation that is coextensive with the rights of native Cherokees." Under the Constitution of the Cherokee Nation, Judge Thomas Hogan emphasizes, the "fates" of native Cherokees and Cherokee freedmen "rise and fall equally and in tandem" (*Cherokee Nation v. Raymond Nash, et al.* 77–78). Following this ruling, the Cherokee Nation began to review applications for citizenship from Cherokee freedmen and eventually granted about seven thousand of them citizenship. To remove what is now considered "a stain on the Cherokee Nation" by tribal leaders, the Cherokee Nation set out to explore its tribal history of slavery. In November 2020, the nation announced that the following year, it would begin the Cherokee Freedmen Art and History Project, which will feature comprehensive research, historical materials, and resources to identify exclusions of freedmen history, taking into account freedmen perspectives.

Besides securing Cherokee freedmen the rights they so long fought for, the 2017 federal ruling also encourages freedmen of other former slaveholding tribes. The Muscogee Creek freedmen, for instance, have since filed two lawsuits to regain their rights; one is in discovery at the moment of this writing. The US Supreme Court's recent decision in *McGirt v. Oklahoma* is also viewed by many freedmen as having the potential to significantly boost their cause. By basing its recognition of a large portion of eastern Oklahoma as Muscogee (Creek) reservation land on the Treaty of 1866, the court stresses the treaty's ongoing validity. If the United States still has to honor this treaty, freedmen argue, Native nations have to do so as well and have to guarantee freedmen equal rights and privileges.[39]

It remains to be seen whether rulings such as these, emanating from the courts of the colonizer, have the power to produce long-lasting changes in the law and social attitudes of Native communities; whether such edicts—as they are often viewed by Native nations due to their interference with Native sovereignty—are able to contribute to the undoing of racial divisions within former slaveholding tribes, to the renewal of inclusive models of Indigenous kinship, and hence to reconciliation and recognition. In tandem with a change in tribal legal codes, novels such as Foster's and Lockhart's, along with community projects such as the Cherokee Freedmen Art and History Project, pave the way for forms of Indigenous peoplehood disconnected from blood lineage and hence from the racial (and racist) logic of federal Indian policy.

CHAPTER 5
"Museumized" *INDIANS*
NATIVE SPECULATIVE REMOVAL FICTION, CULTURAL APPROPRIATION, AND INDIGENOUS FUTURITY

> Unlike the battles of the last century, which involved tangible lands and resources, the battle lines are now lost in a confusing haze of analytically distinct claims centering around a common nexus: cultural appropriation.
>
> Rebecca Tsosie, "Reclaiming Native Stories"

> Only if . . . [Native Americans] refuse to accept and be determined by the romantic linear history which ends with the tragic death or museumization of Indian people, can they continue to imagine their place in the story of ongoing life.
>
> Kimberley Blaeser, "The New 'Frontier' of Native American Literature"

AT FIRST SIGHT, the phrase "Native Speculative Removal Fiction" in the heading of this chapter might appear counterintuitive. Whereas "speculative" suggests a turn away from ordinary reality, a "thought experiment" often concerned with possible futures, "Removal" refers to a historical period of Native–settler history (Oziewicz; see also Gill 72). However, as Ericka Hoagland and Reema Sarwal insist, science fiction, and by extension speculative fiction,[1] does have a "complex relationship with history." In science fiction, "the past is obsessively revisited and reconsidered"; it is revalued in terms of "where it has brought us, and where it might lead us" (9, 10). Indigenous science fiction is particularly invested in creating links between the past (beliefs, stories, histories) and the future (embodied by advanced technologies and alien landscapes). By linking the Indigenous past to "a high-tech or post-tech future," Indigenous writers can assert their continued presence and cultural persistence and envision "possible futures" (Attebery 402; see also 386).

The two novels discussed in this chapter, *Riding the Trail of Tears: A Novel* (2011) by Blake Hausman (Cherokee) and *The Bird Is Gone: A ~~Monograph~~ Manifesto* (2003) by Stephen Graham Jones (Blackfeet), conceptualize past, present, and future not as contiguous, or as chronologically disparate temporalities, but as overlapping and coexistent. They qualify as Native slipstream, "a species of speculative fiction within the sf realm [that] infuses stories with time travel, alternate realities and multiverses, and alternative histories." Slipstream, as Grace L. Dillon has claimed, allows authors "to recover the Native space of the past, to bring it to the attention of contemporary readers, and to build better futures" (3, 4). Hausman's and Jones's novels revisit the history of Indian Removal to make visible and legible what they consider to be the major form of neocolonial regimentation and disenfranchisement that Native Americans face in the present and will continue facing in the future and that threatens the persistence of their peoplehood: cultural appropriation.

Bruce Ziff and Pratima Rao have, in their seminal work on the topic, defined cultural appropriation as "the taking—from a culture that is not one's own—of intellectual property, cultural expressions or artifacts, history and ways of knowledge" (1). These intangible and tangible aspects of culture are subsumed in the legal category of cultural property.[2] With respect to Native America, scholars have emphasized the continuity between battles over land and resources that dominated the relation between tribal communities and the United States until the twentieth century and ongoing battles about the appropriation of cultural property, especially in its intangible form. Angela Riley, for instance, proposes a temporal progression of the settler colonial history of dispossession from real property to intangible property ("Straight Stealing" 75).[3]

Although it is evidently not a new phenomenon, the latter part of the twentieth century witnessed a surge in the appropriation of Native cultural property (Riley and Carpenter 889). Riley goes so far as to speak of a "mass appropriation and dissemination of Indian culture," which she and other scholars have largely attributed to globalization and the emergence of postmodern consumer society ("Straight Stealing" 117; see also 79; P. Deloria 156–57). Stereotypical representations of Native people, cultures, forms of belonging, sacred objects, rituals and songs, stories and history, symbols and designs, clothing, and traditional knowledge have been used both by non-Native individuals, such as environmentalists, artists, and so-called New Agers, and by non-Native educational institutions, business corporations, the tourist industry, and sports teams—sometimes for personal edification yet more commonly for profit. "In short," as Rebecca Tsosie argues, "'Indian' culture is a commodity in modern America. It is sold exploited, probed, catalogued, and controlled by outsiders in many different markets, both economic and intellectual" ("Reclaiming Native Stories" 311–12). Tsosie's use of the term "Indian" points to the fact that the representations of Native identity and culture that are commodified throughout America are, more often than not, colonial inventions. Science,[4] in particular the discipline of anthropology, has played a significant role in the production of these inventions, which is why Pauline Turner Strong has called it "the Indian's Image Maker" (341, 342).

By using the term "Indian," Tsosi and Strong gesture toward Gerald Vizenor's definition of the *indian* (always italicized and never capitalized). For him, "the *indian* is the invention, and *indian* cultures are simulations, that is, the ethnographic construction of a model that replaces the real in most academic references." Vizenor views *indians* as "simulations of the discoverable other. . . . That is to say, the simulations of the other have no real origin, no original reference, and there is no real place on this continent that bears the meaning of that name" (Vizenor and Lee 85). Put differently, "the Indian was an occidental invention that became a bankable simulation" (Vizenor, *Manifest Manners* 11).[5] Cultural appropriation involves the creation and dissemination of simulations of *indianness*. By transforming the appropriated culture into "some quaint aspect" of the dominant society's "culture," the latter obfuscates the political and cultural sovereignty of Native communities and keeps in place structures of colonial domination (Tsosie, "Reclaiming Native Stories" 311, 314, 317).[6] Just like the appropriation of tangible resources, the appropriation and distortion of Native intangible property "diminishes the well-being of individual Indian people and, correspondingly, the health, welfare and self-determination of tribes as collectives" (Riley and Carpenter 930; see also 866).[7] Cultural appropriation is harmful particularly due to its profound effect on the identities of Native individuals and collectives, who increasingly face the pressure to look and act like the simulated *indians* populating the dominant culture's narrations.[8] It thus "interferes with the community's ability to define itself and establish its own identity" and has the potential to "damage or transform cultural practices" (Tsosie, "Reclaiming Native Stories" 313).

The fight against the processes of appropriation and commodification involved in representations of *indianness*, Riley claims, has become at least as important as—in her words—the "'old'" fight for tangible resources and tangible property, such as land, natural resources, sacred objects, and artifacts. Native "destinies," she argues, depend on Native control of their histories and cultures ("Straight Stealing" 75, 76, 77, 83, 90). As Anglo-American property law is of limited use in this struggle,[9] Native activists and legal scholars have been looking for alternative ways to contain Native cultural appropriation and to regain representational authority. Besides intellectual property doctrines, international and tribal law may be of help. Legal scholars also highlight the importance of Native resistance to appropriation through "other mechanisms," such as "social media, art, comedy, film, and technology" (Riley and Carpenter 931; see also Riley, "Straight Stealing" 73–74, 82–91).

This chapter focuses on how Native speculative Removal literature critiques and resists present and future practices of Native cultural appropriation by placing them in relation to past acts of colonial dispossession— first and foremost, Indian Removal. Blake Hausman's novel *Riding the Trail of Tears* is set in the near future, when the history of Cherokee Removal has been appropriated by a non-Native corporation for commercial gains. Besides critiquing recent practices of Native cultural appropriation, it explores the complicity of the Native colonized subject in the commodification of its own culture and history by focusing on Cherokee tour guide Tallulah Wilson's role in this hyperreal theme park of simulations. Stephen Graham Jones's *The Bird Is Gone: A ~~Monograph~~ Manifesto* expands on the implication of Native Americans in processes of cultural appropriation. Jones's text is speculative in the sense that it creates a world radically different from the reader's reality. It is a world after the enactment of the so-called Conservation Act, a federal law passed at some point at the beginning of the twenty-first century and returning all the land between Oklahoma and the Great Plains to Native Americans. What initially appears to be a utopian vision of restitution is revealed to be a modern version of Indian Removal: this time the federal government "removes"

Native Americans from their reservations to a huge outdoor museum, in which they are conserved as scientific objects of anthropological study and encouraged to perform *indianness* for American tourists and anthropologists. With few exceptions, Jones's Native characters internalize the subjectivities created by the dominant culture and are complicit in what Kimberley Blaeser has called the museumization of their own culture and lives (49).

Both Hausman and Jones use their works to explore the contemporaneity of past as well as present and future modes of settler colonial dispossession: the taking of land and the appropriation, commodification, and museumization of Native history, culture, and identity for economic, scientific, and entertainment purposes. By linking these two modes of dispossession within their respective narratives, these texts suggest that the latter is at least as threatening to Indigenous cultural survival and persistent peoplehood as the former, as it keeps the colonial configurations of power intact and entraps Native Americans in a state of psychological dependency. The novels also reflect on the potential ways in which Native Americans could resist non-Native practices of appropriation and the imposition of subjectivities via popular cultural, legal, and scientific discourses. They propose Native reappropriation and self-representation as central in the struggle against colonialism, perhaps even more central than the struggle for restitution. Both these speculative Removal novels thus epitomize what legal scholar Cortelyou C. Kenney has called the "battleground of representation"—the primary battlefield of the twenty-first century—on which Native Americans need to wage their struggle for a self-determined existence as peoples (508).

"THE TRAIL HAD ARRIVED": THE TRAIL OF TEARS AS A THEME PARK IN BLAKE HAUSMAN'S *RIDING THE TRAIL OF TEARS*

On September 16, 2015, the official American Trail of Tears Commemoration Day, Steve Ketchum, then a Choctaw doctoral student of anthropology, posted a piece entitled "(Re)-Remembering the Trail of Tears" in the blog of the American Anthropological Association. In this piece he sarcastically comments on the appropriation of the Trail of Tears in US culture: "Welcome to modernity, a world where an event like the Trail of Tears can be stripped and cleansed of historical significance and context to be appropriated for a social media #campaign. Why engage in being educated about a moment in US history that signaled a legal commitment to the devaluing of Native lives, culture and property when you can just like it as an event on Facebook?"[10] Appropriating this historical event, Ketchum alleges, deprives it of its meaning, context, and significance. The Trail of Tears has become a simulacrum—that is, a pretend representation signifying the absence of the object it claims to represent.

It is such appropriation of the Trail of Tears, along with the appropriation of other intangible property, that Hausman negotiates in *Riding the Trail of Tears*. Drawing on postmodern critiques of globalization, the tourist industry, and "the hyperrealities of neo-colonial consumerism" by Jean Baudrillard, Umberto Eco, and Gerald Vizenor, the novel constructs the Trail of Tears as a hyperreal simulacrum of the past that "bears no relation to any reality whatever" (Baudrillard 1736, 1740; Eco 7; Vizenor, "A Postmodern Introduction" 3; see also Harkin 581). Run by a non-Native corporation, the theme park is located on former Cherokee lands that are now part of Georgia (Hausman, *Riding the Trail of Tears* 34, 39).[11] While such a location might tempt the reader to anticipate that the Tsalagi Removal Exodus Point Park (TREPP) would seek to acquaint visitors with the violent history of Cherokee dispossession, the novel immediately dispels such expectations. For the narrator's description of the TREPP—a virtual reality "tourist trap" (note the intentional near rhyme!)—is saturated with irony and emphasizes its "user-friendly, consumer-driven" design (*RTT* 13, 174). While claiming authenticity and historical accuracy, the TREPP attempts to conceal the violence and suffering of Indian Removal. The customers—mostly "summer travelers and adventure seekers" along with a few students of anthropology from nearby universities—can choose between several levels of violence. Level 1, for instance, is "minimal violence, child friendly" (*RTT* 59; see also 14). In addition, the more visitors pay for their tickets, the more comfort they have on the Trail of Tears: paying high ticket prices allows them to ride with the Cherokee elite rather than with the "commoners." If they ride with the elite, they are also spared witnessing the murder of members of the Treaty Party by opponents of the Treaty of New Echota (*RTT* 85). To make the visitors' experience of "playing Indian"—as Philip J. Deloria has called non-Native performances of *indianness*—most pleasurable and "authentic," the ride makes tourists look *indian*, equipping them with darker skin and higher cheekbones. They also have larger breasts and penises inside the game—"Anything to ensure consumer satisfaction" (*RTT* 93; see also 79). Each game room is equipped with toilets, and everyone is assured by the tour guides that they will be out of the ride in time for dinner, which they can purchase in the two restaurants next to the gift shop, carrying the *indian*-style names Turtleback Café and Soaring Eagle Grill (*RTT* 18, 36, 71, 134). Even though the tourists are constantly reminded "that the ride is like real life," presenting Removal as it really happened, they in fact enter a journey into hyperreality (*RTT* 60, 86, 70–71). Besides revealing to the visitors the ride's built-in scenery, the visors engulfing their heads also show them "what [they] want to see" (*RTT* 74–75).

Hausman's negotiation of the tourists' role inside the ride is reminiscent of Eco's notion of Disneyland as "a place of total passivity" (48). The tour guides regulate the tourists' access to the attraction, suggest certain behaviors and actions, and discourage others. While the illusion of individual agency is maintained, each of the tourists follows a prewritten script. The same is true for the digital Cherokee characters populating the ride. While they appear to be telling their own stories, they are all programmed to represent commonly accepted notions of *indianness*: they feature stereotypically Native names, such as Deer Cooker and Corn Grinder, and behave "as if sprung from a Fenimore Cooper novel" (*RTT* 271; see also 135). They are programmed to suffer, to indulge in their victimhood, and eventually to die.

The Wise Old Medicine Man is the most recognizable character of the ride. Old Medicine, as he is called endearingly by staff members, is encountered by the visitors once they die. He tells them "what [they] want to hear, what [they] think [they] need to hear" and "reaffirms [their] personal ideology by showering [them] with the kind of aboriginal spirituality that only dead people can exude." The Wise Old Medicine Man becomes so popular among customers that some of them consider inducing their own deaths to have that positive experience sooner (*RTT* 57; see also 58). To motivate the tourists to ride the Trail of Tears all the way to Indian Territory, the guides tell them at the beginning of the tour that they will get a $20 voucher and a victory T-shirt (*RTT* 60, 335). The novel's irony becomes even more painful when Tallulah tells her tour group, "So you see . . . there's nothing to stop us from surviving. Nothing except ourselves" (*RTT* 88). Obviously citing the ride's script book of handy phrases, Tallulah suggests that the outcome of the Trail of Tears depends on the performance of every customer. In combination with her insistence that the ride is historically authentic, her words downplay the violence committed by the US military during Removal. If the Cherokees did not survive the trail, it was their own fault: they had chosen the wrong options.

The Trail of Tears ride is therefore a simulation of what Vizenor has called "manifest manners"—that is, "the course of dominance, the racialist notions and misnomers sustained in archives and lexicons as 'authentic' representations of *indian* cultures" (*Manifest Manners* vii; italics in original). The ride engages neither with the Native present nor with an imagined Native future; it is a place steeped in nostalgia and myth and hence signifies ongoing colonial violence (see Baudrillard 1736). "The Trail had arrived," the Nunnehi narrator tells us, after mentioning that several expensive package tours had included admission to the Trail of Tears as part of the bargain (*RTT* 14). The Trail of Tears has finally arrived in the consciousness of postmodern Americans, but not as a historical event signifying colonial violence and intense Native suffering. Rather it is a commodity, an entertaining and consumer-friendly virtual simulation that has "murdered" the real (Baudrillard 1735).

While the Trail of Tears ride is certainly the most prominent act of Native cultural appropriation and commodification in *Riding the Trail of Tears*, it is not the only one. Within the major plot about the ride of one particular tour group on the day before Tallulah's vacation are embedded other stories relating how corporate America and American popular culture exploit Native intangible property. Throughout the novel, references are made to the use of *indian* mascots and racist names (Braves, Chiefs, Redskins) by sports teams and high schools. *indians*, the novel repeatedly reminds the reader, also abound in movie productions, literature, and music (*RTT* 144, 199, 271, 342, 345, 349).

Besides the ride itself, the most central symbol of Native cultural appropriation in the novel is the Jeep Cherokee, an SUV introduced in 1974, replaced by the Jeep Liberty in 2002, and reintroduced by Jeep marketing in 2014 without asking the Cherokee Nation for permission or offering them royalties (Collins). The Jeep Cherokee and the TREPP are deeply entangled. Tallulah works for the TREPP because the Trail of Tears ride was originally her Cherokee grandfather Arthur's invention.

Apparently, to protest the car industry's use of the tribal designation "Cherokee" in the late 1990s, Arthur decided to reappropriate the Jeep Cherokee to develop his own Indigenous, digital version of the history of Indian Removal and to turn a critical lens on Trail of Tears stories told by the dominant society. He equipped the Jeep with numerous "television windows," so that small groups of people could hop in and ride the Trail of Tears together, having "Surround Vision." Arthur was thus the first to bring non-Native appropriations of land and culture together in a powerful act of resistance to both forms of colonial taking (*RTT* 19, 28, 32, 33).

As a pars pro toto of appropriative, corporate America, the Jeep Cherokee is associated with dispossession, harm, and death (*RTT* 27–28, 34). This association continues after Arthur's death, upon which he bequeaths the IP rights to his invention to the Museum of the Cherokee Indian, apparently hoping that the Cherokee staff will incorporate his art into the exhibit or further develop his concept of Surround Vision to confront their visitors with Cherokee history in a novel way (*RTT* 34). Instead, the museum chooses to sell the concept, as well as the Jeep, to the "Atlanta moneyman" Jim Campbell, who uses it as the basic idea for the TREPP. Despite the exchange of money, the novel presents Campbell's purchase of the invention as an act of theft: Tallulah's grandmother obviously never received any royalties for her husband's invention, and Arthur is nowhere mentioned in the TREPP as the actual inventor (*RTT* 28, 34). The Campbell foundation does, however, pay young Tallulah's rent and college bills, but it does this in exchange for her services as the TREPP's "mascot" and her input as "the sole cultural consultant" of the program (*RTT* 14, 27). The involvement of a single enrolled Cherokee enables the TREPP to advertise the ride as authentic and as having received the approval of the entire Cherokee community.[12]

By turning the Trail of Tears into a gigantic simulacrum, Hausman situates the increasing appropriation of Native intangible property (history and culture) within the larger history of colonial land taking. Just as the land has been taken by the colonizer for non-Native use, Native culture and history are increasingly commodified, without proper consultation let alone compensation and attribution. Stereotypical images of Native Americans are omnipresent in American commercials, sports, and the tourist industry, but they themselves are not, or are barely, heard or listened to. They are represented as simulacral specimens of the past, doomed to vanish, having neither a present nor a future. By creating a link between the loss of these two forms of Native belongings (tangible and intangible property), *Riding the Trail of Tears* alerts the reader to the dangers of the loss of the latter. The appropriation of intangible property poses as great a threat to Indigenous ways of living, being, and belonging as does the loss of homeland.

NATIVE AMERICANS AS LIVING SPECIMENS IN A MUSEUM: THE INDIAN TERRITORIES IN STEPHEN GRAHAM JONES'S *THE BIRD IS GONE*

In *The Precession of Simulacra*, Baudrillard explores the role of Western science in the replacement of the real by signs. Along with consumer culture, he argues, science is responsible for turning its objects into signs without referents. He then turns to the discipline of ethnology and analyzes its relation to its most favorite objects of study: Indigenous people (1737, 1739):

> For ethnology to live, its object must die. But the latter revenges itself by dying for having been "discovered," and defies by its death the science that wants to take hold of it. . . . It was against this hades of paradox that the ethnologists wanted to protect themselves by cordoning off the Tasaday with virgin forest. . . . Science loses a precious capital, but the object will be safe—lost to science, but intact in its "virginity.". . . The Indian thereby driven back into the ghetto, into the glass coffin of virgin forest, becomes the simulation model, for all conceivable Indians *before ethnology*. . . . Of course, these particular Savages are posthumous: frozen, cryogenised, sterilised, protected to *death,* they have become referential simulacra. (1737; italics in original)

By categorizing Indigenous culture through scientific taxonomies, Baudrillard says, ethnologists turn their objects of investigation into simulations, replacing their reality with a scholarly account. After killing the real, they seek to conserve the simulated object by cordoning it off, either in the pristine wilderness or in the safe space of the natural history museum, exhibited as a "living specimen." As an example of such a process of museumization, Baudrillard cites Ishi, who lived at the University of California's Museum of Anthropology in Berkeley from 1911 until his death in 1916 and who was advertised as a vanishing Indian: "the last Stone Age man." Like other museumized *indians,* Ishi was made safe for encounters with tourists who craved the exotic other. In museums or cordoned-off spaces, Natives could "once more become 'what they used to be,' or at least that which ethnology has made them—simulacra Indians" (Baudrillard 1737, 1738, 1740).

Baudrillard's theoretical considerations facilitate the interpretation of an otherwise barely accessible text that, to use Stephen Disrud's apt words, "implodes the methodology of close-reading that academics tend to apply to literature": Stephen Graham Jones's *The Bird Is Gone* (27).[13] In light of Baudrillard, the novel's centerpiece, the Conservation Act, which rules the Indian Territories into existence, needs to be interpreted as providing the legal basis on which Western science, in league with US America's environmentalists, is able to cordon off its most cherished object of study—the Native—as a living specimen in a huge outdoor museum and turn it into a simulacrum without a referent.

The Bird Is Gone offers the reader two competing narratives of how the Indian Territories came into being. According to the first narrative, they are the work of Mary Boy, one of the novel's Native protagonists. In the wake of swallowing a peyote button, fed to him by the FBI as part of a government-funded study on the impact of peyote on a "fully-matured male specimen of the Sioux tribe," Mary Boy dreams of making a treaty with a cavalryman. Written by Mary Boy with all the legal language at his disposal, the treaty holds "that DC was hereby giving back all the land it ever took, would take, or was presently taking" (Jones, *The Bird Is Gone* 20; see also 21).[14] When the Conservation Act is passed a few years later and millions of Native Americans from all over the United States arrive in the newly created territories, Mary Boy remembers his treaty and comes to the conclusion that "he'd signed [these Indian Territories] into existence one night on the way back from Whiteclay" (*BG* 21).

Mary Boy's imagined treaty is the work of a radical visionary who transcends Western notions of time and makes strategic use of the paradoxes of American law. Western chronology collapses in this vision, in which past, present, and future acts of dispossession converge. As practiced by the federal government, dispossession has been characterized by what Robert Nichols terms a "recursive logic": the settler colonial state dispossesses (deprives of property) a group of people whose ownership of the land has been denied in the first place; that is, theft precedes, rather than presupposes, property (6–7, 18). In a similar move, Mary Boy makes the government give back land it has not yet taken. He thus signs back into existence a North American continent entirely owned by Native Americans. Not only does his treaty undo all the geopolitical maneuvers of the settler nation in the past, but it undoes the settler nation itself. By depriving the United States of its past, present, and future territory, Mary Boy's imagined treaty sounds the death knell of US political sovereignty, which is grounded in a clearly demarcated territory.

The second explanation for the Indian Territories' existence the novel offers stands in stark contrast to this radically utopian vision. In the glossary of terms, written and "dictat[ed] to America" by LP Deal, another Native character, the act is defined as follows (*BG* 158):

> **Conservation Act**—the accidental solution to the "Indian Problem" (under pressure from Keep America Beautiful, the American Congress signed into law an aggressive bill requiring "the restoration of all indigenous flora and fauna to the Great Plains." As wildlife biologists pointed out, though, for a disturbance-dependent landscape to regain anything approaching self-sufficiency—to say nothing of momentum—the reintroduced grass (*buchloe dactyloides*) needed buffalo (*bison bison*) to "disturb" it, and, just as the prairie dog (*cynomys ludovicianus*) needed the disturbance of the blackfooted ferret (*mustela nigripes*), so did the burgeoning herds of reintroduced buffalo need the INDIAN (*canis latrans*)). (*BG* 164; bold print in original)

According to this definition, the Conservation Act must be read neither as an apologetic gesture on the part of the colonizer nor as an act of restitution geared toward creating a sovereign Indian territory. Instead, by creating the Indian Territories in an area in the United States that is neither densely populated nor a storehouse of resources,[15] the federal government finally realizes a goal that Removal advocates pursued throughout the early nineteenth century: the containment of *all* Native Americans in one part of the domestic territory. On the one hand, such containment would guarantee ethnic separatism. On the other hand, it would secure the homogenization of US domestic space, replacing what

CHAPTER 5

Tom Biolsi has termed "a checkerboard pattern" (244). Just like Removal, the Conservation Act also facilitates the taking of Native land. For in its wake comes the so-called Huna Deal, "controversial land exchanges . . . where the total acreage of the temporarily 'abandoned' reservations was traded for BLM [Bureau of Land Management] land immediately surrounding the TERRITORIES, sometimes at the request of the tribe or nation, but, in the case of some of the tribes or nations holding land bordering national parks, without consent, too. *see also: PENNIES DOWN SYNDROME*" (*BG* 166; italics in original). The Huna Deal becomes possible through the enthusiastic reaction to the Conservation Act by Native Americans all over the United States, who flock to the newly created territory in a "mass exodus" called Skin Parade. The federal government uses this temporary abandonment of reservation lands to annex these lands, giving the Native Americans less valuable land surrounding the territories in exchange (*BG* 171). If the reader looks up "Pennies Down Syndrome" in the glossary, they will learn that this is the "vacant stare associated with those INDIANS who . . . find Americans living in their homes, courtesy of the HUNA DEAL, which auctioned their 'abandoned' land for 'pennies on the dollar'"—another thinly veiled reference to settler practices during the Removal era (*BG* 169).

But the Conservation Act goes one step further than the Indian Removal Act: it relocates Native Americans not as individuals and communities but as ethnographic specimens, reintroduced to the Great Plains along with other flora and fauna. The federal government creates a symbiotic biotope, a pre-conquest wilderness fostering specific plants and animals, with the "INDIAN" being one of them. By writing "INDIAN" in all capital letters, LP Deal asks the reader to look up the term in the glossary, where it is defined as "adj. a mode of dress which peaked when eleven-year-old Norseman Leif Garrett walked onto the production stage of *The Dating Game* wearing beads and buckskin. The girls in the front row screamed and plain fainted. They were all INDIAN" (*BG* 166). The novel here clearly gestures the reader toward Baudrillard's claim that "*We are all Tasaday,* or Indians," once ethnology "is applied to all living things and becomes invisible" (1738; italics in original). This omnipresence of ethnology suggests that even though the immediate passage of the Conservation Act is attributed to the environmentalists, the ideological groundwork behind it has been laid by the disciplines of anthropology and ethnology with their elaborate taxonomies, into which Native Americans have been incorporated.

The glossary definition of "Indian" thus conceptualizes *indianness* as a white simulation popularized by the media, in particular through a "reality" show that turns its (female) viewers into *indians*, reminiscent of Baudrillard's diagnosis of postmodern subjectivity as a state of simulated *indianness*. Popular culture establishes notions of *indianness* that are cherished by consumers due to their exotic otherness and nostalgia. Such medial representation of Native Americans, however, leads to what the glossary calls the "ivory trade," which precipitates the extinction of a species, in this case the Native (*BG* 167). The Conservation Act is the logical consequence of the ivory trade—it constitutes anthropology's and ethnology's effort to save their objects of study.

The objective to create a self-sufficient, self-perpetuating biotope makes necessary a cordon sanitaire that properly contains, controls, and regulates the Natives. The border that the federal government establishes—closely patrolled and featuring a tollbooth (*BG* 32, 35, 36)—is defined in the glossary as the "no man's land between America and the INDIAN TERRITORIES," synonymous with "1. . . . end of the end of the trail, 2. RMZ [remilitarized zone], 3. the looking glass" (*BG* 163–64). The first synonym points toward the 1915 sculpture *The End of the Trail* by American artist James Earle Fraser, which signifies the vanishing of a noble race. While Fraser's sculpture embodies the vanishing Indian, the border signifies the "end of the end of the trail"—that is, the end of the idea of the *indian* as vanishing. Read in light of Baudrillard's idea of the "glass coffin of virgin forest," the border cordons off an area in which simulacra *indians* are "cryogenised." It is a militarized zone, through which the flow of people and goods to and from the Indian Territories is regulated. It is also a looking glass: just as Alice climbs through the mirror in Lewis Carroll's *Through the Looking-Glass, and What Alice Found There* (1871)—a spectator entering an exotic fantasy world—the "anthropologists and ethnologists and enthusiasts [are] stacked belly to back watching through binoculars their saliva coating the bricks for stories" (*BG* 113; see also Baudemann). Whenever the inhabitants leave the territories, they are hunted down by the anthropologists, who want them "to confirm their pet theory" (*BG* 32). The residents poke fun at the scholars by shooting wooden arrows at them; the scholars eagerly pick them up as scientific evidence (*BG* 115).

If anthropologists want to cross the border, they can do so only secretly so as not to impair the authenticity of their objects of study. As Rosemary Coombe puts it, "For an object to be accepted as an authentic artifact, it must locate itself in an untouched, pristine state that bespeaks a timeless essence in a particular cultural tradition. That which is recognized as authentic to a culture cannot bear any traces of that culture's contact with other cultures" (218). In order not to contaminate their specimens through their presence, the anthropologists shoot themselves across the border with catapults so they can take photos, descend with parachutes, and make sure to get back to America unnoticed (*BG* 145–47).

The border is thus not a device to mark off sovereign lands or a sign of Native political independence and self-determination. The novel portrays the Indian Territories as "dominoes" or "a house of cards" and therefore as a fragile geopolitical space (*BG* 141). In a similar vein, the glossary describes this bordered geopolitical space not as an Indian nation but as "INDIANation"—that is, as the process of *indianizing* (*BG* 167). Rather than an autonomous body politic, the Indian Territories are a large outdoor museum, a "petting zoo" (*BG* 45). As the reader learns in the novel's artifact section, every living *indian* specimen is assigned an identification number upon entering the territories (*BG* 178). To be allowed to pass the tollbooth and to cross the border, potential specimens need to successfully perform colonial notions of *indianness:* they have to produce "old turtle rattles and scars and dances they knew and stories they didn't" (*BG* 44). In addition, they have to accept the so-called Code, a "pamphlet distributed to all INDIANS at the BORDER" and "a cultural primer or guidebook on INDIAN etiquette." While the reader never learns who has written the Code, it is not too far-fetched to suggest that this was the work of the numerous anthropologists who flock along the border (*BG* 164; see also 32).[16]

In contrast to the anthropologists' wish to conserve Native Americans as simulations, the federal government soon begins to engage in a secret plan to extinguish them. To maintain a racially homogenous biotope, the Indian Health Service (IHS)—a federal agency—comes up with "pink eye," a drug that is distributed among the Native Americans and that turns their pupils red (*BG* 122). But pink eye was "retroengineered . . . from the smallpox America was supposed to still have, was supposed to be wafting over the border at us for stealing back the Great Plains." When this genocidal scheme fails ("the smallpox never came"), "America" offers Native Americans "bargains for bulk razor blades," a deal that has a more "favorable" effect: a year after the creation of the Indian Territories, 20 percent of its people are floating dead in bathtubs (*BG* 121, 122). Within the first year of the territories' existence, many inhabitants also die from alcohol poisoning or from car accidents on their way home from the bar, and many Native women have stillborn children (*BG* 165–66). While these deaths are not explicitly attributed to the federal government, the reader suspects that the IHS had its hands in causing them. For who else could have been responsible for the import of huge amounts of alcohol capable of killing almost half the territories' population? If readers look up the term "trick" in the glossary, they find the following explanation: "*n. colloq.* what the older generation told us the SKIN PARADE was: a TRICK to get all the INDIANS in one place. The Gatling gun they imagined was huge, locked in a geostationary orbit somewhere over the Great Plains" (*BG* 172). While the anthropologists want to conserve *indianness* for scholarly purposes, the federal government envisions the Conservation Act as a secret weapon to solve the "Indian Problem" once and for all.

Jones's use of irony throughout the text evokes painful laughter. For the Indian Territories he constructs in his novel are not a space of political and economic opportunity in the sense that Mary Boy has envisioned them. Their creation does not imply, as TV sets announce, "that the Dakotas [a]re Indian again" (*BG* 14). By contrast, the Indian Territories as they come to exist are a profoundly dystopian space. They are the result of a twenty-first-century version of the Removal policy that combines the appropriation of Native tangible property (land) and intangible property (culture). By extending the reach of Removal to include intangible belongings, the federal government succeeds at incorporating Native lands and homogenizing and commodifying Native culture in one sweep. Native individuals and communities and their culture become museum objects arrested in settler colonial time, bound by manifest manners and ready to be digested by American scientists and consumers. The settler colonial desire for land in the Removal era has thus given way to a far more all-encompassing desire to consume Native culture and identity in its entirety and to turn it into a "white epistemological possession" (Moreton-Robinson, *The White Possessive* 82).

CHAPTER 5

OF ELVES AND AUTHENTICITY SHUFFLES: NATIVE PERFORMANCES OF *INDIANNESS* IN HAUSMAN AND JONES

In his 2016 "Letter to a Just-Starting-Out Indian Writer—and Maybe to Myself," Jones appeals to prospective writers not to be "elves," his term for simulacra *indians*. He states, "That's what America wants you to be. Elves are liminal beings. They live close to the spiritual source. They commune with nature. They're stewards of the trees. They belong in the forests. They cry because of Dr. Pepper bottles in the creek. Also, as it turns out, they're made-up, they're not real. If you're an elf, you don't exist, and like that America's won" (124). Jones also warns them not to participate in what he calls the "authenticity shuffle," which results from the attempt to hierarchize people's respective "Indian experiences." To him, it is "an ugly, ugly dance to do for all the people who really want us to do it" (126–27). Jones thus addresses the effect of the precession of simulacra, the parade of representations of *indianness*, on Native Americans themselves. Accepting definitions of *indianness*, he says, "that's playing their game, that's submitting to being an entry in an encyclopedia. That's saying yes, you drew the boundaries well, I will live just in this little block of text" (128).

Jones's appeal offers an interpretive inroad into both Hausman's *Riding the Trail of Tears* and his own novel *The Bird Is Gone*. These novels do not limit themselves to critiquing practices of Native cultural appropriation; they also analyze Native Americans' involvement in the settler colonial appropriation and dissemination of *indianness*. Both Tallulah Wilson and most inhabitants of the bowling alley Fool's Hip—the Indian Territories' microcosmic center—perform, rather than resist, *indianness*, sometimes for economic profit, other times to compensate their supposedly insufficient knowledge about Native cultures. While they occasionally employ irony to counter prevalent stereotypes, most of the time they accept, even invite, these essentialist notions of identity and lose each other in debates about cultural authenticity. Especially in *The Bird Is Gone*, Native identity politics is portrayed as repressive and exclusionist. Judging one another's degree of compliance with the subjectivities determined by the colonizer makes the novel's characters blind to the structures of colonial domination that keep them trapped and dependent and prevent them from establishing meaningful forms of belonging.

Hausman's protagonist, Tallulah, is deeply insecure about her own Native identity: she wonders whether she is racially "enough" Cherokee and whether she has sufficient knowledge about Cherokee culture to function as a token employee of TREPP. While she is an enrolled member of the Eastern Band of Cherokees and the Cherokee Nation, she suffers from the fact that she is "three quarters white American" (*RTT* 147; see also 24, 39). She learned about her Native heritage only when she was nine years old, when, after her father's death, her mother acquainted her with her Cherokee grandparents, who then introduced her to aspects of Cherokee culture during her summer visits (*RTT* 31). Whatever else she knows about Cherokee culture and history, including Indian Removal, she has drawn from James Mooney's *Myths of the Cherokee* from 1900. As she considers the book authentic information, she bases her undergraduate thesis on the book and uses it to write the program of the TREPP (*RTT* 14, 57).

Tallulah subjects herself to the clichés created and perpetuated by dominant culture even though she is aware that these clichés are signs without referents. To look more *indian*, she has grown long hair and she braids it. She also exposes herself to the sun to get a dark tan. And she is relieved to have high cheekbones, so her appearance in TREPP's promotional literature is more convincing (*RTT* 16, 361). Moreover, Tallulah accepts that the Trail of Tears ride she has helped create abounds with clichés. When researching the history of Indian Removal as a student, she realized "that the Trail was intentionally undocumented and that the quotations were anonymously concocted post-Removal by writers who melded shards of memory in the fires of nostalgia" (*RTT* 173), the kind of nostalgia that, according to Baudrillard, "assumes its full meaning" "when the real is no longer what it used to be" (1736). Despite such insights, she proceeds to employ these clichéd Removal fictions in her writing of the TREPP tour guide phrasebook and the script for the ride. Hence she contributes to their further dissemination. In a truly postmodern move, Hausman has Tallulah wonder whether these standard accounts of Removal were in reality "a grand fiction" serving some other purpose. However, she is unwilling to think through what this suspicion means for her own work at the TREPP (*RTT* 173).

In her daily work as a tour guide—a job that, as she repeatedly points out, pays very well (*RTT* 15, 27, 324)—Tallulah is asked, and agrees, "to perform as [an] authentic cultural [subject]," which makes her the personal hero of an anthropology professor at a nearby university (Clifford 47; see also *RTT* 46). Even though she occasionally corrects her tourists' misconceptions about Native America, her primary objective is to entertain them and to make them tip her well. Thus she strategically regulates the information she conveys, and her responses are often "noncommittal" in order not to offend anyone (*RTT* 80; see also 19, 23, 25, 62, 65, 97, 101). The role she encourages her tourists to play on the Trail of Tears is that of a "model American Indian": traumatized, weary, not fighting back, and not harboring negative sentiments toward the soldiers. She wants them to follow her prewritten script, just as the vanishing Indian—the born victim—has always followed the immutable and linear progression of history. Agency and resistance are not part of that script. By motivating her tourists to be victims without agency, Tallulah inevitably becomes a proponent of this simulated history of Indian Removal (*RTT* 180).

The novel blurs the lines between Tallulah, a living human being, and the digital *indians* populating the ride, who act according to the program she has developed with the tech crew. Upon being attacked by soldiers, Tallulah behaves exactly like these digital *indians*: she "defaults to passivity" and walks with the same stoicism as her digital counterparts. Like Corn Grinder and his family, Tallulah performs victimhood. She also realizes that just like the digital *indians*, she does not have any feelings for the dying tourists and hence wonders if she too is not human (*RTT* 172; see also 266). Tallulah is also programmed—programmed not by technology but by the stereotypical representations that American consumer society and popular culture have spoon-fed her all her life.

The so-called Misfits are another group of characters that are not officially part of the TREPP's system but for some hazy reason exist and are programmed to behave according to manifest manners.[17] As their name implies, the Misfits "don't fit very well into reality"; they instead "fit into all the stories that have been recorded" (*RTT* 6). They are an assemblage of stereotypes ranging across historical time, as their baseball hats with different *indian* mascots on them suggest. They are also "collective communalists," a phrase spoofing the fact that postmodern consumer culture appropriates even Native forms of belonging—ownership and group identity—for entertainment purposes (*RTT* 116; see also 111, 112). Most importantly, they are victims trapped in a nineteenth-century stockade—just like those used by the US military during the Trail of Tears—and they begin to abuse themselves after the Suits'[18] departure (*RTT* 112, 165, 164–65): they "[whoop] and [holler], Hollywood style," and the young women offer themselves to be raped (*RTT* 106; see also 166, 169).[19]

The Misfit stockade thus represents two forms of entrapment. It stands for the physical entrapment the Cherokees had to face during Removal, yet it also embodies the symbolic entrapment of Native Americans in a Baudrillardian world of simulations (*RTT* 232).[20] The Misfits' state of victimhood is perpetual: "'With each new loop,' says Indians Hat, 'we all begin again. . . . We are targets. We were programmed to be killed, then brought back to life.'" The only way to survive in such a world of simulations, the Misfits' leader, the Chef, tells tourist Irma, is to give up your name, to "become no one" and not to "act like a real person" (*RTT* 118, 119, 161; see also 117). Loss of personhood and identity, however, leads to self-effacement, symbolized in the novel through the Misfits' empty eyes, which make Irma feel guilty for her complicity in stereotyping Native Americans and "for ever appearing at this digital death house in the first place" (*RTT* 232). Hausman uses the Misfits to illustrate the impact of representations of *indianness* on the psyche of Native Americans: due to their inability to establish their own identity, they cease to exist as persons and (as the novel later shows) as peoples.

Tallulah's complicity in this giant simulation takes a heavy psychological toll on her. Contributing to the creation of "this single, inflexible, and violent narrative" and then having to live through it time and again creates self-doubts and leads to a lack of self-respect (Spiers 65): while "Grandpa Art," as his nickname implies, was an artist, a "cultural emissary of the Cherokee Nation," Tallulah views herself as "a history whore," as "a tourist bullshit artist," as "a poseur and a hack . . . who sold her fucking soul to Coca-Cola for [her] air-conditioning" (*RTT* 27, 145, 324). Her own contribution to the dissemination of *indianness* reveals itself to her in the form of a vision of "an Oklahoma Cherokee man driving a big red Jeep Cherokee with multiple American-flag bumper stickers. Driving to Kansas City to watch a Chiefs-Redskins game, listening to the song 'Indian Outlaw' on repeat, and howling along with the lyrics as he swerves between highway lanes, absolutely loving every minute of it" (*RTT* 144). Just like the man in her vision, Tallulah allows herself to be defined by

CHAPTER 5

dominant society and accepts the imposed subjectivities. She has become an externally determined, "metonymical object" in a part-digital exhibit literally embodying *indianness* (see Kenney 509). She is certainly not, as one reviewer of the novel has claimed, what Vizenor calls a "postindian," who uses simulations "for reasons of liberation rather than dominance" (Gannon). While Vizenor's "postindian" stands for "an active, ironic resistance to dominance," Tallulah epitomizes compliance, if not complicity. Even though she suffers from her inability to establish herself as a self-determined individual, she does not manage to quit working for the TREPP (Vizenor and Lee 85; see also *RTT* 343).

The performance of *indianness* and Native compliance/complicity also looms large in Jones's *The Bird Is Gone*. Well before the creation of the Indian Territories, the majority of Fool's Hip's inhabitants already capitalized on performing *indianness*. Denim Horse danced for crowds across the Northern Hemisphere. Cat Stand was "Dairyland's Indian princess," featuring in a dairy company's commercials and on its milk containers (Jones's nod to the Land O'Lakes Indian). And Courtney Peltdowne bewitched white men by playing the exotic *indian* princess (*BG* 22, 37). Once inside the Indian Territories, these performances do not stop but are perfected to satisfy the hankering of the great numbers of tourists pouring into Fool's Hip to see "real Indians." Denim Horse continues to style himself as a sexualized *indian* object of desire that the female tourists cannot get enough of. Mary Boy mints tokens with the face of Back Iron, looking and posing like a noble savage. Residents also try to reinforce the tourists' preconceived notions of *indian* secrecy and magic by teaching them supposedly authentic hand signals and by telling them about their supernatural powers (*BG* 24, 25, 28, 31, 36, 46).

Fool's Hip, as the novel hence suggests, is a gigantic simulacrum, a neocolonial space populated by simulacra *indians* misled by manifest manners. Even the name Fool's Hip hints at the bowling alley's colonial genealogy. Until Mary Boy sold the name and had the letters rearranged,[21] Fool's Hip was called Ship of Fools, just like the eponymous Bacteen tale, in which Bacteen tries in vain to prevent Columbus's fleet, the Ship of Fools, from anchoring and thereby tries to undo the history of colonization (*BG* 82). As the play *Susannah of the Mounties*, staged by the inhabitants of Fool's Hip, depicts it, this history is characterized by the Natives' dispossession of tangible goods: of Native cultural artifacts ("some Mister

X stealing into the reliquary at Pine Ridge, driving the truck out") and of Native land and bodies ("The second episode was a complete replay of the Indian Wars . . . the bodies stacked up so high") (*BG* 129). The theft of Native intangible property is also omnipresent throughout the novel. All chapter headings framing the novel's descriptions of Fool's Hip and its residents refer to stereotypical representations of Native Americans popularized by American popular culture and thus to the appropriation of Native culture, values, and forms of living and being: the vanishing Indian ("Ten Little Indians," "The Only Good Indian," "A Good Day to Die Again," "Indian Burn"), the ecological Indian ("Indian Corn"), and the redskin ("Red Dawn," "Skin Deep," "Roses Are Red"). "It all ended here, at Fool's Hip," the reader is told (*BG* 129). Fool's Hip is presented as the outgrowth of the appropriation of Native land, culture, values, and bodies by dominant society. Its residents lack agency: they are pawns in a colonial game. The novel likens them to the pins of the bowling alley, whose only function is to be knocked down for the game to be over (*BG* 67, 156). They are also characterized as "conscripted actors" by agent Chassis Jones (also known as Pink Eye), trapped in a large-scale performance of stereotypes and clichés imposed on them by the settler society (*BG* 148).

Considering the novel's use of irony, one is tempted to interpret the Native residents' performances of *indianness* as sheer mockery, as acts of resistance to the average American tourist's clichés and as a way of making money out of the tourists' ignorance and naivety. However, Fool's Hip's residents perform *indianness* even when the tourists are absent; in fact, such clichés become the internal yardstick with which the pan-Native population of the Indian Territories measures identity and belonging. Rather than coming up with new, anticolonial categories of identification and recognition, the inhabitants of the territories revert to and implement the subjectivities created by dominant society, all summarized in the Code given to them upon entering the Indian Territories. To repeat Baudrillard's idea of nostalgia once again, "When the real is no longer what it used to be, nostalgia assumes its full meaning. There is a proliferation of myths of origin and signs of reality; of second-hand truth, objectivity and authenticity" (1736). This vision of the postmodern consumer society can be applied to the colonial situation of Jones's Indian Territories: myths of origin proliferate, and there develops among residents a nostalgic attachment to colonial notions of tradition, authenticity, and "INDIAN etiquette" (*BG* 64).

Therefore the Native inhabitants' uppermost priority is to live authentically *indian* lives. They rename themselves, as well as geographical and temporal designations. For their own names, they revert to *indian* naming conventions (modifier and noun). Rivers receive Lakota appellations, which most inhabitants have a hard time pronouncing; months are called "moons" (*BG* 14, 15; see also Disrud 28). Their new motto, aired through their own radio station, is "Keeping the tradition alive" (*BG* 73). They initially even lived in tipis, but this appears to have become impracticable in the long run (*BG* 125). They grow their hair long and remind each other that with short hair you are not "a real Indian" (*BG* 36, 163). Their new currency is "dentalia or blankets or hides" (*BG* 24). "Salad was suddenly Anglo" and is dropped from the menus of the territories' restaurants (*BG* 23). They even readopt band and clan structures and begin to observe the "maniacally strict family lines" (*BG* 17; see also 16). All these efforts are part of a greater program called Indian Days, which seeks to enforce pan-tribal notions of *indian* traditionalism (*BG* 23). Tradition, as Rifkin argues, implies temporal stasis. It "serves as the opposite of modern, indicating not simply chronological dating but qualities that belong to a different epoch—that do not fit the contours of the present." To be traditional means stepping back from modernity and "staging a version of pastness that disavows the 'complexities' of Native life" (Rifkin, *Settler Time* 6, 30; see also Barker, *Native Acts* 221).

Western science's involvement in the inhabitants' enforcement of "tradition" is carried to its extremes by the Aborigine Hotline run by American anthropologists. Whenever the residents need information about Native culture in general or specific tribal cultural practices they are unfamiliar with, they can "telepawn" (here, "pawn" once again evokes the lack of Native agency)—that is, call the hotline (*BG* 172). Telepawning, as the glossary tells us, equals "sell[ing] your soul to the devil" (*BG* 172); it means allowing one's present-day Native identity to be ossified and to be exchanged for "second-hand truth," as Baudrillard characterizes it (1736). What the self-taught ethnographer James Mooney is for Hausman's Cherokee characters, the Aborigine Hotline is for Jones's Fool's Hip community. Both novels thus point at the central involvement of (self-appointed) scientists in the production of "traditional," "authentic"

Native identities and cultures. Their theories are put into practice with the help of American law (the Conservation Act), popularized by American popular culture (the numerous films and novels mentioned in both texts), and, eventually, performed by the Native characters themselves, who rely on them as "expert witnesses" when practicing their culture (see also Barker, *Native Acts* 20).

Jones employs the character Courtney Peltdowne to highlight how the subjection to "tradition" constrains Indigenous forms of living and belonging. One of the saddest episodes in the novel is Courtney's desperate turn away from her cherished vegetarianism due to pressure from Mary Boy, who takes her key away and does not let her enter Fool's Hip as long as she resists established notions of *indianness* (*BG* 22, 23).[22] The social ostracism Courtney experiences for not complying with the Code leads to her binge eating of buffalo, as eating buffalo is considered a sign of cultural authenticity. Even though she finds this enforced traditionalism ridiculous, she finally gives in in order to belong, even though this means sacrificing parts of herself (*BG* 23).

Courtney also has difficulties accommodating herself to what Mishuana Goeman calls the "spatial politics" inextricably linked to "real" *indianness* (103): only those admitted to the Indian Territories and residing there are considered "proper Indians." Courtney, however, cannot identify with the land. Used to living in the urban areas of the Dakotas, she perceives the territories as "empty," in particular at night, and is afraid to go outside for fear of the "Old Ones . . . out there." Her forced return to the "bow and arrow days" and to a securely bordered Native space deeply alienates and terrifies Courtney. She finds the traditional stories oppressive, feels trapped in this outdoor museum of enforced *indianness*, as her wistful walks along the border fence suggest, and is afraid of "disappearing" (*BG* 23). While in urban Dakota she used to visually stand out, in the Indian Territories she has become the visual standard; in terms of culture, she is even below standard due to her difficulty adopting to the prescribed, supposedly authentic traditional lifeways.

The worst crime in the Indian Territories is to be accused of treason by one's fellow residents. Treason means being identified as a "tomato": "red on the outside *and* the in-, yet white just the same" (*BG* 172; italics in original). This definition is one example of the omnipresence of the color red in *The Bird Is Gone*. Other examples are the many synonyms for "Skin

Parade" in the glossary of terms ("Red Tide," "Red Shift," "Red Dawn") and the many synonyms for "Indian Territories" ("Brave Red World, "Red Earth," "Red Sport," "Red Sea") (*BG* 166, 171). The novel thus marks the project of creating the Indian Territories as racial at its core, reminding the reader of the blood degree criteria regulating belonging in federally recognized tribes. Residents must be red "on the outside"—that is, they need to have all the phenotypic markers attributed to *indianness*. Being red "on the inside" gestures toward the idiom of blood, according to which proper lineage is a prerequisite for living and working in the territories (*BG* 14). "Blood quantum and phenotypically 'Indian' features," as Daniel Heath Justice has deplored, "are the fullest measure of cultural authenticity and ... those who are lacking in these qualities are, by definition, no longer Indian—if they ever were" ("'Go Away, Water'" 156). Being "white just the same" refers to those people who are racially red yet who refuse to perform culturally pure *indianness* and who are critical of the territories' identity politics.

In the transcript of the audio cassette that is part of the novel's "artefacts" section, LP Deal is identified as a tomato (*BG* 178).[23] The transcript further informs the reader how tomatoes are treated—that is, how *indianness* is enforced—in the Indian Territories. If a resident is identified as a tomato, they will be exiled, meaning the culprit is "deposited at the border between the Indian Territories and America-proper" by Native American guards. Exile is part of the Indian Days program; after all, it constitutes the most traditional form of Native punishment. If the guards refuse to punish their own people, they risk their employment as well as further betrayals committed by the tomato in the territories. To get out of this quandary, they help the tomatoes they are driving to the border commit suicide on the way (*BG* appendix). Tomatoes, such as Courtney and LP Deal, are deeply scared to be exiled. Besides not daring to go out at night, they desperately try to put up an air of compliance (*BG* 23). *The Bird Is Gone* thus spells out the complex relationship between the wholesale appropriation of Native tangible and intangible property, an exclusionist identity politics, and a narrow understanding of belonging within Native communities. The fate and suffering of the novel's tomatoes reminds the reader of the many Native Americans who "have been dismissed [by their tribes] as anti-Indian and anti-sovereignty" and who have been "accused of being complicit with assimilationist efforts aimed at eroding the integrity of tribal cultures," of being the enemies of "tradition" (Barker, *Native Acts* 15).

When asking prospective Native writers not to be elves, Jones explains his aversion to elves as follows: "They're silhouettes. They're the shape of us but it's that End of the Trail mode, that says we've come as far as we can, and it was a good fight, but now it's time to die, now it's time to fade into that sunset looming behind us" ("Letter" 124). For the larger part of both novels, Hausman's and the majority of Jones's protagonists are elves. While Tallulah's complicity with colonial representations is the act and choice of one individual, Jones's characters communally adopt the subjectivities constructed by scientific, legal, and popular cultural discourses and make them the bedrock of their pan-Native community. They partake in acts of "cultural conditioning," as it is once phrased in *The Bird Is Gone*, imposing externally defined notions of *indianness* upon the territories' multiethnic set of residents, and they oppress and exclude those who refuse to comply (*BG* 178). In his glossary, LP Deal lists "Brave Red World" as one synonym for the Indian Territories (*BG* 166). Through this intertextual reference, Jones relates the workings within the Indian Territories to the intricate mechanisms of conditioning, programming, surveillance, and (threatened) banishment at work in the Central London Hatching and Conditioning Centre, around which Aldous Huxley's 1932 classic *Brave New World* revolves. While the worlds they describe are no less dystopian than the world state, neither *Riding the Trail of Tears* nor *The Bird Is Gone* end on a note of stasis, alienation, and disempowerment. What Hausman has the Misfit Giants Hat state, "in a trick of optimism," also reflects the hopeful ending of Jones's novel: "a house of death could become a house of life" (*RTT* 122).

THE ROLE OF THE PAST IN THE STRUGGLE FOR SELF-DEFINITION AND A SELF-DETERMINED FUTURE

In his book *The Wretched of the Earth*, Frantz Fanon reflects on the appropriate way of using the past in literature written by the colonized: "When the colonized intellectual writing for his people uses the past he must do so with the intention of opening up the future, of spurring them into action and fostering hope" (167). This quotation seems a fitting starting point to discuss how Hausman and Jones envision in their novels the transition from the "house of death," populated by simulacra *indians* trapped in colonial structures of domination, to a "house of life," populated by self-defined and self-determined Native Americans capable of moving into the future as peoples. As both texts engage intensely with the history of Indigenous dispossession, one can safely assume that the past plays a central role in facilitating this transition.

While the choice of Fanon as a theoretical inroad into the novels might at first sight appear rather random, it is in fact *The Bird Is Gone* that nudges the attentive reader to view it through the lens of this foundational text of postcolonial studies. There are references in the novel that immediately lead to Fanon's works. Jones begins his novel with an epigraph by Jean-Paul Sartre taken from the preface to Fanon's *The Wretched of the Earth:* "We only become what we are by the radical and deep seated refusal of that which others have made of us." Sartre reflects on how, in order to regain their humanity, Europeans need to become conscious of and then refuse their own role in colonialism—that is, the role of the perpetrator (*Wretched* li, lvii). By contrast, Fanon explores what Homi Bhabha so fittingly paraphrases in his foreword as the "psycho-affective predicament [of the colonized subject]." Colonialism, Fanon argues, does not merely use force and violence to advance its goals; it also "snare[s] the people in its net or . . . drain[s] the colonized brain of any form of substance" (xix, 149). For the colonized subject internalizes the subject position imposed by the colonizer and thus becomes an instrument of its own dispossession.[24]

Riding the Trail of Tears and *The Bird Is Gone* also direct the reader's attention to the psychological effects of colonialism. Even though the history of land loss is the *primum movens* of their plots,[25] it is not land loss but the representations of manifest manners and their internalization by the colonized subjects that both novels portray as the major stumbling blocks to a self-determined peoplehood in both present and future. In *The Bird Is Gone*, it becomes particularly evident that colonialism cannot simply be overturned through the restitution of land. Despite their newly won, securely bordered land base, the mythologized Great Plains, the territories' inhabitants continue to be trapped within settler colonial representations and simulations, and they rely too heavily on what Glen Coulthard calls "the subjectifying apparatus of the state or other dominant institutions of power" (23). Jones questions Native performances of *indianness* with the objective of land restitution by introducing the figure of Waymon Tise in the glossary. The word "fauna" in the Conservation Act allowed Tise, a Navajo lawyer, to argue that Native Americans are part of the fauna (*BG* 173). Through his acceptance of this subjectivity, Tise manages to reclaim the Great Plains. In their enthusiasm about restitution, his fellow Native Americans seem not to mind being classified by law as fauna and do not question the ulterior motives behind the Conservation Act (*BG* 14).

Riding the Trail of Tears similarly questions the focus of the colonized on the restitution of land in the struggle to overcome the structures of colonial oppression. Thinking about how to escape from their entrapment in the simulations of *indianness* for which the stockade stands, the Misfits decide to go back east to reclaim their "motherland" in North Carolina. This is for them the place of their "deliverance"; only there will they be able "to begin again" and to live self-determined lives (*RTT* 123–24, 194, 281). What is problematic about this "vision," however, is that it is grounded in the subjectifying apparatus of the Trail of Tears ride (*RTT* 263). This nostalgic and clichéd idea of the motherland is an invention of Tallulah's and part of the TREPP phrase book (*RTT* 53, 248, 281). By going back to this cliché-ridden place of longing, the Misfits—yet again—follow a prewritten script (see Deetjen, *Re-Imagining* 187). This may be the reason why Hausman has them fail in their mission: the Misfits' journey ends abruptly when they are killed by a flood (*RTT* 320).

Hausman's and Jones's novels thus decenter the fight for the reclamation of land in favor of a rejection of the subject positions imposed by the colonizer as an essential step in resisting settler colonial structures of oppression. Here the epigraph by Sartre comes to mind again, reminding the reader that to gain self-determination as peoples, the colonized have to refuse colonial subject positions and resist co-optation, on both an individual and a collective level. They need to create their own definitions, based on both their own contemporary values and their shared history of dispossession, to make visible the wide gulf that exists between colonial simulations of *indianness* and the Indigenous real. Self-recognition must replace the desire for recognition by others. In Hausman's narrative, this position is first voiced by the Misfits, the only characters in the novel who sense that their imprisonment in the digital stockade has to do with their internalization of subjectivities: "'We cannot leave while we still think we're the people we were programmed to be,'" Two Hats opines.

And White Sox asserts "that knowledge is power and that self-knowledge would grant them the power they needed to accomplish their mission." Despite their clichéd idea of motherland, their march east (instead of west) and their effort to "[unlearn their] programs" need to be read as first steps toward self-empowerment (*RTT* 119, 237, 240).

The Misfits' insights help Tallulah to gain self-knowledge and to "[question] the logic of her own clichés" that she has been using for many years. She finally wonders whether she is "the cause of [her] own worst problems" (*RTT* 127, 324). Tallulah realizes that she will never be able to measure up to non-Native notions of Native cultural authenticity and that it is time to stop trying. She seems to realize that to achieve self-determination, she needs to "disrupt" derogatory representations based on racist ideologies and must decolonize her own concepts of identification that are grounded in such notions of authenticity (Barker, *Native Acts* 7). Hence, after getting back to the "real" world, Tallulah proceeds to divest herself of her most *indian* feature: her long hair (*RTT* 355–56). "'They'll say an Indian can't be an Indian without long hair,' she says. 'But that's ridiculous'" (*RTT* 365). Tallulah then quits her job for good and embarks on her own trip to the Cherokee motherland, the North Carolina mountains, where she visits her Cherokee grandmother (*RTT* 343).

At first sight, the ending of Hausman's novel appears rather clichéd. Reading it in conjunction with the legal debates about cultural appropriation, however, brings to light the novel's vision of peoplehood. To move into the future, *Riding the Trail of Tears* seems to suggest, Native Americans need to refuse to fashion themselves as the other and to engage in what Vizenor has called "reverse striptease," the donning of *indian* garb and fetishized objects that serve to please the colonizer ("Socioacupuncture" 181). Tallulah leaves the "house of death" not only physically but, more importantly, mentally, through a literal striptease: she gets rid of her hair and, in the sex scene at the end, the clothes she has worn at work. She refuses to further perform *indianness*. Instead she expresses herself without external regulation via her sexuality and decides to reconnect with the Cherokee part of her family. Tallulah's effort to define herself according to her own desires and her family's values and experiences is a first step toward moving into a self-determined future rather than congealing in an externally determined *indianness* that is always on the brink of vanishing. The novel's final tentative sentences and questions,[26] voiced by the Indigenous Nunnehi narrator as he is being washed down the drain, echo Baudrillard, who describes the Americans' justification for creating simulations of *indianness* with the following words: "Everything is obliterated only to begin again" (1740). The novel's allusion to Baudrillard encourages the reader to reflect on the relationship between obliteration and beginning anew. Vizenor insists on a "sensation of a new tribal presence in the very ruins of the representations of invented Indians" (*Manifest Manners* 3). It is such a sense of presence, the potential for a new beginning, with which Hausman leaves the reader at the end of his novel. Tallulah might use her personal crisis to move beyond her former life as a simulacrum *indian*, to live a more self-determined life, and to become a "cultural emissary," just like her grandfather Arthur. She might relapse into the old clichés because, as she herself admits, she needs clichés and has become used to them (*RTT* 328). She might finally also come up with new clichés about her culture (such as her own version of the motherland) that fail to grasp the complex reality of a "three-quarters white American" "indigenous Southerner" living in urban America (*RTT* 147, 349).

The Bird Is Gone provides the reader with far more concrete and complex notions of how Native Americans could overcome the simulations that imprison them and deprive them of a self-determined existence as peoples. Simply quitting performances of *indianness* (in the way Tallulah sets out to do it) will not free Native Americans from the oppressive colonial structures of domination. Instead, as *The Bird Is Gone* suggests, they need to counter the colonial simulations and representations on the level of representation itself.

The Fool's Hip community is taught strategies of resistance by the Native theater troupe performing its own "Dramatic Reversion" of the 1939 American film *Susannah of the Mounties*, a stereotypical rendition of Native–settler relations at the frontier (*BG* 125). Just like Grandpa Art in Hausman's *Riding the Trail of Tears*, the troupe reappropriates colonial stereotypes in order to destabilize them (*BG* 124). It "replace[s]" the "real *Susannah*"—that is, the Native cultural appropriation—"show by show, performance by performance," with a number of episodes all geared toward unsettling the clichés about Native Americans that this film has disseminated (*BG* 126).[27] The troupe's lesson appears to sink in, because soon after the play, Fool's Hip's residents begin a bowling tournament that ends with the destruction of Fool's Hip (*BG* 143, 152, 158). That this destruction is not merely physical but also metaphorical, implying the destruction of Fool's Hip as a simulacrum, is intimated by Cat Stand's striptease while slamming the bowling ball into Fool's Hip. She takes a deep breath and finally takes off the flannel shirt she has been wearing ever since massaging all the milk from her breasts into toilets and showers rather than feeding it to her infant son. And in an act of colonial refusal, she reveals her "great brown breasts" and thereby restores her bodily integrity. For the commercial producers had forced her to bind her breasts in bandages "to look wholesome, like the cartoon pictures on the cartons"—to embody "pure homogenized goodness." Rather than dressing as "Dairyland's Indian Princess" and remaining dispossessed of her own body, Cat Stand "*un*dresse[s]." She regains ownership of her own body by making it visible as a site of sexuality and reproduction. She thus emancipates herself from a colonial subject position defined by the suppression of personal autonomy, sexuality, reproduction, and cultural distinctness. It is at this very moment of refusal and self-assertion that she for the first time scores three hundred points, slamming the ball on the lane with so much force that the wood splinters (*BG* 34, 35, 155–57; italics in original).

The destruction of Fool's Hip inspires the community's other inhabitants to take the first tentative steps toward collective self-fashioning and self-definition:

> This is the way it is: after the massacres and the cigar stores, we gathered around the fire, told stories and watched each other's faces for signs of ourselves.
> It was a third world country, but we called it the first.
> It was a good day to die, but nobody did. (*BG* 160)

For the first time since moving to the Indian Territories, the residents decide to deviate from the prewritten colonial script. They do not call the territories third world and refuse to die. And they do not judge each other's degree of *indianness* according to an externally defined scale of authenticity but begin to determine who they are and what it means to be Native American in the present by telling each other stories from their own lives, by comparing their life stories, hence trying to find themselves in each other. It is their appreciation of the multiplicity of Native experience and their respect for ways of Native living and being that they had previously disrespected for their supposed lack of authenticity that form the basis for a refusal of deeply internalized subjectivities and that lead to the establishment of more inclusive forms of belonging.

In the tradition of Fanon, Jones considers the writer to be the central weapon in the struggle against internalized forms of recognition and the colonial edifice of representations. The "colonized writer" has the power to "loosen up" in his art what Fanon has described as the "congealed" and "petrified" forms of culture that have emerged after a century of colonial domination and to "become the spokesperson for a new reality in action" (159, 172, 175). Like Vizenor's "postindian warrior," the colonized writer has the power to challenge colonial control over images of those colonized. Their writing has the potential to encourage a "tribal striptease"—for Vizenor, a prerequisite for the reappropriation of "captured images" and a "reversal" of "inventions" that makes "the inventors and consumers vanish" (*The Trickster of Liberty* 44, 47).[28] LP Deal is the writer in *The Bird Is Gone*, feverishly working on a manifesto in which he criticizes the colonized minds of the Indian Territories' residents and their subjugation to the subjectivities created by dominant culture (*BG* 15). As the novel's subtitle suggests, LP Deal's manifesto seems to correspond to *The Bird Is Gone*, which is why LP Deal might be conceived of as Jones's alter ego. LP Deal's (and Jones's) manifesto also evokes another Indigenous manifesto, *Peace, Power, Righteousness: An Indigenous Manifesto*, first published in 1998 by Indigenous scholar and activist Taiaiake Alfred. Alfred's manifesto thinks through in theory what Jones negotiates in his fiction. Just like *The Bird Is Gone*, Alfred proposes that decolonization cannot solely be achieved through a regaining of political space but depends on the "unravelling of a colonized Indian identity" and the "recover[y] of oneself as a true Native" (*Peace, Power* 6; see also 3, 4). He asks Indigenous people to cease their "tacit acceptance" of "the imposition of labels and definitions of identity on Indigenous people" by the settler state and to "reject the assumptions that legitimize their subjugation" (106–8). Alfred's manifesto, as well as Jones's/LP Deal's manifesto, propagates writing as a strategy to escape the definitional confines and to—in Vizenor's words—"contend with manifest manners, the 'authentic' summaries of ethnology, and the curse of racialism and modernism in the ruins of representation" (*Manifest Manners* 13). In short, writing is presented as a way to challenge the "terms" of colonial discourse itself and to imagine possible alternative futures.

The Bird Is Gone suggests that overcoming colonial oppression requires the intense engagement of the colonized writer with the dominant language itself. Besides writing the manifesto, LP Deal works on "the terms he was dictating to America—transcriptions of clippings from newspapers and history books, done up in alphabetical order, like the entries in a dictionary" (*BG* 158). These terms are likely to be the glossary appended to the main narrative of *The Bird Is Gone*—that is, to LP Deal's manifesto. This glossary calls the user's attention to the arbitrariness of meaning. Meaning is determined by those in power, but its instability means that it can be changed in an act of Native empowerment. The glossary gives examples of such linguistic acts of self-empowerment. "Vanishing Indians," for instance, are redefined as "masters of camouflage" (*BG* 172). And "full-blood" comes to mean the degree of blood alcohol rather than the blood degree as defined by federal law (*BG* 165). "By attributing a new signified, i.e. new meaning, to signifiers . . . the entire sign is dissolved from its fixed place in colonial discourse," as Kristina Baudemann observes.

Jones's frequent placement of words *sous rature* ("under erasure") in the tradition of Jacques Derrida similarly serves to point to the arbitrariness of meaning and, moreover, to the necessity for the colonized subject to question the accepted usage of colonial designations. In her preface to Derrida's *Of Grammatology*, Gayatri Spivak explains the use of *sous rature*: "Since the word is inaccurate, it is crossed out. Since it is necessary, it remains legible. . . . In examining familiar things we come to such unfamiliar conclusions that our very language is twisted and bent even as it guides us. Writing 'under erasure' is the mark of this contortion" (xxxii). Placing familiar words on paper and then assessing whether or not they accurately represent the things for which they stand is both aesthetic and political praxis. By using *sous rature*, Jones proposes that colonial designations need to be overwritten rather than simply erased. As he writes in his letter to prospective Native writers, "Overwrite the world with *us*. Because we are everywhere. We're in the soil, yes, but we're in the future too. Insist upon that" ("Letter" 129; italics in original). For him, Native American writers are what Vizenor has described as postindian warriors, who overcome "the manifest manners of scriptural simulations and 'authentic' representations of the tribes," not by achieving an "authentic" presence or definitional precision but by critically observing existing simulations and the work they do in undermining a Native presence and by unsettling them (*Manifest Manners* 17; see also 5, 11–12). By inserting a glossary, Jones openly questions the very possibility of defining per se.[29] Definitions are incapable of capturing the things they describe or, to use Baudrillard's phrase, "the real." In this insight lies hope. This hope is expressed in the question and answer functioning as a bridge between the novel's ending—the residents of Fool's Hip listening to one another's stories and watching one another's faces—and LP Deal's "terms":

Is this how it begins?
    yes. (*BG* 161; italics and font in original)

Native scholar Joanne Barker has claimed "that the political and social efficacy of decolonization projects . . . rest[s] *principally* and *principledly* on the radical reformation of Native social and interpersonal relations" (*Native Acts* 227; italics in original). The ending of *The Bird Is Gone* seconds Barker's insistence on the need to reform Native social relations. However, it challenges the oft-voiced conviction that alternative definitions of Native culture and identities from within the Native community itself are needed in order to achieve decolonization and self-determination (see, e.g., Barker, *Native Acts* 225). Jones's novel rather suggests that trying to define Native American identity in precise terms, both externally and internally, is from the outset doomed to failure.

Both Hausman and Jones assign an important role to the past in the affirmative reconstruction of Indigenous identity with which settler colonial designations are to be overwritten. What they share with Fanon is the rejection of a nostalgic past in the form of traditionalist practices going back to a time before colonization that the latter describes as "some congealed mass of noble gestures . . . less and less connected with the reality of the people" (168). This is the kind of past to which the Misfits seek to return by going back to the motherland. It is the past the residents of the Indian Territories seek to re-create as the basis for a new pan-Indian identity. They turn so-called traditions, supposedly untainted by colonialism, into the yardstick for determining Native identity and communal belonging in the present but do not realize that their "antiquated attachment" to a nostalgic past "divert[s] attention away from the present and future needs of Indigenous populations" (Coulthard 147). Such a past, as Barker argues, is "unknowable" and "unattainable." It is gone, like the bird in the title of Jones's novel.[30] There is no "possibility of knowledge and authenticity before history and change affected them" (*Native Acts* 221, 228). Reliance on traditionalism implies stasis (a "house of death") rather than a dynamic movement into the future (a "house of life").

Such rejection of traditionalism as a resource for identity formation, however, does not mean that both novels negate the usefulness of the past in the struggle against the oppressive structures of colonialism and for the construction of Native peoplehood. Right below the epigraph containing Sartre's notion of refusal in *The Bird Is Gone* the reader finds another epigraph by the Afrofuturist science fiction writer Samuel Delany. As Delaney states, the past must be exhausted to finish with the present and, by implication, to move into the future. In both Hausman and Jones, the past is presented not as past but as coexisting with the present and the future; it is, as Rifkin has phrased it in a different context, "a horizon for unfolding dynamics of being and becoming" (*Settler Time* 171).[31] From the perspective of both these novels, past and present are overlapping temporalities, characterized by various forms of dispossession, by "the *longue durée* of settler colonial violence" (*Settler Time* 156; see also 149). The dispossession experienced in the Removal era resonates with the current experiences of Native cultural appropriation; in fact, Removal highlights the destructive impact of current modes of appropriation on Native forms of being and belonging. Hausman's and Jones's novels also emphasize the past's significance for the desubjectification of the colonized subject. All Indigenous characters across historical time have experienced some form of appropriation. Such cross-temporal experiences of dispossession are presented in both texts as having the potential to "decoloniz[e] the mind," to use Barker's words ("Decolonizing the Mind" 208). They are also repositories of identificatory potential and foster group cohesion in the struggle against colonial subjection and co-optation.

The future is imagined in Hausman and Jones as deeply embedded in past and present experiences of appropriation. On the one hand, both novels emphasize the cross-temporal, perpetual nature of Native appropriation, visualized by the lemniscate on the cover of *Riding the Trail of Tears*. On the other hand, both texts suggest that Indigenous futures emerge through what James Clifford has described as "a kind of return [to the past] without going backward in time" (42). In both novels, anger is the sentiment expressing the interconnection between the past and the future.[32] "Anger," as Sara Ahmed argues, "is constructed . . . as a response to the injustice of racism; as a vision of the future; as a translation of pain into knowledge; and as being loaded with information and energy. Crucially, anger is not simply defined in relationship to a past, but as opening up the future." She continues, "In other words, being against something does not end with 'that which one is against.'. . . Being against something is also being for something, but something that has yet to be articulated or is not yet" (175). In *Riding the Trail of Tears* and *The Bird Is Gone*, the anger expressed by the protagonists manifests a vision of the future in which Native Americans will look at one another, rather than being alienated from one another, and in which tribally specific and pan-Native collective identities are created from within on the basis of a wide range of Indigenous experiences of appropriation across historical time. This identity "has yet to be articulated or is not yet"; it is situated outside the diegetic worlds of both novels.

When defining Afrofuturism, Mark Dery wonders whether "a community whose past has been deliberately rubbed out, and whose energies have subsequently been consumed by the search for legible traces of its history, [can] imagine possible futures?" (180). Hausman and Jones employ the genre of speculative fiction to suggest the imagining of Indigenous futures by revisiting and drawing on the past—the history of Indian Removal. They do so to disrupt and reject the romantic and linear settler colonial narrations of *indianness* that lead to an ossification of Native identity and end with the museumization of Native Americans. Through their novels, they seek to identify possible ways of achieving decolonization, Indigenous self-determination, and the transformation of the social fabric of Native communities.

Epilogue

IN THIS EPILOGUE I pursue a twofold purpose. On the one hand, I want to create a dialogue between the visions of Native peoplehood and Indigenous futurity that the Native Removal writings discussed in the previous chapters develop. On the other hand, I intend to engage in a final, in-depth meditation on the reasons why Native writers across the tribal spectrum have over the past centuries felt compelled to go back to just this particular historical act of settler colonial violence. To shed light on these issues, I turn to one of the most recent Native Removal writings, Gerald Vizenor's *Chair of Tears: A Novel* (2012), a highly ironic and self-reflexive fictionalization of Indian Removal.

The works I have discussed in each of my five chapters have in common that they all criticize the terms of colonial discourse and expose the racism and self-interest that they see at the heart of federal Indian law and settler colonial regimes of domination and ownership. They differ, however, in their judgment of the usefulness of non-Native forms of subjectivity in the struggle for Native rights and self-determination. John Ross, Elias Boudinot, John Ridge, John Rollin Ridge, Rachel Caroline Eaton, and John Milton Oskison are mainly concerned in their works with how Native political autonomy, land rights, and culture can be recognized by the settler state. They use their writings to mediate and navigate between tribally specific epistemologies, histories, cultural practices, and forms of belonging and the Native subjectivities constructed by federal Indian law and state law with the objective to deflect the US politics of dispossession. They repurpose settler colonial legal rhetoric if it suits Native political ends or corresponds to their own, tribally specific ideas of peoplehood while disavowing those US impositions of legal subjectivity that they perceive to be corrupted, self-serving, and to the detriment of Native survival and flourishing. In their Removal novels, Robert Conley and Diane Glancy move beyond the territorial boundaries of the settler nation, whose body of law concerning Native Americans and whose celebration of an unfettered individualism they critique severely. They engage Indian Removal to reflect on whether international law with its more capacious concept of self-determination could function as an alternative source of recognition for Native Americans. They gauge to what extent the notion of indigeneity can be useful to resist dispossession and to advance struggles for Native rights on the domestic level.

In comparison to these writers, Sharon Ewell Foster, Zelda Lockhart, Blake Hausman, and Stephen Graham Jones appear far more skeptical of the usefulness of non-Native forms of subjectivity in the struggle against colonial subjugation, disenfranchisement, and dispossession. Their Removal writings explore the psychological and real costs of Native adoption of and reliance on settler colonial frameworks of belonging and recognition, and they emphasize that the internalization of Native subjectivities by Indigenous individuals and communities devastates Native kinships networks, destroys communities, and petrifies Native cultures and identities. They appeal to Native individuals and collectives to remember that decolonization also requires attention to the psyche of the colonized subject. Native empowerment through self-assertion, self-definition, and self-representation on the basis of Native values and shared historical experience, the practice of tribal culture, and a commitment to Native communities are, hence, central to their works. Despite such emphasis on self-empowerment, these authors also point out how difficult it is for the survivors of (ongoing) territorial and cultural appropriation to formulate collective identities and notions of an Indigenous futurity outside the disruptive influence of the settler state and in rejection of its blood ideologies and clichéd notions of *indianness*. Significantly, both Hausman's and Jones's novels end at the very moment when settler colonial ascriptions have been deconstructed but when the precise forms of a continued existence beyond these ascriptions are diegetically still located in the future.

My case studies of Native Removal writing across the centuries thus reveal that peoplehood is a dynamic and shifting category and that survival can take many forms, even what, in a decontextualized reading, could be interpreted as assimilation (as in Oskison's *The Singing Bird*, for instance) or acquiescence to a racial system grounded in the discourse of blood (as in Foster's *Abraham's Well*, for example). Each of the Removal texts I have discussed needs to be viewed as a singular product of a specific individual who returns to Indian Removal at a particular moment in time and in response to a distinct constellation of external and internal forces. But it would simplify the complex politics of Native Removal writing if one merely insisted on its tribal and historical specificity and ignored its representation of Removal as a synecdoche for dispossession and hence as an experience common to all Native Americans and Indigenous people in other settler nations. While Native Removal writers do vary in their respective articulation of how precisely to respond to and resist dispossession and of how to structure Indigenous relations with one another, the settler state, and (from the 1990s onward) the international community, they all agree on the tremendous impact of settler colonial dispossession on Native forms of living, being, and belonging. Moreover, they all represent resistance to dispossession as an integral aspect of enslaved/colonized existence and as a prerequisite for moving into the future and, hence, for survival. Besides addressing Removal from a distinctly Cherokee perspective, in *Pushing the Bear,* for instance, Glancy highlights the potential of the Trail of Tears to forge a pan-Native/Indigenous identity. Being Blackfeet and hence not a member of a tribal community immediately affected by Indian Removal, Jones frames Removal in *The Bird Is Gone* less as a tribally specific event than as a foundational moment in a perpetual process of settler colonial dispossession that has encompassed both tangible and intangible forms of Native property and affected a multitude of tribal communities across the United States. Foster and Lockhart, in turn, both address Indian Removal from a distinctly Cherokee/Choctaw perspective and conceptualize it as constituting the ground for other forms of dispossession, most notably bodily dispossession—that is, the enslavement of people of African descent. To them, (re)turning to Indian Removal means to think together forms of divestment usually conceived of as distinct from each other. In all these textual examples, therefore, Indian Removal not only represents a tribally specific set of experiences, but it also functions as a universal trope of Native/Indigenous, even Afro-Native experience. And it is in this latter sense that the #NoDAPL protesters at Standing Rock, with whom I begin this book, referred to Indian Removal as well. They invoked the Trail of Tears less as a tribally specific historical episode than as an experience common to *all* colonized subjects and communities. For them, the Trail of Tears evokes resilience and capacity for resistance. So it is viewed as having the power to foster mobilization and identification across tribal communities and as having the potential to draw the support of other oppressed groups.

Gerald Vizenor (Anishinaabe) uses his fictional work to reflect extensively on the function of Indian Removal as a universal trope of Native experience. His *Chair of Tears: A Novel* (2012)[1] serves as a source of inspiration for a final, in-depth meditation on the meaning of Indian Removal for the present that each Native Removal writer moves in and on the role of Native Removal writing, in particular fiction, in the Native American struggle against dispossession.

Chair of Tears revolves around a reenactment of Indian Removal in the present time, which takes place on the campus of the University of Minnesota and is performed by Indigenous professors of Native American studies dressed in their twenty-first-century professional attire. What this present-day Removal has in common with its historical role model is its involuntary nature. The Native professors are "removed" from their private offices. However, they are "removed" not—as one would expect based on the Native Removal writings discussed so far—by settler colonial forces but by a Native American trickster figure and the novel's protagonist, Captain Shammer—the new chairman of the Native American Indian Studies Department and the so-called Chair of Tears:

> Captain Shammer delivered the treaty termination notice that removed the faculty from private offices to the conference room one early morning in late autumn. The fragile color of the leaves shivered in the bright sunlight and reflected on the dead river. The faculty was anxious, a common trait on the entire campus, slow and moody, gloomy, a rather solemn procession of native scholars in the throes of an authentic academic removal, but the obvious declarations of resistance were only tentative. (Vizenor, *Chair of Tears* 38–39)[2]

The novel's depiction of the professors' ensuing walk from their private offices to the conference room is saturated with irony and criticism. Like the digital characters in Hausman's *Riding the Trail of Tears* or the inhabitants of Fool's Hip in Jones's *The Bird Is Gone*, the protagonists of Shammer's Trails of Tears behave like they are supposed to do upon being "removed": like victims. Rather than resisting Shammer's "removal," they grudgingly accept their fates, concentrating on retaining their individual gain (private offices) and academic status (reputation). Their "tentative" interventions are limited to a rehearsal of American legal terminology ("treaty rights"). And it is such behavior that makes Shammer's "removal" "authentic." The Native characters appear to be acting out the roles laid out for them in the supposedly authentic Removal narratives penned by the colonizer.

In fact, the Native professors' complicity with acts of domination long predates Shammer's "removal." As the narrator emphasizes, the Native American Indian Studies Department was created by the settler state to control and regulate the production and dissemination of Native culture and history and as evidence of its multicultural recognition politics. The department's Native scholars have been playing along with the state's policies for many years: they have performed their roles as *indians* and have never resisted the fabrications and containment of knowledge about Indigenous cultures and lives. Until Shammer's arrival, they practiced a "politics of atonement and victimry." They tacitly accepted the policies of the former departmental chairmen, who turned tribal cultures into simulations ("ersatz traditions") and fashioned themselves as the victims of a violent settler colonial history in exchange for "the privileges of tenure and the expectation of treaty rights to private offices" (*CT* 24, 27, 28, 29, 32–34, 36–37).

Shammer's reenactment of the Trail of Tears functions as a scathing critique of "authentic" American Removal narratives. What is more, it serves to expose the Native professors' performance of *indianness*, their compliance, and hence their complicity with the forces that strive for their continued subjugation. Shammer invokes a *historical event* that still haunts many Native communities and that most Native Americans are fully conscious of. Through the jarring juxtaposition of the struggle and resistance that the Trail of Tears embodies with the professors' own victimry and anxiety, and their tacit enjoyment of the privileges awarded to them by the American educational system, Shammer throws into relief their blatant neglect of what Weaver has called "communitism" in favor of the individualistic ethos of Western academia (xiii). By creating a subtext of resistance and determined struggle for the perseverance of Native peoplehood that operates in stark contrast to the professors' passivity and acquiescence, Shammer puts them to shame for the role they play in stabilizing the structures of colonial domination.[3]

Shammer also employs Indian Removal as it metonymically embodies a *structure* that constitutes the beating heart of settler colonialism: dispossession. Indigenous studies scholars such as Audra Simpson and Glen Coulthard have defined settler colonialism as "an ongoing structure of dispossession" and as a "form of structured dispossession" with the objective of eliminating Indigenous peoples (Simpson, *Mohawk Interruptus* 74; Coulthard 7). By using the Trail of Tears as a trope, as a synecdoche for all kinds of experiences of dispossession extending beyond particular tribal historical experiences, Shammer makes faculty members aware of the parallels that exist between past and present forms of dispossession. In fact, by going back to the past, he makes present forms of dispossession legible. Read in light of Indian Removal, the state's invention and containment of knowledge about Indigenous cultures within Minnesota's educational system becomes recognizable as a form of dispossession. Thus perspectivized, it needs to be viewed as a continuation, rather than a renunciation, of earlier colonial policies. Just like Removal in the past, dispossessive educational policies in the present exert a tremendous influence on Native modes of subjectivity and are often to the detriment of Indigenous forms of living, being, and belonging, as the Native professors' behavior and the sense of "native absence" in the department highlight so vividly (*CT* 40).

Shammer's invocation of Indian Removal to decolonize the Native American Indian Studies Department and the professors' minds eventually shows the desired effect. After having completed Shammer's program of decolonization, the Native professors in *Chair of Tears* "[renounce] the sentiments of academic treaty rights of privacy, and instead [celebrate] survivance." They form a self-determined Native academic community with a strong sense of rights and Native liberty (*CT* 49).

Chair of Tears hence suggests that Indian Removal as a literary and political practice is so effective because it has both a tribally specific and a pan-tribal universal dimension. It references a particular historical event reminiscent and evocative of tremendous tribal suffering, resistance, and a specific set of Native subjectivities; yet at the same time Removal embodies a universal structure detached from a specific time and place. Removal in this latter sense encapsulates the common experience of dispossession that is "perpetually incomplete," continuing unabated (Byrd et al. 2, 3).[4] Vizenor's novel illustrates that the awareness of cross-temporal experiences of dispossession as being closely related to and in fact growing out of each other has the power to "decoloniz[e] the mind"—that is, it facilitates recognizing one's own subject position in an ongoing structure of domination (Barker, "Decolonizing the Mind" 208).

The way Vizenor conceptualizes Indian Removal in *Chair of Tears* is helpful for understanding the enduring appeal of Native Removal writing and its significance as a critical practice of resistance. Just like Indian Removal itself, the writings about it negotiate both the tribally specific and the pan-tribal universal. All Native authors discussed in this study (re)turn to the history of Removal to respond to specific immediate political concerns and legal debates at the moment of their writing. Going back to the time of Removal enables them to critically reflect on the modes of subjectivity that the settler nation produced in the wake of dispossession and their effect on tribal group identification and practices of belonging up until the moment of their writing, reaching down to the most intimate levels of interaction. Engaging the history of Removal also enables Native writers to gauge the limits of settler colonial ascriptions and knowledge frameworks and to develop tribally specific, alternative modalities of living, being, and belonging, sometimes in dialogue with and at other times in opposition to settler colonial interpellations. It allows them think through forms of Native peoplehood across historical time and to assess the internal and external prerequisites for Native persistence as peoples.

By engaging Indian Removal, Native writers also expound on the pan-tribal universal: in particular they unearth the hidden parallels and argumentative continuities between past, present, and, as in speculative Removal fiction, future forms of dispossession. Native writers represent Removal as an *ongoing* process—a temporal structure rather than a finished event—that affects Indigenous peoples from all settler nations and that is inextricably intertwined with forms of colonial dispossession traditionally seen as unrelated to Indigenous peoples, such as enslavement. In their writings, Removal becomes a foil through which the ongoing structures of settler colonialism are made legible and their devastating effects on Indigenous peoples—their cultures, psyches, and forms of belonging—become understandable. Due to this universal dimension of Removal, Native Removal writings are repositories of identificatory potential. Through their articulation of the experience of dispossession and the struggle against colonial subjection and co-optation, they speak, and appeal, to Indigenous peoples across the tribal spectrum and also to other oppressed communities, such as African American and Afro-Native communities. They have the power to foster group cohesion. While there is great disagreement in these writings on the measures to be taken in the fight against dispossession and subjugation, which modes of subjectivity to rely on, and which forms of Native peoplehood to endorse, there prevails a strong sense that dispossession needs to be confronted and resisted. Common resistance to dispossession, in fact, is elevated in those texts as being constitutive of what it means to be Native American. Glancy's *Pushing the Bear* even demonstrates that a return to the history of Indian Removal can foster the embrace of new modes of legal subjectivity. For the novel's negotiation of the potential of the language of indigeneity, Indigenous rights, and pan-Indigenous collaboration immediately grows out of its representation of the Trail of Tears and Cherokee resistance to it.

Dynamically engaging the past of Indian Removal is thus a critical practice for engaging with the tribally specific *and* the pan-tribal universal Indigenous present and for imagining and enacting Indigenous futures in which regimes of dispossession are overturned. Functioning as imaginative spaces for envisioning forms of Native peoplehood and strategies of resistance to dispossession, Native Removal writings work against what Jodi Byrd has termed the continual deferral of Indigenous peoples and nations "into a past that never happened and a future that will never come" (*Transit* 221). Storying Removal, to borrow Rifkin's formulation, serves to "remak[e] the potentially rupturing effects of settler colonial violence . . . into part of the affective repertoire through which indigeneity persists as such despite the force of non-native occupation" (*Settler Time* 46).

From the body of Native Removal writings, fictional Removal texts stand out in terms of sheer number. This raises the question as to why Native American authors have tended to turn to fiction when seeking to represent Removal. *Chair of Tears* is, once again, useful for addressing this question. Throughout the novel, Vizenor has various characters emphasize the significance of historical storytelling (in contrast to Western forms of historiography). Once cured by Shammer of her former habit of always imagining narratives of victimry, Trauma Queen, as the Chair of Tears fittingly calls her, explains in a rousing speech to her fellow students that the only way for Native Americans to counter American narratives of victimry is to write *"stories of survivance . . . supported by documents and actual testimony"* (*CT* 126; italics in original). And from the many buyers eventually interested in purchasing the department, Shammer, himself a storyteller, selects the Earthdivers, "an association of native storiers," because they promise to "overturn" "[t]he notion that history is a more significant narrative than native stories and literature" (*CT* 132).

Chair of Tears considers Native stories and literature superior to Western historiography for three reasons. First, while the latter tends to result in "historical representations of absence" working toward *"the closure of memory as mere victimry,"* the former help Native listeners and readers establish "epochs of memory" (*CT* 11, 111, 125; italics in original). Such epochs are broad units of time and stand in stark contrast to the "sharp succession between [the] temporal moments" that are constitutive of what James Clifford has called "a Western historical ontology" (Harootunian 124; Clifford 27). Vizenor's phrase "epochs of memory" also resembles Clifford's image of "looping lines of recollection and specific paths forward," which he develops to explain the alternative temporalities of Native forms of storytelling (Clifford 25). Collating past, present, and future, these alternative temporalities challenge the colonial idea of modernity as "unfold[ing] in a linear, developmental fashion with the non-European world placed either at some earlier stage of development or outside of history altogether" (Bhandar, *Colonial Lives of Property* 23). Second, unlike Western historiography, Native stories depict the lives of ordinary people, such as Shammer's Grandmother Quiver's "unnamed mother," and hence spell out the impact of settler colonialism not only on communities and individual community leaders but also on average community members and their most intimate relations with one another (*CT* 14). Third, the narrator tells the reader that, in comparison to conventional histories, Native stories and literature have far greater power over their readers and listeners: while being deeply grounded in fact, negotiating history, law, and politics (using "documents and actual testimony"), they also create imaginary worlds in which the supposedly impossible becomes possible (*CT* 21–22).[5]

It is particularly this last aspect that distinguishes nonfictional and fictional Native Removal writings. Immediately responding to the legal and political actions of the settler nation, for instance, Ross and Boudinot often were compelled to accept the authority of settler law as a given and to dress their claims and resistance in the language of Western law. They had to carefully navigate when trying to insert Indigenous interpretations of the world, as well as Indigenous ideas of sovereignty and belonging. As a historian trained in Western academia, Eaton also felt bound when composing her history of Indian Removal: by the rules and conventions of Western historiography—its archives, its focus on community leaders rather than on average people, and its grounding in the idea of history/modernity progressing in linear fashion. And, as a recent study of the language and arguments used during the #NoDAPL protests has revealed, to be heard by the courts, Native protesters had to move away from framing the harm done to them by the construction of the pipeline in terms of tribal epistemologies and increasingly relied on Western legal language (Delaney 303, 322, 328).

Native stories, by contrast, are *un*bound. They have the power to imagine the disruption and dismantling of forms of subjectivity imposed by the settler state, the refashioning of the Indigenous self and its relations to others. They have the power to imagine alternative forms of living, being, and belonging that do not conform to the settler colonial order with its racial regimes of ownership and modes of governance and that hence have been suppressed by it. Not forced to be politically or legally efficacious, they can use a vocabulary other than that offered to them by Western law and politics and can advance alternative epistemologies and interpretations of the world. They can think through alternative grammars of resistance. In short, they can imagine the world as it could be. "Only in a native trickster story," the narrator in *Chair of Tears* explains, "would my cousin [Shammer] be named an academic administrator" (*CT* 21–22). By using the force of imagination to unhinge deeply ingrained structures of domination, Native fictional texts, in particular, have tremendous transformative power. They can "rouse [the reader's] sense of liberty" in ways that nonfictional texts often cannot (*CT* 15).

In *Chair of Tears*, Captain Shammer teaches his students that only Native stories of survivance have such transformative and affective force

(*CT* 126). He clearly functions as Vizenor's mouthpiece in his demand that Native writers need to resist the demands of the reading public and stop writing stories of victimry, as the latter "*are a cultural and psychological burden, and the causes of historical absence*" (*CT* 126; italics in original; see also 125).[6] As my contextualized readings of Native Removal writings throughout this book have demonstrated, all these writings, be they fictional or not, are "stories of survivance" in the Vizenorian sense of the term: while remembering and rewriting the past from the perspective of those silenced and obscured and thus "*honor[ing] the memory of traumatic experiences,*" they cannot be reduced to trauma narratives (*CT* 126; italics in original). They go back to the past to critically revise it from an Indigenous point of view and to (re)examine and (re)create both present and future. They go back to foster a sense of Native agency, sovereignty, and persistence.

"Communities can and must reconfigure themselves, drawing selectively on remembered pasts," Clifford claims. Such pasts are necessary to "convince and coerce insiders and outsiders, often in power-charged, unequal situations, to accept the autonomy of a 'we'" (62). Indigenous scholars, in particular, have emphasized the significant role that stories and literature play in processes of Native collective identity formation and the alternative temporalities they establish. "We create and recreate ourselves in the past, present, and future in story," Anishinaabe scholar Jill Doerfler says. "The power of stories cannot be measured. The relationship between past, present, and future cannot be separated; it is unbreakable and calls to mind the ways in which familial relationships intertwine individuals together in enduring ways across time and space" (ix). In a similar vein, Craig S. Womack (Muskogee Creek-Cherokee) explains, "The ongoing expression of a tribal voice, through imagination, language, and literature, contributes to keeping sovereignty alive in the citizens of a nation and gives sovereignty a meaning that is defined within the tribe rather than by external sources." Stories, he continues, "help [a community] imagine who they are as a people, how they came to be, and what cultural values they wish to preserve" (14, 26). My reading of Native Removal writings across the centuries has made visible that Indian Removal has become what Rogers M. Smith has called "a story of peoplehood" (*Stories of Peoplehood* 45). It is a story transmitting to its listeners and readers a tribally specific yet also pan-tribal universal sense of belonging.

It encourages them to continue to fight against dispossession in all its forms; to disrupt or even break free of settler colonial ways of knowing, seeing, and thinking; and to define the contours of what it means to be Native/Indigenous from within.

The preceding thoughts finally also shed light on the #NoDAPL protesters' frequent invocation of Indian Removal and the Trail of Tears at Standing Rock. Framing the incidents at Standing Rock in light of the history of Removal served to orient Native protesters with respect to the events unfolding around them as well as to their own role in them. It made Standing Rock legible not so much as an exceptional incident but as just another act of settler colonial violence and as just another attack on Native sovereignty, lives, cultural practices, and forms of belonging. Invoking Removal reminded Native Americans across the United States of both incidents of expulsion and forced relocation in their own tribal histories and the pan-tribal history of dispossession that extends into present and future. Invoking Removal fostered critical self-reflection, a sense of group identity and unity, and collaborative practices of resistance. Invoking Indian Removal also generated hope and confidence in the endurance of the Standing Rock Sioux as a people.

I end this book by turning to Joy Harjo's poetry collection *An American Sunrise*, which I highlight in my introduction as one of the most recent Native Removal writings. Harjo, too, conceives of Indian Removal as both a momentous event for her own tribal community and as a structure that continues until the here and now of her writing and that has affected Indigenous peoples all over North America as well as across the world (xv). This understanding of Removal is also encapsulated in the last lines of her poem "Cehotosakvtes," which contains a song two beloved women allegedly sang along the Trail of Tears whenever any of their band members faltered:

> *Cehotosakvtes*
> *Chenaorakvtes Momis komet*
> *Awatchken ohapeyakares hvlwen*
> Do not get tired.
> Don't be discouraged. Be determined.
> Come. Together let's go toward the highest place. (99; italics in original)

"Cehotosakvtes" derives its power from its mobilization of Muscogee Creek Removal history, cultural traditions, and language praxis and its emphasis on Native American unity, determination, and resistance in the fight against settler colonial dispossession. The poem also testifies to the ongoing power and significance of Native Removal writing—to its capacity of engaging the past to (re)envision both present and future.

Notes

INTRODUCTION

1. I am conscious that the term "Indian Removal" was coined by proponents of the policy and is an extremely ill-fitting and unfortunate designation. On the one hand, "Indian," as it was used when the policy was devised and implemented, was a settler colonial fabrication and did not represent Indigenous forms of living and being. On the other hand, "Removal" reflects neither the settler colony's agency nor the force and violence that it meant for the affected Native communities. Meaning something like emigration or relocation from one place to another, "Removal" is in fact a euphemism, a cover-up for a policy seeking to expulse and forcibly relocate, and on many occasions even exterminate, the communities targeted (Banner 192–93). Having said this, I still use the term "Indian Removal" in this book, as it has come to stand for a particular policy and era in Native-settler relations and is used by Indigenous peoples themselves when referring to that time. Native Removal writing is hence the literature written by Natives that engages with this particular policy. When I refer to other "removals" before or after Indian Removal, I always place the term in quotation marks to emphasize its settler colonial genesis and ill fit with reality.

2. Writing about the racial subject, Bhandar and Bhandar have also emphasized that "there is an inescapable relation between processes of subjectivation and material forms of dispossession" ("Cultures of Dispossession"). See also Alyosha Goldstein's astute analysis of the legacy of Removal policy in past and contemporary neoliberal forms of Native dispossession, in particular in adoption cases ("Jurisprudence").

3. Indian Removal has also figured prominently in Native media productions. See, for instance, the "Trail of Tears" installment of the PBS series *We Shall Remain*, directed by Chris Eyre (Cheyenne and Arapaho).

4. See my discussion of Native conceptualizations of peoplehood later in this chapter. Other disciplines have also started to reflect on "the complexities of the relationship between material engagement and group identity" (Klevnäs 7). See, for instance, the introduction to the edited volume by archaeologists Alison Klevnäs and Charlotte Hedenstierna-Jonson.

5. The writers I examine are not the only ones drawing on Indian Removal in their work. Beginning with the 1922 poem "The Trail of Tears," written by Ruth Margaret Muskrat, whose paternal ancestors walked the Trail of Tears, Native

American poets have made Indian Removal the topic of their poetry. See, for example, Sherman Alexie's "Poem," Qwo-Li Driskill's "Love Poems: 1838–1839," and Linda Hogan's "Trail of Tears: Our Removal." Indian Removal is also at the narrative center of a number of Native family histories and autobiographical texts. See, for example, Glenn J. Twist's "The Dispossession" and "The Promised Land" from his story collection *Boston Mountain Tales: Stories from a Cherokee Family*, Jerry Ellis's *Walking the Trail: One Man's Journey along the Cherokee Trail of Tears* (1991), and Wilma Mankiller's *Mankiller: A Chief and Her People* (1993). Native writers of young adult fiction have published Indigenous versions of Indian Removal to provide young readers with alternative Removal (hi)stories. These include Beatrice Harrell's *Longwalker's Journey* (1999), Joseph Bruchac's *The Journal of Jesse Smoke: A Cherokee Boy* (2001), and Tim Tingle's *How I Became a Ghost: A Choctaw Trail of Tears Story* (2013). Finally, archives have been making available an ever-growing body of Indigenous historical sources on Indian Removal, such as the "Family Stories from the Trail of Tears" collection digitized by the American Native Press Archives and Sequoyah Research Center, as well as the works of Native historians such as DeWitt Clinton Duncan and Emmett Starr. The publication of further Native Removal novels, such as Le Triplett's *American Exodus: A Historical Novel about the Indian Removal* (2006) and Daniel Heath Justice's *The Way of Thorn and Thunder: The Kynship Chronicles* (2011), testifies to the ongoing significance of Indian Removal for Native writers.

6. The Trail of Tears evokes multiple other "removals," such as the Potawatomis' Trail of Death or the Long Walk of the Navajos (Riley and Carpenter 876). Indigenous intellectuals also read more recent government policies, such as the termination and relocation programs of the 1950s and 1960s, as yet another forced "removal" (Mankiller 62–74; Conley, *The Cherokee Nation* 204).

7. In its approach, my work has resonance with Daniel Heath Justice's *Our Fire Survives the Storm* (2006), Joshua Nelson's *Progressive Traditions* (2014), and Kirby Brown's *Stoking the Fire* (2018), which all address Cherokee conceptions of peoplehood and ongoingness and address some of the same writers (especially Ross, Boudinot, and Eaton). Yet those works have more in common with each other than with this monograph, working as explicitly Cherokee nationalist genealogies. In its focus on both politics and aesthetics, my work is also indebted to Lucy Maddox's 1991 monograph *Removals*. Her work, however, focuses on nineteenth-century American literary responses to Indian Removal and therefore follows a different intellectual trajectory.

8. As Denson states, the "Trail of Tears remains a safe and settled topic among non-Indians, one that allows white Americans to acknowledge suffering and injustice in the national past without having to reconsider much of anything in the present" (*Monuments to Absence* 194).

9. Notable exceptions are the scholarly contributions by Mark Rifkin and Lionel Larré, who have offered insightful readings of and comments on the writings of John Ross, Elias Boudinot, and John Milton Oskison (Rifkin, *Manifesting America*, "'For the Wrongs,'" "Making Peoples into Populations"; Larré, Introduction, "John Milton Oskison").

10. In an interview, Lockhart talks about her family's hidden Native heritage: her maternal great-grandmother was of Choctaw and possibly Creek heritage (Greenlee-Donnell). Sharon Ewell Foster also claims to be of mixed heritage. Her great-grandmother was Cherokee ("Q&A with *Abrahams's Well* Author Sharon Ewell Foster").

11. Foster's Removal novel has been analyzed only by Tan; Lockhart's *Cold Running Creek* has so far been interpreted only by Deetjen, and Vigil and Miles.

12. The book here speaks to the emerging and significant field of Indigenous Black studies, including Rifkin's *Fictions of Land and Flesh*, Tiffany King's *The Black Shoals*, and works by historians such as Tiya Miles and Kyle T. Mays.

13. See the works of Daniel F. Littlefield, Patrick Minges, Tiya Miles, Celia E. Naylor, Barbara Krauthammer, and Christina Snyder and the volume on African-Native American literature edited by Jonathan Brennan.

14. For a discussion of the relationship between law and Native American literature as well as a scholarly overview, see Meyer, "The Marshall Trilogy and Its Legacies."

15. In line with Duncan Ivison, Paul Patton, and Will Sanders, I consider "Western political thought" to be "that body of political, legal and social theory developed by European, American, Australian and New Zealand authors and practitioners from the beginning of the modern period in Europe to the present" (2).

16. For a longer discussion of Indigenous uses of Western political thought in Indigenous rights claims, see Ivison et al. (2).

17. See also discussions about the appropriateness of the concept of "sovereignty" in Barker's "Sovereignty" and Deloria and Lytle. For a detailed overview of the history of the concept of sovereignty in both Western and Indigenous intellectual histories, see Carlson, *Imagining Sovereignty*, chapters 1 and 2.

18. Jeff Corntassel declares the concept of peoplehood to be an important step toward terminological decolonization and praises "its non-Western approach to identity, its flexibility, comprehensiveness, and allowance for cultural continuity and change" (94; see also Alfred and Corntassel 610, 614. For a reflection on nationhood versus peoplehood, see Carroll 81; Lyons, *X-Marks* 132–60). Billy Stratton and Frances Washburn have hailed the peoplehood matrix as "a new theory for American Indian literature" and "a useful method to analyze the dynamic and complex nature of American Indian literature" (51, 70; see also Carpenter, "Real Property and Peoplehood"). The concept of peoplehood has also gained increasing prominence in the social sciences. See Rogers M. Smith's monographs *Stories of Peoplehood: The Politics and Morals of Political Membership* (2003) and *Political Peoplehood: The Roles of Values, Interests, and Identities* (2015).

19. "All native peoples use 'people' to refer to themselves," Tom Holm has argued. "Several tribes use a word to convey 'peoplehood' or perhaps the 'way of the people.'" For instance, the term the Cherokees have used for themselves is *aniyunwiya*, which translates as "people" and "the principal people" ("Re: the peoplehood matrix").

20. The US Supreme Court has ruled that Native tribes are "a separate people" within the American polity (*United States v. Mazurie* qtd. in Carpenter et al. 1057). Scholars of international law have shown peoplehood to be capitalized on in the fight for Indigenous rights (Carpenter, "Real Property and Peoplehood" 348; Corntassel).

21. Thomas, in turn, based his concept of peoplehood on Edward H. Spicer's idea of "enduring peoples" to describe "human enclaves" emerging as a result of colonialism and having distinct languages, territories, and religions (qtd. in Holm et al. 11).

22. Rebecca Tsosie makes a similar point: "They [the Native nations] also know that their sovereignty depends upon a corollary notion of property" ("Land, Culture" 1306).

23. Holm and his colleagues see peoplehood as an alternative to the concept of nation, which they view as inextricably linked to modernity and as deeply imbued with Western interpretations of history and notions of political organization. They thus depart from trends in recent Indigenous studies scholarship to "[co-opt] the term's ['nation'] narrower conceptions to demonstrate how thoroughly it characterizes the numerous and varied tribes in the pre-contact and pre-colonial world" (Andersen 183). Indigenous scholars such as Audra Simpson ("Paths toward a Mohawk Nation"), Daniel Heath Justice ("The Necessity"; *Our Fire Survives the Storm*), and Scott Lyons ("Actually Existing Indian Nations"; *X-Marks*) emphasize that those designated by the settler nations as "'others' are and have always been nations" but highlight the fact that Indigenous nationhood draws from Indigenous teachings and responds to (neo)colonial realities (Andersen 183; Simpson, "Paths" 118, 221).

24. Herman Paul points out that White's statement about the centrality of the state for writing history is hyperbolic and should not be taken too literally (112).

25. In conceptualizing subjectivity, I rely in part on Louis Althusser's and Michel Foucault's theorizations of the subject and subjectivity as products of ideological state apparatuses and knowledge systems. In contrast to Althusser, I view the subject as an agent capable of resistance to dominant ideologies. For a recent comparative analysis of theories of subjectivity, see Blackman et al.

26. The only novel published in this time period is Denton R. Bedford's *Tsali* (1972).

27. Among the examples he cites are James Welch's protagonist Jim Loney (in *The Death of Jim Loney*) and Leslie Marmon Silko's Tayo (in *Ceremony*).

28. See, for instance, the publications on Indian Removal by Gary Moulton (*The Papers of Chief John Ross*, 1985), Theda Perdue (*Cherokee Editor: The Writings of Elias Boudinot*, 1996), Perdue and Michel D. Green (*The Cherokee Removal: A Brief History with Documents*, 1995), and Donna L. Akers ("Removing the Heart of the Choctaw People"), which not only made accessible Cherokee primary sources but also highlighted the legal dimensions of Removal and the human suffering it caused. It was also in the 1980s and 1990s that Native scholars such as Vine Deloria, David E. Wilkins, Robert A. Williams, and N. Bruce Duthu began

investigating federal Indian law versus Native American legal traditions and orders; they also emphasized Indigenous sovereignty and rights in light of an ongoing settler colonialism. See Deloria and Clifford M. Lytle's *American Indians, American Justice* (1983) and *The Nations Within* (1984), Deloria and Wilkins's *Tribes, Treaties, and Constitutional Tribulations* (1999), Williams's *The American Indian in Western Legal Thought* (1990) and *Linking Arms Together* (1997), and Duthu's "Implicit Divestiture" (1995).

29. The National Park Service's development of the national trail during the late 1980s and early 1990s also led to the founding of the Trail of Tears Association in 1993, with the aim to promote trail research, contribute to the development of new historic sites, and educate the public about the history of Indian Removal (Denson, *Monuments to Absence* 203, 204).

CHAPTER 1

1. The Marshall Trilogy is generally credited with being the foundation of federal Indian law (see, e.g., Fletcher, "Iron Cold" 627). However, Gregory Ablavsky reminds scholars of the "forgotten origins of federal Indian law" by taking a close look at the Indian Commerce Clause. "Indian law . . . ," he concludes, "is the product of constitutional thought that has been forgotten" (1021, 1088).

2. As Rifkin has pointed out, the great number of English speakers and writers in the Cherokee government has left scholars with a rich body of documents in English for analysis. Moreover, the Cherokees were among the first tribal communities that signed treaties with the US government (Rifkin, *Manifesting America* 39, 205n2; Denson, *Demanding the Cherokee Nation* 3).

3. By the mid-eighteenth century, official British colonial policy was firmly based on the assumption that Native Americans owned all their land, which could be obtained from them through purchase only. While individual settlers often violated this colonial policy by trespassing on Native lands, it remained firmly in place, even after the American Revolution. The early nineteenth century, however, witnessed a transformation in legal thought. Because of an ever-expanding market in preemption rights, Native Americans came to be considered occupants rather than owners of the land, with the fee simple resting with the state and federal governments (Banner 150, 157, 174).

4. "The United States . . . hold and assert in themselves the title by which it was acquired. They maintain, as all others have maintained, that discovery gave an exclusive right to extinguish the Indian title of occupancy either by purchase or by conquest, and gave also a right to such a degree of sovereignty as the circumstances of the people would allow them to exercise" (*Johnson v. McIntosh* 21 U.S. 587).

5. The law of nations, as well as "humanity . . . acting on public opinion," prescribed that "the rights of the conquered to property should be unimpaired" and that the conquered "can be blended with the conquerors, or safely governed as a distinct people" (*Johnson v. McIntosh* 21 U.S. 589–90).

6. For an insightful analysis of the arguments of state courts in favor of state regulation of Native Americans in the face of the supposed federal authority over Indian affairs, see Rosen, *American Indians* 57–75.

7. For a similar argument, see Ross, "Annual Message," 10 Oct. 1832, qtd. in Moulton 252.

8. While the Cherokee leaders, in most of their writings, emphatically "protest against being considered as tenants at will, or as mere occupants of the soil, without possessing the sovereignty" (Memorial of 18 December 1829, rpt. in *Cherokee Phoenix* 20 Jan. 1830:1), in some documents they adopt the language of occupancy: in a letter to the Senate and House of Representatives from February 27, 1829, Ross and several other Cherokees argue in favor of "the preservation of a people whose title to the soil they now occupy, is lost in the ages of antiquity" (qtd. in Moulton 156). In an annual message the following October, Ross and George Lowrey speak about the Cherokees' "occup[ying] the soil inherited from the Great Author of our existence" (qtd. in Moulton 172).

9. While Banner points out that it is not clear why Marshall shifted from discovery to conquest in his opinion (185), a reading of Ross's interpretation of the ruling sheds light on this shift. Ross reads Marshall as interpreting the Revolutionary War, in which the Cherokees fought on the side of the British, as a war of conquest.

10. For further information on the significance of treaties for Native nations, see Carlson, *Sovereign Selves;* Prucha, *American Indian Treaties;* Williams, *Linking Arms*.

11. Locke himself endorsed Native lack of possession (Fitzmaurice 384, 387). Boudinot and Ross thus turned Locke against himself.

12. Georgia's state authorities quickly made sure that the US Supreme Court did not get the opportunity to review the case: they hanged George Tassel. Their action was also evidence of the contempt the state held for Native rights, the US Supreme Court, and federal authority over Indian affairs (Garrison 120, 122–23). The Cherokees' legal counsel William Wirt immediately filed a suit challenging Georgia's extension laws, asking the US Supreme Court to grant an injunction that interdicted enforcement of these laws within the territory of the Cherokee Nation (Norgren 99–100; Burke 503; Fletcher, "Iron Cold" 639).

13. See also Konkle's reading of Marshall's ruling as a response to the Cherokee memorials and the writings of Jeremiah Evarts (65–66).

14. For similar arguments, see J. Ridge; Ridge qtd. in Dale and Litton 8; Ross qtd. in Moulton 241–42.

15. In their opinions, each of the Tennessee judges relied on a different Marshall decision. Whereas Catron argued in line with *Johnson,* Judge Nathan Green relied on *Cherokee Nation* in his characterization of the Cherokee Nation as dependent yet as retaining important powers of self-government. Jacob Peck was the only judge to speak out against the extension laws, supporting Marshall's argumentation in *Worcester* (Garrison 211).

16. According to the treason law of 1829, ceding tribal land without authorization was punished by death (Perdue, *Cherokee Editor* 30, 1506n3).

17. To ensure Cherokee continuity as a collective, the Cherokee National Council, as one of its last acts before Removal, passed a resolution declaring the tribal government to be transferred intact to the new homeland (Denson, *Demanding the Cherokee Nation* 41).

18. Lisa Brooks claims that these descriptions were meant to argue against the idea of *terra nullius* (4–10).

19. Contemporaries such as John B. Weller, a US senator from California, also compared the situation of Natives in California to that of Cherokees in Georgia (Lindsay 276). Several scholars before me have also interpreted the novel as an allegory of Removal. See, for instance, Jordan; Rifkin, "'For the Wrongs'"; Owens; Sweet; Cox.

20. American literary politics at the turn of the century connected the genre of romance "to a national culture of imperial assumption and violence" (Hebard 23), and numerous American studies scholars, such as Amy Kaplan, have emphasized the close relation between Romantic aesthetics and empire building ("Romancing the Empire"). Reading *The Life and Adventures* as a critique of empire, I disagree with Cheryl Walker, who characterizes the novel as "a fantasy [more] than a serious literary undertaking" (119).

21. All further references to this work will be cited in the text as *JM*.

22. See Theda Perdue's work on the development of gender roles in the Cherokee Nation around the time of Indian Removal (e.g., "Cherokee Women and the Trail of Tears").

23. In the incident of the young Americans spared by Murieta because of their promise not to turn him in, the narrator also advances natural law arguments along the lines of Aquinas. Rather than being bound to society and its laws, the narrator argues, the young Americans are "morally bound" to stand up to their bargain. "Society has no right . . . to wring from them a secret which belongs to them and not to the world. In such matters God is the only judge" (*JM* 79–80).

24. In the edition issued by the University of Oklahoma Press, which is used throughout this chapter, the sentence goes, "He had committed deeds that made him amenable to the law, and his only safety lay in a persistence in the unlawful course that he had begun" (*JM* 14). In the 1854 version by Cook and Company, however, the reader finds the sentence as quoted in this chapter (Yellow Bird 6).

25. An example of racist state law in the novel is the mention of the "Foreign Miners' Tax" (*JM* 130) enforced by the state government in 1850. It severely discriminated against foreign miners and led to vigilantism, violence, and unjust accusations (Parins 96–97).

26. Lindsay considers Chapter 133, or "An Act for the Government and Protection of Indians," implemented in 1850, "the cornerstone of legal genocide in California." It legalized genocidal crimes, such as the enslavement of Native Americans and the indenture of Native children. Chapter 133 granted jurisdiction in all complaints by, for, or against Native Americans to the justices of peace. It also ensured that a white man could not be convicted on any offence upon the testimony of a Native American (245, 251, 252).

27. The term "Judge Lynch" is no invention of Ridge's but was commonly used in California at the time. This was a form of justice to which the vigilante committees treated Native Americans. It consisted of a decision by the mob and the immediate hanging of the accused (Lindsay 247).

28. The narrator's admiration of the outlaw calls to mind the "secret admiration" of the "figure of the 'great' criminal" by the public that Walter Benjamin mentions in his "Critique of Violence" (281).

29. As the novel concludes, "He [Murieta] also leaves behind him the important lesson that there is nothing so dangerous in its consequences as *injustice to individuals*—whether it arises from prejudice of color or from any other source; that a wrong done to one man is a wrong to the society and to the world" (*JM* 158; italics in original).

30. See, for instance, Hsu's recent assessment of the novel's ambivalences, most notably its representation of Murieta and his men as noble heroes and murderous monsters and its meandering between condemning and endorsing extralegal violence in newly domesticated spaces, where the rule of law has not yet been firmly established. See also Mondragón 179; Harvard 324.

31. The Cherokees were divided into Old Settler, Treaty, and Anti-Treaty factions, with all of them striving for power. Hostilities began to subside with the Treaty of 1846 but lasted until after the Civil War. They threatened to divide the Cherokee Nation permanently and led to violent killings and acts of revenge (Perdue and Green, *Cherokee Nation* 146–61).

32. This biographical constellation has prompted Louis Owens to argue that Murieta acts out Ridge's own desire for revenge (38). And in a letter, Ridge indeed confessed to Stand Watie that "there is a deep-seated principle of revenge in me which will never be satisfied until it reaches its object" (letter from 2 July, 1849, qtd. in Dale and Litton 64).

33. Ridge here reflects on his personal situation. After killing a fellow Cherokee, he feared to return to the Cherokee Nation due to what he considered the partisan trials implemented by the Ross Party against their political enemies (*Trumpet* 19; see also his letter to Stand Watie, 23 Sept. 1853, qtd. in Dale and Litton 77).

34. The Cherokees' arguments resonated with early theories of natural law advanced by members of the Salamanca School in Spain in the sixteenth century. They turned to natural law to argue that the subject or individual possesses rights, and then employed the idea of the existence of such rights to defend Indigenous peoples against Spanish colonization. Their works were well-known among Anglo-American colonizers. Fitzmaurice describes the turn that occurred in the English reception of the arguments advanced by Salamanca theologians such as Francisco de Vitoria. The promoters of Virginia, he argues, simply reversed the argument of *ferae bestiae*, the strongest pillar in the Salamanca theologians' defense of Indigenous rights, to justify their dispossession of Native Americans (383, 399).

35. Petra T. Shattuck and Jill Norgren also draw a connection between the legal actions of the Cherokees in the context of Removal and the later legal

battles about civil rights, tribal land, and the exploitation of Native resources fought by Native communities in federal courts (5–6).

CHAPTER 2

1. This policy began in the 1870s in the form of President Ulysses Grant's "Peace Policy" and lasted until the 1930s, when John Collier, then commissioner of Indian Affairs, gave federal Indian policy a new direction through the Indian Reorganization Act (Larré, Introduction 14).

2. Eaton revised this publication into her dissertation and was granted her PhD in 1919. She was thus the first woman from Indian Territory to receive a doctorate (Brown 72).

3. The date of *The Singing Bird* remains a mystery. Oskison's sister donated the undated manuscript to the University of Oklahoma's Western History Collection at the time of his death, in 1947. The novel may have been completed shortly before his death—hence his inability to publish it—but it was at this time that he worked on his autobiography. Thus he most likely wrote it between 1925, the year he published a short story called "The Singing Bird," and the early 1940s, before starting to work on his autobiography (Powell and Mullikin xxii).

4. While the speeches by Dawes and Painter, the Dawes and Meriam Reports, and the writings by John Collier that I read alongside Eaton and Oskison do not—in the strict sense of the term—belong to the body of federal Indian law and policy (see, e.g., Duthu, "Federal Indian Law"), scholars have emphasized their central role in shaping the congressional legislation of the assimilation and allotment era (Prucha, *Documents*). They are the argumentative foundations on which the laws implementing (and later superseding) assimilation and allotment rested. The legal subjectivities constructed by these laws stand in direct relationship to the depiction and assessment of Native individuals and collectives by these political writings.

5. Brown also characterizes civilization as a "recognizable shared discourse through which [Cherokee and American Indian writers] could leverage popular sentiments to their own ends" (77; see also 75, 76).

6. Whether Eaton's advocacy of civilization is strategic or expresses her own convictions cannot be established with certainty. For Eaton's rhetoric of civilization has a particular Cherokee inflection and, hence, subversive potential.

7. For an extensive discussion of the rhetoric of "Indian reformers" and US government officials, see Black 81–102.

8. The commission report was, for instance, cited in several court rulings. See, for instance, *Stephens v. Cherokee Nation* 174 U.S. 445 (1899) and *Seminole Nation v. United States* 316 U.S. 286 (1942).

9. For an excellent extensive analysis of Eaton's choice of sources and archives, see Brown 94–104.

10. For a similar reading, see Brown 81.

11. All further references to this work will be cited in the text as *JR*.

12. Such depictions of the period between Removal and the Civil War have persisted well into the twenty-first century. Thus in his *The Cherokee Nation: A*

History, Robert Conley describes this time period as the Cherokees' golden age, during which "the federal government was not coming around demanding new treaties or land cessions"; it was a period when "tremendous strides [were] made by the Cherokees . . . toward becoming a so-called modern nation" (167).

13. Here comes to the fore Eaton's occasional condescension toward Cherokee cultural and political conservatism, which is also present in Oskison's work.

14. This vision of US history as driven by acquisitive interests is an early Indigenous version of what historian Anthony J. Hall, almost two centuries later, describes as the "empire of private property," whose growth was dependent on the transformation of "new frontiers of matter," most notably land, into private property (xxix, 21).

15. Ever since the 1920s, Collier had worked to improve Native health care and other social programs and had fought for the protection of Native land rights, first and foremost through the American Indian Defense Association, which he had founded in 1923 (Genetin-Pilawa 157).

16. For a more detailed discussion of Collier's original bill and the bill finally passed, see Talbot (555–59). Oklahoma was initially excluded from the provisions of the law. In 1936, the Oklahoma Indian Welfare Act brought some of the principles of the Indian Reorganization Act to the state of Oklahoma (Denson, *Demanding the Cherokee Nation* 247; Holm, *The Great Confusion* 188).

17. Oskison's literary strategies are in keeping with those of other Native authors at the time. See, for instance, Sophia Alice Callahan's novel *Wynema, a Child of the Forest* (1891) and D'Arcy McNickle's "The Hungry Generations," the early draft of what would in 1936 become *The Surrounded*.

18. In their analysis of *The Singing Bird*, Powell and Mullikin argue that the novel's characters evolve "from romantic racialism to political empathy for the Cherokees"; they thus do not differentiate between the various approaches to Native American culture each of them represents (xxx).

19. All further references to this work will be cited in the text as *SB*.

20. Oskison juxtaposes Paul's belief in the necessity of Cherokee civilization with the tremendous cultural and political achievements of individual Cherokees and the Cherokees as a group. Just like Eaton, Oskison emphasizes throughout the novel the Cherokees' self-reliance, self-governance, competence, entrepreneurship, and capacity for advancement. He thus refutes the premises underlying the policy of assimilation and allotment and points out the limits of Paul's humanitarianism. For passages in the novel describing Cherokee advancement, see *SB* 56, 73–74, 119, 143, 157–58, 167.

21. Boas still believed, however, that tribal societies were in the process of disappearing, not because this was their inevitable destiny but because of cultural destruction and population loss (Clifford 163; Crawford and Kelley 3–5).

22. Oskison remains vague about the precise shape of Sequoyah's work throughout the novel. Only toward the end of the novel does Paul learn from one of Dan's letters that Sequoyah was writing a history of his people and had traveled to Mexico to find some long-lost sacred symbols that he considered essential for this endeavor (*SB* 149).

23. This is probably also why Oskison has the monoracial leaders Dan and Sequoyah never return from their journey to Mexico.

24. Oskison's mother was one-quarter Cherokee, while his father was an English immigrant. Before attending Stanford and Harvard Universities, never to return to Oklahoma to live, he spent his entire childhood in Indian Territory (Powell and Mullikin xix).

25. Brown 13–14. Christopher B. Teuton beautifully describes the significance of movement for Cherokees: "We separate from our homelands, our communities, our kin and friends, and, of course, from our best selves. And we return home, reunite with each other, and reestablish connections with our communities and homeland. We learn something about the world, about diversity, and about each other in the process" (83).

26. Oskison gave up his journalistic career and began writing novels after serving in World War I (Powell and Mullikin xxi).

27. In the end, *The Singing Bird* remains ambivalent. While it clearly positions itself against Ellen's fervent assimilationism (Oskison first has her change and then die), the novel falls short of taking a firm stand concerning the positions represented by Paul/Miss Eula and Dan/Sequoyah, respectively. While the story centers on Dan and his collaboration with Sequoyah, in the end both of them fail to realize their vision. It is instead Paul, the more moderate reformer, who takes over Oak Hill, together with his new wife, Miss Eula. Catherine's endorsement of her own biracial son as a potential leader is also somewhat tentative and is located in the future.

28. The term "transculturation" was introduced into scholarship by the Cuban anthropologist Fernando Ortiz in his 1940 work *Contrapunteo Cubano del Tabaco y el Azúcar* (*Cuban Counterpoint: Tobacco and Sugar* 102–3). Oskison's endorsement of an Anglo–Native society, based on the fusion of the best traits of both cultures, demonstrates Native American intellectuals' formulations of similar theories on the mutual, reciprocal influences between cultures.

29. Besides Larré's, see also Daniel Heath Justice's, Beth Piatote's, and Kirby Brown's productive engagements with Oskison's work (Justice, *Our Fire Survives the Storm;* Piatote, *Domestic Subjects,* "Domestic Trials"; Brown).

30. The only scholarly text so far dealing with Eaton's book is Brown's *Stoking the Fire.*

31. Vigil draws a link between the advocacy of assimilation by Native intellectuals around the turn of the century and the dearth of scholarly output dealing with their writings, speeches, and public performances (10, 14). Nelson criticizes the tendency of scholars "to describe American Indian identities, cultures, and literatures by oppositions," such as assimilationism versus traditionalism (3).

32. For a description of the Indian New Deal, see Black 149–56. See also Stephen Cornell's assessment of the Indian New Deal. To him, it "set out to grant to Indians a limited but enlarged degree of control over their affairs and destinies but did so in the service of the ends pre-selected by the dominant society" (94–95).

CHAPTER 3

1. Federal support of tribal self-determination has continued until the present day. According to a recent Harvard study, this policy "has clearly empowered the Indian nations to assert themselves [culturally and politically], and has enabled Native communities and tribal governments to begin to break long-standing patterns of dependency and second-class status" (Cornell and Kalt 27).

2. In *The Elusive Promise of Indigenous Development*, Karen Engle analyzes in great detail the discursive shift taking place in the use of self-determination in the late 1980s and early 1990s. While early advocates of self-determination defined it as conferring attributes of statehood, citing documents from the decolonization movement, later advocates—in particular those interpreting it as suggesting autonomy within a state—began to reference human rights documents as the basis for Indigenous peoples' rights to self-determination (96–98, 100–140).

3. The Draft Declaration on the Rights of Indigenous Peoples was adopted by the UN General Assembly in 2007, with 143 votes in favor of, 11 abstentions, and 4 votes against its passage. Australia, Canada, New Zealand, and the United States voted against UNDRIP and upheld this position until 2010 (Pulitano 1–2).

4. It was in the context of preparations for the Columbus Quincentennial, on October 22, 1991, that the city council of Berkeley, California, first recognized Indigenous Peoples' Day, which was observed the following year (Archives of Indigenous Peoples Day).

5. These include *United States v. Kagama* (1886) and *Lone Wolf v. Hitchcock* (1903) (see chapter 2). In *Tee-Hit-Ton Indians v. United States* (1955), the court contended "that seizure by the federal government of Indian property held under original Indian title does not constitute a taking of property under the fifth amendment" (Singer 17–18, 29; Getches 1585).

6. This kind of scholarly criticism has continued into the twenty-first century. See Tsosie and Coffey 194; Anaya, "Indian Givers" 108; Echo-Hawk 5.

7. Treaties, as Allen and other scholars have illustrated, embody an agreement of "the essential—albeit supervised—sovereignty of Indian nations" and of "substantial separatism as well as federal protection" from the infringement of Native rights by states (Allen 69; Wilkinson, *Time* 15–16).

8. In the course of the novel, additional nonfictional records are included in the fictional narrative, either as free-standing chapters, such as Ralph Waldo Emerson's letter opposing Removal to President Martin Van Buren in chapter 8, or as part of existing chapters, such as excerpts from the works of Charles C. Royce (Conley, *Mountain Windsong* 126–28, 145) and James Mooney (80–81, 128–29, 145–46). These historical documents are not commented upon on the level of discourse.

9. Royce's work, which was included in the *Fifth Annual Report of the Bureau of American Ethnology*, was republished at the request of the governing body of the Cherokee Nation and is hence an ethnological text approved by the tribe ("The Cherokee Nation by Charles C. Royce").

10. All further references to this work will be cited in the text as *MW*.

11. See, for instance, the grandfather's insinuation that the first rebellion in the New World against an autocratic regime and the first major struggle for individual rights were not the American Revolution but the rebellion of a Cherokee individual against the priests (*MW* 9). See also the grandfather's emphasis on the significance of individual opinions, including women's opinions, in the context of Cherokee nation building (35, 168).

12. See the anti-elitist discourse in the novel (*MW* 155, 189–90).

13. See also the excerpt from Mooney in the novel (*MW* 127).

14. *Mountain Windsong* is haunted by another treaty, President Jackson's "oral treaty" with Oconeechee's father, Janaluska, through which he thanked him for his support in the Battle of Horseshoe Bend in Alabama in 1813: "'As long as the sun shines and the grass grows, you and me are going to be friends, and the feet of the Cherokees will be pointed East'" (*MW* 8). Just like the Treaty of New Echota, this verbal treaty is proven to be empty rhetoric and nonbinding by the novel.

15. In *Imperialism, Sovereignty and the Making of International Law*, Antony Anghie sheds light on the colonial origins of international law.

16. A similar view is held by Robert Laurence, who insists "that a recognition of tribal sovereignty under domestic law . . . is the best hope of improving the lot of Indian peoples in the United States." In contrast to Getches, Laurence openly dismisses international law as an avenue for securing Native rights: "I'm not optimistic that international forums hold any real promise for the protection of American Indian rights. . . . To the extent that advocating a place for the Indian nations among the states of the world distracts tribal advocates from the vigilance that this balance of contradictory forces at work in the domestic law requires, I think it to be a folly" (429–30).

17. The soldiers violate the Cherokees' rights to life, liberty, and security (UDHR art. 1); subject them to cruel, inhuman, or degrading treatment (UDHR art. 5); arrest them arbitrarily and deprive them of their property (UDHR art. 9, 17).

18. As their influence on the development of the individual is recognized, groups do receive some protection in international law (Xanthaki 19, 23). If considered, however, they have tended to be perceived not as collectives but as "aggregates of individuals whose status in law and politics arises not from their collective identity, but from the rights and interests of the individuals of which they are composed" (Svensson 421).

19. Such fears are reflected in debates about self-determination, the most central collective right demanded by Indigenous peoples ("Consideration–Addendum" 7–8; see also 11). States such as France and Japan shared the American representatives' aversion to Indigenous collective rights (see "Consideration—Addendum" 2; Barsh, "Indigenous Peoples and the UN Commission" 795–96).

20. Australia and Canada, for instance, insisted that the recognition of a new category of collective rights was "the whole point of the declaration" and admitted the need for "something more" than traditional notions of human rights (qtd. in Barsh, "Indigenous Peoples and the UN Commission" 795–96).

21. All further references to this work will be cited in the text as *PB*.

22. Theft, as Robert Nichols has stated, would usually assume that "'property' is logically, chronologically, and normatively prior to 'theft.'" In the settler colonial context, however, this is not the case. Here, "theft is the mechanism and means by which property is generated." Only in hindsight are the Indigenous dispossessed figured as "the original owners." Based on such reflections, Nichols introduces the concept of recursive dispossession, which he defines as "a form of property-generating theft." Indigenous property, he says, "is only cognizable by Western law in and through its alienation . . . *it is fully realized only in its negation*" (8–9, 33; italics in original).

23. As Glancy indicates in a footnote, the property lists are taken from the Cherokee Register of Valuations, part of the records of the Bureau of Indian Affairs housed in the National Archives in Washington, DC (*PB* 78).

24. The agents produced detailed records, which listed the name of each homestead owner, the location of the homestead, and the type, number, and value of all improvements (Wilms 18).

25. Quaty Lewis implies that sleeping with the soldier equals agreeing with Georgia Cherokees who signed the Treaty of New Echota (*PB* 167; see also Allen, "Discourse of Treaties" 81). And as a reaction to her father's admonition that Knobowtee is still her husband and that the trail does not change this, Maritole thinks, "I don't remember signing any treaty" (*PB* 210).

26. Glancy's representation of traditional Cherokee group practices and interpersonal relations corresponds with scholarly findings. Robert K. Thomas, for instance, emphasizes the significance of communal action, working together for the good of all, harmonious relationships, and institutionalized sharing across kin lines within Cherokee communities (7–8).

27. James Mooney re-narrates various Cherokee stories about the origin of the bear. At the center of these stories is a Cherokee boy who starts eating bear food and, as a consequence, increasingly turns into a bear (325). From this story, Mooney argues, derives the Native belief that "a continuous adherence to the diet commonly used by a bear will finally give to the eater the bear nature, if not also the bear form and appearance. A certain term of 'white man's food' will give the Indian the white man's nature." (472). Thus, even in Mooney, the bear story deals with adaptation and assimilation, which is probably why Glancy chose to employ it.

28. For a summary of the various scholarly positions in the debate, see P. Jones 80n1 and 80n2.

29. Scholars such as Peter Jones and Allen Buchanan also speak out against a fundamental incompatibility of individual and collective rights within international law if the collective rights at hand are embedded in a framework of individual rights (Buchanan 103, 207). Jones claims "there is . . . a continuity and complementarity between individual and collective rights: respect and concern for the individual drive both" (90). Buchanan even goes so far as to claim that "the indigenous peoples' movement's emphasis on collective rights . . . enriches, rather than undermines, international human rights law" (108).

30. See chapter 2.

31. One exception is the scholarly writings of Theda Perdue, many of which focus specifically on Cherokee women ("Cherokee Women and the Trail of Tears").

32. Sometimes the signing of the Act of Union is dated to July 12, 1838.

33. The preamble of the Constitution of Massachusetts announces the formation of a "body politic" "to furnish the individuals who compose it with the power of enjoying in safety and tranquility their natural rights, and the blessings of life" ("Constitution of the Commonwealth of Massachusetts").

34. For further critical Indigenous voices on UNDRIP, see, for instance, the contributions by Irene Watson, Aileen Moreton-Robinson, and Ward Churchill in the special Issue of the *Griffith Law Review* "The 2007 Declaration on the Rights of Indigenous Peoples: Indigenous Survival—Where to from Here?"

CHAPTER 4

1. The term "Cherokee freedmen" refers to those formerly enslaved by members of the Cherokee Nation, as well as to their descendants. Although the majority of Cherokee freedmen have predominantly African and African American ancestry, some of them also have Cherokee ancestors. The percentage of Cherokee freedmen with Cherokee ancestry is a question of debate, with estimates ranging from one-tenth to one-third (Sturm, "Race" 575, 596).

2. In 1908 Congress held that if a Native allottee had 50 percent or more Indian blood, their allotment was held in trust by the federal government and was restricted from sale and taxation. Allottees with less Indian blood, including intermarried whites and freedmen, had to pay taxes but could sell their allotments (Sturm, *Blood Politics* 79).

3. For a superb overview of the development of federal conceptions of "Indianness" and their impact on Indigenous notions of belonging from the eighteenth to the twentieth centuries, see Adams 2–20.

4. Seventy percent of all tribal constitutions now contain a blood quantum rule (Gover 251). For an astute analysis of the significance of blood for Native forms of belonging, see also Adams.

5. While Kirsty Gover also highlights the appeal of blood quantum rules for tribal membership practices, especially after 1970, she encourages scholars to differentiate between "Indian blood" (the federal category) and "tribal blood" (a tribe-specific descent rule). While "Indian blood rules allow the admittance of persons with high aggregate multi-tribal blood quantum," tribal blood "is a tribally endogenous concept that does not weigh ancestry from 'outside' the tribe" (251). "The genealogic shift in tribal membership reduces the relevance of Indian blood derived from other tribes and so leans against the colonial concept of an undifferentiated Indian population organized into tribal communities." She thus sees tribal blood quantum as a "tribal innovation" and not as a mere "[replication of] the federal category of Indian blood" (252; see also 247). The Cherokee Nation is one of those tribes displaying what Gover calls "the growing

tribal preference for descent rules" and thus a growing "'genealogic' tribalism" (244–45, 250).

6. Johnson also emphasizes that it is anti-Black racism that underlies the controversy. Individuals with Cherokee and white ancestry are, in discourse and practice, treated differently from the Cherokee freedmen (166, 197).

7. In 1998, in its ruling *Riggs v. Ummerteskee*, the tribunal judged the blood requirement to be consistent with the 1975 Cherokee Constitution and claimed that the Cherokee Nation "is a Sovereign Nation with the absolute right to determine it's [*sic*] citizenship." It thus ruled against the African-Cherokee plaintiff's claim for citizenship and argued in favor of decisions on a case-by-case basis, leaving unresolved the question of freedmen group rights to tribal citizenship (Sturm, "Race" 578).

8. For a detailed history of the relationship between the Cherokee Nation and persons of African descent, see Johnson (176–204).

9. This opinion is widely shared by members of the Cherokee pro-freedmen camp and scholars in the field of Native American studies (see, e.g., Sturm, "Race" 591, *Blood Politics* 3, 248; Wilkins, "Grievous" 338; Johnson 197).

10. The relationship between Removal and slavery has also been generally ignored by historians, so that it remains "one of the little known facts of American history" (Minges xix).

11. Foster professes "to speak in slave narrative format" (*Abraham's Well* 325). As Kathy-Ann Tan has pointed out, with its "reliance on mimetic representation and traditional historiography" the novel "shares more in common with forms of witness and religious narratives than postmodern slave narratives" that resort to nonrealistic representations of reality (239).

12. Historically speaking, the Mississippi Band of Choctaw Indians belonged to "a remnant population" that stayed behind after the forced relocation of the Choctaw Nation. According to the Choctaw Removal treaty, those staying behind continued to be citizens of the Choctaw Nation despite living outside its national territory (Adams 21).

13. In his critique of the Cherokee politics of exclusion, Robert Warrior highlights, with indignation, that the Cherokees had disenfranchised the freedmen, "freed slaves who trod the Trail of Tears with their Native American owners" ("Cherokees Flee").

14. As a reason for the tribal communities' increasing reliance on base rolls, Gover cites their desire for asserting "historical continuity." Lineal descent rules, she says, "serve to 'bridge the gap' between the current community and its last written roll" (262). Not incidentally, the regulations governing the federal recognition of tribes are also organized around the notion of continuity (276).

15. Five times does *Pushing the Bear* briefly mention the fact that some Cherokees, especially "rich landowners," had adopted chattel slavery and took enslaved Black people with them on the Trail of Tears (46; see also 31, 47, 56, 78). By embedding the commodification of Blacks by one privileged group of Cherokees into a narrative on Cherokee dispossession, the novel establishes a tentative

relationship between the settler colonial policy of Removal and Native participation in the settler colonial politics of Black enslavement. However, it does not expound these entanglements in more detail.

16. All further references to this work will be cited in the text as *AW*.

17. The representation of clan relationships in *Abraham's Well* is consistent with scholarly analyses of traditional Cherokee kinships systems (see, e.g., Sturm, *Blood Politics* 28–31; Thomas 1, 4, 7, 8, 26).

18. In many southern states, slave masters managed to implement laws that punished those teaching slaves to read in order to increase their social control over their property (see also Hadden).

19. The Treaty of Dancing Rabbit Creek from 1830 was a Removal treaty the US government negotiated with a small group of Choctaw representatives, who ceded their remaining eastern lands and agreed to move west (Kidwell, *Choctaws* xvi, 3–4; Adams 96).

20. All further references to this work will be cited in the text as *CRC*.

21. The novel thus deviates from the historical timeline established by scholars. Barbara Krauthamer dates the emergence of chattel slavery in Native American tribal communities in the American South to the late eighteenth century. While scholars before her attempted to establish a connection between Native practices of captivity and chattel slavery, Krauthamer emphasizes the differences between the former and the latter. According to her, unlike captivity, chattel slavery was grounded in a racial ideology positing Black inferiority (13, 17–45).

22. In her depiction of Jacques and Grey Fox, Lockhart draws on the history of the LeFlore family, Louis and his son Greenwood LeFlore, albeit with considerable license (see also Pate; Adams 103–4).

23. According to the Treaty of Dancing Rabbit Creek's provisions, the Choctaws who stayed in Mississippi indeed did not lose their citizenship in the Choctaw Nation (Adams 96).

24. The novel here adheres to the historical record. Although the Choctaws in Mississippi in the post-Removal years recognized their shared heritage with African Americans, whom they called Sukanatches, they questioned their Choctaw identity and considered them merely Black (Adams 105).

25. Foster also comments on the racialization of Cherokee nationhood in her novel by mentioning anti-Black laws, which were passed in Indian Territory after Removal (*AW* 206). For another Agambenian reading of *Cold Running Creek*, see Deetjen, "Native Nationalisms."

26. The critique of race and blood is reinforced later in the novel, when Armentia gives birth to Abraham Proof, fathered by her white master Jacob McDowell. Her son has blond, curly hair and blue eyes and is viewed by the plantation slaves as "a light-skinned piece of possibility" (*AW* 231; see also 268). Though legally a slave, Abraham Proof could "pass for a White man" (*AW* 231, 268).

27. Master Cauley's racial background is never made explicit in the novel. The aforementioned quote, along with Armentia's assertion that his plantation "was bigger than anything I had ever seen fenced in by White men," could be interpreted as evidence of both his whiteness and his Cherokee heritage (*AW* 129).

28. Lockhart makes a similar point by elaborating on Lilly's socialization as a plantation mistress.

29. Raven (*CRC* 37–39); Grey Fox (*CRC* 284); Lilly (*CRC* 270–72).

30. Armentia's later husband, Willie, thinks fondly of the time "when they [his people] were brothers—a time before the Trail" (*AW* 285).

31. The novel here relies on the historical record. According to a Cherokee law from 1840, free Blacks and "mulattos" were considered not to be of Cherokee blood and hence were excluded from ownership within the nation (Sturm, *Blood Politics* 71).

32. Neither can Lilly connect to her lover, whom she calls Man, because she is convinced of her racial superiority. "'I ain't no nigger,'" she says to him (*CRC* 241).

33. For other references to the importance of shared suffering along the Trail of Tears, see *AW* 113, 169, 181.

34. See also Tan's withering assessment of the novel and Foster's final note: they "[amount] to little more than a personal testimony of the Christian faith rather than a social critique of the double marginalization of black Cherokee subjects by both Indigenous and non-Indigenous concepts of nationhood and citizenship." Tan judges *Abraham's Well* to be "a fictional exploration of one woman's journey from slavery into freedom against all odds rather than a critical commentary on the complex issues of sovereignty and self-determination, race, ethnicity, kinship, place, and community that factor into contemporary discussions of Indigenous nationhood, citizenship, and belonging" (242).

35. As the swamp undermines proprietary relations, Lilly will cease to be Willie's property. Her escape to the swamp can also be read as an act of emancipation, an escape from the bonds of patriarchy to a more self-determined existence.

36. Denson argues that much current heritage work also ignores the place of African Americans in Cherokee history (*Monuments to Absence* 219). Within the last two decades, scholarship on the history of African–Native relations, in particular on the question of slavery among the Cherokees, Seminoles, Creeks, Choctaws, and Chickasaws, has proliferated. See Miles; Krauthamer; McCray Pearson; Saunt; Chang.

37. As Gover has outlined, "over-inclusive membership rules could legally transform a tribe from a sovereign political entity to a racial association and release the federal government from its trust obligations" (169).

38. This call for historical truth concerning practices of Native slaveholding and racial discrimination has been answered by a group of Cherokee authors, Deborah L. Duvall, Murv Jacob, and James Murray, who in 2012 published *Secret History of the Cherokees: A Novel*, which retells the history of Indian Removal and Cherokee nation building up until the Civil War through the lens of slavery.

39. Johnson 200–201; Monet; Hansen; "Cherokee Nation Announces New Initiative"; Healy; Somvichian-Clausen; Carter.

CHAPTER 5

1. "Speculative fiction" is "a generic umbrella term that allows grouping of diverse forms of nonmimetic fiction—from fantasy and science fiction to

derivatives and hybrids that draw on the fantastic for specific purposes but often elude easy classifications" (Oziewicz).

2. While cultural property was initially limited to tangible objects, since the early 2000s its definition encompasses both "the tangible and intangible effects of an individual or group of people that define their existence, and place them temporally and geographically in relation to their belief systems and their familial and political groups, providing meaning to their lives" (Sherry Hutt et al. qtd. in Riley, "Straight Stealing" 77; see also Carpenter et al. 1032; Kenney 505–6).

3. For a similar argument, see also Riley and Carpenter 859, 866; Blaeser 38; Tsosie, "Reclaiming Native Stories" 310; Alfred, *Wasase* 58; Berman 383.

4. This chapter uses "science" in the broad sense of the term and not as merely denoting the natural and physical sciences.

5. Following Vizenor, this chapter employs the terms *indian* and *indianness* to denote settler colonial inventions and representations of dominance; it uses tribal designations and the collective terms "Natives" and "Native Americans" to refer to Indigenous people themselves.

6. See also Riley and Carpenter 889–90; Riley, "Straight Stealing" 78; Coulthard 16.

7. Rebecca Tsosie seconds this: "The failure to protect Native cultures . . . perpetuates significant harm to Native people as distinctive, living cultural groups" ("Reclaiming Native Stories" 310).

8. Scholars, for instance, have shed light on how modern Indian law imposes notions of *indianness* (Riley and Carpenter 890; Barker, *Native Acts* 20; Berkhofer 33–69; Castile 269–80).

9. Until the present day, the domination of the idea of an "expressive, inventive, and possessive" individual author in intellectual property law continues to exclude collectively authored Native intangible property from protection (Coombe 209, 219, 220; Berman 384, 387; see also Tsosie, "Reclaiming Native Stories" 315; Riley and Carpenter 865; Riley, "Straight Stealing" 79–81).

10. For other recent criticism of Trail of Tears appropriations, see Marissa Payne's article in the *Washington Post* and Cherokee Adrienne Keene's blog *Native Appropriations*.

11. All further references to this work will be cited in the text as *RTT*.

12. This procedure might be read as an allusion to the federal government's conclusion of treaties, such as the Treaty of New Echota, with a small, unauthorized faction of the Cherokee Nation.

13. The novel (is it a novel at all or rather a political manifesto?) features more than forty characters and confuses the reader with its nonlinear narration, multiple time shifts, and wild mix of settings, plotlines, and narrative techniques. Moreover, Jones uses different font types and sizes, a glossary in which he explains a great number of terms, and an appendix with facsimiles of original documents. As Birgit Däwes rightly states, all these supposedly explanatory tools are, in fact, "simulacra of navigational devices rather than actual compasses in the maze of the plot." As such, "they turn out to be unreliable or contradictory signifiers, pointing on to further signifiers rather than offering orientation" (116).

14. All further references to this work will be cited in the text as *BG*.

15. John Gamber has fittingly called this area a "hinterland disposal site" (36).

16. The border zone has also turned into a popular tourist site: a decade after the territories were established, hotels sprang up like mushrooms, with all their windows facing west toward the territories (*BG* 113). The American tourists, arriving by busloads, want to look west—they want to watch the living specimens in action to have their notions of *indianness* confirmed. The most popular of these hotels is the Mayflower, a hotel and casino just inside the territories. The name of the resort symbolizes the colonial nature of the encounter between tourists and the territories' inhabitants (*BG* 168).

17. The Nunnehi narrator tells the reader that no TREPP employee knows about the Misfits (*RTT* 194). He gives the reader two reasons for their existence. First, they are "manifestations of our own labor"—that is, they are created by the Nunnehi (*RTT* 5). Second, the "Suits" created them and gave them names (*RTT* 6, 117).

18. It never becomes entirely clear who the Suits are. The reader learns only that they wear dark power suits and resemble the Spanish conquistadores in their armor (*RTT* 161). At the end of the novel, the reader is told that the homeland security agents wear dark suits (*RTT* 343). The novel thus establishes a link between the homeland security's fight against terrorism and the representation of Native culture in the TREPP.

19. Hausman has the Misfits drop self-reflexive and humorous comments on their performances of *indianness* (*RTT* 114, 123).

20. By calling the Chef's apprentice Ish, Hausman suggests that Tallulah and the other digital characters in the ride are museum artifacts, just like Ishi, who was turned into a museum object under the guidance of an(other) anthropologist, Alfred Kroeber (Kroeber and Kroeber xiii; Clifford 95–96).

21. Instead of rearranging the letters into Fools' Ship, the illiterate maintenance man comes up with Fool's Hip (*BG* 165).

22. Jones creates a very compelling image signifying exclusion: Courtney cupping her hands against the glass to look through the locked entry door of Fool's Hip (*BG* 22, 23).

23. Throughout the novel, he is asked several times why he does not wear long hair like "*a real Indian*," but he does not dare to answer the question (*BG* 15, 36; italics in original). He finally etches his answer to the question—"because I'm not"—on the stall of the men's bathroom (*BG* 119).

24. Another reference to Fanon in *The Bird Is Gone* can be found in the glossary of terms (*BG* 171). "Red Dawn" gestures toward the Guinean Kéita Fodéba's poem "African Dawn," about the colonized subject Naman, "the hero of the battlefields of Europe," which Fanon cites in *The Wretched of the Earth* as an example of protest poetry, portraying how the colonial powers (ab)used the colonized as soldiers, both in foreign wars and to put down independence movements (168). But the poem also problematizes the attitude of the village elders, who decide "to send the young man who best represents our race so that he can prove to the white man the courage we Mandingos have always been known for" (164–65).

Their eagerness to prove themselves worthy and their desire to be recognized by the colonizers result, according to Fanon's analysis, in their acceptance of the derogatory images and the structural relations they help implement as more or less natural (167; see also Coulthard 31, 32).

25. The ride only exists because of the historic Trail of Tears, and the Native Americans only return to the Indian Territories because of their prior dispossession.

26. "Endless water, underground, moving somewhere. Maybe it all flows back to where it began? Do you know where it comes from? Do you know where it goes?" (*RTT* 370).

27. The episode "Make Him Dance," which is included in the novel as a typescript, features the Lone Ranger and his Native sidekick Tonto, another famous pair from American popular cultural lore. In this Indigenous reappropriation, Tonto appears not as sidekick but as the puppeteer in charge of the Lone Ranger, who is portrayed as a robot (*BG* 134–36).

28. In his short story "Tune Brown: Graduation with Ishi," Vizenor tells the story of the trickster Tune, who begins to adopt poses of *indianness* ("a proud invention and the reversal of tribal striptease") only to reject the "captured images," again in an act of tribal striptease (*The Trickster of Liberty* 44; see also 45).

29. Under the heading "non-dairy creamer," for instance, the reader finds a reference to "Manifest Destiny," which leads to *Susannah of the Mounties* (*BG* 168).

30. This bird refers to the passenger pigeon, a once numerous species of bird that became extinct in the early twentieth century and that cannot be brought back to life (*BG* 169; see also Gamber 35).

31. In Hausman, all characters—both digital and nondigital—transcend temporal planes: Tallulah and her tourists move in between the Removal era and present-day Georgia. Despite being part of the ride, the Misfits wear outfits representing several centuries. And while being figures from Cherokee mythology and past, the Nunnehi and the digital stock characters also inhabit the present. Jones, in turn, intersperses his novel with chapters containing episodes engaging the history of colonization and Native–settler relations (see the Bacteen tale and "Indian Corn").

32. Tallulah cuts off her hair out of anger (*RTT* 352, 357), and LP Deal writes his manifesto in "small, angry letters" (*BG* 16).

EPILOGUE

1. For a more extensive discussion of the novel, see Meyer, "From Domestic Dependency to Native Cultural Sovereignty."

2. All further references to this work will be cited in the text as *CT*.

3. To make his critique more explicit, Shammer puts on various masks during the Trail of Tears, among them those embodying the Native scholar Elizabeth Cook-Lynn and the American movie actor John Wayne (*CT* 39–30). In her writings, Cook-Lynn has repeatedly asked Native scholars to dedicate themselves to the exercise of political, social, and territorial sovereignty (see also Justice, "'Go Away, Water!'" 161). The Cook-Lynn mask can thus be read as reminding

the professors on the trail of the deficiency of their work with regard to Native sovereignty. The John Wayne mask, in turn, is used by Shammer to critique the faculty members' performance of *indianness* according to the scripts provided to them by American popular culture. Moreover, by instituting "last lectures," in which selected Native Americans confess their lifelong performance of *indianness* in order to be absolved by the audience, Shammer similarly seeks to alert Native faculty members to the cost involved in being "*Indian poseurs and fakers*" who satisfy the colonizer's needs and desires (*CT* 84; italics in original; see also 83).

4. See also Glen Coulthard, who in *Red Skin, White Masks* characterizes settler colonialism as "territorially acquisitive in perpetuity" (152).

5. As the previous chapters show, almost all Native writers discussed in this book address the power of Native storytelling more or less explicitly. They suggest Indigenous stories to be far more truthful than Western historical accounts of Native–settler relations as they foreground settler colonial violence, correct settler colonial misrepresentations, and, by focusing on the impact of Indian policies on the lives of ordinary people, allow listeners and readers to develop a heightened sense of the real. They serve to disentangle past and present Native ways of living, being, and belonging from settler colonial simulations of *indianness* and categories of identification and to establish connections among people.

6. In his theoretical writings, Vizenor voices a similar position (see, e.g., *Manifest Manners* 16; *Fugitive Poses* 15; "Aesthetics of Survivance" 11).

Works Cited

Ablavsky, Gregory. "Beyond the Indian Commerce Clause." *Yale Law Journal* 124.4 (2015): 1012–90. Web. 12 Aug. 2016.
Adams, Mikaëla M. *Who Belongs? Race, Resources, and Tribal Citizenship in the Native South*. Oxford: Oxford UP, 2016. Print.
Adamson, Joni. "Seeking the Corn Mother: Transnational Indigenous Organizing and Food Sovereignty in Native North American Literature." *Indigenous Rights in the Age of the Declaration*. Ed. Elvira Pulitano. Cambridge: Cambridge UP, 2012. 228–49. Print.
Agamben, Giorgio. *Homo Sacer: Sovereign Power and Bare Life*. Trans. Daniel Heller-Roazen. Stanford: Stanford UP, 1998. Print.
Ahmed, Sara. *The Cultural Politics of Emotion*. New York: Routledge, 2004. Print.
Akers, Donna L. "Removing the Heart of the Choctaw People: Indian Removal from a Native Perspective." *Native Historians Write Back: Decolonizing American Indian History*. Ed. Susan A. Miller and James Riding In. Lubbock: Texas Tech UP, 2011. 105–16. Print.
Albrecht, James M. *Reconstructing Individualism: A Pragmatic Tradition from Emerson to Ellison*. New York: Fordham UP, 2012. Print.
Alexie, Sherman. "Poem." *Old Shirts and New Skins*. Los Angeles: American Indian Studies Center, 1996. 77. Print.
Alfred, Taiaiake. *Peace, Power, Righteousness: An Indigenous Manifesto*. 2nd ed. Oxford: Oxford UP, 2009. Print.
———. *Wasase: Indigenous Pathways of Action and Freedom*. Peterborough, ON: Broadview P, 2005. Print.
Alfred, Taiaiake, and Jeff Corntassel. "Being Indigenous: Resurgences against Contemporary Colonialism." *Government and Opposition* 40.4 (2005): 597–614. *Wiley Online Library*. Web. 1 Aug. 2016.
Allen, Chadwick. "Postcolonial Theory and the Discourse of Treaties." *American Quarterly* 52.1 (2000): 59–89. *Project Muse*. Web. 11 Nov. 2013.
Allen v. Cherokee Nation Tribal Council, et al. JAT-04-09. Cherokee Nation Judicial Appeals Tribunal. 2006. Web. 2 Apr. 2014.
Althusser, Louis. "Ideology and Ideological State Apparatus (Notes Towards an Investigation)." *Lenin and Philosophy and Other Essays*. Trans. Ben Brewster. New York: Monthly Review P, 2001. 85–126. Print.
Anaya, S. James. "Indian Givers: What Indigenous Peoples Have Contributed to International Human Rights Law." *Washington University Journal of Law and Policy* 22 (2006): 107–20. Web. 12 Dec. 2015.

WORKS CITED

———. *Indigenous Peoples in International Law*. 2nd ed. Oxford: Oxford UP, 2004. Print.

———. "Indigenous Rights Norms in Contemporary International Law." *Arizona Journal of International and Comparative Law* 8.2 (1991): 1–39. *HeinOnline*. Web. 22 Jan. 2016.

———. "Superpower Attitudes toward Indigenous Peoples and Group Rights." *Proceedings of the Annual Meeting of the American Society of International Law* 93 (1999): 251–60. *JSTOR*. Web. 15 Dec. 2015.

Andersen, Chris. "Indigenous Nationhood." *Native Studies Keywords*. Ed. Stephanie Nohelani Teves, Andrea Smith, and Michelle H. Raheja. Tucson: U of Arizona P, 2015. 180–98. Print.

Anderson, Gavin W. "Post-colonial Legality and Legitimacy: The Challenge of Indigenous Peoples." *Legality and Legitimacy: Normative and Sociological Approaches*. Ed. Chris Thornhill and Samantha Ashenden. Baden-Baden, Germany: Nomos, 2010. 235–53. Print.

Anghie, Antony. *Imperialism, Sovereignty, and the Making of International Law*. Cambridge: Cambridge UP, 2004. Print.

Archambault, David, II. "Taking a Stand at Standing Rock." *New York Times* 24 Aug. 2016. Web. 1 May 2017.

Archives of Indigenous Peoples Day. Curated by John Curl. Web. 8 Nov. 2020.

Attebery, Brian. "Aboriginality in Science Fiction." *Science Fiction Studies* 32.3 (2005): 385–404. *JSTOR*. Web. 1 Feb. 2017.

Banner, Stuart. *How the Indians Lost Their Land: Law and Power on the Frontier*. Cambridge, MA: Belknap P of Harvard UP, 2005. Print.

Barker, Joanne. "Decolonizing the Mind." *Rethinking Marxism: A Journal of Economics, Culture and Society* 30.2 (2018): 208–31. Web. 4 Feb. 2021.

———. "For Whom Sovereignty Matters." *Sovereignty Matters: Locations of Contestation and Possibility in Indigenous Struggles for Self-Determination*. Ed. Joanne Barker. Lincoln: U of Nebraska P, 2005. 1–32. Print.

———. *Native Acts: Law, Recognition, and Cultural Authenticity*. Durham, NC: Duke UP, 2011. Print.

Barrera, Jorge. "US President Donald Trump's Actions on DAPL Like Andrew Jackson's Trail of Tears." *Aboriginal Peoples Television Network*, 25 Jan. 2017. Web. 1 Feb. 2017.

Barsh, Russel Lawrence. "Indigenous Peoples and the UN Commission on Human Rights: A Case of the Immovable Object and the Irresistible Force." *Human Rights Quarterly* 18.4 (1996): 782–813. *HeinOnline*. Web. 3 July 2015.

———. "Indigenous Peoples in the 1990s: From Object to Subject of International Law." *Harvard Human Rights Journal* 7 (1994): 33–86. *HeinOnline*. Web. 2 July 2015.

Barton, LaQuaria. "Dakota Access Pipeline: The New Trail of Tears." *Our Political Revolution: Government Reform NOW*, 16 Nov. 2016. Web. 1 Feb. 2017.

Baudemann, Kristina. "Removed to the Signifier: Utopia in Stephen Graham Jones's *The Bird Is Gone: A monograph Manifesto* (2003)." *Open Library of Humanities* 4.1 (2018). Web. 18 May 2021.

Baudrillard, Jean. "*From* The Precession of Simulacra." *Norton Anthology of Theory and Criticism.* Ed. Vincent B. Leitch. New York: Norton, 2001. 1732–40. Print.

Bedford, Denton R. *Tsali.* San Francisco: Indian Historian Press, 1972. Print.

Benjamin, Walter. "Critique of Violence." *Reflections: Essays, Aphorisms, Autobiographical Writings.* Ed. Peter Demetz. New York: Schocken Books, 1986. 277–300. Print.

Bentham, Jeremy. *Theory of Legislation.* Trans. from the French of Etienne Dumont by R. Hildreth. London: Trübner, 1871. *HathiTrust.* Web. 12 July 2016.

Berkhofer, Robert. *The White Man's Indian: Images of the American Indian from Columbus to the Present.* New York: Knopf, 1978. Print.

Berman, Tressa. "Cultural Appropriation." *A Companion to the Anthropology of American Indians.* Ed. Thomas Biolsi. Hoboken, NJ: Blackwell, 2004. 383–97. Print.

Bernstein, Robin. *Racial Innocence: Performing American Childhood from Slavery to Civil Rights.* New York: New York UP, 2011. Print.

Bhandar, Brenna. *Colonial Lives of Property: Land, Law, Racial Regimes of Ownership.* Durham, NC: Duke UP, 2019. Print.

———. "Property, Law, and Race: Modes of Abstraction." *UC Irvine Law Review* 4.1 (2014): 203–18. Web. 12 July 2016.

Bhandar, Brenna, and Davina Bhandar. "Cultures of Dispossession: Critical Reflections on Rights, Status, and Identities." Special issue on "Reflections on Dispossession: Critical Feminisms." Ed. Brenna Bhandar and Davina Bhandar. *Darkmatter* 14 (May 2016). Web. 17 Feb. 2021.

Biolsi, Thomas. "Imagined Geographies: Sovereignty, Indigenous Space, and American Indian Struggle." *American Ethnologist* 32.2 (2005): 239–59. Web. 11 Aug. 2016.

Black, Jason Edward. *American Indians and the Rhetoric of Removal and Allotment.* Jackson: UP of Mississippi, 2015. Print.

Blackman, Lisa, John Cromby, Derek Hook, Dimitris Papadopoulos, and Valerie Walkerdine. "Editorial: Creating Subjectivities." *Subjectivities* 22 (2008): 1–27. Web. 1 Feb. 2017.

Blaeser, Kimberley M. "The New 'Frontier' of Native American Literature: Dis-Arming History with Tribal Humor." *Native American Perspectives on Literature and History.* Ed. Alan R. Velie. Norman: U of Oklahoma P, 1994. 37–50. Print.

Bobroff, Kenneth. "Retelling Allotment: Indian Property Rights and the Myth of Common Ownership." *Vanderbilt Law Review* 54.4 (2001): 1559–1623. Web. 12 June 2015.

Borrows, John J. *Recovering Canada: The Resurgence of Indigenous Law.* Toronto: U of Toronto P, 2002. Print.

Brennan, Jonathan. "Introduction: Recognition of the African-Native Literary Tradition." *When Brer Rabbit Meets Coyote: African-Native American Literature.* Ed. Jonathan Brennan. Urbana: U of Illinois P, 2003. 1–97. Print.

Brooks, Lisa. *The Common Pot: The Recovery of Native Space in the Northeast.* Minneapolis: U of Minnesota P, 2008. Print.

Brown, Kirby. *Stoking the Fire: Nationhood in Cherokee Writing, 1907–1970*. Norman: U of Oklahoma P, 2018. Print.

Bruchac, Joseph. *The Journal of Jesse Smoke: A Cherokee Boy*. New York: Scholastic, 2001. Print.

Bruyneel, Kevin. *The Third Space of Sovereignty: The Postcolonial Politics of U.S.-Indigenous Relations*. Minneapolis: U of Minnesota P, 2007. Print.

Buchanan, Allen. "The Role of Collective Rights in the Theory of Indigenous Peoples' Rights." *Transnational Law and Contemporary Problems* 3 (1993): 89–103. *HeinOnline*. Web. 22 Dec. 2015.

Bunch, Mary. "Outlawry and the Experience of the (Im)possible: Deconstructing Biopolitics." PhD thesis, U of Western Ontario, 2010. Print.

Burke, Joseph C. "The Cherokee Cases: A Study in Law, Politics, and Morality." *Stanford Law Review* 21.3 (1969): 500–31. *JSTOR*. Web. 2 Apr. 2016.

Byrd, Jodi A. "'Been to the Nation, Lord, but I Couldn't Stay There': American Indian Sovereignty, Cherokee Freedmen and the Incommensurability of the Internal." *Interventions* 13.1 (2011): 31–52. Web. 6 July 2015.

———. "Introduction. Forum: Indigeneity's Difference: Methodology and the Structures of Sovereignty." *J19* 2.1 (2014): 131–36. *Project Muse*. Web. 28 Nov. 2017.

———. *The Transit of Empire: Indigenous Critiques of Colonialism*. Minneapolis: U of Minnesota P, 2011. Print.

Byrd, Jodi A., Alyosha Goldstein, Jodi Melamed, and Chandan Reddy. "Predatory Value: Dispossession and Disturbed Relationalities." *Social Text* 36.2 (2018): 1–18. Print.

Callahan, Sophia Alice. *Wynema: A Child of the Forest*. Lincoln: U of Nebraska P, 1997. Print.

Carlson, David J. *Imagining Sovereignty: Self-Determination in American Law and Literature*. Norman: U of Oklahoma P, 2016. Print.

———. *Sovereign Selves: American Indian Autobiography and the Law*. Urbana: U of Illinois P, 2006. Print.

Carpenter, Kristen A. "Contextualizing the Losses of Allotment through Literature." *North Dakota Law Review* 82 (2006): 605–26. Web. 5 Feb. 2016.

———. "Real Property and Peoplehood." *Stanford Environmental Law Journal* 27 (2008): 313–95. *Social Science Research Network*. Web. 2 Aug. 2016.

Carpenter, Kristen A., Sonia K. Katyal, and Angela R. Riley. "In Defense of Property." *Yale Law Journal* 118 (2008–2009): 1022–1125. Web. 11 Aug. 2016.

Carroll, Clint. *Roots of Our Renewal: Ethnobotany and Cherokee Environmental Governance*. Minneapolis: U of Minnesota P, 2015. Print.

Carter, Ray. "Slave-Owning Past Remains Problem for Choctaws." *Oklahoma Council of Public Affairs*, 19 Aug. 2020. Web. 26 Jan. 2021.

Castile, George Pierre. "Federal Indian Policy and Anthropology." *A Companion to the Anthropology of American Indians*. Ed. Thomas Biolsi. Hoboken, NJ: Blackwell, 2004. 268–83. Print.

Champagne, Duane. "UNDRIP (United Nations Declaration on the Rights of the Indigenous Peoples): Human, Civil, and Indigenous." *Wicazo Sa Review* 28.1 (2013): 9–22. *Project Muse*. Web. 30 June 2015.

Chang, David A. *Race, Nation, and the Politics of Land Ownership in Oklahoma, 1832–1929*. Chapel Hill: U of North Carolina P, 2010. Print.

Chávez, Luis Enrique. "The Declaration on the Rights of the Indigenous Peoples Breaking the *Impasse*: The Middle Ground." *Making the Declaration Work: The United Nations Declaration on the Rights of Indigenous Peoples*. Ed. Claire Charters and Rodolfo Stavenhagen. Piscataway, NJ: Transaction Publishers, 2009. 96–107. Print.

"Cherokee Nation Announces New Initiative to Explore Freedmen History." *Insight into Diversity*, 12 Nov. 2020. Web. 25 Jan. 2021.

"The Cherokee Nation by Charles C. Royce." *Transaction*. Web. 10 Sept. 2015.

Cherokee Nation v. Georgia. 30 U.S. 1. United States Supreme Court. 1831. *Justia*. Web. 7 Nov. 2015.

Cherokee Nation v. Raymond Nash, et al., Marilyn Vann, et al., Ryan Zinke. United States District Court for the District of Columbia. 2017. Civil Action No. 13-01313. attorneygeneral.cherokee.org. Web. 1 July 2018.

Cherokee Phoenix Feb. 21, 1828—June 11, 1831. *Hunter Library*. Web. 30 Oct. 2015.

Cheyfitz, Eric. "The (Post)Colonial Construction of Indian Country: U.S. American Indian Literatures and Federal Indian Law." *Columbia Guide to American Indian Literatures of the United States since 1945*. Ed. Eric Cheyfitz. New York: Columbia UP, 2006. 3–124. Print.

Churchill, Ward. "A Travesty of a Mockery of a Sham: Colonialism as 'Self-Determination' in the UN Declaration on the Rights of Indigenous Peoples." *Griffith Law Review* 20.3 (2011): 526–56. *HeinOnline*. Web. 11 July 2016.

Clifford, James. *Returns: Becoming Indigenous in the Twenty-First Century*. Cambridge, MA: Harvard UP, 2013. Print.

Clinton, Robert N. "Peyote and Judicial Political Activism: Neo-Colonialism and the Supreme Court's New Indian Law Agenda." *Federal Bar News and Journal* 38 (1991): 98–100. Web. 22 May 2015.

Cobb, Amanda J. "Understanding Tribal Sovereignty: Definitions, Conceptualizations, and Interpretations." *American Studies* 46.3–4 (2005): 115–32. Web. 7 July 2015.

Coffey, Wallace, and Rebecca Tsosie. "Rethinking the Tribal Sovereignty Doctrine: Cultural Sovereignty the Collective Future of Indian Nations." *Stanford Law and Policy Review* 12.2 (2001): 191–221. Web. 3 Aug. 2014.

Cohen, Felix S. *Handbook of Federal Indian Law*. Washington, DC: GPO, 1941. Print.

———. *Handbook of Federal Indian Law*. Washington, DC: GPO, 1982. Print.

Collier, John. *From Every Zenith: A Memoir and Some Essays on Life and Thought*. Denver: Sage, 1963. Print.

———. "Office of Indian Affairs." *Annual Report of the Secretary of the Interior for the Fiscal Year Ended June 30, 1938*. Washington, DC: GPO, 1928. 209–63. *Internet Archive*, 2012. Web. 15 Mar. 2016.

———. "The Red Atlantis." *Survey* 49.1 (October 1922): 15–20, 63, 65. *Internet Archive*, 2007. Web. 10 Mar. 2016.

Collins, Glenn. "When Cars Assume Ethnic Identities." *New York Times* 21 June 2013. Web. 1 Apr. 2017.

Conley, Robert J. *The Cherokee Nation: A History*. Albuquerque: U of New Mexico P, 2008. Print.

———. *Mountain Windsong: A Novel of the Trail of Tears*. Norman: U of Oklahoma P, 1992. Print.

"Consideration of a Draft United Nations Declaration on the Rights of Indigenous Peoples—Information Received from Governments: Addendum (Geneva: Economic and Social Council, Commission on Human Rights, Open-ended Inter-sessional Working Group on a Draft UN Declaration on the Rights of Indigenous Peoples, First Session, E/CN.4/1995/WG.15/2/Add.1, 1994)." *Official Document Service of the United Nations*. Web. 22 Aug. 2015.

"Constitution of the Cherokee Nation." *Cherokee Phoenix* 21 Feb. 1828. 1–2. *Hunter Library*. Web. 30 Oct. 2015.

"Constitution of the Commonwealth of Massachusetts 1780." General Court of the Commonwealth of Massachusetts. *MyLegislature*. Web. 2 Feb. 2016.

Coombe, Rosemary J. *The Cultural Life of Intellectual Properties: Authorship, Appropriation, and the Law*. Durham, NC: Duke UP, 1998. Print.

Cornell, Stephen. *Return of the Native: American Indian Political Resurgence*. New York: Oxford UP, 1988. Print.

Cornell, Stephen, and Joseph P. Kalt. "American Indian Self-Determination: The Political Economy of a Policy that Works." HKS Faculty Research Working Paper Series. Cambridge, MA: Harvard University, 2010. Web. 12 June 2016.

Corntassel, Jeff. "Who Is Indigenous? 'Peoplehood' and Ethnonationalist Approaches to Rearticulating Indigenous Identity." *Nationalism and Ethnic Politics* 9.1 (2003): 75–100. Web. 2 Feb. 2015.

Coulthard, Glen Sean. *Red Skin, White Masks: Rejecting the Colonial Politics of Recognition*. Minneapolis: U of Minnesota P, 2014. Print.

Cox, James H. *Muting White Noise: Native American and European American Novel Traditions*. Norman: U of Oklahoma P, 2006. Print.

Crawford, Suzanne J., and Dennis F. Kelley. "Academic Study of American Indian Religious Traditions." *American Indian Religious Traditions: An Encyclopedia*. Vol. 1. Ed. Suzanne Crawford and Dennis F. Kelley. Santa Barbara, CA: ABC CLIO, 2005. 1–10. Print.

Daes, Erica-Irene A. "The Concepts of Self-Determination and Autonomy of Indigenous Peoples in the Draft United Nations Declaration on the Rights of Indigenous Peoples." *St. Thomas Law Review* 14 (2001–2002): 259–69. *HeinOnline*. 10 July 2015.

Dale, Edward Everett, and Garston Litton, eds. *Cherokee Cavaliers: Forty Years of Cherokee History as Told in the Correspondence of the Ridge-Watie-Boudinot Family*. Norman: U of Oklahoma P, 1995. Print.

Daniel, Michelle. "From Blood Feud to Jury System: The Metamorphoses of Cherokee Law from 1750 to 1840." *American Indian Quarterly* 11.1 (1987): 97–125. *JSTOR*. Web. 12 Dec. 2013.

Dawes, Henry L. "Defense of the Dawes Act." *Americanizing the American Indians: Writings by the "Friends of the Indian" 1880–1900*. Ed. Francis Paul Prucha. Cambridge, MA: Harvard UP, 1973. 100–10. Print.

———. "Solving the Indian Problem." *Americanizing the American Indians: Writings by the "Friends of the Indian" 1880–1900*. Ed. Francis Paul Prucha. Cambridge, MA: Harvard UP, 1973. 27–30. Print.

Däwes, Birgit. "'Back to before All This,' He Said": History, Temporality, and Knowledge in Stephen Graham Jones's *The Bird Is Gone*." *The Fictions of Stephen Graham Jones: A Critical Companion*. Ed. Billy J. Stratton. Albuquerque: U of New Mexico P, 2016. 111–31. Print.

Deetjen, Claudia. "Native Nationalisms and African-Native Experiences: Zelda Lockhart's *Cold Running Creek* (2007)." *Transnational American Studies*. Ed. Udo Hebel. Heidelberg: Winter, 2012. 269–81. Print.

———. *Re-Imagining Nature's Nation: Native American and Native Hawaiian Literature, Environment, and Empire*. Heidelberg: Winter, 2016. Print.

Delaney, Danielle. "Under Coyote's Mask: Environmental Law, Indigenous Identity, and #NoDAPL." *Michigan Journal of Race and Law* 24 (2019). 299–333. *University of Michigan Law School Scholarship Repository*. Web. 15 Mar. 2021.

Deloria, Philip J. *Playing Indian*. New Haven, CT: Yale UP, 1998. Print.

Deloria, Vine, Jr., and Clifford Lytle. *American Indians, American Justice*. Austin: U of Texas P, 1983. Print.

———. *The Nations Within: The Past and Future of American Indian Sovereignty*. New York: Pantheon Books, 1984. Print.

Deloria, Vine, Jr., and David E. Wilkins. *Tribes, Treaties, and Constitutional Tribulations*. Austin: U of Texas P, 1999. Print.

Dennison, Jean. "The Logic of Recognition: Debating Osage Nation Citizenship in the Twenty-First Century." *American Indian Quarterly* 38.1 (2014): 1–35. *JSTOR*. Web. 12 Feb. 2018.

Denson, Andrew. *Demanding the Cherokee Nation: Indian Autonomy and American Culture, 1830–1900*. Lincoln: U of Nebraska P, 2004. Print.

———. *Monuments to Absence: Cherokee Removal and the Contest over Southern Memory*. Chapel Hill: U of North Carolina P, 2017. Print.

Dery, Mark. "Black to the Future: Interviews with Samuel R. Delany, Greg Tate, and Tricia Rose." *Flame Wars: The Discourse of Cyberculture*. Ed. Mark Dery. Durham, NC: Duke UP, 1994. 179–222. Print.

Dillon, Grace L. "Imagining Indigenous Futurisms." *Walking the Clouds: An Anthology of Indigenous Science Fiction*. Ed. Grace L. Dillon. Tucson: U of Arizona P, 2012. 1–14. Print.

Disrud, Stephen Chris. "A Reading of Parody as Resistance in Stephen Graham Jones's *The Bird Is Gone*." Graduate paper, North Dakota State U, April 2006. Web. 5 May 2015.

Doerfler, Jill. *Those Who Belong: Identity, Family, Blood, and Citizenship among the White Earth Anishinaabeg.* Winnipeg: University of Manitoba Press, 2015. Print.

Driskill, Qwo-Li. "Love Poems: 1838–1839." *Walking with Ghosts: Poems.* Cambridge: Salt, 2005. 56–57. Print.

Drysdale, David J. "States of Insurgency: Dismemberment and Citizenship in the American 1848." PhD thesis, U of Western Ontario, 2011. Print.

Duthu, N. Bruce. *American Indians and the Law.* London: Penguin, 2008. Print.

———. "Federal Indian Law." *Oxford Research Encyclopedia of American History. Oxfordindex,* Dec. 2014. Web. 3 Mar. 2018.

———. "Implicit Divestiture and Tribal Powers: Locating Legitimate Sources of Authority in Indian Country." *American Indian Law Review* 19.2 (1994): 353–402. *JSTOR.* Web. 2 July 2019.

Duvall, Deborah L., Murv Jacob, and James Murray. *Secret History of the Cherokees: A Novel.* Tahlequah, OK: Indian Territory P, 2012. Print.

Eaton, Rachel Caroline. *John Ross and the Cherokee Indians.* Menasha, WI: George Banta, 1914. Print.

Echo-Hawk, Walter R. *In the Courts of the Conqueror: The Ten Worst Indian Law Cases Ever Decided.* Golden, CO: Fulcrum, 2010. Print.

Echo-Hawk, Walter R., and James S. Anaya. *In the Light of Justice: The Rise of Human Rights in Native America and the UN Declaration on the Rights of Indigenous Peoples.* Golden, CO: Fulcrum, 2013. Print.

Eco, Umberto. *Travels in Hyperreality: Essays.* Trans. William Weaver. San Diego: Harcourt Brace, 1990. Print.

Eide, Asbjørn. "The Indigenous Peoples, the Working Group on Indigenous Populations and the Adoption of the UN Declaration on the Rights of Indigenous Peoples." *Making the Declaration Work: The United Nations Declaration on the Rights of Indigenous Peoples.* Ed. Claire Charters and Rodolfo Stavenhagen. Piscataway, NJ: Transaction Publishers, 2009. 32–47. Print.

Elias, Amy J. "Fragments That Rune Up the Shores: *Pushing the Bear,* Coyote Aesthetics, and Recovered History." *Modern Fiction Studies* 45.1 (1999): 185–211. *Project Muse.* 13 Nov. 2013.

Ellis, Jerry. *Walking the Trail: One Man's Journey along the Cherokee Trail of Tears.* New York: Dell, 1991. Print.

Engle, Karen. *The Elusive Promise of Indigenous Development: Rights, Culture, Strategy.* Durham, NC: Duke UP, 2010. Print.

———. "On Fragile Architecture: The UN Declaration on the Rights of Indigenous Peoples in the Context of Human Rights." *European Journal of International Law* 22.1 (2011): 141–63. Web. 12 Jan. 2016.

Fanon, Frantz. *The Wretched of the Earth.* Trans. Richard Philcox. With a Commentary by Jean-Paul Sartre and Homi K. Bhabha. New York: Grove, 2004. Print.

Fitz, Karsten. *Negotiating History and Culture: Transculturation in Contemporary Native American Fiction.* Frankfurt: Peter Lang, 2001. Print.

Fitzgerald, Stephanie, and Hilary E. Wyss. "Land and Literacy: The Textualities of Native Studies." *American Literary History* 22.2 (2010): 271–79. Web. 17 Apr. 2015.

Fitzmaurice, Andrew. "Moral Uncertainty in the Dispossession of Native Americans." *The Atlantic World and Virginia, 1550–1624*. Ed. Peter C. Mancall. Chapel Hill: U of North Carolina P, 2007. 383–409. Print.

Fletcher, Matthew L. M. "The Iron Cold of the Marshall Trilogy." *North Dakota Law Review* 82 (2006): 627–96. Michigan State University Legal Studies Research Paper 04-07. Web. 5 Nov. 2014.

———. "Looking to the East: The Stories of Modern Indian People and the Development of Tribal Law." *Seattle Journal for Social Justice* 5.1 (2006): 1–26. *Seattle U School of Law Digital Commons*. Web. 3 Sept. 2014.

Foster, Sharon Ewell. *Abraham's Well: A Novel*. Bloomington, MN: Bethany House, 2006. Print.

Frickey, Philip P. "Doctrine, Context, Institutional Relationships, and Commentary: The Malaise of Federal Indian Law through the Lens of Lone Wolf." *Tulsa Law Review* 38 (2002): 5–36. *HeinOnline*. Web. 12 Jan. 2016.

———. "Domesticating Federal Indian Law." *Minnesota Law Review* 81 (1996): 31–95. *Berkeley Law Scholarship Repository*. Web. 22 Jan. 2016.

Gallatin, Albert. "A Synopsis of the Indian Tribes within the United States East of the Rocky Mountains, and in the British and Russian Possessions in North America" (1836). Zea E-Books in American Studies. Book 16. Web. 5 May 2021.

Gamber, John Blair. "The End (of the Trail) Is the Beginning: Stephen Graham Jones's *The Bird Is Gone*." *Western American Literature* 49.1 (2014): 29–46. *Project Muse*. Web. 21 Nov. 2016.

Gannon, Tom. Review of *Riding the Trail of Tears* by Blake M. Hausman. Web. 5 May 2016.

Garrison, Tim Alan. *The Legal Ideology of Removal: The Southern Judiciary and the Sovereignty of Native Americans*. Athens: U of Georgia P, 2002. Print.

Garroutte, Eva Marie. "Defining 'Radical Indigenism' and Creating an American Indian Scholarship." *Culture, Power, and History: Studies in Critical Sociology*. Ed. Stephen Pfohl, Aimee Van Wagenen, Patricia Arend, Abigail Brooks, and Denise Leckenby. Leiden: Brill, 2006. 169–95. Print.

Genetin-Pilawa, C. Joseph. *Crooked Paths to Allotment: The Fight over Federal Indian Policy after the Civil War*. Chapel Hill: U of North Carolina P, 2014. Print.

Getches, David H. "Conquering the Cultural Frontier: The New Subjectivism of the Supreme Court in Indian Law." *California Law Review* 84.6 (1996): 1573–1655. *Berkeley Law Scholarship Repository*. Web. 28 Dec. 2015.

Gill, R. B. "The Uses of Genre and the Classification of Speculative Fiction." *Mosaic* 46.2 (2013): 71–85. *Project Muse*. 15 Dec. 2016.

Glancy, Diane. Afterword. *Pushing the Bear: After the Trail of Tears*. Norman: U of Oklahoma P, 2009. Print.

———. *Pushing the Bear: A Novel of the Trail of Tears*. New York: Harcourt Brace, 1996. Print.

Goeman, Mishuana. *Mark My Words: Native Women Mapping Our Nations*. Minneapolis: U of Minnesota P, 2013. Print.

Goldstein, Alyosha. "The Jurisprudence of Domestic Dependence: Colonial Possession and *Adoptive Couple v. Baby Girl*." Special Issue on "Reflections on

Dispossession: Critical Feminisms." Ed. Brenna Bhandar and Davina Bhandar. *Darkmatter* 14 (May 2016). Web. 17 Feb. 2021.

Gover, Kirsty. "Genealogy as Continuity: Explaining the Growing Tribal Preference for Descent Rules in Membership Governance in the United States." *American Indian Law Review* 33.1 (2008): 243–309. *HeinOnline*. Web. 30 Jan. 2018.

Greenlee-Donnell, Cynthia. "Native and African Americans: The Red and the Black." *Indyweek*, 28 Mar. 2007. Web. 10 Aug. 2016.

Gross, Ariela J. *What Blood Won't Tell: A History of Race on Trial in America*. Cambridge, MA: Harvard UP, 2008. Print.

Hadden, Sally E. "The Fragmented Laws of Slavery in the Colonial and Revolutionary Eras." *Cambridge History of Law in America*. Vol. 1. Ed. Christopher Tomlins and Michael Grossberg. Cambridge: Cambridge UP, 2008. 253–87. Print.

Hall, Anthony J. *The American Empire and the Fourth World: The Bowl with One Spoon*. Vol. 1. Montreal: McGill-Queen's UP, 2003. Print.

Hansen, Lani. "Freedman Case Exhausts Tribal Remedy." *Mvskokemedia*, 5 Jan. 2021. Web. 26 Jan. 2021.

Harjo, Joy. *An American Sunrise: Poems*. New York: W. W. Norton, 2019. Print.

Harkin, Michael Eugene. "Staged Encounters: Postmodern Tourism and Aboriginal People." *Ethnohistory* 50.3 (2003): 575–85. *Project Muse*. Web. 24 Jan. 2017.

Harootunian, Harry. "Uneven Temporalities/Untimely Pasts: Hayden White and the Question of Temporal Form." *Philosophy of History after Hayden White*. Ed. Robert Doran. London: Bloomsbury, 2013. 119–50. Print.

Harrell, Beatrice O. *Longwalker's Journey: A Novel of the Choctaw Trail of Tears*. New York: Dial Books for Young Readers, 1999. Print.

Harris, Cheryl I. "Whiteness as Property." *Harvard Law Review* 106.8 (1993): 1707–91. *JSTOR*. Web. 15 June 2017.

Harvard, John C. "John Rollin Ridge's *Joaquín Murieta*: Sensation, Hispanicism, and Cosmopolitanism." *Western American Literature* 49.4 (2015): 321–49. *JSTOR*. Web. 12 Apr. 2015.

Hausman, Blake M. *Riding the Trail of Tears: A Novel*. Lincoln: U of Nebraska P, 2011. Print.

Healy, Jack. "Black, Native American and Fighting for Recognition in Indian Country." *New York Times* 8 Sept. 2020. Web. 26 Jan. 2021.

Hebard, Andrew. *The Politics of Sovereignty in American Literature, 1885–1910*. Cambridge: Cambridge UP, 2013. Print.

Henriksen, John B. "The UN Declaration on the Rights of Indigenous Peoples: Some Key Issues and Events in the Process." *Making the Declaration Work: The United Nations Declaration on the Rights of Indigenous Peoples*. Ed. Claire Charters and Rodolfo Stavenhagen. Piscataway, NJ: Transaction Publishers, 2009. 78–85. Print.

Herman, Mathew. *Politics and Aesthetics in Contemporary Native American Literature: Across Every Border*. New York: Routledge, 2010. Print.

Hoagland, Ericka, and Reema Sarwal. "Introduction: Imperialism, the Third World, and Postcolonial Science Fiction." *Science Fiction, Imperialism, and the Third World: Essays on Postcolonial Literature and Film.* Jefferson, NC: McFarland, 2010. 5–20. Print.

Hobsbawm, Eric J. *Bandits.* London: Weidenfeld and Nicolson, 1969. Print.

Hogan, Linda. "Trail of Tears: Our Removal." *Dark Sweet: New and Selected Poems.* New York: Coffee House P, 2014. 357–59. Print.

Holder, Cindy L., and Jeff J. Corntassel. "Indigenous Peoples and Multicultural Citizenship: Bridging Collective and Individual Rights." *Human Rights Quarterly* 24 (2002): 126–51. *HeinOnline.* Web. 3 July 2015.

Holm, Tom. *The Great Confusion in Indian Affairs: Native Americans and Whites in the Progressive Era.* Austin: U of Texas P, 2005. Print.

———. "Re: the peoplehood matrix—questions from a German scholar." Email received by Sabine N. Meyer, 13 Feb. 2015.

Holm, Tom, J. Diane Pearson, and Ben Chavis. "Peoplehood: A Model for the Extension of Sovereignty in American Studies." *Wicazo Sa Review* 18.1 (2003): 7–24. *Project Muse.* Web. 1 Dec. 2015.

hooks, bell. "Postmodern Blackness." *Postmodern Culture* 1.1 (1990). *Project Muse.* Web. 7 Mar. 2017.

———. *Yearning: Race, Gender, Cultural Politics.* Toronto: Between the Lines P, 1990. Print.

Horsmann, Reginald. *Race and Manifest Destiny: The Origins of American Racial Anglo-Saxonism.* Cambridge, MA: Harvard UP, 1981. Print.

Hoxie, Frederick E. *A Final Promise: The Campaign to Assimilate the Indians, 1880–1920.* Lincoln, NE: Bison Books, 2001. Print.

Hsu, L. Hsuan. "The Legend of Joaquín Murieta: A History of Racialized Violence." *Paris Review* 9 July 2018. Web. 14 Aug. 2020.

Huang, Hsinya. "Memory, Community, Historicity in Joseph Bruchac's *The Journal of Jesse Smoke, a Cherokee Boy, The Trail of Tears, 1838.*" *Twenty-First Century Perspectives on Indigenous Studies: Native North America in (Trans)Motion.* Ed. Birgit Däwes, Karsten Fitz, and Sabine N. Meyer. New York: Routledge, 2015. 217–35. Print.

Huxley, Aldous. *Brave New World: A Novel.* London: Chatto and Windus, 1960. Print.

Institute for Government Research. *The Problem of Indian Administration: Report of a Survey Made at the Request of Honorable Hubert Work, Secretary of the Interior, and Submitted to Him, February 21, 1928.* Baltimore: Johns Hopkins, 1928. Web. 3 Mar. 2016.

Ivison, Duncan, Paul Patton, and Will Sanders, eds. Introduction. *Political Theory and the Rights of Indigenous Peoples.* Cambridge: Cambridge UP, 2000. 1–24. Print.

Jackson, Joseph Henry. Introduction. *The Life and Adventures of Joaquín Murieta: The Celebrated California Bandit.* By John Rollin Ridge (Yellow Bird). Norman: U of Oklahoma P, 1969. 11–50. Print.

James, Trechia C. "Standing with Standing Rock on the Trail of Tears." *Facebook*, 12 Nov. 2016. Web. 2 Dec. 2016.

Johnson, Hannibal B. *Apartheid in Indian Country? Seeing Red over Black Disenfranchisement*. Fort Worth, TX: Eakin, 2012. Print.

Johnson v. McIntosh. 21 U.S. 543. United States Supreme Court. 1823. *Justia*. Web. 1 Oct. 2014.

Jones, Peter. "Human Rights, Group Rights, and Peoples' Rights." *Human Rights Quarterly* 21.1 (1999): 80–107. Web. 3 Apr. 2015.

Jones, Stephen Graham. *The Bird Is Gone: A ~~Monograph~~ Manifesto*. Tallahassee: FC2, 2003. Print.

———. "Letter to a Just-Starting-Out Indian Writer—and Maybe to Myself." *Transmotion* 2.1–2 (2016): 124–30. Web. 6 Mar. 2017.

Jones, Timothy S. *Outlawry in Medieval Literature*. New York: Palgrave Macmillan, 2010. Print.

Jordan, Tracey. "Joaquín Murieta, Cherokee Outlaw-Hero: Yellow Bird's Vindication of Cherokee Nature." *Arizona Quarterly* 60.3 (2004): 1–32. *Project Muse*. Web. 21 Apr. 2015.

Justice, Daniel Heath. "'Go Away, Water!' Kinship Criticism and the Decolonization Imperative." *Reasoning Together: The Native Critics Collective*. Ed. Craig S. Womack, Daniel Heath Justice, and Christopher B. Teuton. Norman: U of Oklahoma P, 2008. 147–68. Print.

———. "The Necessity of Nationhood: Affirming the Sovereignty of Indigenous National Literatures." *Moveable Margins: The Shifting Spaces in Canadian Literature*. Ed. Chelva Kanaganayakam. Toronto: TSAR, 2005. 143–59. Print.

———. *Our Fire Survives the Storm: A Cherokee Literary History*. Indigenous Americas Series. Minneapolis: U of Minnesota P, 2006. Print.

———. *The Way of Thorn and Thunder: The Kynship Chronicles*. Albuquerque: U of New Mexico P, 2011. Print.

Kaplan, Amy. "Romancing the Empire: The Embodiment of American Masculinity in the Popular Historical Novel of the 1890s." *American Literary History* 2.4 (1990): 659–90. *JSTOR*. Web. 21 Apr. 2015.

Keene, Adrienne. "Gawker Uses 'Mail of Tears' for a Cheap Pun." *Native Appropriations*, 17 Jan. 2016. Web. 12 Jan. 2017.

Kelly, Lawrence C. *The Assault on Assimilation: John Collier and the Origins of Indian Policy Reform*. Albuquerque: U of New Mexico P, 1983. Print.

Kenney, Cortelyou C. "Reframing Indigenous Cultural Artifacts Disputes: An Intellectual Property-Based Approach." *Cardozo Arts and Entertainment* 28 (2011): 501–52. Web. 12 Jan. 2017.

Ketchum, Steve. "(Re)-Remembering the Trail of Tears." *American Anthropological Association Blog*, 16 Sept. 2015. Web. 12 Jan. 2017.

Kidwell, Clara Sue. *The Choctaws in Oklahoma: From Tribe to Nation, 1855–1970*. Norman: University of Oklahoma P, 2005. Print.

King, Tiffany Lethabo. *The Black Shoals: Offshore Formations of Black and Native Studies*. Durham, NC: Duke UP, 2019. Print.

Klevnäs, Alison. "Introduction: The Nature of Belongings." *Own and Be Owned: Archaeological Approaches to the Concept of Possession*. Ed. Alison Klevnäs and Charlotte Hedenstierna-Jonson. Stockholm: Department of Archaeology and Classical Studies, Stockholm University, 2015. 1–22. Print.

Konkle, Maureen. *Writing Indian Nations: Native Intellectuals and the Politics of Historiography, 1827–1863*. Chapel Hill: U of North Carolina P, 2004. Print.

Krauthamer, Barbara. *Black Slaves, Indian Masters: Slavery, Emancipation, and Citizenship in the Native American South*. Chapel Hill: U of North Carolina P, 2013. Print.

Kroeber, Karl, and Clifton Kroeber. Editors' introduction. *Ishi in Three Centuries*. Ed. Karl Kroeber and Clifton Kroeber. Lincoln: U of Nebraska P, 2003. xiii–xxi. Print.

Krupat, Arnold. *Ethnocriticism: Ethnography, History, Literature*. Berkeley: U of California P, 1992. Print.

———. *Red Matters: Native American Studies*. Philadelphia: U of Pennsylvania P, 2002. Print.

———. "Representing Cherokee Dispossession." *Studies in American Indian Literatures* 17.1 (2005): 16–41. Web. 3 Apr. 2015.

Kymlicka, Will. *Multicultural Citizenship: A Liberal Theory of Minority Rights*. Oxford: Oxford UP, 1996. Print.

———. *Politics in the Vernacular: Nationalism, Multiculturalism, and Citizenship*. Oxford: Oxford UP, 2001. Print.

Larré, Lionel. Introduction. *Tales of the Old Indian Territory and Essays on the Indian Condition*. By John Milton Oskison. Ed. Lionel Larré. Lincoln: U of Nebraska P, 2012. 1–64. Print.

———. "John Milton Oskison and Assimilation." *American Indian Quarterly* 37.1–2 (2013): 3–33. *Project Muse*. Web. 18 Nov. 2015.

Laurence, Robert. "Learning to Live with the Plenary Power of Congress over the Indian Nations: An Essay in Reaction to Professor Williams." *Arizona Law Review* 30.3 (1988): 413–37. Web. 17 Oct. 2015.

Leroy, Justin. "Black History in Occupied Territory: On the Entanglements of Slavery and Settler Colonialism." *Theory and Event* 19.4 (2016): 1–10. *Project Muse*. Web. 3 Mar. 2018.

Lindsay, Brendan C. *Murder State: California's Native American Genocide, 1846–1873*. Lincoln: U of Nebraska P, 2012. Print.

Littlefield, Daniel F., Jr. *Africans and Seminoles: From Removal to Emancipation*. Westport, CT: Greenwood, 1977. Print.

Locke, John. *Two Treatises of Government*. Ed. Thomas Hollis. London: A Millar et al., 1764. *Online Library of Liberty*. Web. 3 Mar. 2019.

Lockhart, Zelda. *Cold Running Creek*. Hillsborough, NC: LaVenson, 2007. Print.

Lyons, Scott Richard. "Actually Existing Indian Nations: Modernity, Diversity, and the Future of Native American Studies." *American Indian Quarterly* 35.3 (2011): 294–312. *Project Muse*. Web. 11 July 2016.

———. "Rhetorical Sovereignty: What Do American Indians Want from Writing?" *College Composition and Communication* 51.3 (2000): 447–68. Web. 11 Sept. 2016.

———. *X-Marks: Native Signatures of Assent*. Minneapolis: U of Minnesota P, 2010. Print.

Macpherson, C. B. *The Political Theory of Possessive Individualism: Hobbes to Locke*. Oxford: Oxford UP, 1962. Print.

Maddox, Lucy. *Removals: Nineteenth-Century American Literature and the Politics of Indian Affairs*. Oxford: Oxford UP, 1991. Print.

Mays, Kayle T. *Hip Hop Beats, Indigenous Rhymes: Modernity and Hip Hop in Indigenous North America*. New York: SUNY P, 2018. Print.

Mankiller, Wilma Pearl. *Mankiller: A Chief and Her People*. New York: St. Martin's, 1993. Print.

Mbembe, Achille. "Necropolitics." *Public Culture* 15.1 (2003): 11–40. Print.

McCray Pearson, Joyce A. "Red and Black—A Divided Seminole Nation: Davis v. U.S." *Kansas Journal of Law and Public Policy* 14 (2004–2005): 607–38. *HeinOnline*. Web. 11 July 2016.

McCrudden, Christopher. "Human Dignity and Judicial Interpretation of Human Rights." *European Journal of International Law* 19.4 (2008): 655–724. Web. 22 Apr. 2015.

McNickle, D'Arcy. *The Surrounded*. Albuquerque: U of New Mexico P, 1978. Print.

Meyer, Sabine N. "From Domestic Dependency to Native Cultural Sovereignty: A Legal Reading of Gerald Vizenor's *Chair of Tears*." *Native North American Survivance, Memory, and Futurity: The Gerald Vizenor Continuum*. Ed. Birgit Däwes and Alexandra Hauke. New York: Routledge, 2017. 119–34. Print.

———. "The Marshall Trilogy and Its Legacies." *Routledge Companion to Native American Literature*. Ed. Deborah L. Madsen. New York: Routledge, 2015. 123–34. Print.

Miles, Tiya. Foreword: "All in the Family: A Meditation on White Centrality, Black Exclusion, and the Intervention of Afro-Native Studies." *Race, Roots, and Relations: Native and African Americans*. Ed. Terry Straus and Denene DeQuintal. Chicago: Albatross, 2005. 1–7. Print.

———. *Ties That Bind: The Story of an Afro-Cherokee Family in Slavery and Freedom*. Berkeley: U of California P, 2005. Print.

———. "Uncle Tom Was an Indian: Tracing the Red in Black Slavery." *Confounding the Color Line: Indian-Black Relations in Multidisciplinary Perspective*. Ed. James Brooks. Lincoln: U of Nebraska P, 2002. 137–60. Print.

Miner, Joshua D. "Beasts of Burden: How Literary Animals Remap the Aesthetics of Removal." *Decolonization: Indigeneity, Education and Society* 3.2 (2014): 60–82. Web. 10 Aug. 2015.

Minges, Patrick Neal, ed. *Black Indian Slave Narratives*. Winston-Salem, NC: Blair, 2004. Print.

Mondragón, Maria. "'The [Safe] White Side of the Line': History and Disguise in John Rollin Ridge's *The Life and Adventures of Joaquin Murieta: The Celebrated California Bandit*." *ATQ* 8.3 (1994): 173–84. Print.

Monet, Jenni. "Decision in Cherokee Freedmen Case Offers Opportunity for Healing." *Indianz.com*, 7 Sept. 2017. Web. 21 Oct. 2017.

Mooney, James. *James Mooney's History, Myths, and Sacred Formulas of the Cherokees: Containing the Full Texts of* Myths of the Cherokee *(1900) and* The Sacred Formulas of the Cherokees *(1891) as Published by the Bureau of American Ethnology*. Introd. George Ellison. Fairview, NC: Bright Mountain Books, 1992.

Moreton-Robinson, Aileen. *The White Possessive: Property, Power, and Indigenous Sovereignty*. Minneapolis: U of Minnesota P, 2015. Print.

———. "Virtuous Racial States: The Possessive Logic of Patriarchal White Sovereignty and the United Nations Declaration on the Rights of Indigenous Peoples." *Griffith Law Review* 20.3 (2011): 641–58. *HeinOnline*. Web. 11 July 2016.

Moulton, Gary E., ed. *The Papers of Chief John Ross*. Vol. 1. Norman: U of Oklahoma P, 1985. Print.

Muskrat, Ruth Margaret. "The Trail of Tears." *University of Oklahoma Magazine* 10 (1 Feb. 1922): 14. Web. 12 May 2015.

Nash, et al., vs. Cherokee Nation Registrar. CV-07-40. District Court of the Cherokee Nation. 2011. Web. 17 Apr. 2015.

Naylor, Celia E. *African Cherokees in Indian Territory: From Chattel to Citizens*. Chapel Hill: U of North Carolina P, 2008. Print.

———. "'Born and Raised among These People, I Don't Want to Know Any Other': Slave's Acculturation in Nineteenth-Century Indian Territory." *Confounding the Color Line: The Indian-Black Experience in North America*. Ed. James F. Brooks. Lincoln: U of Nebraska P, 2002. 161–91. Print.

Nelson, Joshua B. *Progressive Traditions: Identity in Cherokee Literature and Culture*. Norman: U of Oklahoma P, 2014. Print.

Nichols, Robert. *Theft Is Property! Dispossession and Critical Theory*. Durham, NC: Duke UP, 2020. Print.

Niezen, Ronald. *The Origins of Indigenism: Human Rights and the Politics of Identity*. Berkeley: U of California P, 2003. Print.

Norgren, Jill. *The Cherokee Cases: Two Landmark Federal Decisions in the Fight for Sovereignty*. Norman: U of Oklahoma P, 2004. Print.

Ortiz, Fernando. *Cuban Counterpoint: Tobacco and Sugar*. 1940. Durham, NC: Duke UP, 1995. Print.

Oskison, John Milton. "Cherokee Migration." *Tales of the Old Indian Territory and Essays on the Indian Condition*. Ed. Lionel Larré. Lincoln: U of Nebraska P, 2012. 349–52. Print.

———. "The Closing Chapter: Passing of the Old Indian." *Tales of the Old Indian Territory and Essays on the Indian Condition*. Ed. Lionel Larré. Lincoln: U of Nebraska P, 2012. 429–36. Print.

———. "Friends of the Indian." *Tales of the Old Indian Territory and Essays on the Indian Condition*. Ed. Lionel Larré. Lincoln: U of Nebraska P, 2012. 362–64. Print.

———. "Making an Individual of the Indian." *Tales of the Old Indian Territory and Essays on the Indian Condition*. Ed. Lionel Larré. Lincoln: U of Nebraska P, 2012. 380–690. Print.

———. "The Outlook for the Indian." *Tales of the Old Indian Territory and Essays on the Indian Condition*. Ed. Lionel Larré. Lincoln: U of Nebraska P, 2012. 358–61. Print.

———. "The President and the Indian: Rich Opportunity for the Red Man." *Tales of the Old Indian Territory and Essays on the Indian Condition*. Ed. Lionel Larré. Lincoln: U of Nebraska P, 2012. 353–57. Print.

———. "Remaining Causes of Indian Discontent." *Tales of the Old Indian Territory and Essays on the Indian Condition*. Ed. Lionel Larré. Lincoln: U of Nebraska P, 2012. 372–79. Print.

———. *The Singing Bird: A Cherokee Novel*. Ed. Timothy B. Powell and Melinda Smith Mullikin. Norman: U of Oklahoma P, 2007. Print.

Owens, Louis. *Other Destinies: Understanding the American Indian Novel*. Norman: U of Oklahoma P, 1992. Print.

Oziewicz, Marek. "Speculative Fiction." *Oxford Research Encyclopedia of Literature*, 2016. Web. 12 Jan. 2017.

Painter, Charles. "Our Indian Policy as Related to the Civilization of the Indian." *Americanizing the American Indians: Writings by the "Friends of the Indian" 1880–1900*. Ed. Francis Paul Prucha. Cambridge, MA: Harvard UP, 1973. 66–73. Print.

Parins, James W. *John Rollin Ridge: His Life and Works*. Lincoln: U of Nebraska P, 1991. Print.

Parins, James W., and Jeff Ward, eds. "The Poems of John Rollin Ridge—A Reproduction of the 1868 Publication Plus Fugitive Poems and Notes." *Sequoyah Research Center, American Native Press Archives, U of Arkansas*. Web. 10 May 2015.

Parrish, Austen L. "Changing Territoriality, Fading Sovereignty, and the Development of Indigenous Group Rights." *American Indian Law Review* 31.2 (2007): 291–313. Faculty Publications 889. *Digital Repository@Maurer Law*. Web. 10 Aug. 2015.

Pate, James P. "LeFlore, Greenwood (1800–1865)." *Encyclopedia of Oklahoma History and Culture*. Web. 27 Oct. 2015.

Pattaro, Enrico. "An Overview on Practical Reason in Aquinas." *Stockholm Institute for Scandinavian Law*, 2010. Web. 22 May 2015.

Paul, Herman. *Hayden White: The Historical Imagination*. Cambridge: Polity, 2011. Print.

Payne, Marissa. "Ohio High School Cheerleaders Taunt Opposing 'Indians' with 'Trail of Tears' Banner." *Washington Post* 29 Oct. 2016. Web. 12 Jan. 2017.

Perdue, Theda, ed. *Cherokee Editor: The Writings of Elias Boudinot*. Athens: U of Georgia P, 1996. Print.

———. "Cherokee Women and the Trail of Tears." *Journal of Women's History* 1.1 (1989): 14–30. *ProQuest*. Web. 12 Aug. 2020.

———. *Slavery and the Evolution of Cherokee Society, 1540–1866*. Knoxville: U of Tennessee P, 1979. Print.

Perdue, Theda, and Michael D. Green. *The Cherokee Nation and the Trail of Tears*. New York: Viking, 2007. Print.

———. *The Cherokee Removal: A Brief History with Documents.* Boston: St. Martin's, 1995.

———. *North American Indians: A Very Short Introduction.* New York: Oxford UP, 2010.

Petersen, Niels. "Human Dignity, International Protection." *Max Planck Encyclopedia of Public International Law,* Oct. 2012. Web. 16 Sept. 2015.

Peyer, Bernd C. *American Indian Nonfiction: An Anthology of Writings, 1760s–1930s.* Norman: U of Oklahoma P, 2007. Print.

———. *The Tutor'd Mind: Indian Missionary Writers in Antebellum America.* Amherst: U of Massachusetts P, 1997. Print.

Piatote, Beth H. *Domestic Subjects: Gender, Citizenship, and Law in Native American Literature.* New Haven, CT: Yale UP, 2013. Print.

———. "Domestic Trials: Indian Rights and National Belonging in Works by E. Pauline Johnson and John M. Oskison." *American Quarterly* 63.1 (2011): 95–116. *Project Muse.* Web. 7 May 2014.

Powell, Timothy B., and Melinda Smith Mullikin. Introduction. *The Singing Bird: A Cherokee Novel.* By John Milton Oskison. Norman: U of Oklahoma P, 2007. xix–xlvii. Print.

Prucha, Francis Paul. *American Indian Treaties: The History of a Political Anomaly.* Berkeley: U California P, 1994. Print.

———, ed. *Documents of United States Indian Policy.* 3rd ed. Lincoln: U of Nebraska P, 2000. Print.

———. Introduction. *Americanizing the American Indians: Writings by the "Friends of the Indian" 1880–1900.* Ed. Francis Paul Prucha. Cambridge, MA: Harvard UP, 1973. 1–10. Print.

Pulitano, Elvira. "Indigenous Rights and International Law: An Introduction." *Indigenous Rights in the Age of the Declaration.* Ed. Elvira Pulitano. Cambridge: Cambridge UP, 2012. 1–30. Print.

"Q&A with *Abrahams's Well* Author Sharon Ewell Foster." *Christianbook,* 20 Mar. 2007. Web. 10 Aug. 2016.

Radin, Margaret Jane. "Property and Personhood." *Stanford Law Review* 34 (1982): 957–1015. *HeinOnline.* Web. 15 Jan. 2016.

Ray, S. Alan. "A Race or a Nation? Cherokee National Identity and the Status of Freedmen's Descendants." *Michigan Journal of Race and Law* 12 (2007): 387–463. Web. 2 Feb. 2017.

Reed, Julie L. *Serving the Nation: Cherokee Sovereignty and Social Welfare, 1800–1907.* Norman: U of Oklahoma P, 2016. Print.

"Remembering the Trail of Tears." *ProQuest,* 16 Sept. 2016. Web. 12 Nov. 2016.

"Report of the Dawes Commission." *Documents of United States Indian Policy.* 3rd ed. Ed. Francis Paul Prucha. Lincoln: U of Nebraska P, 2000. 189–93. Print.

"Report of the Working Group on Indigenous Populations on the Eleventh Session." 23 Aug. 1993. E/CN.4/Sub.2/1993/29. Dag Hammarskjöld Library. Print.

Ridge, John. "Speech of John Ridge, A Cherokee Chief." *Liberator* 17 Mar. 1832, 44; col. B. Print.

Ridge, John Rollin (Yellow Bird). *A Trumpet of Our Own: Yellow Bird's Essays on the North American Indian: Selections from the Writings of the Noted Cherokee Author John Rollin Ridge*. Ed. and comp. David Farmer and Rennard Strickland. San Francisco: Book Club of California, 1981. Print.

———. *The Life and Adventures of Joaquín Murieta: The Celebrated California Bandit*. Introd. Joseph Henry Jackson. Norman: U of Oklahoma P, 1969. Print.

Rifkin, Mark. *Beyond Settler Time: Temporal Sovereignty and Indigenous Self-Determination*. Durham, NC: Duke UP, 2017. Print.

———. *The Erotics of Sovereignty: Queer Native Writing in the Era of Self-Determination*. Minneapolis: U of Minnesota P, 2012. Print.

———. *Fictions of Land and Flesh: Blackness, Indigeneity, Speculation*. Durham, NC: Duke UP, 2019. Print.

———. "'For the Wrongs of Our Poor Bleeding Country': Sensation, Class, and Empire in Ridge's *Joaquín Murieta*." *Arizona Quarterly* 65.2 (2009): 27–56. *Project Muse*. Web. 21 Apr. 2015.

———. "Indigenizing Agamben: Rethinking Sovereignty in Light of the 'Peculiar' Status of Native Peoples." *Cultural Critique* 73 (2009): 88–124. Web. 23 Apr. 2015.

———. "Making Peoples into Populations: The Racial Limits of Tribal Sovereignty." *Theorizing Native Studies*. Ed. Audra Simpson and Andrea Smith. Durham, NC: Duke UP, 2014. 149–87. Print.

———. *Manifesting America: The Imperial Construction of U.S. National Space*. Oxford: Oxford UP, 2009. Print.

Riggs v. Ummerteskee. JAT-97-03-K. Judicial Appeals Tribunal of the Cherokee Nation. 2001. Web. 12 Nov. 2015.

Riley, Angela R. "The History of Native American Lands and the Supreme Court." *Journal of Supreme Court History* 38.3 (2013): 369–85. *Wiley Online Library*. Web. 12 Dec. 2015.

———. "Straight Stealing: Towards an Indigenous System of Cultural Property Protection." *Washington Law Review* 80 (2005): 69–164. Web. 17 May 2015.

Riley, Angela R., and Kristen A. Carpenter. "Owning *Red*: A Theory of Indian (Cultural) Appropriation." *Texas Law Review* 94.5 (2016): 859–931. Web. 7 Jan. 2017.

Robertson, Lindsay G. *Conquest by Law: How the Discovery of America Dispossessed Indigenous Peoples of Their Lands*. Oxford: Oxford UP, 2005. Print.

———. "The Judicial Conquest of Native America: The Story of *Johnson v. M'Intosh*." *Indian Law Stories*. Ed. Carole Goldberg, Kevin K. Washburn, and Philip P. Frickey. New York: Foundation, 2011. 29–59. Print.

Ronnow, Gretchen Lyn. "John Milton Oskison: Native American Modernist." Dissertation, U of Arizona, 1993. *UA Campus Repository*. Web. 2 Aug. 2016.

Rosen, Deborah A. *American Indians and State Law: Sovereignty, Race, and Citizenship, 1790–1880*. Lincoln: U of Nebraska P, 2007. Print.

———. "Slavery, Race, and Outlawry: The Concept of the Outlaw in Nineteenth-Century Abolitionist Rhetoric." *American Journal of Legal History* 58.1 (2018): 126–56. Print.

Rozema, Vicki. *Voices from the Trail of Tears.* Winston-Salem, NC: John F. Blair, 2003. Print.
Saunt, Claudio. *Black, White, and Indian: Race and the Unmaking of an American Family.* Oxford: Oxford UP, 2005. Print.
———. "'The English Has Now a Mind to Make Slaves of Them All': Creeks, Seminoles, and the Problem of Slavery." *Confounding the Color Line: The Indian-Black Experience in North America.* Ed. James F. Brooks. Lincoln: U of Nebraska P, 2002. 47–75. Print.
Schulte-Tenckhoff, Isabelle. "Treaties, Peoplehood, and Self-Determination: Understanding the Language of Indigenous Rights." *Indigenous Rights in the Age of the Declaration.* Ed. Elvira Pulitano. Cambridge: Cambridge UP, 2012. 64–86. Print.
Schweninger, Lee. "'Use and Control': Issues of Repatriation and Redress in American Indian Literature." *Indigenous Rights in the Age of the Declaration.* Ed. Elvira Pulitano. Cambridge: Cambridge UP, 2012. 250–75. Print.
Seal, Graham. *The Outlaw Legend: A Cultural Tradition in Britain, America and Australia.* Cambridge: Cambridge UP, 1996. Print.
Shattuck, Petra T., and Jill Norgren. "Political Use of the Legal Process by Black and American Indian Minorities." *Howard Law Journal* 22.1 (1979): 1–26. *HeinOnline.* Web. 6 Aug. 2016.
Simpson, Audra. "Paths toward a Mohawk Nation: Narratives of Citizenship and Nationhood in Kahnawake." *Political Theory and the Rights of Indigenous Peoples.* Ed. Duncan Ivison, Paul Patton, and Will Sanders. Cambridge: Cambridge UP, 2000. 113–36. Print.
———. *Mohawk Interruptus: Political Life across the Borders of Settler States.* Durham, NC: Duke UP, 2014. Print.
Singel, Wenona T. "Cultural Sovereignty and Transplanted Law: Tensions in Indigenous Self-Rule." *Kansas Journal of Law and Public Policy* 15 (2005–2006): 357–69. *Digital Commons at Michigan State U College of Law.* Web. 3 Sept. 2014.
Singer, Joseph William. "Sovereignty and Property." *Northwestern University Law Review* 86.1 (1991): 1–56. *HeinOnline.* Web. 12 July 2015.
Smith, Rogers M. *Political Peoplehood: The Roles of Values, Interests, and Identities.* Chicago: U of Chicago P, 2015. Print.
———. *Stories of Peoplehood: The Politics and Morals of Political Membership.* Cambridge: Cambridge UP, 2003. Print.
Smithers, Gregory D. *The Cherokee Diaspora: An Indigenous History of Migration, Resettlement, and Identity.* New Haven, CT: Yale UP, 2015. Print.
Snyder, Christina. *Slavery in Indian Country: The Changing Face of Captivity in Early America.* Cambridge, MA: Harvard UP, 2010. Print.
Somvichian-Clausen, Austa. "The Creek Freedmen Push for Indigenous Tribal Rights Decades after Being Enfranchised." *Hill* 7 Dec. 2020. Web. 21 Jan. 2021.
Spiers, Miriam C. Brown. "Reimagining Resistance: Achieving Sovereignty in Indigenous Science Fiction." *Transmotion* 2.1–2 (2016): 52–75. Web. 10 Dec. 2016.

Spivak, Gayatri Chakravorty. "Translator's Preface." *Of Grammatology* by Jacques Derrida. Trans. Gayatri Chakravorty Spivak. Introd. Judith Butler. Baltimore: Johns Hopkins UP, 2016. xxvii–cxii. Print.

Stratton, Billy, and Frances Washburn. "The Peoplehood Matrix: A New Theory for American Indian Literature." *Wicazo Sa Review* 23.1 (2008): 51–72. Project Muse. Web. 11 July 2016.

Streeby, Shelley. *American Sensations: Class, Empire, and the Production of Popular Culture*. Berkeley: U of California P, 2002. Print.

Strickland, Rennard. *Fire and the Spirits: Cherokee Law from Clan to Court*. Norman: U of Oklahoma P, 1975. Print.

Strong, Pauline Turner. "Representational Practices." *A Companion to the Anthropology of American Indians*. Ed. Thomas Biolsi. Hoboken, NJ: Blackwell, 2004. 341–59. Print.

Sturm, Circe. *Becoming Indian: The Struggle over Cherokee Identity in the Twenty-First Century*. Santa Fe, NM: School for Advanced Research P, 2011. Print.

———. *Blood Politics: Race, Culture, and Identity in the Cherokee Nation of Oklahoma*. Berkeley: U of California P, 2002. Print.

———. "Race, Sovereignty, and Civil Rights: Understanding the Cherokee Freedmen Controversy." *Cultural Anthropology* 29.3 (2014): 575–98. Web. 12 July 2016.

Suzack, Cheryl. "The Transposition of Law and Literature in *Delgamuukw* and *Monkey Beach*." *South Atlantic Quarterly* 110.2 (Spring 2011): 447–63. Print.

Svensson, Frances. "Liberal Democracy and Group Rights: The Legacy of Individualism and Its Impact on American Indian Tribes." *Political Studies* 27.3 (1979): 421–39. *Wiley Online Library*. 10 Aug. 2015.

Sweet, Timothy. *American Georgics: Economy and Environment in Early American Literature*. Philadelphia: U of Pennsylvania P, 2002. Print.

Talbot, Steve. "Indian Reorganization Act." *Encyclopedia of American Indian History*. Vol. 1. Ed. Bruce E. Johansen and Barry M. Pritzker. Santa Barbara, CA: ABC-CLIO, 2008. 555–59. Print.

TallBear, Kim. *Native American DNA: Tribal Belonging and the False Promise of Genetic Science*. Minneapolis: U of Minnesota P, 2013. Print.

Tan, Kathy-Ann. *Reconfiguring Citizenship and National Identity in the North American Literary Imagination*. Detroit: Wayne State UP, 2015. Print.

Teuton, Christopher B. *Cherokee Stories of the Turtle Island Liars' Club*. Chapel Hill: U of North Carolina P, 2012. Print.

Teuton, Sean Kicummah. "The Native Novel." *Oxford History of the Novel in English*. Vol. 6: *The American Novel 1870–1940*. Ed. Priscilla Wald and Michael A. Elliott. Oxford: Oxford UP, 2014. 423–35. Print.

Thomas, Robert K. "Cherokee Values and World View." Unpublished paper, 1958. Web. 11 Jan. 2019.

Tingle, Tim. *How I Became a Ghost: A Choctaw Trail of Tears Story*. Oklahoma City: RoadRunner, 2013. Print.

Tocqueville, Alexis de. *Democracy in America*. Vol. 1. Trans. Harry Reeve. New York: Vintage Books, 1990. Print.

Triplett, Le. *American Exodus: A Historical Novel about Indian Removal.* Lincoln, NB: iUniverse, 2006. Print.

Tsosie, Rebecca A. "Land, Culture, and Community: Reflections on Native Sovereignty and Property in America." *Indiana Law Review* 34 (2001): 1291–312. Web. 4 Sept. 2016.

———. "Reclaiming Native Stories: An Essay on Cultural Appropriation and Cultural Rights." *Arizona State Law Journal* 34 (2002): 299–358. Web. 12 Nov. 2015.

Tsosie, Rebecca, and Wallace Coffey. "Rethinking the Tribal Sovereignty Doctrine: Cultural Sovereignty the Collective Future of Indian Nations." *Stanford Law and Policy Review* 12.2 (2001): 191–221. Web. 29 Sept. 2015.

Twist, Glenn J. *Boston Mountain Tales: Stories from a Cherokee Family.* Greenfield Center, NY: Greenfield Review, 1997. Print.

Universal Declaration of Human Rights (UDHR). 1948. *United Nations.* Web. 12 Apr. 2015.

Vann, Marilyn. "Cherokee Chief Moves to Remove Cherokee Citizens from Tribal Membership Status." *African-Native American Genealogy Forum,* 15 Mar. 2016. Web. 6 June 2016.

Vigil, Kiara M. *Indigenous Intellectuals: Sovereignty, Citizenship, and the American Imagination, 1880–1930.* Cambridge: Cambridge UP, 2015. Print.

Vigil, Kiara, and Tiya Miles. "At the Crossroads of Red/Black Literature." *Oxford Handbook of Indigenous American Literature.* Ed. James H. Cox and Daniel Heath Justice. Oxford: Oxford UP, 2014. 31–49. Print.

Vizenor, Gerald. "Aesthetics of Survivance: Literary Theory and Practice." *Survivance: Narratives of Native Presence.* Ed. Gerald Vizenor. Lincoln: U of Nebraska P, 2008. 1–24. Print.

———. *Chair of Tears: A Novel.* Lincoln: U of Nebraska P, 2012. Print.

———. *Fugitive Poses: Native American Indian Scenes of Absence and Presence.* Lincoln: U of Nebraska P, 2000. Print.

———. *Manifest Manners: Narratives on Postindian Survivance.* Lincoln: U of Nebraska P, 1998. Print.

———. "A Postmodern Introduction." *Narrative Chance: Postmodern Discourse on Native American Indian Literature.* Ed. Gerald Vizenor. Albuquerque: U of New Mexico P, 2008. 1–12. Print.

———. "Socioacupuncture: Mythic Reversals and the Striptease in Four Scenes." *The American Indian and the Problem of History.* Ed. Calvin Martin. New York: Oxford UP, 1987. 180–91. Print.

———. *The Trickster of Liberty: Native Heirs to a Wild Baronage.* Norman: U of Oklahoma P, 2005. Print.

Vizenor, Gerald, and A. Robert Lee. *Postindian Conversations.* Lincoln: U of Nebraska P, 1999. Print.

Walker, Cheryl. *Indian Nation: Native American: Literature and Nineteenth-Century Nationalism.* Durham, NC: Duke UP, 1997. Print.

Warrior, Robert Allen. "Cherokees Flee the Moral High Ground Over Freedmen." *News from Indian Country,* 9 Aug. 2007. Web. 31 Oct. 2016.

Watson, Blake A. "The Doctrine of Discovery and the Elusive Definition of Indian Title." *Lewis and Clark Law Review* 15.4 (2011): 995–1024. Web. 10 Aug. 2016.

Watson, Irene. "The 2007 Declaration on the Rights of Indigenous Peoples: Indigenous Survival—Where to from Here?" *Griffith Law Review* 20.3 (2011): 507–14. *HeinOnline.* Web. 11 July 2016.

Weaver, Jace. *That the People Might Live: Native American Literatures and Native American Community.* Oxford: Oxford UP, 1997. Print.

White, Hayden. "The Value of Narrativity in the Representation of Reality." *Critical Inquiry* (Autumn 1980): 5–27. *JSTOR.* Web. 16 Aug. 2016.

White, Michael J. "On the Use of '*Ius*' (and '*Lex*')." Unpublished article. Web. 10 May 2015. Quoted with permission from the author.

Wicke, Jennifer. "Postmodern Identity and the Legal Subject." *University of Colorado Law Review* 62 (1991): 455–73. *HeinOnline.* Web. 22 May 2017.

Wiessner, Siegfried. "Indigenous Self-Determination, Culture, and Land: A Reassessment in Light of the 2007 Declaration on the Rights of the Indigenous Peoples." *Indigenous Rights in the Age of the Declaration.* Ed. Elvira Pulitano. Cambridge: Cambridge UP, 2012. 31–63. Print.

Wilkins, David E. *American Indian Sovereignty and the U.S. Supreme Court: The Masking of Justice.* Austin: U of Texas P, 1997. Print.

———. "A Most Grievous Display of Behavior: Self-Decimation in Indian Country." *Michigan State Law Review* 2 (2013): 325–38. Web. 8 May 2015.

Wilkins, David E., and Tsianina Lomawaima. *Uneven Ground: American Indian Sovereignty and Federal Law.* Norman: U of Oklahoma P, 2001. Print.

Wilkinson, Charles F. *American Indians, Time, and the Law: Native Societies in a Modern Constitutional Democracy.* New Haven, CT: Yale UP, 1987. Print.

———. *Blood Struggle: The Rise of Modern Indian Nations.* New York: Norton, 2005. Print.

Williams, Robert A., Jr. *The American Indian in Western Legal Thought: The Discourses of Conquest.* Oxford: Oxford UP, 1990. Print.

———. *Like a Loaded Weapon: The Rehnquist Court, Indian Rights, and the Legal History of Racism in America.* Minneapolis: U of Minnesota P, 2005. Print.

———. *Linking Arms Together: American Indian Treaty Visions of Law and Peace, 1600–1800.* New York: Routledge, 1997. Print.

Wilms, Douglas C. "Cherokee Land Use in Georgia before Removal." *Cherokee Removal: Before and After.* Ed. William L. Anderson. Athens: U of Georgia P, 1991. 1–28. Print.

Wolfe, Patrick. "Settler Colonialism and the Elimination of the Native." *Journal of Genocide Research* 8.4 (2006): 387–409. Web. 21 Oct. 2015.

Wong, Julia Carrie. "Police Remove Last Standing Rock Protesters in Military-Style Takeover." *Guardian* 23 Feb. 2017. Web. 5 May 2017.

Womack, Craig S. *Red on Red: Native American Literary Separatism.* Minneapolis: U of Minnesota P, 1999. Print.

Worcester v. Georgia. 31 U.S. 515. United States Supreme Court. 1832. *Justia.* Web. 13 Nov. 2015.

Worland, Justin. "What to Know about the Dakota Access Pipeline Protests." *Time* 28 Oct. 2016. Web. 12 Nov. 2016.

Worster, Donald. *A River Running West: The Life of John Wesley Powell*. New York: Oxford UP, 2001. Print.

Xanthaki, Alexandra. *Indigenous Rights and United Nations Standards: Self-Determination, Culture and Land*. Cambridge: Cambridge UP, 2007. Print.

Yellow Bird. *The Life and Adventures of Joaquín Murieta, the Celebrated California Bandit*. San Francisco: W. B. Cooke, 1854. Print.

Ziff, Bruce, and Patima V. Rao. "Introduction to Cultural Appropriation: A Framework for Analysis." *Borrowed Power: Essays on Cultural Appropriation*. New Brunswick, NJ: Rutgers UP, 1997. 1–30. Print.

Index

Acosta, José de, *De procuranda Indorum*, 36
Act of Union between Eastern and Western Cherokees (1839), 133–35, 243n32
Adamson, Joni, 11
adaptation (of Natives to settler colonial customs), 67, 86–93, 119, 137, 144, 146, 149–52, 158, 170–71, 242n27
advancement (Native capacity for), 19, 71, 75, 77–79, 81–83, 85–86, 102, 238n20
African-Native literature, 10, 138–79, 231n13
African Natives, 10, 21, 138–79, 218–19, 223, 246n36. *See also* Cherokee freedmen debate; slavery (African Americans as slaves of Native Americans)
Afrofuturism, 214–15
Afro-Natives. *See* African Natives
Agamben, Giorgio, 155–57, 245n25
agency (of Natives), 9, 19, 78, 201–2, 226
agriculture, 7, 31–32, 35–36, 51, 75, 80–81, 87, 121, 123, 125, 129, 133, 173
Ahmed, Sara, 215
Alabama, 24, 40–41, 46–47, 241n14
alcohol, 195, 212
Alexie, Sherman, 230n5
Alfred, Taiaiake, 12, 211
allegory, 6, 26, 50–51, 54, 98, 235n19
Allen, Chadwick, 11, 108

Allen v. Cherokee Nation Tribal Council, et al. (2006), 138–40
allotment, policy of, 5, 19, 48, 68–78, 80, 83, 85–88, 95–96, 98, 100, 138–40, 148, 159, 173, 237n4, 238n20, 243n2. *See also* Dawes Act (1887)
Althusser, Louis, 16, 232n25
amalgamation (Oskison), 19, 72, 97–100
American Indian Defense Association, 238n15
American Indian Studies Association, 135
Anaya, James S., 11, 111, 113–14, 118
ancestors, 32–33, 65, 73, 111, 145, 162, 172, 175, 229n5, 243n1
anger (Ahmed), 215
Anishinaabe, 7, 219, 226
anthropology, 13, 16, 73, 182, 184–85, 189–90, 192–95, 198, 202, 207, 239n28, 248n20
anticolonial strategies, 26, 49, 62, 66, 163–64; reappropriation, 16–17, 184, 188, 209, 211, 249n27; repurposing, 116, 216. *See also* decolonization; resistance, Native forms of
appropriation as perpetual Native experience, 214–15. *See also* cultural appropriation; dispossession
Arbuckle, Matthew, 81
Archambault, David, II, 1–2. *See also* Standing Rock protests (2016–17)

275

INDEX

Aristotle, 78
assimilation, 5, 9, 19, 27, 35, 68, 71–73, 77, 83–89, 91, 93, 95–100, 204–5, 217, 233n5, 237n4, 238n20, 239n27, 239n31, 242n27
atavism, 81
authenticity, 22, 60, 139, 185, 187–88, 194, 196–98, 200–204, 208, 210–12, 214, 219–20

Banner, Stuart, 1–2, 11, 122
bare life (Agamben), 155, 157
Barker, Joanna, 105, 139, 213–14
Battle of Horseshoe Bend, 241n14
Baudemann, Kristina, 212
Baudrillard, Jean, 185, 189–90, 192–93, 197, 202, 209
Bedford, Denton R., 232n26
belonging (Native forms of), 3–5, 8, 14, 21–22, 24–27, 30, 67, 69, 83, 87, 100, 111, 124–25, 127–28, 140, 144, 147–51, 153, 156–59, 162, 164–65, 167, 169–77, 182, 189, 196, 198, 201, 203–4, 211, 213–14, 216–18, 221–22, 225–27, 243nn3–4, 246n34, 250n5. *See also* Cherokee collective identity; Native collective identity
Benjamin, Walter, 236n28
Bentham, Jeremy, 152–53
Bernstein, Robin, 160
Bhabha, Homi, 206
Bhandar, Brenna, 31, 35, 229n2
Biolsi, Tom, 191–92
biracial (Native-White): as intratribal elites, 72, 78, 82–83, 92, 98, 150, 161, 239n27. *See also* multiracialism
Black, Jason Edward, 101
Blackfeet, 7, 181, 218
blood feud, 27, 45
blood quantum rules, 138–41, 143, 145, 155, 157, 159, 166, 168–70, 176, 179, 204, 212, 217, 243n2, 243nn4–5, 244n7, 244n14, 245n26, 246n31, 246n37

blood requirement, 138–39, 244n7
Blood Rolls. *See* blood quantum rules; tribal membership
Boas, Franz, 94–95, 238n21
Bobroff, Kenneth H., 11, 120–21
Boudinot, Elias, 6, 18, 25–26, 28, 36–37, 39–46, 48–50, 53, 61, 63–64, 91, 109, 216, 225, 230n7, 230n9, 232n28, 234n11
Brennan, Jonathan, 10
British colonial policy, 30, 32–33, 233n3. *See also* Revolutionary War
Brown, Kirby, 79, 100, 132, 230n7, 239n29
Bruchac, Joseph, 230n5
Buchanan, Allen, 117, 121, 131, 242n29
Bureau of American Ethnology, 240n9
Bureau of Indian Affairs, 87, 242n23
Byrd, Jodi, 88–89, 139, 143–44, 223

Caldwell, Charles, 90
Caldwell v. Alabama (1831), 40–41
California, racist legal practices in nineteenth century, 49–50, 52–54, 56–60, 62, 65, 235n19, 235nn25–26, 236n27
Callahan, Sophia Alice, 238n17
capitalism, 26, 92, 122–23, 143, 154, 158, 167. *See also* property
Carlson, David J., 11
Carpenter, Kristen, 11, 13, 126
Carroll, Lewis, 193
Cass, Lewis, 46
Catron, John, 25, 43, 234n15
Champagne, Duane, 135
Chang, David, 11, 167
chattel slavery, 143, 147, 149–54, 156–57, 162, 166–67, 169, 176, 244n15, 245n21. *See also* slavery (African Americans as slaves of Native Americans); slavery (Native Americans as slaves)
Chavis, Ben, 13

INDEX

Cherokee citizenship. *See* tribal membership
Cherokee clans, 26–27, 45, 129, 145, 147, 168, 173, 245n17
Cherokee collective identity, 7, 26, 31, 44, 125, 137, 165, 167. *See also* Native collective identity
Cherokee constitutions, 27, 29–32, 40, 47, 77, 79–80, 139–41, 178, 243n4, 244n7
Cherokee Freedmen Art and History Project, 178–79
Cherokee freedmen debate, 5, 21, 138, 140–41, 143–44, 169, 173, 177–79, 243n1, 244nn6–9, 244n13. *See also* African Natives; slavery (African Americans as slaves of Native Americans)
Cherokee General Council, 37
Cherokee governance, 34, 49, 52, 109. *See also* Act of Union between Eastern and Western Cherokees (1839); tribal governance
Cherokee intratribal conflicts, 21, 78, 236nn31–33. *See also* Cherokee freedmen debate; Treaty of New Echota
Cherokee language/*Tsalagi*, 91, 121, 127, 132, 144–45
Cherokee legal system, 27–28, 30, 44, 246n31
Cherokee legends, 89, 128, 242n27, 249n31
Cherokee life in Indian country, 63–64, 166–67. *See also* Indian Territory
Cherokee National Code, 138
Cherokee National Council, 47, 235n17
Cherokee Nation Tribal Council, 138–40
Cherokee Nation Tribal Council Legislative Act, 138
Cherokee Nation v. Georgia (1831), 24, 37–39, 64

Cherokee Nation v. Raymond Nash, et al. (2017), 178
"Cherokeeness," 27, 98, 140, 159, 174. *See also* Cherokee collective identity
Cherokee peoplehood. *See* peoplehood
Cherokee Phoenix, 33, 36, 39–40, 43, 234n8
Cherokee society, 124–30, 241n26
Cherokee Trail of Tears, 20, 25, 109–11, 119–27, 129, 142–43, 145, 147, 149, 158, 166, 172, 174, 183–88, 197–98, 207, 221, 223, 244n13, 244n15, 246n33. *See also* Trail of Tears
Cherokee women. *See* gender issues
Cheyenne River Sioux, 1
Cheyfitz, Eric, 9–11
Chickasaws, 2, 141, 170, 246n36
childhood innocence, 160–61
Chinese in California, 56–57
Choctaw clans, 148–49, 154–55, 162, 175
Choctaw governance, 155, 157
Choctaws, 1, 7, 21, 141–43, 148–50, 154–57, 161–62, 164, 169–71, 175–77, 184, 218, 230n5, 231n10, 232n28, 244n12, 245n19, 245nn23–24, 246n36
Choctaw slave codes, 156–57, 162, 171
Christianity, 35–36, 40, 75, 91, 93–94, 96, 129, 246n34
Cicero, *De Legibus*, 54
citizenship. *See* tribal membership
civilization (settler colonial concept), 19, 35–36, 39, 42, 46, 51, 53–54, 57, 59, 61–62, 65, 68–79, 81–84, 86, 89–97, 99–100, 113–15, 120, 124, 128, 134, 137–38, 143, 150–52, 237nn5–6, 238n20
Civil War, 74, 78, 82, 142, 163, 168–69, 172, 236n31, 237n12, 246n38
clans. *See* Cherokee clans; Choctaw clans

cliché. *See* "Indianness" (settler colonial invention); stereotypes (of Natives)
Clifford, James, 103, 214, 224, 226, 238n21, 248n20
Clinton, Robert N., 103
Cohen, Felix S., 10, 106
Cold War, 118
Collier, John, 72, 87–89, 92, 101, 237n1, 237n4, 238nn15–16
collective identity. *See* Cherokee collective identity; Native collective identity
collective land ownership. *See* communal land ownership
collective rights (vs. individual rights), 103, 105, 117–19, 131–34, 241nn19–20, 242n29
collectivism, 80, 117, 119–20, 129–31
colonialism (ideology), 16–17, 26, 33, 74, 108–10, 122, 134, 144, 164, 176–77, 181, 184–85, 196, 201–2, 206–7, 209–17, 222–24, 227–28, 232n21, 241n15, 248n16, 248n24. *See also* civilization (settler colonial concept)
Columbus, Christopher, 104, 200, 240n4
Combe, George, 90
commemoration, 4, 7–8, 20, 184
communal land ownership, 19, 48, 69, 71, 73, 76, 80–81, 83, 87, 96, 120, 122, 143, 145, 148, 167, 173–74
communitism (Weaver), 172, 177, 220
Conley, Robert, 6, 9, 70, 230n6, 237n12; *Mountain Windsong: A Novel of the Trail of Tears*, 20–21, 104–5, 107–12, 114–16, 136–37, 216, 240n8, 241n14
conquest, 29, 32–34, 41, 106, 111, 122, 150, 233n4, 234n9. *See also* discovery doctrine
Constitution of the Cherokee Nation (1827). *See* Cherokee constitutions

Constitution of Massachusetts, 133, 243n33
Constitution of the United States. *See* US Constitution
consumerism, in Foster's and Lockhart's novels, 181, 185–87, 189, 193, 198, 201
Cook-Lynn, Elizabeth, 249n3
Coombe, Rosemary, 194
Cooper, James Fenimore, 186
co-optation, and colonialism, 207, 214, 223
Corntassel, Jeff, 11, 131, 231n18
corruption, 56, 62, 76–77, 109, 216, 219–20
Coulthard, Glen, 206, 221, 250n4
Creeks, 1, 40, 246n36. *See also* Muscogee (Creek)
crime, 27, 50, 55, 58, 60, 62, 76, 203, 235n26
Cripps, John, 141
cross-temporality, 181, 202, 214, 222, 224–25
cultural appropriation, 5, 22, 180–84, 187, 196, 208–9, 214, 217, 247n10; complicity of Natives in, 183–84, 196–200, 205–6, 220; as modern form of dispossession, 181, 183–84, 188–89, 195, 214
cultural integrity, 107, 118
cultural property. *See* intangible property
cultural relativism, 89, 94–96
Curtis Act, 69–70, 77

Dakota, 2
Dakota Access Pipeline protests (#NoDAPL). *See* Standing Rock protests (2016–17)
Dakotas (states), 1–2, 195, 203
Dawes, Henry L., 71, 74–75, 91, 237n4
Dawes Act (1887), 68–70, 138–40
Dawes Commission/Report, 68, 71, 75–77, 80–81, 140, 237n4
Dawes Rolls. *See* blood quantum rules

INDEX

Declaration on the Granting of Independence to Colonial Countries and Peoples. *See* United Nations
decolonization, 103, 177, 208, 211, 213–15, 217, 221–22, 231n18, 240n2
Deer Clan (Cherokee), 145, 147. *See also* Cherokee clans
Delaney, Samuel, 214
Deloria, Philipp J., 185
Deloria, Vine, 11, 103, 116
Dennison, Jean, 177
Denson, Andrew, 7–8, 246n36
Dery, Mark, 215
Derrida, Jacques, 212
Descendants of Freedmen Association, 140–41
dignity, human, 114–16
Dillon, Grace L., 181
discovery doctrine, 28–33, 41, 122, 233n4, 234n9, 235n18. *See also* conquest
disenfranchisement, 2, 16, 40, 47, 62, 71, 119, 133, 135, 141, 143, 173, 181, 217, 244n13
displacement, 7, 68, 113
dispossession, 2, 8, 10, 14, 21, 24, 35, 59, 69–70, 79, 122, 129, 154–57, 184–85, 188, 190–91, 195, 200–201, 204, 217–18, 227; as general "structure," 221–22, 229n2; impact on Native lives, 122–26, 132, 152–53, 210, 222; legal issues, 25, 28–36, 236n34; Native resistance to, 16, 20, 22, 27, 34, 49, 62–63, 73, 100–101, 108, 135, 207, 214, 216–19, 222–23, 227–28; relation to slavery, 10, 143, 151–53, 165, 173–74, 177, 218, 222, 244n15; as theft, 33, 122–23, 191, 242n22. *See also* allotment, policy of; cultural appropriation; Indian Removal; Marshall Trilogy; property
Disrud, Stephen, 190
District Court of the Cherokee Nation, 141
Doerfler, Jill, 226
domestic dependency, 18–19, 37, 39–42, 64, 66, 155, 249n1
domination, and colonialism, 66, 150, 152, 182, 196, 206, 209, 211, 216, 220, 222, 225
Drysdale, David J., 66
Duthu, N. Bruce, 11
Duvall, Deborah L., 246n38
dystopia, 195, 205

Eaton, Rachel Caroline, 6, 9, 19, 71–74, 77, 83–84, 86, 89, 91, 99–102, 132, 216, 225, 230n7, 237n2, 237n4, 237n6, 237n9, 238n13, 238n20; *John Ross and the Cherokee Indians*, 6, 19, 71–72, 77–84, 89, 100–101, 239n30
Echo-Hawk, Walter, 107, 111
Eco, Umberto, 185
economic theory, 128–29. *See also* property
education, 35–36, 54, 70, 72, 75, 78, 80, 83, 85–87, 91–92, 97–98, 111, 146, 160–61, 182, 220–21, 245n18
egalitarianism, 89, 100, 129
Elias, Amy J., 128
Ellis, Jerry, 230n5
Emerson, Ralph Waldo, 110, 240n8
empowerment/self-empowerment, 62, 118, 208, 212, 217, 240n1
Engle, Karen, 240n2
environmental issues, 118, 182, 190, 192
equality (legal principle), 40–41, 56, 60, 62, 117
essentialism, 144, 196
ethnic identity, 7, 51, 135, 138, 162, 246n34
Eurocentrism, 85, 88, 94
exile, 174, 204
extension laws (southern states), 34, 37, 40–41, 43, 52, 60, 234n12, 234n15

279

extermination, and Indian Removal policy, 150, 221, 229n1
Eyre, Chris, 229n3

family. *See* kinship practices (Native)
Fanon, Frantz, 205–6, 211, 213, 248n24
farming. *See* agriculture
federal Indian law, 4, 11, 13–14, 21, 46, 50, 72–73, 75, 77, 89, 99–101, 106–8, 111–16, 136, 156, 216, 232n28, 233n1, 237n4
fence (as symbol), 124, 145, 166–67
fictional writing, as strategy of Native resistance, 22, 49–50, 63, 73, 85, 89, 99, 143, 180–81, 215–16, 219, 223–25, 229n5. *See also* narrativity (in historiography); resistance, Native forms of
Final Rolls. *See* blood quantum rules; tribal membership
Fitz, Karsten, 134
Fitzgerald, Stephanie, 9
Five Civilized Tribes, 68–71, 75–77, 138, 143
Five Civilized Tribes Act (1906), 70
Fletcher, Matthew, 11–12
Fodéba, Kéita, 248n24
Foster, Sharon Ewell, 6, 10, 21, 142–44, 148–50, 156–57, 177, 217–18, 231n10; *Abraham's Well: A Novel*, 10, 21, 142–50, 152–54, 158–61, 165–69, 171–74, 179, 217, 231n11, 244n11, 245n17, 245n25, 246n34
Foucault, Michel, 232n25
Fraser, James Earle, 193
freedmen, 21, 138–39, 141, 143–44, 177–78, 243n2. *See also* Cherokee freedmen debate; slavery (African Americans as slaves of Native Americans)
Frickey, Philip P., 107, 111, 113–14
Friends of the Indian, 19, 74, 99
frontier, 58, 89, 209, 238n14

full-blood, 76–77, 80, 147, 159, 161, 212. *See also* blood quantum rules

Gallatin, Albert, 121
Garrison, Tim Alan, 11, 42–43, 48
Garroutte, Eva, 176
gender issues, 51–52, 79, 114, 117, 132–33, 145, 149, 160–61, 163–66, 175–76, 199, 235n22, 237n2, 241n11, 243n31. *See also* matrilineality
General Allotment Act. *See* allotment, policy of; Dawes Act (1887)
genocide, 195, 235n26
Georgia: Indian legislative acts, 24, 29–30, 32–34, 37–46, 50, 52, 56, 60, 78–79, 81–82, 110, 234n12, 235n19; setting of Hausman's novel, 185, 249n31
Georgia v. Tassel (1830), 30, 37, 234n12
Getches, David H., 11, 106–7, 113
Glancy, Diane, 6, 132, 136, 216–17; *Pushing the Bear: A Novel of the Trail of Tears*, 20–21, 104–5, 119–37, 143, 149, 166, 216–18, 223, 242n23, 242nn26–27, 244n15
globalization, 113, 181, 185
Goeman, Mishuana, 203
Gover, Kirsty, 139, 243n5, 244n14, 246n37
Grant, Ulysses, 237n1
Great Plains, 183, 191–92, 194–95, 206–7
Green, Nathan, 234n15
Groom, Don, 107
Gross, Ariela, 158–59

hair (as racial indicator), 159–61, 197, 202, 208, 245n26, 248n23, 249n32
Harjo, Joy, *An American Sunrise*, 3, 227
Harrell, Beatrice, 230n5
Harris, Cheryl, 150–52
Harvard University, 72, 97–98, 239n24, 240n1

INDEX

Hausman, Blake, 6, 9, 217; *Riding the Trail of Tears: A Novel*, 22, 181, 183–89, 196–200, 202, 205–9, 213–15, 217, 219, 248nn19–20, 249n31
health issues (Native), 54, 85, 87, 109–10, 131, 182, 194, 238n15
Hegel, Georg Wilhelm Friedrich, *Lectures on the Philosophy of History*, 15–16
Hicks, Elijah, 43
historical particularism. *See* Boas, Franz; cultural relativism
historicity, 15–17
historiography (Western), 4, 6, 20, 77, 99, 180, 198, 223–25, 244n11
Hoagland, Ericka, 180
Hobbes, Thomas, 128
Hobsbawm, Eric, 50
Hogan, Linda, 230n5
Hogan, Thomas, 178
Holder, Cindy L., 131
Holm, Tom, 13–14, 84, 231n19, 232n23
homesteads, 68–69, 242n24
hooks, bell, 144
Hopkins, Ruth, 2
House of Representatives. *See* US Congress
Huang, Hsinya, 8–9
human dignity, 114–16
humanitarianism, 76, 238n20
human rights, 20, 58, 103–5, 112–18, 120, 131, 134–36, 240n2, 241n20, 242n29
Huxley, Aldous, 205
hyperreality, 183, 185–86

identity politics, 97, 144, 173, 196, 204
imagined futures. *See* peoplehood
improvement of land, 30–32, 35, 48, 80–81, 110, 121–25, 167, 242n24. *See also* property
(in)alienability: of land, 31, 44, 68, 122–23, 125; of people, 122, 153, 169

Indian country, 2, 21, 80, 91–93, 138, 142, 177
"*indian/indianness*" (Vizenor). *See* "Indianness" (settler colonial invention)
"Indianness" (settler colonial invention), 21, 83, 97, 140, 182–87, 193–210, 215, 217, 220, 243n3, 247n5, 247n8, 248n16, 248n19, 249n28, 249n3, 249n5. *See also* simulation
Indian New Deal, 88, 101, 239n32
"Indian Problem," 72, 191, 195
Indian Reform, 74–75, 84, 90–91, 93, 237n7
Indian Removal, 1–10, 17–22, 47, 49–50, 57, 66–67, 71, 82, 89, 91, 111, 114, 122, 125, 132, 136, 142–44, 148, 152, 173, 177, 181, 183–85, 188, 192, 197–98, 215–23, 225–27, 229n1, 229n3, 229n5, 230n7, 232n28, 233n29, 235n22, 246n38; evoked during Standing Rock protests, 2, 218, 227; still haunting Native Americans, 2–3, 5–6, 8–9, 20–22, 215, 218–20, 222–23, 227, 229n5, 232n28; tied to slavery, 10, 143, 165, 174, 177, 222, 244n10, 244n15, 246n38; universal trope and ongoing process, 219, 221–22, 226; US mismanagement, 2, 48, 70, 81–82, 109–10, 114–15, 123
Indian Removal Act (1830), 47, 192
Indian Reorganization Act (1934), 70, 88, 237n1, 238n16
Indian Rights Association, 75
Indian Territories (in Jones's novel), 189–96, 200–205, 210–11, 213, 249n25
Indian Territory, 19, 21, 25, 68–72, 75–78, 80–82, 85, 91–93, 96, 98, 127, 133, 142, 148, 154, 166–69, 172, 177, 186, 191, 237n2, 239n24, 243n1, 245n25

281

indigeneity, 135–37, 217, 223
indigenization of Western practices. *See* adaptation; resistance, Native forms of
Indigenous Black studies, 231n12
Indigenous futurity. *See* Native futurity
Indigenous peoplehood. *See* peoplehood
Indigenous Peoples' Day, 240n4
Indigenous rights, 5, 11, 20–21, 25, 67, 104–5, 112–18, 131, 134–37, 223, 231n16, 232n20, 236n34. *See also* Native rights
individualism, and law, 105, 117, 119–21, 126, 128–31, 134, 217, 220
individual rights. *See* collective rights; individualism, and law
Institute for Government Research, 85–86
intangible property, 181–82, 185, 187–89, 195, 201, 204, 218, 247n2, 247n9. *See also* cultural appropriation
intellectual property. *See* intangible property
Intercourse Acts, 34, 40
interculturalism, 91, 94, 96, 99
interdisciplinarity, 8, 11
interests, individual vs. collective, 20–21, 81, 119–20, 129, 131–32, 134, 241n18
intermarriage, 19, 72, 78, 97–98, 122, 129, 171, 243n2
internalization, and colonialism, 21, 184, 206–7, 211, 217
International Labor Organization, 113
international law, 4–5, 11–15, 20, 105, 112–14, 117–19, 131, 134–36, 217, 232n20, 241nn15–16, 241n18, 242n29
International Year/Decade of the World's Indigenous People. *See* United Nations
interpellation (Althusser), 4, 16, 222

interpersonal/intratribal relations (impact of Removal on), 3–4, 21, 69, 78, 96, 111, 125, 146, 154, 166, 168, 170–71, 213, 222, 224, 242n26. *See also* kinship practices (Native)
interracial relations, 19–20, 72, 96–97, 174
intertribal relations, 2, 78, 243n5. *See also* tribal membership
ius, 54

Jackson, Andrew, 32, 43–44, 109, 241n14
Jacob, Murv, 246n38
Jeep Cherokee, 187–88, 199
Johnson, Hannibal B., 139, 177, 244n6
Johnson v. McIntosh (1823), 24, 28–30, 32, 34–35, 38, 41–43, 233nn4–5, 234n15
Jones, Stephen Graham, 22, 196, 205, 211; *The Bird Is Gone: A Monograph Manifesto*, 22, 181, 183–84, 190–96, 200–207, 209–15, 218–19, 247n13, 248nn14–16, 248nn21–24, 249n27, 249nn29–32
Judicial Appeals Tribunal of the Cherokee Nation, 138–40, 174, 244n7
Justice, Daniel Heath, 3–5, 8, 176, 204, 230n5, 230n7
justices of the peace, 57, 60, 235n26

Kansas City Chiefs, 187, 199
Katyal, Sonia, 13, 126
Keene, Adrienne, 247n10
Kelly, Lawrence C., 75
Kenney, Cortelyou C., 184
Ketchum, Steve, 184–85
kinship practices (Native), 21, 144–45, 147–51, 153–55, 157, 162, 165, 167–73, 175–76, 179, 217, 245n17, 246n34
Krupat, Arnold, 20, 26, 108
Kymlicka, Will, 117

INDEX

Lake Mohonk Conference, 74–75, 84. *See also* Friends of the Indian

Lakota, 2, 202

land. *See* place

land, Native loss of. *See* dispossession; Indian Removal

land ownership, 5, 17, 28–35, 37, 48, 67, 83, 150–51, 169, 181, 233n3. *See also* communal land ownership; property

Larré, Lionel, 230n9

law and (Native American) literature, 8, 10–12, 231n14

law of nations, 29, 233n5

Leflore, Greenwood, 245n22

legal philosophy, 39, 53

legal positivism, 19, 26

legal subjectivities, 5–6, 11–12, 14–18, 24–25, 28, 49, 67, 100, 104, 113, 119, 134, 136, 140, 184, 205, 216, 223, 237n4

Leroy, Justin, 10, 177

Le Triplett, 230n5

lex, and Cicero, 54

lex aeterna, divina, humana, naturalis (Thomas Aquinas), 54–56, 60–64. *See also* natural law

Lindsay, Brendan C., 59, 235n26

linear progression, of races or cultures, 19, 72, 89, 93–94, 96

Locke, John, 126, 128, 234n11; *Second Treatise on Government*, 31–32, 35–37

Lockhart, Zelda, 6–7, 10, 21, 142, 217, 231n10; *Cold Running Creek*, 10, 21, 142–44, 148–50, 154–58, 161–66, 169–71, 175–79, 217–18, 231n11, 245nn19–24, 246nn28–29, 246n32

Lone Ranger and Tonto, 249n27

Lone Wolf v. Hitchcock (1903), 69, 240n5

Lumbee, 13

lynching, 60, 236n27

Lytle, Clifford M., 103, 116

Macpherson, C. B., 128

Manifest Destiny, 53, 249n29

manifest manners (Vizenor), 187, 195, 198, 200, 206, 211–12

Mankiller, Wilma, 230nn5–6

Marshall, John, 24, 28–33, 37–38, 40–42, 64, 67, 234n9, 234n13, 234n15

Marshall Trilogy, 24–25, 28, 35, 37, 41, 106, 231n14, 233n1. See also *Johnson v. McIntosh* (1823); *Cherokee Nation v. Georgia* (1831); *Worcester v. Georgia* (1832)

matrilineality, 145, 150–51, 168, 170, 175–76

Mbembe, Achille, 65

McGirt v. Oklahoma (2020), 178

McNickle, D'Arcy, 238n17

memory culture. *See* commemoration

Meriam, Lewis, 85

Meriam Report, 72, 83, 85–87, 237n4

Mexicans, 49–51, 57–59, 61–62

Miles, Tiya, 176

Miner, Joshua D., 8

Minnesota, 219, 221

mission. *See* Christianity

Mississippi (state), 142–43, 148, 154–55, 161, 176, 244n12, 245nn23–24

Mississippi River, 129, 156

Mississippi Band of Choctaw Indians, 244n12

Missouri River, 1

Mix, Charles E., 59

mixed-blood. *See* multiracialism

Mooney, James, 197, 202, 240n8, 241n13, 242n27

Morgan, Lewis Henry, 73

Morton, Samuel George, 90

Mount Shasta, 53–54, 64–66

Mullikin, Melinda Smith, 89–90, 238n18

multiracialism: as hallmark of Native society before Removal, 145–47, 165–66, 171; as ideal, 147, 164–65, 172–76. *See also* African Natives;

283

multiracialism (*continued*)
    biracial (Native-White); interracial relations
Murray, James, 246n38
Muscogee (Creek), 3, 141, 178, 228
museumization, 21–22, 66, 180, 184, 189–90, 215
Muskrat, Ruth Margaret, 229n5
mythology, 187, 201, 249n31. *See also* Cherokee legends

narrativity, in historiography, 15–17
National Park Service, 233n29
nationhood (Native), 27, 34, 36, 42, 47, 71, 134, 246n34; as racialized, 144, 149, 156–57, 165–66, 169, 171, 174, 245n25; vs. peoplehood, 144, 232n23
Native absence. *See* "vanishing Indian"
Native collective identity, 4–5, 10, 12–16, 20, 31, 69, 104–5, 111, 177, 215, 217, 226, 241n18. *See also* Cherokee collective identity; pan-Native/pan-Indigenous perspectives
Native cultural appropriation. *See* cultural appropriation
Native family relations. *See* kinship practices (Native)
Native futurity, 3–6, 9, 17–18, 22, 25, 28, 97–98, 116, 129, 134, 137, 171–72, 174, 177–78, 180–81, 183–84, 187, 189, 205–6, 208, 212–18, 223–24, 226–28. *See also* peoplehood
Native peoplehood. *See* peoplehood
Native property rights, 11, 30–33. *See also* dispossession; property
Native Removal writing, 3–9, 11–12, 16–17, 22–23, 217, 222–28, 229n1, 229n5; aesthetic aspects, 6, 8–10, 12, 23, 212, 230n7; as challenge to settler colonial legal order, 17, 216–18, 221–28; distinct genre, 4, 7; pan-Indigenous appeal, 222;

as political and legal intervention, 12
Native rights, 16, 20, 26, 38, 46, 103, 107, 109, 135, 216–17, 234n12, 240n7, 241n16
Native self-government, 16, 27, 35–36, 41, 45, 70–71, 76, 79, 82, 88–89, 103, 106–7, 113, 116, 136, 234n15, 238n20
Native sovereignty. *See* sovereignty
Natives in US or Western popular culture, 16, 22, 181–82, 184, 187, 193, 198, 201, 203, 205, 249n27, 249n3. *See also* "Indianness" (settler colonial invention); stereotypes, of Natives
Native statehood, 65–66, 240n2
Native survival, 14, 19, 43, 48–49, 68, 82, 87, 96, 127, 129, 131–32, 134, 173, 184, 199, 216–18, 243n34. *See also* survivance (Vizenor)
Native tradition(alism), 11, 14, 18, 26–28, 49, 67, 74, 79, 86, 88, 91, 94, 96, 105, 128, 144, 151, 155, 158, 161, 166, 168–70, 176, 182, 202–5, 213–14, 220, 228, 232n28, 239n31, 242n26, 245n17
natural law: mobilized by Native Americans against Removal, 19, 25–26, 30–32, 35–37, 66–67, 128, 236n34; in Ridge's novel, 49, 55–57, 62, 235n23
Navajos, 207, 230n6
Naylor, Celia E., 8, 231n13
Nelson, Joshua B., 26–28, 67, 230n7, 239n31
neocolonialism, 113, 181–85, 200
neoliberalism, 229n2
Nichols, Robert, 190, 242n22
Niezen, Ronald, 11, 112
Nixon, Richard, 102,
noble savage, 51, 92, 200
#NoDAPL. *See* Standing Rock protests (2016–17)
North Carolina, 107, 207–8

INDEX

nostalgia, 187, 193, 197, 201, 207, 213
Nunnehi, 187, 209, 248n17, 249n31

occupancy (vs. ownership), 27–30, 32, 38, 48, 233nn3–4, 234n8
occupation (of Native land). *See* dispossession; Indian Removal
Oklahoma, 2, 70, 99, 107, 140–42, 172–73, 178, 183, 199, 238n16, 239n24. *See also* Indian Territory
Oklahoma Enabling Act (1906), 70
Oklahoma Indian Welfare Act (1936), 238n16
Oklahoma land rush, 172–73
Oklahoma Territory, 70
Old Settler (Cherokee), 64, 236n31
one-drop rule, 138. *See also* blood quantum rules
Ortiz, Fernando, 239n28
Oskison, John Milton, 6, 9, 19, 70–72, 84–85, 96–100, 136, 216, 230n9, 237nn3–4, 238n13, 239n24, 239n26, 239nn28–29; *The Singing Bird: A Cherokee Novel*, 19, 72, 84, 89–101, 216, 237n3, 238nn17–20, 238n22, 239n23, 239n27
outlawry, 44–45, 47–51, 56, 60–66, 236n28
ownership. *See* communal land ownership; land ownership; property

Painter, Charles, 71, 75, 237n4
pan-Native/pan-Indigenous perspectives, 3–5, 136, 215, 218, 221–23, 226–27
Pattaro, Enrico, 55–56
Pearson, J. Diane, 13
Peck, Jacob, 234n15
peoplehood: alternative conceptions, 6, 12–15, 17–18, 20–22, 25–27, 46, 48–49, 64, 67, 71, 89, 100, 119, 129–31, 133, 135, 137, 144–45, 148, 163–64, 171–79, 208, 214, 216–17, 220, 222–23, 225–26; concept and traditional forms, 3–6, 8–9, 12–15, 17–18, 42, 44, 46, 63, 158, 166, 181, 184, 206, 216, 229n4, 230n7, 231nn18–19, 232nn20–21, 232n23. *See also* anticolonial strategies; collective identity; Indigenous futurity; resistance, Native forms of
Piatote, Beth, 11–12
place: boundedness of Native American identity to, 5, 13, 31, 43, 47, 91, 125, 207, 246n34; as central factor for peoplehood, 13, 44, 48; vs. "land" (as commodity, property, resource), 13–14, 44; spiritual meaning, 73
plantation slavery. *See* chattel slavery; slavery (African Americans as slaves of Native Americans)
positive law, 19, 26
postindian (Vizenor), 200, 211–12
postmodernism, 181, 185, 187, 193, 197–98, 201, 244n11
Potawatomis, Trail of Death, 230n6
Powell, John Wesley, 72–75
Powell, Timothy B., 89–90, 238n18
power, Indigenous vs. Western notions of, 12–13
pre-contact/-conquest Native American history, 13, 27, 134, 192, 232n23
preservation/self-preservation of Native culture (vs. modernization), 79, 84, 87–88, 92, 99, 113, 127, 131, 226
Principal People/*Aniyunwiya* (Cherokee self-denomination), 144–45, 148, 172, 174, 231n19
progress. *See* civilization (settler colonial concept)
property: communal household property, 149; private property of increasing importance in Native communities, 19, 69, 73, 75–76, 80–81, 99, 119–28, 146–50, 152–56, 161–62, 164–69,

285

property (*continued*)
232n22; inheritance, 26–27, 33; labor theory (Locke), 30–32, 37; land as property, 14, 17, 30–31, 65, 76, 195, 233n5, 238n14; link between property and personhood, 123–24, 145–46; racialized, 21, 150, 156, 164–65, 169, 172, 177. *See also* communal land ownership; dispossession; intangible property; Native property rights; natural rights

Pueblos, 87

purchase of Native lands, 29, 32–33, 41, 233nn3–4. *See also* dispossession; land ownership

race: and federal Indian policy, 4, 21, 86, 138, 150; impact on Indigenous belonging, 94–95, 99, 136, 138–41, 144, 149–79, 244n8, 245n26; and property, 150–53, 167, 169, 172, 177; as social construct, 138–39, 144, 158–59, 161, 164–65, 168, 170, 176, 245n26. *See also* blood quantum rules; blood requirement; racism; slavery (African Americans as slaves of Native Americans)

racism: Native Americans against African Americans or African Natives, 21, 138–79, 244n6; white against Native Americans, 21, 35–36, 86, 90, 114, 139, 179, 187, 208, 216; white against other groups, 56–57, 60, 138–39, 143, 160, 235n25

Radin, Margaret Jane, 123

Rao, Pratima, 181

realism, literary, 60–61, 244n11

reappropriation, of colonial stereotypes. *See* anticolonial strategies

recognition, of Natives by settler state or international law, 13, 14, 16, 19, 21, 37, 38, 41, 46, 69, 105, 116, 135, 177, 204, 211, 216–17, 220, 241n16, 241n20, 244n14, 248n24. *See also* self-recognition, as strategy of resistance

Reconstruction treaties (1866): Cherokee, 78, 140, 178; Muscogee (Creek), 178

reenactment, of "Indianness" and Native history, 185–88, 197–200, 219–20

Rehnquist, William H., 103

Rehnquist Court, 103, 106, 111, 120

relocation. *See* Indian Removal

Removal. *See* Indian Removal

repurposing of laws or rhetoric for decolonial goals. *See* anticolonial strategies

reservations, 2, 20, 59, 69, 74–75, 87, 102, 120, 175, 178, 184, 192

resistance, Native forms of: disobedience, 49, 63, 66, 155; insurrection, 26, 49, 56, 62; legal resistance, 1–2, 19–20, 25–26, 37, 45–46, 66–67, 95, 105, 184, 225; violence, 49–50, 63, 236n30; writing/media, 100, 135, 183–84, 188, 209, 222–23, 226–28. *See also* anticolonial strategies; decolonization; dispossession, Native resistance to; legal subjectivities; indigeneity; outlawry; peoplehood; Standing Rock protests (2016–17)

restitution (of Native lands), 183–84, 191, 206–7

Revolutionary War, 33, 234n9

Ridge, John (father), 6, 18, 25–26, 28, 42–43, 46, 49–51, 63, 109, 216, 234n14

Ridge, John Rollin (son), 19, 25–26, 28, 49, 51–52, 62–66, 91, 114, 216, 236nn32–33; *The Life and Adventures of Joaquín Murieta*,

6, 25–26, 49–65, 114, 235n20, 236n27, 236n32; "Mount Shasta, Seen from a Distance," 53–55
Rifkin, Mark, 4, 11–12, 14, 18, 26, 42, 65, 102, 155, 157, 202, 214, 223, 230n9, 233n2
Riley, Angela, 11, 13, 126, 181–83
Robertson, Lindsay G., 11, 42
romance (literary genre), 49–50, 56, 61–62, 107, 235n20
Roosevelt, Theodore, 69–70
Rosen, Deborah, 45, 60
Ross, John, 6, 18, 25–26, 34, 37, 41, 43–50, 53, 61–65, 71, 77, 80, 82–83, 91, 95, 124, 126, 216, 225, 230n7, 230n9, 232n28, 234nn7–9, 234n11, 234n14; message to Cherokee Nation of 1828, 32–33; memorial of 1829, 33–34; letter to Congress of 1829, 35; message to Cherokee General Council of 1830, 37–39; message to Cherokee Nation of 1830, 40; memorial to Congress of 1834, 44–45; letter to Lewis Cass of 1835, 46–47, petition to Congress of 1836, 47–48
Ross party. *See* Treaty of New Echota
Royce, Charles C., 108–9, 240nn8–9
rule of law, 15–16, 28, 36, 40, 45–46, 50, 65–67, 236n30

Salamanca School, 236n34
Sartre, Jean-Paul, 206–7, 214
Sarwal, Reema, 180
savagism, 19, 29–30, 33, 35–36, 40, 42, 51, 61–62, 71, 73–75, 77, 79, 90–92, 97, 114–15, 120, 124, 189, 200
schools. *See* education
Schweninger, Lee, 11
science fiction, 180, 214, 246n1
self-definition/knowledge (Native), 12–13, 16, 23, 105, 174–75, 206, 208, 210, 217

self-determination, in international law, 103–4, 112, 135–36, 217, 240n2, 241n19
self-determination, Indigenous conceptions of, 83, 104–5, 112, 116, 136, 182, 206–9, 213, 215–16, 240n2, 241n19
self-determination, US policy of, 20, 102–5, 240nn1–2
self-interest, economic, 77, 81, 126
self-recognition, as strategy of resistance, 207, 222
Seminole Nation v. United States (1942), 237n8
Seminoles, 2, 141, 237n8, 246n36
Senate. *See* US Congress
Senate Committee on Indian Affairs, 74
Sequoyah (proposed Indian state), 70
Sequoyah Research Center, 230n5
sexuality, 125, 160, 162–63, 200, 208, 210
Shawnee, 136
Silko, Leslie Marmon, 232n27
Simpson, Audra, 221
simulacrum, 185, 188–90, 193, 196, 200, 205, 209–10, 247n13
simulation, 182–83, 187–89, 193–94, 199–200, 206–7, 209, 212–13, 220, 250n5
Singer, Joseph, 11
Sioux, 190. *See also* Cheyenne River Sioux; Standing Rock Sioux
slave narrative/neo–slave narrative, 142, 244n11
slavery (African Americans as slaves of Native Americans), 10, 21, 45, 81, 124, 129, 133, 141–44, 147–48, 151–71, 173–79, 218, 222, 235n26, 243n1, 244n11, 244n13, 244n15, 245n21, 245n26, 246n34, 246n36, 246n38
slavery (Native Americans as slaves), 235n26

slipstream (genre), 181
Smith, Chad, 141
Smith, Rogers M., 226, 231n18
Smithers, Gregory, 141
social media, 2, 183, 185
Society of American Indians, 84, 136
Socrates, 95
"sovereign law" (John Rollin Ridge), 53–57, 66
sovereignty, 4, 8, 12–14, 16–17, 19, 24, 28, 30, 34, 38–39, 41, 43, 46, 50, 54–56, 64–66, 69–73, 75, 77, 79, 81, 103, 105–9, 114, 116, 119, 134, 139–40, 155–57, 178, 182, 191, 194, 204, 225–27, 231n17, 232n22, 232n28, 233n4, 234n8, 240n7, 241nn15–16, 244n7, 246n34, 246n37, 249n3
speculative fiction, 180–81, 215, 246n1
Spivak, Gayatri Chakravorty, 212
sports (cultural appropriation), 182, 187–88, 199
Standing Rock protests (2016–17), 1–2, 218, 225, 227
Standing Rock Sioux, 1–2, 227
Stand Watie, 63, 236nn32–33
Stanford University, 72, 239n24
Starr, Emmett, 230n5
Starr, James, 63
Starr, Tom, 63
state legislature (vs. federal law), 24–25, 30, 41–42, 46, 48, 50, 59–60, 64–67, 234n6, 234n12. See also Georgia
state of exception (Agamben), 155, 157
Stephens v. Cherokee Nation (1899), 237n8
stereotypes (of Natives), 92, 181–82, 186, 188–89, 196–99, 201, 207–9, 217. See also "Indianness" (settler colonial invention); racism
storytelling (Native), 12, 77, 120, 127, 129, 132, 180, 182–83, 186, 194, 198, 203, 210, 223–26, 242n27, 250n5

Strickland, Rennard H., 106
Strong, Pauline Turner, 182
Sturm, Circe, 138–41, 165
subaltern resistance. 26, 49–50, 65–66.
  See also resistance, Native forms of
subjectivity, Native modes of, 4–6, 16–18, 21, 28, 184, 196, 200–201, 205, 207, 211, 216–17, 221, 232n25.
  See also legal subjectivities
Supreme Court of the United States, 20, 24, 37–39, 43, 50, 64, 69, 77, 102–3, 106–7, 110, 178, 232n20, 234n12
survival. See Native survival
survivance (Vizenor), 221, 224–26, 250n6
Susannah of the Mounties, 209, 249n29
Suzack, Cheryl, 11
Sweet, Timothy, 53

Tan, Kathy-Ann, 173, 244n11
Tassel, George, 234n12. See also *Georgia v. Tassel* (1830)
Tecumseh, 136
Tee-Hit-Ton Indians v. United States (1955), 240n5
Teller, Henry M., 73
tenancy, 29, 234n8
Tennessee, 2, 24–25, 43, 46–47, 234n15
Tennessee v. Forman (1835), 43
termination policy, 102, 230n6
territorial appropriation. See dispossession; Indian Removal
Teuton, Christopher B., 71, 239n25
Texas, 1, 169
theft. See dispossession
Thomas, Robert K., 13, 232n21, 242n26
Thomas Aquinas, 235n23; *Summae Theologicae*, 54–55; Treatise on Law, 56
Tingle, Tim, 230n5
title (property), 28–30, 33–34, 38, 41, 46–48, 233n4, 234n8, 240n5. See also dispossession; property

288

Tocqueville, Alexis de, 57–58
tourism, 7, 22, 182, 184–86, 188, 190, 198–201, 248n16, 249n31
Trail of Tears, 2–3, 7–9, 111, 115, 143, 227, 229n3, 229n5, 230n6, 230n8, 233n29, 247n10; as pan-tribal symbol of anticolonial resistance, 218–19, 221; reenacted in Vizenor's novel, 219–22, 249n3; relation to Standing Rock protests, 2, 218, 227; reenacted in Hausman's novel, 183–88, 197–99, 207, 219, 249n25. *See also* Cherokee Trail of Tears
Trail of Tears Association, 233n29
Trail of Tears Commemoration Day, 184
Trail of Tears National Historic Trail, 20, 233n29
transculturation, 99, 128, 229n28. *See also* amalgamation (Oskison); interculturalism
trauma, 3, 8, 80, 224, 226
treason law (1829), 234n16
Treaty of Dancing Rabbit Creek, 142, 148, 154, 245n19, 245n23
Treaty of 1866. *See* Reconstruction treaties (1866)
Treaty of Hopewell, 34, 41
Treaty of New Echota, 44, 46–48, 51, 63–64, 82, 108–10, 115, 124–25, 168, 185, 236n31, 236n33, 241n14, 242n25, 247n12
tribal governance, 12–13, 20–21, 24, 69–70, 76, 83, 102, 105, 166, 225, 240n1. *See also* Cherokee governance; Choctaw governance; self-government
tribal law, 4–5, 11–12, 21, 46, 139, 183
tribal membership, 21, 138–40, 143–44, 167–68, 177, 243n5, 244n7. *See also* African Natives; blood quantum rules; blood requirement
trickster, 219, 225, 249n28
Trump, Donald, 1
Tsalagi. *See* Cherokee language/*Tsalagi*

Tsosie, Rebecca, 11, 120, 180, 182–83
Twist, Glenn J., 230n5

United Nations: Commission on Human Rights, 116; Declaration on the Granting of Independence to Colonial Countries and Peoples (1960), 103; Declaration on the Rights of Indigenous Peoples (UNDRIP, 2007), 104, 113, 134–36, 240n3, 243n34; Human Rights Commission, 113; International Year/Decade of the World's Indigenous People, 113, 135–36; Sub-Commission on Prevention of Discrimination and Protection of Minorities, 116; Universal Declaration of Human Rights (1948), 115, 131; Working Group on Indigenous Populations, 113, 117–18, 120
United States v. Kagama (1886), 69, 240n5
Universal Declaration of Human Rights. *See* United Nations
University of California, Berkeley, 190, 240n4
University of Oklahoma, 237n3
urbanization of Native Americans in 1950s–1960s, 20, 230n6
US Congress, 20, 24–25, 35, 43–44, 47–48, 65, 68–70, 74–75, 77, 87, 99, 102, 106, 191, 234n8, 237n4, 243n2
US Constitution, 27, 34–35, 37, 40–41, 43, 50, 59, 113, 115, 133, 138, 233n1; Commerce Clause, 34, 41–42, 233n1; Supremacy Clause, 34
US Department of the Interior, 70–71
utopianism. *See* peoplehood

Van Buren, Martin, 110, 240n8
"vanishing Indian," 7–8, 84, 189–90, 193, 198, 201, 208, 212, 221, 224, 226

Vann, Marilyn, 140, 144
victimry (Vizenor), 220, 224, 226
Vigil, Kiara M., 100, 239n31
vigilantism, 50, 57–58, 60, 235n25, 236n27
violence (settler colonial against Natives and others), 22, 47, 49, 51–52, 56–57, 59–60, 62–63, 70–71, 114, 155–56, 170, 185, 187, 206, 214, 216, 220, 223, 227, 229n1, 235n25, 236n30, 241n17, 250n5. *See also* vigilantism
Vitoria, Francisco de, 236n34
Vizenor, Gerald, 6–7, 9, 22, 182, 185, 187, 200, 208–9, 211–12, 216, 219, 222, 226, 247n5, 249n28, 250n6; *Chair of Tears*, 9, 22, 216, 219–26, 249n3. *See also* "*indian/indianness*"; manifest manners; postindian (Vizenor); survivance (Vizenor); victimry (Vizenor)

Walker, Cheryl, 53–54, 235n20
Warrior, Robert, 139, 244n13
Washington Redskins, 187, 199
Weaver, Jace, 172, 220
Welch, James, 232n27
Weller, John B., 235n19
Western (legal) thought and institutions (vs. Native), 7, 12–13, 15, 45, 58, 67, 77, 80, 88, 99–100, 118–19, 123–24, 127–29, 134, 137, 144, 148, 166, 176, 189–90, 202, 220, 224–25, 231nn15–18, 232n23, 242n22. *See also* civilization (settler colonial concept); colonialism (ideology); historiography
White, Hayden, 15
whiteness, 83, 150–52, 154, 156, 158, 160–61, 163–65, 175, 245n27
white supremacy, 160
Wicke, Jennifer, 16
Wiessner, Siegfried, 117
Wilkins, David E., 11
Wilkinson, Charles, 102
Williams, Lucy Ward, 77
Williams, Robert A., 11, 113–14, 232n28, 234n10
Willie Halsell College, 72
Wirt, William, 234n12
World War I, 239n26
World War II, 103, 112, 117
Womack, Craig S., 226
women (Native). *See* gender issues
Worcester, Samuel, 121
Worcester v. Georgia (1832), 24, 41–44, 64, 110, 234n15
Wyss, Hilary E., 9–10

Ziff, Bruce, 181